DEMOCRACY VERSUS SUSTAINABILITY

ALSO BY BORIS FRANKEL

Capitalism Versus Democracy?
Rethinking Politics in the Age of Environmental Crisis

Fictions of Sustainability:
The Politics of Growth and Post-Capitalist Futures

Zombies, Lilliputians and Sadists:
The Power of the Living Dead and the Future of Australia

When the Boat Comes In:
Transforming Australia in the Age of Globalisation

From the Prophets Deserts Come:
The Struggle to Reshape Australian Political Culture

The Post Industrial Utopians

Beyond the State?
Dominant Theories and Socialist Strategies

Marxian Theories of The State: A Critique of Orthodoxy

DEMOCRACY VERSUS SUSTAINABILITY

INEQUALITY, MATERIAL FOOTPRINTS AND POST-CARBON FUTURES

BORIS FRANKEL

GREENMEADOWS

First published in 2021 by Greenmeadows

P.O. Box 128

Elsternwick,

Melbourne 3185

A catalogue record for this book is available from the
National Library of Australia

Name: Frankel, Boris, author.

Title: Democracy Versus Sustainability: Inequality, Material Footprints and Post-Carbon Futures/Boris Frankel.

Includes Notes and References and Index.

Subjects:

1. Politics of environmental sustainability. 2. Democracy.

3. Degrowth. 4. Post-capitalism – post-growth societies. 5. Social reform – alternative policies

ISBN: (pbk) 978-0-6483633-7-8
ISBN: (epub) 978-0-6483633-6-1

Cover Design by Emile Frankel

CONTENTS

PREFACE

Democracy Versus Sustainability is the third volume in a larger project that began with the publication of *Fictions of Sustainability: The Politics of Growth and Post-Capitalist Futures* (2018). It was followed by *Capitalism Versus Democracy? Rethinking Politics in the Age of Environmental Crisis* (2020). Each book has focussed on distinct aspects of the political, socio-economic, and environmental crises that have confronted us over the past decade, as well as the strengths and weaknesses of proposed solutions. Some parts of *Democracy Versus Sustainability* were originally published in a different version in Book Three of *Capitalism Versus Democracy?*. These sections have been extensively revised and together with the inclusion of additional chapters and updated material largely constitute a new book.

In a world of continuing unresolved crises and rapidly fluctuating political scenarios, *Democracy Versus Sustainability* is not only an analysis of carbon capitalism and prospective post-carbon socio-economic developments. It also offers a critical examination of why many political parties, governments, businesses, and social movements have either failed to break the current political impasse or come to terms with the enormous scale of ongoing political economic and environmental challenges.

While there is now endless discussion of climate breakdown, this book goes beyond the climate emergency and focuses on the deeper struggles over material resources and biodiversity that will shape future societies.

Writing these three books was made possible by the support given to me by the Melbourne Sustainable Society Institute at the University of Melbourne. I thank Director Brendan Gleeson and the folks at MSSI such as Sam Alexander, the MSSI Fellows and others for their convivial and stimulating discussion of topics over the years. I also thank David Spratt for keeping me alert about the climate emergency with his informative discussion and regular supply of relevant articles.

Once again, my deepest appreciation and love go to Julie Stephens for her detailed discussion of the material in the text, her long labour in editing the manuscript, and for her many years of continued love and intellectual exchange. My heartfelt thanks go to our son, Emile Frankel, who has produced a striking new cover to add to his previous two attractive covers in this project and for his invaluable typesetting and design.

I dedicate this book to the millions of innocent victims who died needlessly, and continue to die, as a result of living in capitalist societies where governments systematically cut or under-resourced their health and care systems in the years before the pandemic, while playing down the threat of COVID-19 to either keep markets open for as long as possible or reopen them prematurely. The rising global death toll and the distribution of vaccines continues to reflect gross social and political economic inequalities. Let us hope that one day we can replace such destructive market systems with more care-centred and socially just societies that respect the fragile and precious nature of our shared biosphere.

Boris Frankel
30th September 2021.

INTRODUCTION

WE LIVE in a world where there is no consensus about how to define 'democracy' or 'environmental sustainability' let alone what their future relationship should or could be. Is the attainment of one, only possible at the expense of the other? What would be necessary for both to flourish? This lack of clarity and the widespread dearth of public discussion of the actual and potential relationship between distinct types of democracy and various levels of environmental sustainability will become increasingly crucial in coming years as the conflict between democratic rights and desirable goals of sustainability help shape public policies. It is also important to distinguish between immediate urgent issues of sustainability and medium to longer term questions of what kind of future society simultaneously maximises social justice while best safeguarding biodiversity and overall environmental sustainability.

At the moment, the conflict between democracy and sustainability is most visible in the voluminous but also narrow public debate over how to deal with the climate crisis. Existing democratic processes uphold market capitalist practices and the ideology of 'choice'. These are seen by many others as essentially legitimising and fuelling inequality. Increasingly, democratic processes are also viewed as too cumbersome, too self-interested, and too slow to be able to reach agreement on the scale, depth, and urgency of action necessary to prevent climate catastrophe.[1] Conversely, it is argued that without open democratic public debate, we cannot afford to trust governments to make unilateral decisions that could possibly turn out to be irreversible social and environmental disasters.

Thirteen years before the IPCC invoked 'code red' in 2021, David Spratt and Philip Sutton published *Climate Code Red: the case for action*.[2] What they described as the 'normal political-paralysis mode' still prevails across the world and is characterised by the following:

- lack of urgency and 'politics as usual' based on spin or denial.
- market needs dominate political responses.
- budgetary allocations are restrained.
- socio-economic targets and goals are determined by political trade-offs, compromise, and systemic inertia.
- there is an absence of national and international leadership as politics is adversarial, slow, and incremental.

Spratt and Sutton argued in 2008, that the urgency of the climate crisis requires that we implement similar methods as were adopted by the US and its allies during the Second World War. This 'emergency mode' recognises that speed of response is crucial; all necessary available resources should be mobilised and devoted to the emergency; non-essential functions and consumption should be curtailed or rationed; planning and innovation are necessary to foster rapid transition to a post-carbon future that is initiated and coordinated by government; emergency measures are endorsed by bi-partisan political leadership and broad public support; and, very importantly, failure is not an option.

Although this book is about the wider and deeper conflict between democracy and sustainability that goes well beyond the immediate issue of climate breakdown, it is the global scale of the climate emergency – regardless of whether countries have representative democracies or authoritarian regimes – that provokes much anxiety and deep political divisions. Of the 189 countries that ratified the Paris 2015 climate accord, just two, China and the US plus the European Union (EU) bloc, account for half of global emissions. China's emissions are now larger than the combined emissions of the US and EU. Add another seven countries – India, Russia, Japan, Brazil, Indonesia, Iran, Canada – and we have nine countries and the EU that are not only responsible for almost 70% of total global emissions but also play a disproportionate role in fossil fuel extraction, production, and consumption. Meanwhile the bottom and poorest 100 countries were responsible for only 3.6% of world emissions.[3] The burning political question becomes whether all or most of the top emitters would enter 'emergency mode' given their quite different domestic institutions and distribution of political power?

Despite the Biden administration's welcome commitment to decarbonisation after Trump's aggressive pro-fossil fuels regime, it is certainly not pursuing an emergency response. On the contrary, the symbolic declaration of protecting American public lands has been undermined by the US government approving within the first three months of 2021 a total of 1,179 drilling permits and 207 offshore drilling permits, almost as high as the record set by the Trump administration.[4] Although appearing to be substantial amounts in dollar terms, Biden's expenditure proposals are actually extremely modest. When rapid decarbonisation requires a minimum of 5% to 7% of GDP expenditure annually, Biden has allocated a tiny 0.5% of GDP spread out over eight years.[5] Similarly, his infrastructure plans are 1.9% of GDP or $500 billion annually over the same period but military expenditure will be 3.3% of GDP![6] The US is not alone. The G7 powerful countries – the UK, US, Canada, Italy, France, Germany, and Japan committed $US189 billion to support oil, coal and gas between January 2020 and March 2021 but only $US147 billion on clean forms of energy.[7] By September 2021, *Climate Tracker* rated proposed decarbonisation commitments by most leading G20 countries as either 'critically insufficient' or 'highly insufficient'.[8] So much for the climate emergency and building an ecologically sustainable world.

Leaving aside the current low level of expenditure allocated to decarbonisation, defenders of either democracy or markets are divided for quite different reasons over whether we should temporarily suspend democratic rights, subordinate businesses to 'wartime' controls and generally implement sweeping emergency action in the name of the climate crisis. As the exasperated graffiti on street walls declared: "if the climate were a bank, it would have already been saved." Other environmentalists such as Laurence Delina and Mark Deisendorf concede that wartime measures can rapidly achieve many goals but that without democratic public support these emergency measures will ultimately not succeed.[9] They nonetheless also acknowledge that democratic processes have failed to bring about urgent international policies to prevent climate breakdown, hence they focus primarily on the limited arenas of the national and the local.[10] Meanwhile, no anti-democratic authoritarian government or Right-wing movement is implementing or advocating emergency solutions to deal with the climate emergency. On the contrary, most defend fossil fuels, attack environmentalist and social justice movements or ignore the issue.

In other words, there is a divisive stalemate over whether emergency processes or 'normal politics' is best suited to prevent climate disaster. A fine line exists between creating powerful government institutions that could rapidly implement decarbonisation but also snuff out democratic rights. Is the cacophony of voices and disparate interests that currently deliver political paralysis and ineffective government the price we have to pay for preventing authoritarian rule? This question is part of a dangerous political myopia concerning emergency action. We are living in the worst of both worlds where class power rather than democracy prevails, and authoritarian measures are being increasingly enacted by parliamentary government in the name of 'democracy'.

The COVID-19 pandemic has already produced exaggerated fears of a new authoritarian state voiced by critics from the Right and Left. Notably, Italian philosopher, Giorgio Agamben has attacked lockdown measures, mask wearing, and social distancing as the end of democracy and freedom via the imposition of a 'state of exception' – emergency measures legitimised by the new religion called 'medicine'. He argues that modern societies have divided human experience into the biological 'bare life' and separated it from the 'social and cultural life' of humans. "Never before," he declares, "not even under Fascism and during the two world wars, has the limitation of freedom been taken to such extremes: people have been confined to their houses and, deprived of all social relationships, reduced to a condition of biological survival."[11] (Except, as he later notes, for the inmates of Nazi concentration camps who were reduced to 'bare life' vegetative states.)

What Agamben completely devalues is that there will no 'social and cultural life' for the more than four million people (and increasing, at the time of writing) who have officially already lost their 'bare life' and much higher numbers that have not been officially counted in many countries. The conflicting interests of 'the market' and 'medicine', including the inconsistencies of imposing lockdowns, leaving the production and distribution of vaccines in the hands of corporations and governments more committed to business as usual than public health, has ensured that waves of the virus will continue to plague many countries. Agamben assumes that there is a homogeneous 'medicine' when in fact 'expert' opinion varies considerably in regard to the viruses, infection rates and preventative measures.

Another interpretation is offered by French social theorist, Bruno Latour, who sees the emergency measures brought about by the pandemic as a dress rehearsal for the difficulties of dealing with climate change. In March 2020, before the massive global death toll rolled on in successive waves, Latour speculated:

> Imagine that President Macron came to announce, in a Churchillian tone, a package of measures to leave gas and oil reserves in the ground, to stop the marketing of pesticides, to abolish deep ploughing, and, with supreme audacity, to ban outdoor heaters on bar terraces. If the gas tax triggered the yellow-vests revolt, then imagine the riots that would follow such an announcement, setting the country ablaze. And yet, the demand to protect the French people for their own good and from death is infinitely more justified in the case of the ecological crisis than in the case of the health crisis, because it affects literally everyone, not a few thousand people – and not for a time but forever.[12]

Ironically, in May 2021, Macron had 'the supreme audacity' to ban outdoor heaters but unsurprisingly, none of the other measures Latour had hoped for or imagined. If the pandemic is a dress rehearsal for climate emergency measures, then heaven help us. By late 2021, the mass bungling, incompetence and political divisions by governments and citizens over vaccines and lockdowns had left millions dead and tens of millions ill. Could such deliberately and unintentionally incompetent governments solve the climate emergency, or had they learnt invaluable lessons from the failed responses to COVID-19?

The fear that preventing climate breakdown would lead to a permanent loss of democracy and civil liberties had already been anticipated before COVID-19. Take, for instance, the view of Stephan Rammler, Director of the Institute for Future Studies and Technology Assessment in Berlin. In May 2019, he proclaimed: "I'd rather die in a democracy than live in a sustainable dictatorship. Climate change is still a better option than losing our civil liberties."[13] It is not clear whether Rammler was merely being provocative or sincerely believed that 'democracy' is an absolute value that should not be compromised or subordinated to other objectives. Whatever the reason, like Agamben, he expressed a short-sighted, exaggerated, and ill-informed opinion. This is because we currently live in a world where most people do not enjoy the luxury of democratic civil liberties and even those living in countries with representative democracies have governments that put their capitalist market economies well above democratic accountability and environmental sustainability. After all, there is little point in a mindless, truncated 'democracy' and 'freedom' if climate break-down leads to major socio-economic crises including food shortages, devastating natural disasters and hundreds of millions affected by epoch-defining death and social dislocation. Likewise, there is little point in a 'green-washed' adulterated form of 'sustainability' if this neither achieves ecological sustainability nor overcomes profound levels of global social inequality with only token forms of democracy.

What Rammler and others alert us to is the difficulty of discussing deep tensions between contemporary democratic practices and the goal of environmental sustainability without simultaneously either endorsing libertarian and abstract notions of freedom or encouraging anti-democratic views that give ammunition to authoritarian political forces. Any critical questioning of what commonly passes for 'democracy' in contemporary societies immediately raises the equally troubling problems that could arise if various advocates of alternative post-capitalist societies continue to hold naïve and innocent notions of the power of 'genuine democracy'. Socialists, anarchists, and advocates of degrowth offer powerful criticisms of capitalist markets and the inadequacy of representative democracies. The essence of their critiques of highly constrained representative democracy is that apart from citizens participating in periodic elections, most institutions operate as 'democracy-free zones' between elections.

Hence, socialists and radical environmentalists believe that once the remote and unrepresentative nature of existing representative democracies are replaced with direct, participatory democracy at community and work-place level, then democracy will flower and cease being in conflict with sustainability. This hope is based on the as yet unproven assumption that participatory direct democracy is inherently far more compatible with ecological sustainability than is representative democracy. But what if it isn't? To be clear, I am not arguing against participatory democracy. Rather, this book will analyse and question the simplistic versions of direct democracy that tend to ignore the potential tensions and incompatible relations between democracy and sustainability at the local and larger national and global institutional level.

Importantly, we must distinguish between theory, policy, and agency. The three are related but not reducible to one another. For example, establishing the theoretical justification for either adopting wartime measures or democratic processes to prevent climate chaos is not equivalent to formulating the policies needed to prevent the latter, nor to mobilising the agents and devising the institutions and organisational strategies necessary to implement these emergency policies. At the theoretical and practical level, I do not believe that we can achieve a mythical full 'reconciliation with nature' that preserves sustainability for all species forever. Rather, we can only aim to maximise sustainability and biodiversity. Therefore, this book deals with some of the central political dilemmas of our time. One of these dilemmas concerns why environmental sustainability is much broader and deeper than widespread popular notions that sustainability is equivalent to adopting renewable energy and aiming for zero carbon emissions.

In *Capitalism Versus Democracy? Rethinking Politics in the Age of Environmental Crisis* (2020), I analysed how and why the fraught and tense relationship between 'capitalism and democracy' changed over the previous one hundred years. The recent revival of neo-fascist movements and the protracted economic and environmental crises threatening fragile representative democracies across the world signifies the continued relevance of the old conflict between 'capitalism and democracy'. Yet, this lengthy battle has also mutated into a new or parallel conflict which I call 'democracy versus sustainability'. Actually, this new political dispute is unintelligible without understanding previous and current conflicts over 'capitalism versus democracy'. Nonetheless, 'democracy versus sustainability' is not reducible to this old conflict. We have seen analyses of 'capitalism versus the climate'[14] but currently the discussion of 'democracy versus sustainability' remains underdeveloped.

Two Parallel Political Struggles

It is abundantly clear that strategic geopolitical scenarios devised in Washington, Beijing, Berlin, Tokyo, Paris, Moscow, and other capitals are focussed on recovering from the socio-economic crises caused by COVID-19.[15] In these policy scenarios, despite the co-ordinated ideological campaign directed at China by America and its allies – under the banner 'democracy versus authoritarianism' – concern for democratic rights ranks incredibly low as a priority issue compared with maintaining military power and industrial capacity as well as energy, food, and natural resources security. The desire of many citizens to protect environments and the biosphere may well threaten the future of capitalism. On the other hand, limited democratic decision-making in different countries (that is, electoral representative democracy) has consistently enabled governments to make policy decisions that either avoid or oppose the need for urgent environmental measures.

Currently, conservative and liberal defenders of this form of representative democracy claim to be more responsive to the peoples' need for jobs, income, and material wellbeing rather than jeopardising the latter by prioritising what they regard as unnecessarily drastic environmental sustainability measures. In opposition, advocates of degrowth and eco-socialism argue that green growth is an environmental fantasy and that the 'ecological modernisation' of the existing system of production and consumption will still make it largely unsustainable. Hence, we are witnessing two parallel political economic struggles that barely engage with each other but will, nonetheless, increasingly clash in coming years. These two struggles over the desirability and viability of either green growth or degrowth do not follow conventional Right and Left positions in regard to the future of capitalism. I will return to the anti-capitalist or post-capitalist positions shortly.

Firstly, the struggle over green growth is a familiar conflict that has been ongoing for at least three decades but will reach its most intense stage during the next five to ten years. I refer here to the conflict at national and international levels between the 'rear-guard' political parties, business groups, media outlets and think-tanks frantically trying to both delay and prevent the abandonment of fossil-fuels. Tied to this 'last stand' politics is a defence of multi-trillion-dollar investments and the desperate need to avoid or delay the restructure of carbon-intensive industries in manufacturing, transport, agriculture, chemicals and so forth. This is a fight that the 'rear-guard' cannot win but, unfortunately, will still have the capacity to inflict enormous damage on the biosphere. It is also essentially a technocratic dispute about moving to a new era of post-carbon capitalism, whether via electoral democracy and new legislation or via authoritarian measures such as government decrees and planned energy and industry transitions in those many countries without free elections.

Defenders of green growth capitalism are essentially divided into two camps. The first camp advocate ecological modernisation in the form of switching energy and production methods to renewables but leaving social inequality within and between countries, as well as private financial services, labour markets and rates of consumption (with a few exceptions) largely untouched. The so-called sustainability of green growth without major social reform is regularly voiced by a mixture of leading international agencies such as the IMF, UN, OECD and pro-business technological innovators and centre/Left parties. It is also evident in the extensive growth in financial markets of all kinds of 'green bonds', derivatives and fintech devices. These are driven by corporate and wealthy investors jumping on the gravy train of what is envisaged to be a new and booming area designed to suck up hundreds of billions of idle dollars in search of new investment outlets rather than constructing a more socially just and reformed 'green society'. I will not devote space to critiquing green growth, as there are many detailed analyses of the serious shortcomings and flaws in this approach to environmental problems.[16]

Within the green growth camp there is also a second group who wish to combine ecological modernisation with limited or greater social and economic reforms. Prominent exponents of social democratic 'mixed economy' agendas are policy analysts in Europe and the US such as Rebecca Henderson, Mariana Mazzucato, Thomas Piketty, Jeffrey Sachs, and Joseph Stiglitz. These policy reformers argue that ecological modernisation should be promoted alongside tax reforms, controls on financial corporations and new public investment in run-down health and social services. In Europe, even pro-competitive market analysts or Schumpeterians, such as Philippe Aghion, see technological innovation combined with state and civil society policies as the solution to the climate crisis and unemployment.[17] Other social democrats and neo-Schumpeterians campaign for more interventionist national government policies, the democratisation of the EU and variations of the 'entrepreneurial state' (Mazzucato[18]) to build a new 'social state'. Beyond switching to renewable energy, they also favour transforming cities and addressing housing needs, radically reducing pollution and waste, promoting healthier workplaces, diets and more investment in education and social care. Online daily journals such as *Social Europe* regularly produce a full range of these state-led green growth, social reform proposals.[19]

By contrast, in the US, anti-free-marketeers such as Rebecca Henderson believe, like Aghion, that innovative businesspeople can save capitalism by adopting a reform agenda based on 'sustainable, socially responsible capitalism'.[20] This latter agenda assumes that most businesses can remain profitable while paying a fair living wage, implementing ecological modernisation combined with adequately funded health and social services and political reform. Henderson acknowledges that the major political caveat or catch to such widespread and fundamental social change is that most businesses would have to adopt these reforms at the same time, as individual businesses would be unable to compete or survive if they implemented wage and social improvements on their own. It is important to note that some of the social democrats and socialists such as Thomas Piketty support far reaching reforms that are closer to proposals advocated by more radical Green New Deals. Across the world, there are now many varying conceptions of Green New Deals that range from social democratic and high-tech reforms (Jeremy Rifkin[21]) to more radical combinations of socialist and anti-capitalist environmental policies.[22]

If green growth is doomed to be an unsustainable 'stop gap' policy option, the question troubling many on the Left or in environmental groups is whether it is better to first achieve 'ecological modernisation' or to oppose it and fight for degrowth. We are not talking here about the classic Marxist debates about first the 'bourgeois revolution' before the final 'socialist revolution'. Remember, that the social justice elements within various Green New Deals are important to fight for but these are not to be confused with the old political distinctions between 'bourgeois' or 'socialist' revolutions; they are simply necessary social and environmental reforms. The political proposals and stakes are much more complex. Riccardo Mastini, Giorgos Kallis and Jason Hickel, for example, make a distinction between the following:

- Green New Deal 1.0 which is essentially a Keynesian stimulus package combined with emissions cuts, new investment in technology and jobs (such as the EU's 2019/2020 European Green Deal).
- Green New Deal 2.0 that supports social and environmental justice as central to economic stimulus (advocated by the Left in the British Labour Party, Green parties, or Left US Democrats); and
- Degrowth which rejects growth and emphasises social justice by abolishing or reducing all pressures on eco-systems (supported by small activist groups and academics).[23]

Spanish activist Alfons Pérez goes further and adds 'Post-Extractive' or 'Southern Green New Deal' and 'Feminist Green New Deal' to make degrowth proposals sensitive to identity politics and post-colonial needs.[24] Others such as Max Ajl reject Keynesian Green New Deals as imperialist and call for a 'peoples' Green New Deal' that combines Leninism with 'Left populism' and degrowth.[25] Similarly, the 'Red Deal' proposed by the Red Nation indigenous group is a crude amalgam of Marxism/Leninism and American cultural politics.[26] Every small political group now has its own version of a Green New Deal which embrace a wide variety of old and new political positions that are either coherent or a mishmash of incompatible tendencies.

Meanwhile, corporations and governments are banking on future technological innovations that will allow the vital room for high growth and high material consumption to continue expanding by *decoupling* economic growth from negative environmental impacts. Pro-marketeers such as Andrew McAfee in his book, *More from Less,*[27] argues that the 1970s claim of natural limits to growth has been completely disproven by fifty years of incredible capitalist growth. While I agree with McAfee that peak oil, peak copper, peak nickel, and the like have not yet occurred, this is not because of the competitive ingenuity of markets. Rather, finite limits of certain raw materials may never be reached as long as more than two-thirds of the world's population are kept in poverty by developed capitalist socio-political systems. Importantly, McAfee's arguments have been attacked by scientists and degrowthers as cherry picking facts and scientifically groundless.[28] He and other believers in the market ignore the already dangerous changes to four out of the nine planetary boundaries identified by earth system scientists.[29] Besides greenhouse gas emissions, there is far too much change to bio-geochemical boundaries such as excessive use of nitrogen in agricultural production, acidification of oceans and loss of biodiversity. It is not a simple matter of just certain natural resources running out, but rather of limits to the capacity of planetary life support systems to cope with excessive toxic pollution, soil erosion and alteration of bio-physical capacities due to incessant capitalist production and consumption.

The rose-tinted faith in free-markets ignores the reality that more than three-fifths of the world's population only consume a fraction of what is the per-capita material consumption in America. If the rest of the world were to enjoy the wages, material consumption and services of most people in OECD countries, there would be no more 'cheap food', 'cheap energy', 'cheap raw materials' or 'cheap manufacturing goods and services' to fuel so-called 'dematerialised' markets.[30] Far too many champions of capitalism also conveniently ignore the fact that the 'digital economy', for instance, is based on digital hardware that is produced in often appalling conditions in Asian and other low- and middle-income countries. Additionally, they remain silent about the millions of rural labourers working on cash crops in low-income countries or the low-paid, precarious immigrant labour that is imported to work under exploitative circumstances in the agricultural sectors of Australia, the US and Europe.[31]

Against the technological cheer squad, whether of the Right or the

Left, rates of *relative* decoupling or efficiency dividends in various indus-tries due to intensified productivity gains, new technologies, and synthetic manufacturing materials are far from adequate to meet present or future global needs based on lifestyles in high-income countries. Relative decou-pling in selected industries does not lead to absolute decoupling and is not translatable to whole economies. The notion that absolute decoupling will produce environmentally sustainable capitalist or post-capitalist societies is based on myth making, selective use of one-off productivity gains in some industries and other such claims. In short, no evidence has been produced in the three decades since 1990 that the extremely difficult or highly improbable technologically driven goal of absolutely decoupling growth from nature is attainable.[32] Similarly, claims that poverty has been falling in most countries is not borne out once China is excluded from global poverty figures.[33] Equally untrue is the assertion that markets are now 'treading lightly on the planet'. This claim ignores 'offshoring' carbon-intensive production and shipping waste to non-OECD countries.

Following the Sixth Assessment Report of the Intergovernmental Panel on Climate Change (IPCC) in 2021 which warned that keeping global warming to just an additional 1.5° Celsius degrees was quite remote, there is now little excuse for governments to avoid urgent action. Apart from almost daily reports of disruptive climate breakdown, the failure to *abso-lutely* decouple incessant economic growth of manufacturing, mining, and construction from the limits of nature, many agricultural scientists, envi-ronmentalists and the United Nations Food and Agriculture Organisation have voiced alarm about current forms of grain stock meat production and chemical agribusiness that only have a life expectancy of about sixty years. This earlier projection assumed the relative absence of massive climatic events now threatening food security. McAfee and others would be more convincing if they could show that food, water, and other vital natural resources could be sustainably produced and equitably consumed without relying on synthetic food, genetically modified ingredients, vitamin supple-ments and other non-natural resources generated by commercial markets.

We can therefore anticipate that two simultaneous and developing political economic struggles will affect the old divisions that characterised the contest between 'capitalism and democracy'. The first dispute between the advocates of pro- or anti-capitalist policies will continue to be charac-terised by struggles over the distribution of wealth and power, despite most of the opposing groups continuing to base their policies on environmen-tally *unsustainable material growth-orientated* futures. A broad range of antineoliberals, including Keynesian and post-Keynesian liberal social democrats, Marxists, and moderate environmentalists all favour action to prevent climate breakdown combined with varying degrees of reform or radical restructuring of markets. Yet, as I will argue, many continue to be stuck in the old distributional struggles between labour and capital, rather than also seeing the deep tension between 'democracy and sustainability'. Crucially, they still believe in the necessity of material *economic growth* rather than the struggles over the qualitative character and size of per capita and national material footprints.

   Whether defending fossil-fuels or championing various forms of ecological modernisation and social reform, most of the latter still have either a relatively impoverished understanding or hostile attitude to the need for high-income OECD countries to reduce affluent production and consumption. Conversely, some environmentalists argue that affluent per capita material consumption will need to be reduced by a massive 80 to 90 per cent of current levels if global equality for billions of impoverished people is to be achieved. Whether this figure proves to be a gross exaggeration in order for global equality to be realised without dangerously transgressing biophysical planetary boundaries is a crucial mainstream debate that is yet to occur.[34] Either way, if 80 to 90 per cent is too high, then we are still left with the task of persuading the affluent to reduce their material consumption by approximately 25 to 60 per cent in order to preserve maximum biodiversity.[35] This in itself constitutes an unimaginable political obstacle if contemporary voting patterns and anti-radical policy preferences become the measure. Importantly, we need to assess the political disputes over how to measure material footprints, which social groups or countries must make sacrifices for global sustainability to be secured and which industry sectors and forms of consumption need to be radically changed as I will discuss in Chapter Three.

   The second concurrent and less visible political struggle between the advocates of growth as opposed to degrowth is a more fundamental and far-reaching conflict between on the one hand, the ascending political economic forces promoting ecological modernisation and on the other side a range of radical environmentalists and eco-socialists who reject green growth as environmentally unsustainable. In opposition to the dominant versions of capitalist ecological modernisation are degrowth movements based on a diverse set of counter-cultural environmentalists, eco-socialists and post-colonial groups who share an anti-capitalist perspective but are presently too weak and too unwieldly in terms of their individual specific political agendas to constitute a coherent political coalition in favour of degrowth.

On current levels of political strength, the advocates of pro-market green growth will almost certainly win over much weaker degrowth movements. However, their success will be a pyrrhic victory and short-lived. This is because green growth can only temporarily postpone the need to resolve far deeper ecological problems generated by the unsustainable consumption of particular material resources associated with capitalist production of biomass, minerals, and metal ores. Whether it be water scarcity, deforestation and desertification, the ravages caused by numerous mining ventures, chemical agribusiness, multiple threats to oceans from pollution, deep sea mining and destruction of coastal habitats, not to mention the still unresolved and escalating problem of global waste disposal,[36] all these unfolding crises driven by material consumption will not be solved by simply switching to renewable energy and illusory panaceas such as electric cars.[37]

Hence, the dilemma facing us in the form of the climate emergency makes old style Left tactical discussions about 'correct line' strategy both a luxury and counterproductive. The political task is first to prevent complete climate breakdown and co-operate with social and political forces across the spectrum that are committed to this very urgent objective. This does not mean rejecting one's belief in degrowth, socialism or whatever, but merely to recognise urgent priorities and the relative political strength or weakness of diverse and often contradictory social forces in the political field. Instead of the conventional distinction between revolutionaries and reformists, the environmental crisis is producing quite different political approaches and strategies that is witnessing greater cross fertilisation of Green New Deal plans and degrowth proposals.

At the heart of the divisions between many alternative conceptions of the relationship between democracy and sustainability are varying emphases on a strong role for either local or national or international state institutions (or combinations of the latter). Clearly, there are major political differences between proposals based on state orientated as opposed to stateless conceptions of democracy, sustainability, and social justice. In recent years, a new ingredient has been thrown into the policy mix, namely, horizontal networks and peer-to-peer digital and other circuits that aim to bypass both corporate and vertical forms of production, distribution, and administration. It remains to be seen whether all kinds of blockchains, the internet of things and peer-to-peer networks constitute the emergence of a new social system or are merely new forms of digital capitalism that leave existing power relations largely untouched.

Different elements within the broad Left and environmentalist movements have long been divided between various forms of local communalist, nationalist, and internationalist tendencies. Each group begins from quite different starting points. Some envision radical or modified alternative institutional practices (whether capitalist or post-capitalist) that retain key features of existing high-tech industrialised societies. Others prioritise changing unsustainable energy and material consumption which requires radically different new modes of living and a drastic overhaul of familiar technologies and socio-political institutions. Regardless of whether alternative political movements grow or not, escalating environmental crises will necessitate citizens and policymakers having to make difficult choices.

As I discussed in *Fictions of Sustainability* (2018), any possible reorganisation of environmentally unsustainable, chemically based food production and consumption processes will have to include:

- the need to drastically reduce greenhouse gases from agricultural production which contributes 35% of global emissions.
- preserve biodiversity and yet produce sufficient affordable food for large numbers of low- to middle-income people.
- change the high dependence of urban residents on large-scale agribusiness based on either capital-intensive production or on the exploitation of rural labour; and
- provide secure employment, community services and improved social relations for both rural and urban residents.

Yet, some Leftists, such as Max Ajl, naively and absurdly believe that technically, "agriculture is ridiculously easy to fix" and that land reform, nationalisation of agribusiness companies, guaranteed living wages for rural producers and so forth are merely political problems.[38] This division between 'technical' and 'political' problems is artificial as they are inseparably fused.[39] Hence, the enormously challenging task of achieving the above as well as many other issues associated with food production, distribution, and consumption. The task is to achieve the goals of sustainability within a democracy and avoid past experiences of authoritarian mass slaughter (such as Stalinist forced collectivisation of agriculture) or major food shortages under nationalised production schemes. This is a challenge that many urban Marxists, anarchists and degrowthers have not yet fully considered. Therefore, this book aims to contribute to an understanding of some of the complex issues and challenges that will need to be resolved if democratic institutions and practices are to become compatible with ecologically sustainable objectives.

Illusions About the Sustainability of Digital Futures

In *Fictions of Sustainability*, I also discussed the radical Left technological utopians who oppose the advocates of degrowth. Like the pro-market believers in techno-fixes, they elaborate a range of technological fantasies about trillions of sensors providing abundance for all via the internet-of-things, zero marginal cost goods, 3D printing, cryptocurrencies or millions of earthlings colonising other planets and replacing scarce natural minerals or food resources. These digital imaginaries are especially popular with young radicals desiring anti-bureaucratic solutions based on post-work and individual or collective autonomy. Sadly, these post-capitalist futures usually ignore elementary but crucial environmental problems.

If far too many Marxists, Keynesians, and Greens have not yet caught up with the digital transformation of capitalist institutions and social practices, the opposite is true of a new generation of digital analysts. Currently there is a profound disconnect between the 'software' creating the images of the future and the major sustainability problems of manufacturing and managing the 'hardware' of digital, cybernetic capitalism or post-capitalism. It is not just the millions of low-paid workers creating high-tech hardware as already mentioned, but the growing crisis of carbon emissions from this faux 'sustainable' production. This is compounded by the inability to reuse much of the toxic materials and equipment through the so-called 'circular economy' and safely manage mountains of E-waste.

Most people supporting green growth ignore the horrific conditions under which rare metals or mineral elements are produced primarily in China and the Republic of the Congo. There would be no mobile phones, wind turbines, LED screens or dozens of other digital products without the 10,000 mines and the 'cancer villages' in China alone, the high volume of water and energy needed to produce each ton of these indispensable rare earth metals precisely in countries that have serious water shortages.[40] All this even before the need and ability to safely dispose of the coming predicted avalanche of batteries for the estimated 2.5 billion electric cars by 2050, the hundreds of millions of past-their-use-date solar power panels and other hardware. It is not that lithium and rare minerals are only available in

China or the Congo. Many countries can supply these metals. Rather, it is the cost of mining that is currently uneconomical for private businesses. Any post-carbon transition will require a thorough reorganisation and 'cleansing' of dangerous, polluting mining industries to minimise current shocking practices affecting both workers and communities suffering the excesses of environmental abuse and quasi-slave labour. Additionally, 3D printing will need to cease its reliance on a multitude of fossil-fuel based chemicals or polymers that pose a massive threat to global warming and waste management.

Technological utopians also seem to dismiss the fact that bitcoin requires enormous amounts of energy or that semi-conductor chips are also incredibly dependent on abundant forms of pure water resources that can be become scarce due to drought conditions (as in Taiwan in 2020-21). Similarly overlooked is the impact of mass space flights on earth's fragile life support systems, not to mention the enormous cost yet negligible impact space colonies may make on resolving natural constraints on earth within the urgent timeframe that is now required. It is quite likely that technological solutions to E-waste and other major environmental problems will be developed. Yet, research and development has never meant that capitalists automatically adopt innovative technology. Currently, many corporations are switching to renewable energy. However, it is far from certain that private businesses will voluntarily and rapidly implement a comprehensive ecological modernisation strategy in the next ten or so years and on a scale necessary to avoid a climate catastrophe.

One should not forget that pre-COVID-19, businesses, and governments could not even find a sustainable fuel solution for mass airline travel. Restrictions on short distance flying are already being imposed in France and other countries due to escalating dangers from carbon emissions and the extremely difficult technological obstacles preventing airlines from replacing fossil-fuels.[41] The tension between local needs and global desires is highly visible in the environmental and social damage caused by escalating air-borne mass tourism, such as lack of affordable housing due to short-stay rental crowding out residents in many cities, and damage to fragile eco-systems.

It is revealing that techno-utopians advocating 'fully automated luxury communism'[42] and their opposites in the form of degrowthers, both fail to offer convincing proposals for solving poverty suffered by billions of people. The former group promote an unsustainable environmental fantasy in claiming to be able to provide affluence for an additional seven billion out of nine billion people in the next thirty years. Meanwhile, degrowth proponents remain unable to outline adequate notions of alternative institutions and political strategy in OECD countries, let alone specify how poverty can be reduced for billions of people without significant material growth in low-income countries. The question of what level of equality is possible is not just an issue that merely affects relations between high-income and low- and middle-income nations. It is very much a political distributional struggle within *all* nations, whether the US, China, India, Brazil, France, South Africa, Indonesia, Italy, or Egypt.

One looming consequence of unsustainable growth is the likelihood that business owners, managers and administrators of capitalist societies will increasingly use police and military apparatuses to either stop citizens from protesting and voting or else prevent potentially newly elected governments from moving away from unsustainable forms of production and consumption. Unpalatable choices between incessant market growth and possible catastrophic environmental pressures face businesses, political parties, social movements, and citizens leading to irreconcilable divisions over desirable policies and solutions. Take for example the violence in France in late 2018 and through 2019 between the *gilets jaunes* ('Yellow Vests') and the police. The fact that this was triggered by the Macron Government's increase in diesel fuel taxes can be interpreted in two ways: deep public hostility to environmental measures when they increase the cost of living; or reaction against the Macron government's deliberate use of 'environmental' policies to cynically increase fuel taxes in order to fund tax cuts for the wealthy while simultaneously slashing and underfunding the 'social state'. It remains to be seen whether the Yellow Vests were a 'once only' reaction, or as Joshua Clover argues, an early example of 'climate riots' that are bound to increase in other countries in coming years.[43]

If minor taxes on carbon emissions have already produced violent reactions, it is a far greater challenge for the much larger agenda of degrowth in material consumption and production to be accomplished democratically. The contest between 'capitalism and democracy' now includes conflicts over energy, transport and other aspects of the *circulation process* and *social reproduction* system (welfare services, health, pensions, child, and aged care) rather than just the goods producing system. In Chapter Six I will discuss how the issue of a financially and environmentally sustainable 'social state' and alternatives to existing welfare regimes will increasingly take centre place in future policy debates. These new areas of dispute are the product of social and political realignments in recent decades. They require a reappraisal of traditional capital-labour conflicts as depicted in pre-1945 notions of the conflict between 'capitalism and democracy'. It is true that the New Left from the 1960s revised old 'classical' concepts of class struggle to embrace white collar workers and new social movements. Now even these 'revisions' are dated or inadequate to grasp the environmental implications and interconnections of 'capitalism versus democracy' *and* 'democracy versus sustainability'.

No society with free elections has ever had to face the decision of whether preserving the 'democratic will' is more important than preventing impending environmental disasters, especially if the majority of voters oppose necessary restrictions on capitalist production and consumption. This is not an argument against democracy, nor is it an abstract philosophical choice. I merely wish to puncture the illusions associated with naïve advocates of the 'infallible' power of democracy. It has long been optimistically assumed by many socialists that the exercise of democratic power by 'the people' is either a threat to, or incompatible with capitalist practices. This has certainly not proved to be the case in most parliamentary democracies where 'democracy' is largely confined to the vote and to free speech. Let us not forget that racist and exclusionary policies have already been reinforced by democratic electorates in OECD countries against refugees and immigrants in the name of 'protecting our communities, jobs and way of life'. We should therefore also not assume that parliamentary democracies will necessarily endorse urgently needed sustainable environment policies at the expense of existing profits, jobs, and consumption.

So far, anti-capitalist movements have produced few alternative planning measures. Instead, various pro-market scientists and government agencies are working on geo-engineering and military 'planning scenarios' concerning controlling greenhouse gases or dealing with national and international climate-induced crises. None of these military and other 'planning scenarios' have anything to do with either democratic participation, reducing inequality or decelerating economic growth. Importantly, the revival of nationalism within the context of 'globalised capitalism' has also created new political realignments across the political spectrum. Much of this new nationalism is hostile to existing civil rights, increased democratisation, equality, and environmental sustainability.

Today, in the midst of major environmental crises, three interrelated, urgent issues prevail. Firstly, whether democracy is the best way of preventing not just climate breakdown but other deeper ecological catastrophes. Secondly, the extent to which the future of capitalist growth depends on curbing or reducing even existing limited forms of democracy. Thirdly, the different ways that post-capitalist scenarios need to be rethought, particularly given that most socialist schemes to date have ignored the ecological constraints for the sustainable delivery of more equitable standards of living for over nine billion people in coming years.

Post-scarcity?

Given the highly fragile state of the biosphere (or the sum total of all world-wide ecosystems) and given the reality that social change will first occur very unevenly at national level rather than globally, it is necessary not to quickly assume that scarcity is an artificial or politically imposed concept that can be solved by radical redistribution of wealth and resources. Of course, attaining political and cultural equality remains an absolutely vital pre-condition for achieving material equality. That said, all future political agendas and social goals will no longer be able to rest on a naïve post-scarcity belief in material abundance. The long historical tradition of 'plenitude', of a supposedly abundant earth that can regenerate habitats and resources denuded by constant extraction and abuse is a dangerous conceit and phantasy that is still unrecognised, especially by far too many policy makers.

We are located at the end of a historical period that despite its setbacks and uneven distribution of material goods and services was driven by the political belief that each new generation would be better off materially than the last. Whether achieved incrementally or through revolution, the belief in material progress of the past two hundred years has not disappeared. Instead, a fundamental reassessment of both the rate and character of environmentally sustainable economic growth will test all shades of public policies across the political spectrum. In particular, advocates of equality will confront the dilemma of how much material redistribution is politically possible in particular societies if it becomes either too ecologically dangerous to keep on growing an unsustainable 'economic pie' or social conflict escalates because there is less to redistribute *without* adequate material growth.

Scarcity and deprivation have been constants throughout history. The so-called cycles of 'fat years' and 'lean years' were often accepted fatalistically as determined by the Gods. We also know that many communities and some civilisations were forced to migrate or collapsed due to inhospitable ecological habitats or depleted resources. From the nineteenth century onwards, 'scarcity' has been used by conservatives such as Thomas Malthus to justify harsh policies towards the poor based on the dubious notion that breeding from lack of constraint on sexual behaviour would see population outgrow food supply. In recent decades, the 'limits to growth' and other environment theories have either fused with a quasi-Malthusian notion of scarcity (Paul Ehrlich and the 'population bomb', for example[44]) or produced a non-Malthusian conception of enlarged material footprints (due to incessant capitalist growth rather than population growth) overshooting the 'carrying capacity of the earth'.

Analysts such as Lyla Mehta, Ian Scoones and others see a division across the political spectrum between those who adhere to notions of 'absolute scarcity' where scarcity is real, physical, and inescapable. They also identify 'relative scarcity' as something that depends on demand that can be allayed by science, technology, and economic policies such as solving under-production of food or goods. Both absolute and relative scarcity are to be distinguished from 'political scarcity' or the deliberate manufacture of 'scarcity' by those who do not wish to solve inequality of power and access to resources.[45] While these distinctions are helpful, the authors fudge the boundaries between those artificial narratives of scarcity that can be remedied by reforms, technological innovation or radical political action, and the non-artificial finite limits of resources that even a socialist revolution cannot overcome. It is the interplay of different real and politically created forms of scarcity that shape this conflict between 'democracy and sustainability'.

Degrowthers such as Jason Hickel risk succumbing to illogical rhetoric when discussing scarcity. While I share his penetrating critiques of pro-market analysts who believe in incessant green growth or create misleading impressions that global inequality is now supposedly much lower, it is important not to dress up degrowth and call it 'radical abundance'. Hickel is responding to sections of the Left whom he claims are smearing degrowth by calling it austerity that will force people to endure miserable lives. Instead, he argues, that exactly the opposite is true.

> While austerity calls for scarcity in order to generate more growth, degrowth calls for abundance in order to render growth unnecessary. Abundance, then, is the solution to our ecological crisis. If we are to avert climate breakdown, the environmentalism of the 21st century must articulate a new demand: a demand for radical abundance.[46]

I have no disagreement with Hickel, particularly if he is merely arguing that a more socially just distribution of resources and goods is needed rather than politically determined inequality, profound waste, and the unnecessary production of a range of goods, whether military weapons or bottled water. However, if scarcity is misconceived as only being artificial and politically determined, then there is no need to worry about the size and extent of material resources extraction and consumption or even Left calls of 'fully automated luxury communism' for all.

Mainstream green growthers have also mouthed cliches about 'sustainable abundance'. United Nation's 'Global Ambassadors' Michael Bloomberg, Saleemul Huq and Agnes Kalibata recently proclaimed that national governments could "heed the chorus of businesses, investors, cities, regions, and citizens calling for a healthier, more resilient future. We can all be winners in the race to sustainable abundance."[47] This 'win-win' market claptrap deliberately ignores that all cannot be winners if businesses and investors have to curb their current levels of resources consumption or investment in ecologically unsustainable production.

Words are important, and what Hickel actually supports is 'sufficiency' for all, rather than 'radical abundance'. Nonetheless, like most degrowthers, he supports reducing annual use of global material resources to the arbitrary figure of only 50 billion tons which has been plucked out of the air with little justification. As I will later discuss, if alternative movements accept this figure as representing the total amount of material resources, then they must also abandon the future goal of lifting between five to seven billion people out of poverty, as 50 billion tons will be insufficient, even after high-income populations reduce their per capita consumption by 90 per cent. Just as a world of nine billion people living affluent high-income lifestyles is environmentally unsustainable, so too, scarce resources and goods mean that 'radical abundance' is not possible especially if total global resources used are kept at such extremely low, unrealistic levels.

Fifty years ago, the notion of post-scarcity prevailed in various anarchist and Leftist circles. In the winter of 1972/73, while staying with radicals Sylvia Federici and Michael Kosok in New York, I remember witnessing the very heated arguments between them over anarchist Murray Bookchin's anti-Leninist collection of late 1960s essays, *Post-Scarcity Anarchism,* published in 1971.[48] However, their disagreements were over political organisation rather than whether or not scarcity could be overcome, such was the optimism of the times. Ironically, a similar disregard for scarcity is held by both utopian capitalists and technological utopian socialists such as

Leigh Phillips who continue to believe in affluence and abundance while rejecting degrowth as austerity-ecology.[49] Displaying either minimal environmental awareness or disregard for what is required to raise several billion poor people to affluence, both corporate capitalists and socialist utopians are in for a rude shock. The harsh reality of scarcity will force a rethink of many policies once the hope of absolutely decoupling economic growth from negative environmental impacts is revealed as a technocratic mirage.[50]

Unfortunately, demystifying utopian notions of decoupling economic growth from nature is only a starting point and will not in itself lead to any clear-cut politics, which will be dependent on the particular socio-political terrain in each different country. To understand how 'democracy versus sustainability' will influence future political struggles, we must first free ourselves from the prison of prevailing concepts and discourses that have helped shape our familiar perceptions of the world. Any new political paradigm must initially use the language of the dominant paradigm before subverting it by asking new questions and moving toward different answers and conclusions. The issues of environmental sustainability force us to rethink conventional politics. This book proceeds to advance an 'internal' critique of conventional liberal social democratic and radical Left and degrowth thinking about transitions to post-carbon democracy and post-capitalist societies.

The different conceptions of the compatibility or incompatibility of 'democracy and sustainability' are closely related to the historical level of capitalist development in particular countries. In the following chapters, I will analyse how past and present theories and movements of social change – whether anti-capitalist or post-capitalist in their green or other forms – understand and attempt to deal with the major problems in the present-day world. At the moment, no party, social movement, government, or business enterprise is adequately prepared for escalating environmental and social crises. Indeed, only preventative action is feasible, as it is impossible to be prepared politically, economically, technologically, or militarily. This is partly due to the unpredictable nature of volatile environmental events. It is also due to deep-seated political divisions amongst decision-makers across the world over how to respond to the climate crisis which currently prevent, or delay coordinated action. David Spratt makes the compelling point that:

> When risks are existential, markets fail because they can neither adequately

assess the risks nor mitigate the threat in the interest of society as a whole. This is true for weapons of mass destruction, for pandemics, and for ecological collapse, where the primary risk management responsibility lies with the state. It is also true for climate disruption, where markets have failed to analyse the high-end risks, especially system tipping points and impacts which are non-linear and difficult to model. When damages are beyond calculation, – or infinite – cost-benefit analyses, economic models, conventional risk analysis and the "learning from failure" approach all break down.[51]

Liberals, social democrats, and other centrists are particularly divided or half-hearted concerning rates of necessary decarbonisation responses to prevent catastrophic conditions. They also fear social conflict and polarisation but are still quite comfortable tolerating major disparities in wealth and power. While recognising the prospect of increased social dislocation caused by climatic and other environmental crises affecting food production, they nevertheless prioritise economic growth driven by private businesses rather than resolving inequality through a range of non-market expenditure and regulatory measures. Similar fears and divisions extend beyond centre/Right and centre/Left parties and are evident in trade unions and civic organisations over how much social justice is necessary in any 'just transition' to a post-carbon society. Pragmatic faith in rational social policy adjustments and technological innovation mixed with ad hoc policy responses continue to drive policy agendas. Whether domestically in OECD countries through the emphasis on education and incremental social reform, or in developing countries via support for 2030 Sustainable Development Goals, liberal social democrats have still not come to terms with the scale and depth of looming social and environmental crises which their incremental policies will do little to resolve.

This book will analyse the relationship between democracy and sustainability and the new challenges that will confront all groups across the political spectrum. In Chapters One and Two, I outline why the emergence of post-carbon societies, whether post-carbon capitalist or post-capitalist, will be quite different to the early development of capitalist societies. What kind of social classes, political organisations and prevalent cultural practices will characterise these transitional societies? In Chapter Three, I attempt to show why the coming political struggle over the size and character of material footprints will become central to policy making in a way that is still barely recognised today. Following on from this, I will discuss in

Chapter Four why the degrowth movement as the most radical challenge to capitalist economic growth, rests on seriously flawed proposals that undermine their otherwise extremely important critique of existing production and consumption processes. The failure of the degrowth movement to have any detailed notion of state institutions and planned degrowth raises the crucial issue discussed in Chapter Five of what kind of reform-orientated or radical politics is possible to break the current political impasse preventing decisive action on environmental and socio-political crises.

No radical or reform-based alternative to existing capitalist systems is adequate without a conception of how to create, organise and fund a 'social state' that provides universal care and satisfies social needs currently neglected in capitalist welfare regimes. In Chapter Six, I discuss the strengths and weaknesses of various social welfare systems and alternatives such as basic income and universal basic services schemes. It is not just conventional Right-wing parties and liberal social democratic policy makers that will be forced to seek novel solutions to maintain political relevance and social order. Radical advocates of alternative societies can no longer rely on historically obsolete modes of organisation or familiar social change agents. It is the emerging challenges and tensions between democracy and sustainability that will affect the shape and content of forthcoming politics and the future character and viability of capitalist societies.

1. FROM CARBON CAPITALISM TO POST-CARBON DEMOCRACIES

THE TRANSITION FROM 'CARBON CAPITALISM' to a 'post-carbon society' is conceptualised as either an ecologically modernised capitalism or as a socialist or ecologically sustainable post-capitalist social order. The way carbon capitalism is seen as a precursor to post-carbon social formations raises many questions. To date, capitalist, communist, monarchist, military and other authoritarian regimes have all relied to different extents on carbon emitting fossil fuels and continue to do so. While the prevailing form of energy is the focus of much environmental activism and thinking, will the adoption of renewable energy be so significantly different that it will disrupt and undermine not only existing forms of production and consumption, but the very distribution of political power and social privilege?

Any transition from capitalist systems driven by fossil fuels to post-carbon capitalism, let alone post-capitalist societies based on renewable energy, requires an understanding of how diverse societies came to be what they are today. It is their diverse histories and social structures that either make possible or severely limit their capacity to develop new socio-economic and political institutions and practices. This truism is often over-looked in the burgeoning literature on the topic of the Anthropocene. Apart from earth scientists warning about how humans now threaten the nine planetary boundaries through carbon emissions and other deleterious activities, no clear politics is so far linked to the concept of the Anthro-pocene. Instead, an army of scholars from the humanities, social sciences and natural sciences continue to explore every facet of this human-induced geological age with only a minority making any connection between academic investigations and political action.[1] There is much discussion of the old boundaries between nature and culture being broken down and how the blending of the constructed, artificial, and human made world ('post-humanism') has brought about the end of 'nature'. Like the nineteenth century dreams of a single universal science that could cover what are commonly called the natural sciences, cultural studies, and social sciences, so the new 'post-humanist' materialists endlessly discuss new theories but, unsurprisingly, fall back on very conventional concepts when trying to explain actual political and social struggles.[2]

Influential historian and theorist of the impact of climate change on the humanities, Dipesh Chakrabarty, has given currency and depth to the concept of the Anthropocene. However, he has redefined the 'political' to the extent that it is little more than a metaphysical combination of earth systems science and conservative Heideggerian and Schmittian philosophy. The problem I have with this kind of theorisation is that everyday politics, such as the pursuit of social justice in human historical time, is now far 'out-scaled' by 'Anthropocene time' which is part of the millions of years old 'earth history'.[3] French theorists Christophe Bonneuil and Jean-Baptiste Fressoz ask a pertinent question about Chakrabarty's depoliticised approach: "What can we still do on the individual and collective scale given the massive scale of the Anthropocene? The risk is that the Anthropocene and its grandiose time frame anaesthetise politics. Scientists would then hold a monopoly position in both defining what is happening to us and in prescribing what needs to be done."[4]

Instead of being a catalyst for mass political action, Bonneuil and Fressoz argue that the concept of 'humanity as geological force' actually reinforces various socio-environmental injustices under the consensual banner of 'the species'. "The subject of the Anthropocene, moreover, appears as an eco-citizen optimising her carbon credits, managing her individual footprint ... And finally, the subject of the Anthropocene is constructed as a passive public that leaves solutions to geocratic experts."[5]

Although Bonneuil and Fressoz highlight the depoliticised character of much of the literature on the Anthropocene, they say little about the potential agents of social change that could bring about a post-carbon society. This is also partly true of Andreas Malm, Jason Moore, and other advocates of the 'Capitalocene'.[6] Instead of focussing on millions of years of geological time, Moore sees the origins of the climate crisis and broader environment crises dating from developments in the long 17th century.[7] It is not an undifferentiated humanity in general (or the human species) that is responsible for our current crisis but the emerging capitalist class that dominated and transformed nature as mere stuff to be used in production and consumption.

One can travel a substantial distance with Moore. After all, it is outrageously unfair of Anthropocene theorists to blame 'humanity', especially billions of poor people who have tiny carbon and material footprints compared to the incessant growth propelled by capitalist industries in leading G20 countries. Yet, ultimately, the 'Capitalocene' is also a limited umbrella concept that bends the stick too far the other way in that it reduces or subsumes the whole natural world to a 'productivist' logic equivalent to the development and practice of capitalist production. In other words, there are no natural processes, no laws of physics, and no evolutionary biology outside capitalism. In many respects, proponents of the 'Capitalocene' are conventional class analysts just as many 'post-humanists' are anti-class analysts. Despite Moore's many valuable insights into how contemporary capitalism is based on the four 'cheaps' of labour power, food, energy, and raw materials,[8] he is unable to tell us how and why conflicts within contemporary capitalist countries will not follow the pattern of earlier forms of class struggle. The same is true of other Marxists such as John Bellamy Foster and Brett Clark who coin the ugly and simplistic term 'Capitalinian' to describe monopoly capitalist environmental impacts since 1945.[9]

Comparing the Origins of Capitalism with Potential Post-Carbon Democracies

Most of the abstract and depoliticised discussions of the Anthropocene do little to help us understand the necessary processes to achieve decarbonisation or whether and in what ways a post-carbon society will differ from existing capitalist systems. Are we currently seeing the origins of post-carbon social formations and if so, are they being driven by social classes that are similar or different to those that produced the emergence of capitalist societies? To answer this question, we have to first dispel the widespread misconception that 'capitalism' or the 'industrial revolution' was a homogeneous system or stage of history that replaced 'feudal' society. There was no uniform 'capitalism' that developed simultaneously in various countries or originated under the same conditions. The voluminous literature on the origins of capitalism reveals no agreement between historians as to whether, for example, capitalism primarily developed in towns or first required the transformation of agricultural production into commercial capitalist agriculture, thus driving surplus populations into expanding urban centres. These and other developmental paths depended on the specific conditions in individual countries.

A range of mainstream analysts have, for instance, argued that capitalism is essentially a more developed form of commercial market relations that existed in rudimentary form in medieval and ancient societies. The full flowering of capitalist commercial life could only proceed after the numerous political, religious, geopolitical, and social constraints on commerce and industry, such as mobile, 'free labour', were weakened or removed. Marxists either reject all or various key parts of this perspective. Many have viewed capitalism as a new mode of production which separated production from consumption, introduced new forms of labour with corresponding social relations that developed quite differently to earlier forms of pre-capitalist commercial activity. Recently, there has been a revival of debates on how 'capitalist' were the so-called 'bourgeois revolutions' from the eighteenth to the twentieth centuries.[10] In other words, there is no agreement between historians on what 'feudalism' was and also how prominent were the bourgeoisie or capitalists in the overthrow of 'feudalism' in France in 1789 or in Ethiopia in 1974.

If capitalism is based on free wage labourers rather than slaves or serfs, what kind of labour system will characterise post-carbon societies? Many who believe that slavery, in its legal or illegal forms, never completely disappeared under capitalism, also assume that emerging post-carbon societies will be capitalist. Others argue that a fully decarbonised society will eventually prove to be incompatible with capitalism. As all industry sectors are forced to decarbonise, the cumulative consequences will be far more destabilising. Employment, consumption, and other social processes will thus require far greater state intervention than previously seen, even compared to the period from the 1940s to the 1960s. According to this perspective, optimistic pro-market analysts mainly focus on a few areas such as renewable energy or transport and do not consider the deeper global implications of decarbonisation. So far, neither the pro-market advocates of smooth continuity, nor the doubters who see disruption creating new post-capitalist social relations have produced convincing evidence to justify their case.

Several questions concerning the character of future post-carbon societies arise from disputes over the emergence of earlier forms of capitalism.

Contrast, for example, Marx's analysis with the conventional history of the change from so-called 'feudalism' to the 'industrial revolution' taught in schools and universities. Volumes one to three of *Capital* were a forensic examination of the component elements of the capitalist mode of production such as labour, rent, land, capital, commodities, value, and circulation. Marx not only argued that each element differed from their earlier historical forms (despite the labels 'rent' or 'labour' creating the false impression that they were similar) but that each of these elements were transformed within countries where the new capitalist class emerged. Landowners and 'land' did not disappear but took on either diminished or transformed political, economic, and cultural roles compared with the power and roles of owners of capital.[11] If so, what are the emerging elements of post-carbon society – apart from new forms of renewable energy – and in what way will these emerging social relations and modes of producing, distributing and consuming goods and services differ from or be a continuation of the capitalist mode of production? Will the possible emergence of new social classes be matched by new political, administrative, legal, and cultural institutions and practices or will the latter be modified versions of existing relations?

Importantly, the deterioration of environmental conditions driven by unsustainable capitalist growth will make it necessary for post-carbon societies to be founded on a new relationship to the natural and constructed environment. To what extent will corporations and small businesses adapt to new environmental constraints or become unviable? Much of the contemporary discussion of post-capitalism ignores the capacity of business to adapt and is preoccupied with speculative outlines and hoped for new institutions and practices. There is a common vision or assumption that post-carbon societies will constitute a complete break with capitalist social institutions and relations. Yet, capitalist socio-political relations and industrial modes of production became dominant in diverse countries and co-existed historically alongside the residues of earlier social classes and political orders, whether agrarian, aristocratic, merchant traders or subordinated Indigenous people.[12] It follows that if emerging capitalist societies were hybrid forms based on a fusion or co-existence with pre-capitalist social practices (whether religious, gendered, cultural or legal), then future post-carbon or post-capitalist social orders will also most likely be hybrid social formations, unless there is wholesale revolutionary destruction of the old order.

Currently, it is difficult to see any significant differences between businesses that use either fossil fuels or renewables. Despite their use of different technologies and energy sources, both practice within the context of local and international capitalist markets structured by government regulations, finance, labour markets or competition with other producers of goods and services. Could post-carbon energy systems and innovative technologies free local communities from dominant markets and gradually unleash new ways of producing, consuming, and sharing? This is the idealised vision of many advocates of alternative technologies who see 3-D printing, the zero-marginal cost of goods, blockchain financial transactions and so forth, as facilitating new social systems even though the latter technologies were developed by capitalist entrepreneurs. Yet, the power of innovative technologies is insufficient on their own to create new social orders.

If the emergence of either post-carbon capitalist or environmentally sustainable post-capitalist societies will not follow the paths that gave rise to the origins of diverse forms of capitalism, how will this new society emerge? Max Weber famously claimed that the development of capitalism required specific Western social conditions such as scientific rationality, Protestant religion and new European urban social classes. Some would argue that Weber displayed a form of Orientalism that depicted the East as dominated by mysticism, magic and spirituality while the West was progressively disenchanting the world through secular technical rationality.[13] Leaving these important historical disputes aside, the acquisition and application of particular levels of knowledge, as also the emergence of new social classes and political cultural conditions required for post-carbon societies will definitely not be associated solely with the West. China, for instance, has more scientists, engineers, and researchers than the US and Europe combined. Unfortunately, most of them, as in the EU and US, are currently not working on environmentally sustainable technology or new organisational social practices.

Regardless of geographical location, it is most likely that new environmentally sustainable societies will emerge from within 'the womb' of existing capitalist societies just like some early capitalist social relations emerged within pre-capitalist societies. Nonetheless, it is unlikely that 'revolution from below' will be the catalyst for social transformation as contemporary capitalist societies do not conform to simple two class models of a ruling class and a subordinate working-class or peasantry. Instead, emerging post-carbon societies may be initially driven by growing protest movements from below, plus expanded government legislation and regulations designed to prevent deepening eco-system crises. It remains to be seen whether currently dominant forms of corporate capitalist power will survive largely intact or be subordinated to emerging post-carbon, democratic or non-democratic state control.

Rather than adhering to the widespread misconception of neatly packaged 'stages' of history that succeed one another in linear fashion, I wish to emphasise the 'messiness' of historical change, its highly conflictual, chaotic, and uneven character, and why any possible transition to environmentally sustainable societies will also be fundamentally different to earlier historical transformations. Momentous social turbulence invariably helps in the development of new social classes or is caused by the prior emergence of new social classes that have refused to continue tolerating being marginalised and exploited by dominant classes. As usual, it is much easier to see the past than to envisage the future. For instance, note the different reception given to historian E. P. Thompson's classic 'history from below', the complex rural and urban origins and processes that led to 'the making of the English working class' from the late eighteenth to early decades of the nineteenth century.[14] In the 1960s, Thompson's account was controversial because it involved certain preconceived notions about what it meant to 'make a class'. Tom Nairn and Perry Anderson challenged Thompson's assertion that "the working class made itself as much as it was made"[15] and that it developed a class consciousness through struggles and common lived experiences of shared antagonisms to employers, landlords and so forth. Nairn, and later Anderson, asked: what did it mean for a class 'to be made', and what constituted 'class consciousness' if the militant English working class before 1832 become so politically docile twenty years later and continued to be non-revolutionary for the next 150 years during the period of its greatest expansion?[16]

I would add that just as 'capitalism' is never 'completed' or 'made', so too, the making of a class, whether it be capitalist or working class is never finished. Rather, there is constant transformation of either occupations, existing industries, living conditions, or larger socio-cultural and political power relations. This is one of the reasons why 'class consciousness' in the 1820s, 1890s, 1930s, 1960s or 2020s is so different in each period, not only in England but comparatively in other countries across the world. We can also never be quite sure when and if capitalist classes have exhausted their capacity to innovate new forms of production and modes of maintaining socio-political power. As we have seen, capitalist classes are themselves in constant flux in terms of the sources of their capital, their preferred investments, their commitment to defending old production processes or supporting innovative technologies and products, such as the current divisions over opposing or supporting ecological modernisation.

The critique of Thompson in the 1960s was quite different to recent criticisms influenced by post-colonial theory and capitalist globalisation. Commenting on *The Making of the English Working Class* (1963) historian Priya Satia argued in 2020 that:

> Expansive as its cast is, its geographical scope is constricting. Though set in the era of British conquest of vast swathes of the world, it barely acknowledges that reality. This is doubly strange, given that Thompson wrote it while decolonisation was forcing Britons to contend with the ethics of empire, and was himself descended from a line of colonial missionaries deeply engaged with such matters. His classic text created an island template for the most progressive British history of the late-20th century, unwittingly legitimising the nostalgic view of 'Little England' that has culminated in Brexit.[17]

How is it, she asks, that Thompson who was a strong critic of colonialism, could present a thesis about how the English working class 'was made' without any analysis of the inseparable relationship of the English factory system to the social conditions that produced Indian cotton and other colonial commodities? Satia notes that despite countless anti-colonial thinkers and historians documenting the British Empire's morally bankrupt foundation in racism, violence, extraction, expropriation and exploitation, recent studies in 2016 and 2020 show that 43 percent of Britons are still proud of their empire and believe it was a good thing. Britons are also more likely than people in other former colonial powers such as France, Germany or Japan to wish that their country still had an empire.[18] She convincingly illustrates that even though "the historical sensibility that enabled imperialism is still intact, despite the seeming end of empire, we have been unable to sustain a consensus around the moral case against empire."[19] Therefore, Satia argues that we need new modes of historical thinking that are less likely to blind us to the crimes of empire.

What, you may ask, has the critique of E. P. Thompson got to do with the transition to post-carbon societies? Part of the answer relates to the transformation of existing social classes and the possible emergence of new social change agents. If the original making of the English working class in the decades leading up to the 1830s was not fully comprehensible without understanding the interconnection of domestic developments in England with activities in Britain's empire, then the notion of autonomous *national* social change in the twenty-first century is even less plausible. Any account of the likely changes to specific industries, labour markets, forms of consumption, financial relations and government social services in particular countries will be extremely limited at best, if we do not grasp the *international* and interconnected factors determining or restraining the possible private and public sector developments of new post-carbon modes of living.

Contemporary international communication networks and trade may instantaneously spread particular social ideas, innovative technologies and help reshape local domestic practices. Nonetheless, the reception of these ideas and the formation of a post-carbon or deeper environmental 'consciousness' can never be identical in its impact and consequences. This is because ideas need to be received and absorbed by different segments of local and national populations and practised by particular political organisations, businesses, social movements, and governments operating under quite different national and local conditions with quite specific socio-political histories.

Those who believe that we are in the 'cancer stage' of capitalism or 'catastrophe capitalism', the 'end times' and other epithets, must differentiate between the so-called political inability of ruling classes to innovate or reform and whether any potential future 'modernisation' such as green growth will save capitalism or only exacerbate deep-seated social and economic crises. In other words, are we in a comparable historical and political economic situation to Gorbachev's 'perestroika', where once the political will to 'reconstruct' the USSR was finally found by the mid-1980s, it was far too late and only escalated the disintegration of the old system? Could leading capitalist societies also be suffering from terminable forms of stagnation and decline or will the transition to green growth restore their vitality rather than hasten their demise?

Crucially, for a new post-carbon social class or classes to emerge, it would require not just a change in occupations but a fundamental alteration in the proportion of people in the paid workforce dependent on wages and salaries as compared to those unemployed, on various state benefits, studying or in retirement. Without this social transformation in the quantity and quality of paid work, there would be little political economic space for the possibility of a new class to survive and function. In short, a new social class must embody socio-economic characteristics that are quite distinct from simply being a variation or part of a reconstituted wage-dependent class. Since the 1940s, we have seen regular discussion of a 'new class' of professionals and managers standing between capitalists and workers. There is no doubt that this category has grown and many now vote for Green parties and centre/Left policies. However, most are not self-employed and are in dependent positions subordinate to private or public employers. Others constitute part of a reconstituted middle class that embrace not just lawyers, doctors, or shop keepers of the old petite bourgeoisie but also new consultants, self-employed contractors and so on. Most of these are in a fragile position dependent on businesses or governments for their services and as such would be unlikely to become the dominant class of a new post-carbon society.

While 'professionals' do not constitute a new class, they carry out key administrative and technical roles and help shape cultural practices. Nonetheless, they lack the economic and political power to create any new social formation on their own without either the support of large capital or unions and other social movements. Many professionals came from working-class families just as former peasants became urban wage workers and developed new socio-cultural relations as part of earlier forms of industrial transformation. The emergence of any sizeable 'post-carbon class' would require existing classes to be dramatically reduced or undermined so that the latter no longer remain central or dominant. Also, what kind of political organisations would represent this new class or strata given that their current support for centre/Left parties or Greens hardly constitutes a major political change to the status quo? Importantly, in what way would this new class change state institutions to reflect such a significant transition to a post-carbon or post-capitalist society? What shape would this class take in the most populous and highly stratified societies such as India or China?

Most current discussions of threats to democracy or how to resolve the climate emergency largely and understandably focus on the familiar rather than the unknown. We are in the midst of the rapid implementation of digital technologies and communications systems to produce consumer goods and military weapons or conduct state and private surveillance. A proliferation of global and regional interlocking corporate supply chains, pervasive cultural marketing techniques and restructured labour markets have already disorganised and undermined the former social and political power of working-class organisations. Capitalist classes for all their internal divisions still remain in the saddle but it is unclear how secure, and durable is their power. COVID-19 has already revealed how fragile is the condition of millions of small and medium sized businesses once health lockdowns jeopardised their viability, with or without government support.

Political conflicts over simultaneously occurring socio-economic and environmental crises could turn out to be very turbulent, perhaps even as volatile as the massive political economic upheavals witnessed during the industrial transformation of agrarian societies between the eighteenth and twentieth centuries. To think that successful decarbonisation strategies can proceed smoothly without significant modification or abandonment of disastrous, short-sighted international financial, production, trade, military, and other policies is to ignore the complexities of the challenges we face.

Declining and Rising Social Classes

To better understand the lack of clarity among theorists and activists about the character of possible emerging new industries, institutions, and societies during the next ten to thirty years, it is sobering to reflect on the failed prophecies that were made in similar but earlier debates from the 1830s to the 1880s. During this period when European and American agrarian societies were being transformed into varying levels of industrial capitalism, most predictions about the character of future societies either failed to materialise or went in a different direction to what might have been expected. These debates centred on identifying which social class or classes would be pivotal in countering existing ruling classes and, equally importantly, recognising which social classes were in decline, as their historical moment had passed. The participants in these earlier debates argued that if the emerging social agents of change were not identified, then it would be difficult to develop appropriate political organisational forms capable or realising the goals necessary for any future alternative society.

The circumstances may be entirely different, but in order to illustrate the dilemma facing those who are currently trying to conceptualise future post-carbon socio-political trends, it is worth reflecting on the conflict over theory and practice between Karl Marx and Mikhail Bakunin (and their followers) in the International Working Men's Association during the 1860s and early 1870s. Both shared many views about the need for socialism but differed on substantive issues including who would make the revolution and whether a state would exist under socialism. Bakunin, the anarchist, was heavily orientated to the past and present size of the peasantry in agrarian

Europe rather than to the rapidly industrialising and urbanising capitalist social structures. He therefore argued that peasants would play a leading revolutionary role, as they were closer to nature. Bakunin also championed what he described as the 'riff-raff' or 'rabble' of society (thieves, prostitutes and others *not* employed as wage labour in factories and other workplaces). While Marx called these sub-proletariat the 'lumpen-proletariat', Bakunin saw them playing a vital role because they were 'uncontaminated' by stuffy, property-orientated, law-and-order bourgeois social practices. He liked the 'riff-raff' because too many 'respectable' workers were conservative and aped the manners and values of the bourgeoisie. Bakunin also opposed Marx's argument for the 'dictatorship of the proletariat', a temporary socialist state that would protect the working-class from any attempt by the capitalist class to reimpose capitalism. Marx saw the state as withering away only in the advanced stage of communism whereas Bakunin objected to a worker's state dictating to the peasantry and especially to the 'rabble' of society.

Although their debate may appear archaic, it remains instructive when considering who will bring about any future ecologically sustainable democracy and what its main characteristics will be. Both Bakunin and Marx were fundamentally wrong insofar as no complex society can function without new coordinating state institutions, especially those concerned with social justice, legal protection of human rights and redistribution of material wealth, whether one calls these societies capitalist, socialist, communist, or post-carbon democracies. Some argue that Bakunin was more prescient in that the major revolutions of the twentieth century occurred in peasant-based societies of Russia, China, Vietnam and so forth. However, in developed industrial capitalist countries most peasants and agricultural labourers were consigned to the 'historical dustbin', as their numerical size rapidly declined during the following four decades until 1914. They were reduced to less than a quarter of the total workforce in Western Europe between 1950 and 1960 and shrunk to fewer than 5 per cent of the workforce in the following decades. In the century after the 1917 Russian revolution, agricultural labour had declined from 62% of the global workforce in 1950 to approximately 28% of total workers by 2016.[20]

As for the 'lumpenproletariat', only handfuls of radicals in the 1960s and 1970s romanticised criminals, prostitutes, and schizophrenics as the 'true revolutionaries'. These groups were seen to violate the norms of private property, bourgeois ideology and cultural taboos. If Freud had attended to the neuroses and psychoses of the bourgeois individual that developed within the bourgeois family, Deleuze and Guattari, among many others, romanticised the power of unconstrained desire, and promoted 'schizoanalysis' (the power of 'schizoid' desire as the basis of revolutionary action) in opposition to what they saw as conservative psychoanalysis.[21] Today, no major radical social movement believes that substance addicted individuals, criminals and the mentally ill are the vanguard of the new society even though they condemn the 'war on drugs' and the over-emphasis on treating the ill individual rather than the 'sick society', as well as the incarceration and appalling treatment of prisoners in many criminal justice systems.

If Bakunin's peasants largely disappeared by the mid-20th century in many OECD countries, the industrial proletariat also began succumbing to the same fate after reaching their high-water mark in these same developed capitalist countries during the 1950s and 1960s. (Globally, total employment in manufacturing industries continued to grow by 1990, due to major increases in low- and middle-income countries.) Despite still retaining strength in some industries in developed capitalist countries and engaging in occasional spasmodic militancy, it has been abundantly clear for over fifty years, that the leading role Marx attributed to the blue-collar indus-trial proletariat is, with a few exceptions, well and truly over in OECD countries. Alas, far too many of the old Left are still too wedded to a deep-seated belief in the leading role of the industrial working class as the vanguard of social change.

Significantly, it should be noted that at present, it is already technologi-cally possible to produce all the manufactured goods in the world with between five and ten per cent of the total global workforce. Some countries have larger percentages involved in manufacturing, but it is highly likely that the percentage of workers employed in factories will experience the same fate of agrarian workers and fall to between 2% and 5% of workforces in coming decades. It will not be automation alone that determines the rate of the demise of the blue-collar proletariat. Rather, the size and power of manufacturing sectors will depend on national employment and industry policies, political struggles over job cuts, levels of private investment and the viability of particular enterprises and industries in the face of regional and global market competition. Aaron Benanav argues that it is not rapid technological innovation that is driving the replacement of workers but rather overcapacity combined with stagnation and low growth rates in the capitalist world.[22] As I will later discuss, Benanav presents only a partial analysis as he ignores environmental factors in his analysis of automation.

In contemporary America, instead of a pre-industrial lumpenprole-tariat, we have seen the emergence in recent decades of what social theo-rist, Clyde Barrow calls a post-industrial lumpenproletariat or 'surplus population' that is either outside or intermittently connected to the production system.[23] It continues to be affected by deindustrialisation, racism, mental illness, addiction, crime, and general social neglect apart from policing and incarceration. White conservatives called this population the 'white underclass' and Right-wing Democrat, Hilary Clinton described them as 'the basket of deplorables'. Other capitalist countries also have 'surplus populations', but the US lacks an adequate social welfare system combined with a history of racism that exacerbates the power of the 'new lumpenproletariat' turning it into an unpredictable political force. Discussing the rise of Donald Trump, Barrow pessimistically declares that: "When the lumpenproletariat becomes politically active, it brings large numbers of desperate people, an unbridled capacity for violence and brutal-ity, and a willingness to side with anyone – or to even change sides in the middle of the struggle – depending on who is willing to pay them, feed them, clothe them, and entertain them. They are effectively the soldiers and police of whichever side is winning the class struggle, and that is usually the ruling class."[24] Barrow does not explain why the 'white lumpen-proletariat' express their politics quite differently to the 'black lumpenpro-letariat' and why Trump's supporters also included many who were in the production system either as workers or businesspeople.

Even if we update the debates between Marx and Bakunin and ask which classes or segments of contemporary society will be indispensable to the creation of environmentally sustainable post-capitalist social forma-tions, there is no simple answer. In low- and middle-income capitalist soci-eties, especially China, India, Indonesia and various Asian countries with substantial industrial working classes and large peasant or agrarian popula-tions, any fundamental social change will likely involve a mixture of the new urban and old rural social forces either in some form of possible polit-ical coalition or in strong opposition to one another. These social classes will either champion reform orientated ideas or pursue higher material standards of living within conservative authoritarian market systems. If global competition and climate breakdown and general eco-system deterio-ration severely constrain economic growth, the consequences will be explo-sive domestic and international distributional struggles.

It is not just that service sector workers now constitute the over-whelming majority of contemporary wageworkers in developed capitalist societies. Importantly, the low-employment and highly capital-intensive character of solar farms and wind turbine grids combined with the dispersal of renewables on domestic rooftops and in small communities means that the former strategic leverage of powerful miners' unions and oil workers will *not* be crucial to the emergence and operation of post-carbon societies. Driverless vehicles will also undermine road transport unions, while the move to cashless transactions will decimate bank employees. Some workers in strategically key areas such as passenger and air freight transport, ware-house logistical distribution of supplies and consumer goods, digital equipment maintenance, hospitals and pathology laboratories, police forces, extraction and mining of natural resources and food production could cause serious immediate or delayed disruptions if they went on strike. Also, given the centrality of property development to financialisation, it is not surprising that governments and businesses will continue to ensure that unions in the construction and infrastructure sectors do not undermine the 'property-industrial complex'.

Yet, with the shift to higher levels of cognitive and care work, or the automation of 20% to 70% of many *job tasks* (rather than full automation of jobs), it is difficult to predict which new clusters of specialised workers will acquire indispensable roles in a range of vital industries. What we do know is that the transition to post-carbon social forms will be affected by two contradictory developments in labour markets. There could be political leverage exercised by strategically placed, highly skilled technical and co-ordinating workers in key sectors which may disrupt businesses if their demands are not met. Or social volatility will be caused by an increasing surplus of low-skilled and single-skilled, middle-wage level workers facing uncertain futures as jobs become either automated or dispensed with due to overproduction. If the latter scenario becomes politically dangerous for ruling classes, new forms of publicly subsidised jobs or income may well be implemented thus laying the foundation for universal basic services, a point I will develop in Chapter Six. Mobilising fragmented workers around clear sets of unified political demands in order to defend work and living conditions will require quite different organising techniques and political strategies compared with the earlier historical mobilisation of factory workers and miners who were densely concentrated in close proximity to one another.

As we know, the Marxist dream of a revolutionary proletariat has never been realised and is not likely in the future. Marx was correct in seeing the working-class as the rising class in emerging capitalist countries in comparison to Bakunin's declining peasant and agrarian class. Yet, nowhere did the industrial proletariat constitute a revolutionary majority of wage workers, certainly not in North America, Europe, Japan, or Australia. Similarly, the revolutions in Russia, China, Vietnam, Cuba, and North Korea were not based primarily on the urban proletariat. In Weimar Germany with its politicised working class mobilised into bitterly divided parties and unions (Social Democratic, Communist, Christian and Nazi), the gap between the symbolic representation of the proletariat in newspapers, films, books, art, theatre and public mobilisation far outweighed the numerical and political strength of the actual revolutionary proletariat.[25] Over the past sixty years, it has become common to read historians, Left theorists and activists acknowledging that most industrial workers were never revolutionary in developed capitalist countries and that in recent years have even, with few exceptions, significantly reduced their support for centre/Left social democratic parties.

The brief upsurge of militant strike action in several countries during the 1960s and 1970s, followed by greatly reduced strike activity in the subsequent forty to fifty years, has merely highlighted how weak and passive the majority of industrial labour movements have become in many countries. Across the world, major disruptions, and political clashes by striking workers are in a distinct minority except for 'wildcat' eruptions in China and other places without supportive free unions. Instead, public protests incurring violent police crackdowns have not been instigated by militant organised workers but by various social movements, disaffected and desperate social strata such as the Yellow Vests in France, anti-corruption activists in Lebanon and Iraq, Extinction Rebellion climate protestors, cross-class anti-austerity Chilean or Colombian protestors or Hong Kong militants opposed to authoritarianism. In France, union activists have even adopted some of the tactics used by the Yellow Vests, as traditional industrial militancy is both less common and less effective today.

A century earlier, the original populists, the Russian *Narodnik* intelligentsia, regarded the peasantry as a revolutionary force against Czarism and capitalism. However, the impoverished rural masses rejected the urban middle-class intelligentsia who during the 1870s had come to villages to help 'liberate' these largely illiterate and conservative masses. So too, the earnest attempts of middle-class students in tiny Trotskyist and Maoist parties to 'enter' the proletarian workplaces (between the 1960s and 1980s) and help agitate for militant action failed abysmally, as the vast majority of workers rejected radical politics. Similar hostile reactions from miners and other fossil-fuel workers have greeted environmentalists protesting in their mining regions.

Contemporary Marxist/Leninists who hold onto the belief in the vanguard party and the politics of industrial class struggle are the latter-day Bakunins. They are blind to the character and evolving structure of present-day societies and cling to a politics based on both a declining and transformed working class just like Bakunin who could not see the disappearing power of peasants. Marxist politics continues to rest on the hope that workers in OECD countries will once again become militant. In their wildest hopes, they tentatively cling to the belief that the mass proletariat in China and other industrialising countries will become the vanguard of revolution. Also, there are a minority of radicals who still dream of the crisis-collapse of capitalism, like the 'mechanical Marxists' of the Second Socialist International prior to 1914. This 'final crisis' has never depended, and still does not depend on the organised power of workers. Instead, the notion of 'crisis-collapse' is the inevitable end product of inbuilt 'economic laws' – such as the so-called law of the 'falling rate of profit' and the inevitable immiseration of the working-class – rather than the politically driven 'contradictions of capitalism' fostering class struggle.

In recent years, the concept of 'crisis collapse' has migrated to sections of the environment movement. Prominent Extinction Rebellion member, Rupert Read, believes that 'this civilisation is finished' and that capitalism will collapse.[26] Crude, apolitical environmental predictions not only see an inevitable collapse of capitalism, but of 'global civilisation' due to ecological overshoot.[27] These 'catastrophists' or 'collapsologists' believe that there will be no post-capitalist society because 'civilisation' itself will perish from climate breakdown. While there are some definite ecological limits to incessant material growth, these 'limits' will *not* be felt evenly across the world and must not be confused with an automatic system-like process based on natural laws that will inevitably lead to either doomsday or to a politics that favours environmental care and sustainable social goals.

Even those who do not subscribe to this view of climate catastrophe continue to express fears that the social breakdown of capitalism – whether slow or rapid – will be characterised by the failure of new post-neoliberal institutions and social relations to triumph while the old order falls apart. In this Gramscian 'interregnum' where 'the new cannot be born', individuals are depicted as increasingly unprotected and exposed to a multitude of socio-economic and political crises as societies become ungovernable.[28] One version of this stalemate is ultra-pessimistic and without a clear politics as it is devoid of any concept of social agency, that is, a notion of social movements or parties struggling to prevent possible chaos. It is also a *homogeneous* conception of 'decaying capitalism' as a *global* phenomenon because it assumes that all capitalist societies will *simultaneously* become *ungovernable* and that all people in these diverse capitalist countries will be left unprotected and helpless as doomsday scenarios of economic collapse and ecocide destroys civilisation. This is an erroneous view of the world that continues to see history moving in *uniform* stages.

Take, for example, the historical analogies that are made between the so-called imminent collapse of capitalism and the collapse of the Roman Empire. What is ignored in these crisis-collapse scenarios is that the crisis of mismanagement and conflict in the Western Empire centred on Rome were quite different to the Eastern or Byzantine Empire based in Constantinople. While the Roman world began to collapse around 400 A.D, the Eastern Empire continued to flourish and reached its peak two centuries after the collapse of Rome.[29] Whether 'Eastern capitalism' centred on Asia continues to thrive while 'Atlantic capitalism' collapses is both speculative and an inappropriate historical analogy, as the manner of capitalist interdependence is quite different to the social orders of pre-capitalist empires.

We should, however, never underestimate the short-sightedness, procrastination, and deliberate attempts by various governments to protect fossil fuel industries for as long as possible. Nevertheless, the twin crises of capitalist growth and the socio-economic impact of global warming will not be felt evenly across the world as some governments manage economic crises better than others and will also implement mitigation and adaptation strategies quicker than others. Whether these national interventions protect societies from cross border climate impacts is highly debatable. The alternative of doing nothing or believing that people in Ethiopia, Sweden, China, or New Zealand will suffer the same consequences is equally untenable.

Misplaced Nostalgia for 'Workerist' Struggles During 'Carbon Capitalism'

The full political economic ramifications of decarbonisation are either unknown or barely explored territory. Timothy Mitchell's book *Carbon Democracy* reminds us of the power of fossil fuels in the twentieth and twenty-first centuries and importantly, their connection to various wars, imperialist struggles, and the development of Western parliamentary democracies. Mitchell rejects a reductionist explanation of how political outcomes (what is 'above ground') can be directly traced back to the coal-face and the oil well ('below ground'). That is, he implicitly rejects the orthodox Marxist 'base' determining the socio-political and legal 'super-structure' and argues that the growing reliance on fossil fuels was not a one-sided history of the rise of democracy produced by social movements in the newly industrialising cities. Rather, it was also the history of the suppression of democratising movements in regions such as Europe and the Middle East, especially the inseparable relation between the exercise of violence and political repression in the quest for control over fossil fuels.

Building on Mitchell, and yet also critiquing his thesis, Israeli scholar, On Barak, has recently presented a more complex analysis of how 'carbon democracy' in Britain was not only inseparably linked to 'carbon autocracy' in the British empire, but why we should stop neatly dividing societies by the types of successive energy (animal power, water power, fossil fuels or renewables) they have used or will use.[30] Instead of the conventional association of the Middle East with oil, Barak shows that the British set up numerous coal hubs or bunkers along their shipping lanes from the Mediterranean to the Red Sea and Indian Ocean to facilitate both carbonisation and multiple forms of food production, desalination of water, and socio-political control both well before and after oil became dominant. As he argues,

> energy regimes are implicitly thought to be predicated on a hegemonic, modelling energy source, both technologically and geographically. The nineteenth-century adoption of fossil fuels, for example, seemed to separate England – the first place to take up coal industrially – from the rest of the world, a "great divergence" as it were. The divergence perspective mapped neatly onto divides between industry and agriculture, modernity and tradition, the artificial (polluting, abnormal) and natural (renewable, sustainable), and the (energetic) West and (lethargic) East, obfuscating important connections among these worlds as well as other kinds of entanglements among machines, humans, animals, and other forces. Contrasting urbanising, industrial, coal-rich Europe with the non- or deindustrialised, non- or underdeveloped agricultural peripheries that fed its working classes and factories missed two key facts: not only were these peripheries themselves dependent on coal steam power from about the same time they were fully adopted in England, but English industrialisation

itself depended on these remote settings as markets and laboratories for coal and coal-burning technologies.[31]

Allowing for these interrelated complexities that Mitchell glossed over, his observations on the role of organised workers' movements such as coal miners and railway workers are still worth noting and discussing. It is the concentrated location of coal and later oil that gave workers in these industries strategic leverage which is also true of rail workers and dockworkers engaged in the distribution of coal and oil. Most coal miners, rail workers and dockers across the world tended to be organised in Communist, social democratic and other Left unions affiliated to major Left parties. They could paralyse production and consumption through their strategically disruptive actions. In some respects, they were the 'shock troops' of democracy and social reform because of their ability to advance society-wide causes on behalf of workers in weaker sectors, particularly unorganised or disadvantaged people.

However, Mitchell's account unintentionally undermines popular Left notions of 'Fordism' – from Gramsci to the Paris Regulation School – that supposedly dominated capitalism prior to the 1970s (see Chapter 8 of my previous book *Capitalism Versus Democracy?*). It is not mass production on assembly lines and the corporatist agreements between capital and labour sanctioned by governments that alone shaped capitalism up until the 1970s. Rather, it was the political struggles over the production and availability of cheap fossil fuels that were, and in many countries continue to be, the necessary material *pre-conditions* for the emergence and sustainability of mass production capitalism.

If coal miners, railway workers and dockers helped advance the 'welfare state' and democracy in the first half of the twentieth century, it was the switch from coal to oil, Mitchell argues, that was used by businesses and governments (both violently and for narrow economic reasons) to weaken powerful miners' unions and thereby also halt or reverse gains made by workers. Thatcher's crushing of the miners in the 1980s would be a particularly strong example. Mitchell's book was published well before the concluding chapter in the long tradition of American and British mining and industrial workers' communities was written in 2016 (with many industrial workers supporting Trump) and in the UK election of December 2019 abandoning the Labour Party. After decades of deindustrialisation and neglect by successive Conservative and Labour governments, various 'Red Wall' Labour electorates with weak local Labour Party community organising switched in large numbers to neoliberals led by Boris Johnson. They eroded more than a century of proud working-class solidarity that in many instances also barely disguised deep-seated racism and nationalism.

Despite Mitchell's insights, his narrow focus on fossil fuels fails to advance a satisfactory explanation of the political and social development of capitalist societies. He says much about carbon but far less about democracy, namely, how particular historical state apparatuses developed and why their origins, character and level of democratic control differ from one capitalist country to another. *Carbon Democracy* is a thesis that claims too much, both indirectly and directly, on behalf of fossil fuels. It overlooks the way the mobilisation of different classes and segments of society helped shape quite diverse political cultures, levels of social welfare and either more individualist or more communitarian traditions and institutional values, despite the fact that they *all relied* on fossil fuels. We need to differentiate the origins and evolution of many of these political institutional forms and cultural values from their direct or indirect connections to coal and oil. This is not to doubt past and current dependence of production and consumption on fossil fuels. However, On Barak makes the valid observation that one 'energy regime' did not and will not neatly replace the previous 'energy regime'.[32] Rather, coal historically coexisted with animal and waterpower, still coexists with oil and gas, while fossil fuels will unfortunately long be present alongside renewable energy unless government action prohibits these fuels.

Mitchell, like the analysts of 'Fordism', ignores the fact that despite giant multinational corporations, most businesses have never been just large mass-producing entities. Similarly, significant numbers of unionists were not in mining, oil, railways, or giant factories. Instead, depending on the country, many workers were members of numerous small and medium craft and post-craft unions or in public sector unions away from factories, mines, and oil wells. This is not to deny Mitchell's important highlighting of the significant role played by miners, oil workers, rail workers and dockers or the wider influence and magnitude of struggles by unionised workers in large manufacturing plants. Rather, it is to recognise that the pre-existing historical institutional and cultural contexts within which 'carbon democracy' and so-called 'Fordism' emerged. This would include nineteenth and early twentieth century nationalist struggles or secular conflicts against the power of organised religion. These were also highly influential in shaping contemporary institutions and political cultures, especially legal statutes, levels of socio-political tolerance and civil rights.

It is important not to reduce struggles for social recognition and political representation by women, non-property owners, people of colour, Indigenous peoples, and other minorities to simply the 'economy'. Moreover, we should not overlook the contradictory and complex conservative or progressive roles of those employed in services, or small business owners, rural movements, and the professions in either strongly opposing democratisation or else advancing social improvements for workers and other disadvantaged people in areas of health, education, housing, and political representation. Without the multifaceted forms of all these socio-political struggles, it is not possible to understand why the characteristics of national voting systems, levels of taxation and public services, social welfare, or legal-administrative institutions, to name just a few areas, vary so considerably in all fossil-fuel based capitalist countries.

Mitchell's over-emphasis on carbon at the expense of democratic struggles concerning the policies and practices of diverse state apparatuses is a lesson in why there will be *no simple correlation* between emerging post-carbon energy systems and the complex component structures and policies of future political regimes. One only has to look at the stimulus packages in response to COVID-19 to see the difference between the modest public expenditure on ecological modernisation in Europe as opposed to the relative lack of such investment in most other countries.

If fossil-fuels laid the preconditions for the growth in manufacturing and thereby the growth of workers' solidarity unions and parties, the dawn of the post-carbon era coincides in OECD countries with widespread de-unionisation, precarity and exploitation. Today, coal miners, rail workers and dockers in most developed capitalist countries are a shadow of their former strength due to mine closures, road transport, containerisation, automation of docks and so forth.[33] The transformation of rail-freight and shipping by containers began in the US in the 1960s before it moved to other countries. Although the teamsters became a powerful road-based union, they were not supportive of radical social reforms as earlier Left-wing rail and dock-worker unions across the world. In recent years, miners can no longer be described as solidly Left-wing and are often opposed to environmentalists including supporting Right-wing nationalist movements and politicians like Trump.

In low- and middle-income societies, the repression of workers attempting to form unions, the annual deaths of more than 15,000 miners in China, India, South Africa, Bolivia and the Congo or the tens of thousands of children working in the mines of Columbia and other countries are all testimony to the vast disparity in social conditions and political rights across the world. As Laleh Khalili shows, now that China is the 'world factory' and ninety per cent of world trade in goods is still carried in ships – 44% of which is dry-bulk cargo (grain, coal, iron ore, bauxite and other minerals) while oil constitutes 30% of all shipping cargo – it is no surprise that the ports on the Arabian Peninsula constitute a strategic part of global capitalism.[34] Not only do immigrant workers from India, Bangladesh and Pakistan constitute the majority of workers in these port cities but shipping itself is dominated by crews from Asia, especially from the Philippines. The big post-1945 labour strikes of Communist-led dockers in Aden and other places are distant memories. Strategic military interventions and infrastructure and trade investments by Saudi Arabia, the US, Iran, China, and other players now determine the last vestiges of carbon capitalism. Democracy is nowhere to be seen in these conflict zones. Yet, it is these widely divergent conditions and global imbalances that will shape the pace, the character, and the extent to which post-carbon societies emerge via democratic processes or undemocratic means.

The Role of Labour Movements in the Transition to Post-Carbon Democracies

In highlighting the role of labour struggles in the development of carbon society, Mitchell and Khalili inadvertently alert us to the *absence* of significant sections of contemporary labour movements in promoting post-carbon sustainable democracies. It is true that the International Labour Organisation and a considerable number of trade unions (in EU member states, Australia, and other countries) have campaigned alongside environmentalists for policies to decarbonise capitalist economies. However, it is also evident that the positive commitments of trade union peak bodies to combat climate breakdown have been hampered in various countries by the opposition to and reluctance of some mining and manufacturing unions to accept environmental crises as urgent issues. Clearly, there are significant disparities between unions in carbon-intensive and non-fossil fuel industries and their level of support for climate emergency action, especially when jobs are threatened. Many weakened union movements have either a diminished capacity or level of commitment to fight for a post-carbon democracy and reclaim the progressive leading roles that they once played in bringing about 'carbon democracy' in capitalist societies.

Class struggle over the control of political and economic power may share the same fate as historical struggles between the Third Estate (commoners) and the First and Second Estates (clergy and nobility) within France and other countries before and after 1789. It is not that the aristocracy and clergy disappeared during the nineteenth century, but rather that these struggles between estates became increasingly politically irrelevant as new classes of capitalists and workers as well as other social strata emerged from the dissolution of the old Third Estate. One hundred and fifty-years later, is it misguided to ask what could emerge from the dissolution of both the capitalist class and the working-class? After all, the Third Estate embraced a more diverse set of classes (including the early bourgeoisie, peasants, and craft workers) rather than just workers or capitalists. Yet contemporary capitalist and working classes are far from homogeneous and also have no political unity at either national or global levels.

In the early twenty-first century, it is evident that the dominant mode of capitalist production will continue to undergo substantial changes driven by intense global and regional market competition, technological innovation, and diverse political responses to unavoidable environmental pressures, not only changes driven by the need to reduce greenhouse gases. It is a brave person who predicts levels of private or public ownership and control, proportions of workers in secure full-time jobs or precarious employment, or such factors as degrees of adequate social welfare coverage or continued impoverishment. Existing organisations such as trade unions are defensive organisations that can sometimes promote new social ideas but are ill-equipped to lead their members in a full-scale challenge to the social system as opposed to specific campaigns about wages, work conditions and other issues. In Europe, at least, there is a growing awareness among trade unions that the future employment and welfare of workers must be inextricably linked to both social and ecological agendas.

It is therefore necessary not to confuse two aspects of class. Firstly, the way classes are constantly changing both in their composition and in their relation to other classes and secondly, why a social 'map' of classes is not equivalent to the way organisations, movements and institutions express or claim to advance particular class policies, especially future political and environmental objectives. In Volume One of *Capital*, for example, Marx cited the 1861 census in England and Wales to show that the largest category of workers were predominantly female domestic servants, an occupation that was double the size of coal and metal miners, three times larger than metal manufacturing workers and double the size of all the workers in cotton and other textile factories.[35] Notably, as we know, it was not isolated domestic servants who led the formation of new trade unions and political parties. One hundred and fifty years later, we superficially appear to have come full circle in developed capitalist countries. While not primarily employed in domestic service, the overwhelming majority of workers are nonetheless once again employed in all kinds of services. What is significant is not their numerical size. Rather, most contemporary service sector workers, like the old domestic servants, are isolated and fragmented, especially in small and medium business workplaces such as shops, offices, leisure, and personal care centres, that are once again largely non-unionised. In some countries, however, levels of unionisation are substantial, particularly among public sector service workers and in occupations with a heavy presence of female workers such as nursing and teaching. Will these unorganised and organised workers play a minor or major role in shaping post-carbon societies?

If 'unity is strength', then low levels of unionisation in many service sector industries and the repression of free trade unions in manufacturing sectors in authoritarian countries constitutes a serious obstacle to the union movement playing a key role in the transition to a post-carbon society. Rebuilding union strength is exceedingly difficult in those countries without government pro-union industrial relations legislation. Most governments prefer protecting employers reliant on casualised, precarious employment rather than fostering 'green jobs' based on organised workers. Little wonder then that large numbers of workers are either anti-green or neutral and 'light green' at best and worry more about their jobs rather than about sustainability.

One of the questions about how the future post-carbon society will be made is whether the previous repression, killings and persistent violence waged by police, armed forces, and private police forces to defend capitalist businesses against industrial workers fighting for social justice will be repeated in the struggle to bring about post-carbon democracy? It is not enough for environmental economists, theorists of the 'environment state', advocates of degrowth and others to devise ideas about how the new sustainable society will function. They also need to specify which social agents will likely carry out this transformation, what level of obstruction they will encounter and whether the transition will be peaceful or violent.

Strategically and politically, the debates during the past five decades over how to define who belongs to the proletariat have been eclipsed by new social change issues. Orthodox Marxists have divided workers into those who produce surplus value, and others who perform so-called 'unproductive labour' in sales, administration, finance, transport, and the circulation of goods, or in nursing, teaching and many other services. They incorrectly assume that the vast majority of these workers in service sectors ultimately depend on those working in 'productive labour' jobs and their degree of exploitation. In other words, if the rate of surplus value extraction falls and thereby also profitability, then all those in 'unproductive labour' jobs in both private and public sectors who help circulate commodities and realise their value through sales and administration – not to forget all the tax revenue derived from production and consumption processes needed to fund social welfare dependents and public services – that all of these 'unproductive' jobs will become unviable and welfare dependents will lose their income as tax revenue declines. If this is true about 'productive labour', then it would be impossible for a post-carbon capitalist society to become economically viable if it sheds many environmentally *unsustainable* but 'surplus value' producing jobs in factories, mines, and other sectors.

This is a case in point where the theory of surplus value is either flawed or inadequate to explain modern capitalist countries where most people are employed in 'unproductive labour'. Any development of post-carbon democratic social formations needs to consider how recent changes in labour markets and production processes affect transition strategies. In both the most technologically advanced sectors of the 'digital economy' and the least developed 'informal' sectors of low- and middle-income countries, exploitation and self-exploitation now take on countless variations. Workers are often not sure who employs them given outsourcing of production and services, shelf-companies, and other business devices such as digital platforms designed to undermine traditional employer-worker relations. Current political debates concern the classification of people working in precarious 'informal' sectors. In low- and middle-income countries, the boundaries between villagers, transitory urban workers, street vendors and numerous other categories of work and income do not conform to employment and work conditions formalised by national state regulations or enterprise agreements. Precarious labour has always existed in capitalist societies. Yet, the 'informal sector' or 'precarity' are very loose concepts that often encompass diverse social groups, from peasants and street vendors right through to university-educated workers in casual 'gig economy' jobs. These workers have little social, cultural and class relations in common apart from their precarious status as they do not even share similar work descriptions and conditions.

To put just one aspect of inequality in stark statistical terms, prior to

COVID-19, official global unemployment hovered around the 170 to 200 million level for the past decade with two billion out of 3.3 billion global workers located in the informal economy and over 1.1 billion working on their own account in subsistence activities without adequate social protection.[36] An International Labour Organization Report in January 2021 estimated that during 2020, the equivalent of 255 million full-time jobs were lost due to unemployment and reduced hours of work.[37] Although mass unemployment hit OECD countries in North America and Europe, the main casualties were in low- and middle-income countries in Latin America, Southern Asia and parts of Africa. Despite partial economic recovery in many countries, scarcity of jobs will continue to remain one of the hallmarks of life within capitalism, a *persistent crisis* well beyond the capacity of markets to resolve on their own. Familiar conditions of underemployment, tens of millions giving up looking for work and the degrading conditions of slavery, child abuse, gender and racial discrimination are merely the beginning when it comes to the deep inequalities that dominate this world.

Depending on national labour market legislation and levels of unemployment, approximately 20 to 30 per cent of workers are employed in either 'informal' markets or casual, precarious jobs in OECD countries with much higher percentages in low- and middle-income countries, including new forms of slavery and about 152 million child labourers.[38] However, there is a difference between part-time employment and 'gig economy' jobs such as those working for platform companies. In many OECD countries, 'permanent' employees have remained stable at approximately 79% for the period between 1996 to 2016,[39] whereas in other countries casual and part-time insecure jobs have accounted for almost half of all new positions in the past decade.

We are yet to see whether the 'gig economy' will increase or whether official statistics tell us little about the insecurity felt by most workers even though they are classified as 'permanent employees'. Certainly, the shutdown by COVID-19 witnessed millions of precarious workers left unemployed and unsupported by governments. Also, such is the impact of 'innovative labour processes' that we cannot ignore the real pressures coming from business groups within member countries of the EU and OECD. One such political pressure by employers is to prevent official labour laws from defining what 'standard employment' is or is not.[40] In the US, some business lobbies are going much further and seek to abolish the category of 'employer'. This would legitimise hyper-exploitation based on so-called 'non-existent' employers free from any legal constraints or moral responsibility thus enabling them to adopt ruthless work practices.

Forty years ago, Andre Gorz and others were already arguing that the conflict between workers and capitalists centred on 'the factory' had long been surpassed as the central conflict in society. The 'working class' in Marx's terms could no longer liberate society by liberating themselves from exploitative alienated labour in the mode of production. Instead, Gorz argued that:

> It is not through identification with their work and their work role that modern wage-earners feel themselves justified in making demands for power which have the potential to change society. It is as citizens, residents, parents, teachers, students or as unemployed; it is their experience outside work that leads them to call capitalism into question.[41]

Gorz was prescient in focussing on the relation between capitalism and ecology, forecasting how modern technology would favour only a minority of skilled/professional workers, and how new work processes such as 'flexi time' and casualisation would undermine the power of unions. Yet, he was wrong in believing that work time would continue to be reduced and hence lose its central meaning in the life of workers. Some countries such as Sweden and Germany have seen particular industries offer four-day weeks in return for higher productivity. But this is atypical of most countries and most industry sectors that have witnessed longer working weeks in the form of involuntary overtime combined with substantial amounts of under-employment.

Old Marxist notions of social change depended on differentiating between two levels of consciousness – a limited 'trade union consciousness' that is mainly preoccupied with improved wage and work conditions, and its opposite, namely, a unifying 'revolutionary class-consciousness'. Both have now lost a significant degree of their former political *raison d'être*. Without a readily identifiable and coherent working class (class-in-itself) let alone a radical proletariat (class-for-itself), there is a question about which social change agents are able to simultaneously represent 'democracy' in its conflict with 'capitalism'. It is little wonder then, that 'democracy' ceases to represent a clear alternative to 'capitalism' or embody a shared political program apart from the belief in the right of all to vote or to make political decisions. This restructuring of the old working class has serious implications for the transition to post-carbon society.

It has also taken the COVID-19 global crisis to reveal why both mainstream analysts and post-work radicals are promoting hollow theories about automation. There have been many economists and sociologists over the years who have argued that 'capital does not need labour' and that business can happily grow while dispensing with most workers. This may be true for individual employers and enterprises but is profoundly untrue for the total private sector in any single country. One only has to see the disastrous economic impact of the lack of working-class consumers on whole industries and economies due to weeks and months of quarantine measures. Recent debates over the extent of job losses due to automation and AI are inconclusive. We know that the overall *quantity* of jobs has not diminished due to technological innovation even though the *quality* of many new jobs has deteriorated in terms of precarity, wages and so forth. If this trend continues and there is no political shift to improving wages and social protection, escalating automation in coming decades will not be about the coming tsunami of job destruction (although this is technically possible) as it will be about the replacement of middle-income jobs thereby reducing overall disposable income in capitalist societies. Capitalism may survive but it cannot thrive once it abolishes most forms of well-paid labour. Conversely, given tight operations margins, will most businesses survive if the past four decades of increasingly relying on de-unionised, precarious, and outsourced forms low-paid labour is ended? In the absence of market-generated wage growth and protracted unemployment, will businesses and voters pressure governments to engage in either the mass subsidisation of wages or the creation of government guaranteed jobs.

As I have argued, there is a major difference between traditional forms of class conflict and the forthcoming politics of transitional innovation in an era of environmental crises. Take, for instance, the issue of unemployment. Under the old paradigm of 'capitalism versus democracy', Polish political economist, Michal Kalecki, famously argued that business and political leaders preferred lower profits than the potentially higher profits coming from increased aggregate demand driven by full employment. This is because full employment caused discipline to break down as workers no longer feared losing their jobs and would demand much better conditions.[42] Capitalists also feared democratic state intervention, he observed, as this enabled governments to make crucial public investment decisions that had formerly been largely in the hands of private market forces.

Importantly, Kalecki's thesis ultimately depended on the strength of organised labour movements that were able to take advantage of low unemployment levels. Trade unions are, however, shadows of their former strength in many countries. Does this mean that capitalist classes have little to fear? This may indeed be the case. Strong organised labour movements remain vital if workers' conditions and rights are to be defended or improved. However, trade unions have historically performed contradictory roles. Apart from defending their members' rights and conditions, they have provided stability for businesses by channelling demands and dissent through recognised processes. Their militancy has also signalled to businesses what kind of technological and organisational innovations are necessary to remain competitive and one step ahead of workers. Take away union strength and all looks rosy for capitalists for a brief period of time. The looming danger for businesses and conservative governments is that the current interregnum of defeated labour movements may not last.

Whether union movements can be revived nationally (despite continuing to be strong in some industries) is not the only factor in play. A minority of owners and shareholders currently recognise that what replaces old labour-capital struggles may be far worse for business than the former 'orderly' channelled character of industrial disputes. Both employers and unions have always feared 'wild cat' strikes because these signalled grass-roots rebellion against conservative union leaders and unpredictable dangers for employers. Without former historical levels of unionisation being restored, the character of present-day and future environmental challenges means that governments, especially in countries with free elections, will come under mounting pressure from electorates, sections of business and a range of social groups to act to prevent catastrophic environmental events occurring on a frequent basis. Combine this with major socio-economic malaise and we are likely to see eruptions that are far more difficult to control by conventional centre/Left parties or Right-wing governments. The 'Yellow Vests' are possibly a small taste of things to come. Such protests are not like most forms of strike action and confined to a single enterprise or industry. Whole city centres, retailing, tourism, communication and so forth are disrupted and dislocated in ways that are not predictable. Of course, if governments combine rapid intervention to prevent climate chaos with significant social reform agendas, then new forms of 'guerrilla' protests will become less effective. Such pro-active government action presupposes the formation of new political alliances which are unlikely at the moment in most countries.

We should also not forget that just as businesses prefer lower profits to full employment, *many companies prefer to live with the risk of global warming* rather than face the consequences of unpredictable and precedent-setting government action on decarbonisation. However, such a choice is not likely to be left to businesses alone. Instead, it is the conflict of 'democracy versus sustainability' that begins to impact or replace old forms of 'capitalism versus democracy'. *Financial Times* columnist, Simon Kuper, declares that: "No electorate will vote to decimate its own lifestyle. We can't blame bad politicians or corporates. It's us: we will always choose growth over climate."[43] Certainly, this is currently true of electorates that haven't yet experienced climate havoc. Questions such as 'how 'urgent is government preventative action' will begin to take on a quite different meaning in the midst of a rapidly unfolding crisis. Even the widespread hostility of a conservative electorate to climate action can be transformed into support for urgent decarbonisation action following major floods, fires, and droughts. President Biden's environment ambassador, John Kerry, acknowledged that three environmental storms recently cost America $265 billion and that: "We've reached a point where it is an absolute fact that it's cheaper to invest in preventing damage or minimising it at least than cleaning up."[44]

Just as historically there was no sudden, ready-formed capitalist class that clashed with various feudal ruling classes or other holders of pre-capitalist power, similarly, there is currently no already formed new social class that is the standard bearer of post-carbon political economic power and alternative social relations. It is not just the working class that is being transformed well beyond former familiar divisions of blue and white collar, male and female dominated industries, unskilled, skilled, and professional occupations. Sections of other older classes are being dissolved or re-made and it is probable that a new class based on a recombination or offshoot of elements and layers from other classes is also 'being made' at this very moment. However, we are unable to predict its future characteristics and how it will help or hinder transforming the structure of power in coming decades.

In fact, there is *no* single class that represents the political economic interests of all who wish to wage political conflict with old social classes in existing 'carbon capitalist' societies. Instead, we have fragments or elements of existing socio-economic classes such as particular non-fossil fuel businesses and self-employed consultants in renewable energy, organic farming and other industry sectors, plus higher educated professionals, urban environment groups and clusters of communities in eco-villages who all favour the establishment of post-carbon democracies. Some of these heterogeneous groups overlap with traditional wage workers and *petite bour-geois* classes but other strata do not.

Let me conclude this discussion of carbon capitalism and class struggle with Andreas Malm's well-known Marxist study of *Fossil Capital.*[45] This is a detailed analysis of the socio-economic reasons why factory owners in the English cotton industry abandoned power generated by workers operating water wheels in favour of coal-fired steam engines in the period beginning in the 1830s. The ability to locate factories away from rivers and other sources of water gave coal a clear advantage and led to its adoption as an energy fuel across the world. However, when it comes to post-carbon technology and non-fossil fuels, it is disappointing that Malm has little to say about class and post-carbon society. Instead, he relies on Nikolai Kondrati-eff's highly problematic Long Wave theory and its interpretation by Trot-skyist Ernest Mandel.[46]

Long Wave theory is based on the notion of 50 to 60-year-long cycles of capitalist expansion and decline and is also used by many non-Marxists such as neo-Schumpeterian green growth analysts Carlota Perez and Mariana Mazzucato.[47] I will not repeat all the reasons why Long Wave theory is at best seriously flawed, and at worst a form of economic voodoo when it comes to explaining the varied forms of capitalist development.[48] Malm is not a technological determinist but unintentionally highlights another reason why innovative technology does not always correlate with periodic upswings of economic growth, whether fossil-based or future renewables.

In attempting to tie class struggle to Long Waves of capitalist growth, Malm argues that neoliberalism of the fifth Long Wave (1992 to 2008) "can only be understood as a way out of the impasses of the fourth, the Keynesianism of the fourth as a response to the imbalances and catastrophes of the third, and so on..."[49] He therefore erroneously assumes homogeneous or unilinear political economic 'stages' of capitalism, such as Keynesianism, that were in fact *not* universally practised in leading capitalist countries such as Germany prior to the 'universal stage' of neoliberalism. This so-called neoliberal uniform stage will also *not* be succeeded by another universal stage such as 'climate post-Keynesianism' or some other so-called world-wide system.

We already know that major capitalist powers such as China and the US may be economically interconnected but that they are driven by quite different domestic and international political goals as well as having dissimilar socio-economic regimes. Hence, the so-called hypothetical future 'sixth

Long Wave' will not be able to solve the problems troubling so-called similar neoliberal countries which were neither uniform nor global. Because Long Wave theory, like neo-classical economics, assumes supposed regular cycles or upswings and downswings of capitalist growth, these theories cannot explain capitalist political economic dynamics when countries will increasingly encounter ecological limits to growth. Since the 1970s, Long Wave theorists have regularly given us false starting dates for the next boom or expansionary wave. Instead, we have witnessed low growth/stagnation in developed capitalist countries for over forty years and rapid growth in China and other capitalist countries in Asia (excluding Japan). For the past decade we have been told that green growth will drive the next world Long Wave, but what if this does not eventuate or cannot substitute for downturns and austerity in other sectors?

Equally importantly, previous Marxist interpretations of Long Waves have linked them to levels of class struggle but have said nothing about environmental factors. Not only is Long Wave theory unable to adequately explain developments in the nineteenth and early twentieth centuries, but it is *not* a theory that can deal with the political conflicts over the formation of post-carbon societies which will most likely occur in a period of low organised class struggle. This is a world where incessant growth does not come up against the militant proletariat but rather the deep-seated and largely insurmountable, and sometimes imperceptible environmental constraints in the form of excessive carbon emissions, deforestation, acidified oceans, and other threats to the safe operating space of planetary life support systems. Long Wave theory is redundant in a world where innovate technology is most unlikely to be able to decouple growth from negative impacts on nature. If so, then capitalist expansion in a varying number of countries will either be curtailed or will lead to escalating ecological disasters that will eventually make growth unsustainable.

Politically and culturally, there has been no equivalent historical precedent to the social and environmental debates that are currently waged over which energy source is preferable to sustain biodiversity and human wellbeing. In fact, there is a fundamental *de-synchronisation* between the reproduction of natural cycles of renewal, that is, the rate at which the biosphere can replenish itself by renewing fragile or irreversibly damaged habitats, and the *speed* at which natural resources are *extracted* and consumed. This means that the conflicting demands by market forces and pluralist democratic movements require distinct levels of acceleration or deceleration, depending on the widely diverse levels of economic development and social needs in low or high-income countries. Such policies need to be debated carefully and democratically.[50]

Technologically, future post-carbon societies could be based on far less geographically concentrated energy sources such as coal, gas, and oil. Two contradictory patterns of implementation of renewable energy are currently visible. One process is the widely dispersed installation of solar panels and wind turbines by communities and households. The other trend is the vigorous attempt by private corporations to capture the renewable energy market via the installation of extensive energy grids to harness renewable solar, wind, hydropower and hydrogen, geothermal and other technologies. This latter trend has the upper hand at the moment and if successful will mean that renewable energy production will likely continue to remain heavily owned by capitalist classes or mixtures of public-private enterprises. Either way, technology and energy do not alone pre-determine how they will be utilised, let alone future social classes or the structure and complexity of prospective political institutions and social relations. Just because renewable energy (such as solar and wind) can be more easily dispersed and decentralised does *not* automatically tell us whether energy will actually become decentralised or crucially, whether political power will also be dispersed, decentralised and re-distributed.

2. INTELLECTUALS, NETWORKS, CULTURE: SHAPING FUTURE POST-CARBON SOCIETIES

IN THE PREVIOUS chapter I discussed the many reasons why the emergence of a post-carbon social order will not mirror the origins of capitalism. Given the diverse character of contemporary developed capitalist societies, the transition to a post-carbon society will not be driven by an industrial working class. If so, who or what movement or social forces will make or reshape the post-carbon or post-capitalist society? In current explanations of major social and cultural transformation, knowledge and technological change continue to be given prominence. Yet, how relevant are theories of post-industrialism and 'network' societies in helping us to understand the coming post-carbon society? In what way will notions of democracy, the role of private and public socio-cultural relations shape the ecological and socio-economic transition from capitalist practices to the as yet unknown cultural processes of post-carbon societies? In this chapter, I will focus on the problematic aspects of influential accounts of the role of both militant worker intellectuals and post-industrial managerial knowledge elites. Most of these theories have either ignored or rest on extremely limited accounts of the interrelation between environmental systems and the dynamics of contemporary capitalism. I will first examine popular radical notions of combatting cultural hegemony in capitalist societies before discussing theories of post-industrial and digital networks. I will then analyse in what way the cultural contradictions of capitalism are relevant to the shaping of socio-cultural relations in future post-carbon societies.

The Political Obsolescence of 'Organic Intellectuals'

It is always a sobering experience for many serious scholars of capitalism or long seasoned political activists to discover that pop-sociologists and futurologists such as Alvin Toffler (*Future Shock,* 1970[1]) were more in touch with changes to developed capitalism in the 1960s and 1970s than a new generation of radicals who revived Marxist theories of class struggle. Leaving aside many of their exaggerated, breathless, and unfulfilled predictions, Toffler and others pointed to the fluidity of contemporary societies, of the growth of subcultures, profound changes in families and social relations, including geographical and social mobility, the rise of temporary relations, the throw-away society, as well as the shift to home-based work, the emergence of biotech, cybernetics, and other technologies. All these changes to cultural and production processes were breaking down standardised, industrial mass production and the cultural foundations of social orders based on more homogenous classes and political identities.

At that time, radicals and social movements also pointed to new gender relations and family types, the ways capitalists utilised innovative technologies, and the growth of subcultures (feminist, ecological, racial, sexual). However, there remained an assumption amongst socialist radicals in particular, that all these profound changes could be explained by updating Marxist analysis and political strategies and uniting the fragments of new social movements into a successful anti-capitalist alliance. Instead, we have witnessed fifty years of continued fragmentation rather than growing mass anti-hegemonic cultural politics. As many have argued, this fragmentation is connected to the eclipse of the former leading role of the proletariat in social change strategies. In addition, the past two decades have witnessed the rise of new digital social media subcultures with new identities and forms of cultural recognition and interaction. What does this changed cultural profile mean for developed capitalist societies positioned on the cusp of transitioning to post-carbon social formations?

It is instructive to compare recent cultural developments with the key role that Italian revolutionary Antonio Gramsci's accorded to 'organic intellectuals'. Unlike the demise and disillusionment with the notion of a mass Leninist vanguard party, Gramsci's work has strangely not suffered a similar fate as Leninism. On the contrary, in recent decades there has been a widespread revival of Gramsci's ideas on how the capitalist class maintain political and economic power through cultural hegemony, even though the capitalism of today is so different to that which Gramsci wrote about in his

Prison Notebooks between 1929 and 1935. Gramsci's influence stretches to many non-Marxists, including supporters of degrowth.[2] Unfortunately, his analysis of hegemony is limited by Gramsci's dated conception of capitalist state institutions and Italian socio-cultural relations. Gramsci never lived to see the emergence of much more complex state apparatuses since the early 1930s and how they are closely interrelated with many private socio-economic practices. Consequently, his conception of 'organic intellectuals' and how to bring about social revolution is largely unsuitable for any transition to post-carbon democracy, as I will elaborate below. One can, of course, recognise some valuable aspects of Gramsci's analysis of culture and hegemony without agreeing with his outdated notion of the role of the working class in countering this hegemony. Also, it is possible to recognise the continued existence of classes and class conflict in capitalist societies while questioning the relevance of his theory of the role of 'organic intellectuals'.

Historically, Gramsci's analysis is trapped within the character of a transformed 'bourgeois public sphere'.[3] The emergence of bourgeois society in the period from the seventeenth century to late nineteenth century was associated initially with new salons and media that were dominated by spokespersons who articulated the ideas and interests of monarchists, republican nationalists, the church, the industrial and commercial bourgeoisie, and agrarian gentry. This 'public sphere' also facilitated the promotion of both the values of individual freedom championed by the urban liberal intelligentsia and even bohemian cultural elements at odds with a business work ethic. The social manifestations of these old and new social classes varied in strength from country to country. In theory, the 'public sphere' mediated relations between state institutions, the capitalist market and civil society via the new print media and the formation of public opinion, political parties and so forth. In reality, these 'boundaries' were artificial, as the 'economic', 'political' and 'social' were directly or indirectly interconnected and affected all social classes. Social theorist, Jürgen Habermas, argues that the industrialisation and the rationalisation of state and market institutions transformed earlier forms of public activity. By the late nineteenth century, religious and other civic organisations, as well as conservative and liberal parties and the 'bourgeois media' were challenged by a 'counter' or 'proletarian public sphere' which functioned in developed or less developed forms, depending on the strength of socialist and labour parties, trade unions and national independence movements in particular countries.[4]

The ability of organisations within the 'counter sphere' to delineate a distinct 'working class culture' in opposition to the dominant bourgeois public sphere depended on the role and activity of working-class militants or 'organic intellectuals'. Whether there ever were clearly defined dominant public spheres and 'counter spheres' is disputed, but their transformation and demise by the second half of the twentieth century helped reshape notions of 'public' and 'private'. By the beginning of the twenty-first century, these earlier definitions of public and private were rendered obsolete by the emergence of social media and a plethora of digitalised marketing relations. I will explain the irrelevance of 'organic intellectuals' to establishing a post-carbon or post-capitalist 'counter sphere' based on environmental sustainability in what follows.

Returning first to the legacy of the original notion of working-class militants, Marxist revolutionaries believed that any political movement or activist committed to radical social change and 'proletarian democracy' must have a conception of the role of political consciousness, an idea of which social agents can carry out the relevant level of social change needed, and the type of organisation best suited to mobilise and develop class-consciousness and realise the needs of the working class. This strategic legacy lives on even among all those social movements that reject class analysis. The significant difference is that when an environmentalist, feminist or other cultural movement rejects the working-class party as a vehicle of change, it has often been either unclear or divided over whether the object of its activism is to change state policy directly by seeking electoral power or indirectly by lobbying, civil disobedience, mass protests, infiltration of mainstream parties, social media mobilisation and other such actions designed to transform 'public consciousness' and policy. In other words, does the movement want to create a totally new society or only change those parts of existing society that oppress, exclude, or threaten the survival of cultures or natural species?

Political strategies based on 'organic intellectuals' are connected to two classical maxims of Marxist-Leninist vanguard theory. These maxims were either challenged or indirectly absorbed and modified by many non-Leninist parties and movements. Firstly, it was claimed that constructing counter-hegemonic power could only succeed when the working-class developed its own culture and 'organic intellectuals' challenged the 'common sense' elements of bourgeois hegemony. In 1923, Hungarian revolutionary György Lukács argued that 'organisation is the form of mediation between theory and practice'.[5] Hence, radical social change could only be brought about by an *extraordinary* political organisation. Likewise, Gramsci (who was claimed as one of their own by both Leninists and anti-Leninists), also argued that Machiavelli's 'prince' was historically obsolete because no single person could capture and hold state power. Consequently, the Communist party had to become the 'Modern Prince' and succeed in the battle of manoeuvre with liberal, fascist, and conservative bourgeois parties, state apparatuses and capitalist businesses.[6]

It will be recalled that Gramsci challenged the traditional notion of an 'intellectual' associated with literature, philosophy and science, that is, those highly educated aristocratic or bourgeois individuals rather than workers and peasants because the latter had minimal formal education or were illiterate. Each type of society, according to Gramsci, had its own 'organic intellectuals', whether the clergy in feudal societies or technicians, ideologues and economists in capitalist society. The role of working-class 'organic intellectuals' was to facilitate and translate the ideas of the advanced sector of the class (read Communist Party activists) to fellow workers in communities and workplaces. In theory, the Party was to educate and simultaneously learn from the daily life experiences of its own class, thereby developing a counter-hegemonic culture. This 'counterculture' would link custom, folk and 'common sense' with grievances against the ruling class and simultaneously develop this suffering and set of grievances into a higher and more elaborate political consciousness necessary for revolutionary action. Preparation for revolution would entail years of strategic tactics in a 'war of position' in which the 'organic intellectuals' simultaneously combatted capitalist ideological hegemony in both the public sphere and amongst working class social institutions, thus helping develop working-class consciousness, solidarity and political action.

Defenders of Gramsci who emphasise the continued relevance of 'organic intellectuals' usually invoke the following points. Firstly, the working class was never homogenous and united, therefore all that has changed is that there are multiple new occupations and new digital media and cultural practices that maintain dominant class views of the world. Secondly, regardless of all the various social movements and identities, most of these people are also members of the working class which is the largest class in society. Thirdly, 'organic intellectuals' who are also feminist, black or LGBTQI people or support ecological sustainability can simultaneously develop a broader counter-hegemony because ultimately, all these diverse interests can only be realised with the replacement of capitalism.

It is true that Gramsci and his generation of Marxists always argued that workers were divided by race, religion, nationalism, and other factors and therefore a developed class consciousness needed to overcome these social divisions. However, a century later, Gramsci's concept of the 'Modern Prince' and what constitutes an 'organic intellectual' is historically obsolete because of more fundamental changes to contemporary capitalist societies.

To begin, the notion of 'organic' is highly problematic and assumes there is a 'working class' that is 'naturally', self-evidently and homogeneously distinct from petite bourgeois strata and 'bourgeois culture' as well as being distinct from other classes and cultures. In the past one hundred and fifty years, peasant cultures in particular countries had been the background of many workers entering factories, mines, and the building construction industry. Disentangling 'working class' culture from the embedded former peasant culture or religiously influenced, *petite* bourgeois culture and commercial 'popular culture' in most workers and their families has never been easy. Gramsci's attempt to construct a revolutionary 'national-popular culture' belonged to an earlier historical era of newly formed nation states such as Italy. Today, the 'national popular' is fraught with dangerous nationalist overtones that are heavily tapped into by the ethno-nationalist Right. It is no longer primarily a battle of fascists against Communists and socialists as in the 1920s and 1930s. Geopolitical power and location in the contemporary national 'pecking order' makes all the difference. Nationalist movement intellectuals in Catalonia or Scotland may be significant locally while having little influence internationally when compared to the global and regional implications of nationalist ideologues. Take for instance calls to 'make America great again' or the promotion of *Hindutva* in Modi's India, an anti-secular, anti-Muslim, populist form of extreme Hindu nationalism.

During the 1930s, Communist-led 'popular front' movements attempted to build national political strategies against fascism. By contrast, Eurocommunism or 'national roads' of the 1970s and 1980s, tried to make Communist parties independent of Moscow. These days, Left nationalism has quite different connotations and has to compete with vigorous neo-fascist ethnonationalist movements. We do not even have the 'constructed' alternative 'working class culture' developed by early twentieth century Left parties through their sports, theatre, music, children's clubs, pubs, housing, community welfare and numerous other social activities. Residues of tradition and political memory are still preserved by some unions, social history museums or via ritual commemorative days such as May Day. In practice, Labour, Social Democratic and radical Left parties, either through their integration into dominant cultural practices, the privatisation of leisure and care, or severe lack of members, now offer flimsy alternatives to commercial popular celebrity culture and social media which dominates the lives of large segments of *all* social classes – from the monarchy and billionaires to the precariat.

At best, Left parties believe in non-profit public cultural institutions rather than media entertainment corporations. Most of the present-day alternative, counter-hegemonic cultural forms, come from anti-consumerist degrowthers living lives of simplicity, or from students and avant-garde artists (such as those working in new digital or audio-visual mediums) and are largely unconnected to working-class organisations. By contrast, in low- and middle-income countries, the absence of large socialist revolutionary parties means that alternative cultures often take the form of religiously influenced movements or traditional indigenous practices and various post-colonial movements, including oppressive fundamentalist, patriarchal religious movements mobilised through mosques, temples and other institutions. Their messages are much more potent than calls for international working-class solidarity because religious communal identity is threatened by capitalist market practices and military intervention. An effective anti-hegemonic position against American or French-backed governments in Africa, the Middle East and Asia is intricately connected to a coherent anti-Western and anti-secular 'counterculture' based on a mixture of both exaggerated and credible critiques of what they see as alcohol-fuelled, vulgar commercial, pornographic capitalist culture. Even those populations of large cities in newly industrialised countries who reject religious fundamentalism are more attracted to liberal political models and globalised consumer cultural practices rather than to socialist working-class mobilisation.

In reality, the new Communist parties founded from 1920 onwards were minority movements because the politically conscious working class was very divided. During the 1920s, the notion of a unified proletarian or bourgeois culture was more myth than reality. In Berlin alone there were 2,633 magazines and journals, and 147 daily newspapers that disseminated a wide variety of perspectives.[7] Today, the print media has been eclipsed in most cities in developed capitalist countries with only one or two newspapers or no papers. The Internet may have more than made up for this decline with thousands of web sites and online blogs. But there is a fundamental difference between the more coherent pattern of workers reading newspapers on the way to or from work (which used to occur within more standardised working hours) rather than the far more random and diverse use of smart phones during an irregular workweek spread over 24/7. Four decades of postmodern culture and the assault on universal political and cultural values and identities has destroyed the former privileged place that socialists allocated to the working class in anti-capitalist political action. The cacophony of tens of thousands of social media sites and subcultures renders a coherent 'class culture' an archaic relic, even though, despite all the changes, the transformed working class remains the largest class in capitalist societies.

However, it is the fragmentation of labour markets and socio-cultural divisions amongst wage workers that reduces the former role of 'organic intellectuals' to a meaningless or ineffective remnant of a bygone age. Four decades of the neoliberal promotion of market individualism has affected political and cultural values and practices across the political spectrum. The rise in support for new forms of Right-wing individualism such as 'sovereign individuals', opposition to social solidarity and collective responsibility in the name of 'freedom' from mask wearing, vaccinations and public health measures such as lockdowns, are all indicative of the larger breakdown of former social relations that Gramsci wrote about. The proliferation of social media abuse, individualist dreams of bitcoin and other digital schemes are not merely confined to market entrepreneurs and Right-wing trolls. The hostility to collective action (unless supporting 'individual freedoms' or specific 'identity' groups) now also permeates those who are critical of capitalism.

It is not just that contemporary identity-driven movements refuse to subordinate or submerge their interests under the umbrella of 'working class consciousness', a concept that socialists still mistakenly assume to be 'universal' and all embracing. Today, it is extremely difficult to construct political coalitions because differences surrounding 'identity' claims trump social solidarity on a range of socio-economic and environmental issues. Despite the attempt to incorporate feminist, green or LGBTQI values into Trotskyist and other Left parties, it is understandable that these identity-based movements see themselves as equally important and not reducible to expedient political strategies devised by vanguard party leaders seeking to lead the working class. In short, the more that capitalist societies evolved into complex social formations, the more that vanguard parties and hierarchical Left parties gradually lost their capacity as organisations to represent diverse social groups that either did not identify as proletarians or rejected the undemocratic political mode of operation of traditional Left parties.

Today, there is neither a 'Modern Prince' that strategically acts on behalf of the proletariat, nor a unified working-class that is able to surmount the multiple racial, gender, ecological, ethno-national and other political interests, and identities. Crucially, the vast majority of Left intellectuals (mainly academics) are isolated and have no 'organic' connection to the working class regardless of whether the latter work in manufacturing, mining, construction, or services. They may be far better read and informed than earlier generations but often they mainly communicate with fellow academics or students. The nearest we have to 'organic intellectuals' are various particularistic rather than universalist 'community organisers' who mobilise ethnic and racial minorities on behalf of candidates or parties. They are unable to surmount wider socio-economic and cultural divisions but hope that being part of the electoral machine campaigning for individual candidates or for a national party will 'deliver' better policies favouring specific 'community' constituencies. Such electoral politics are fragile and fluctuate due to the rise and decline of support by multicultural voters for different candidates and parties.

Similarly, it is questionable whether marketing software engineers, biotech researchers, fintech analysts and other so-called 'knowledge economy' technoscience 'intellectuals' would abandon their crucial roles in contemporary capitalist industries and become alternative 'organic intellectuals' advancing eco-socialism. If they did, what alternative non-capitalist vision of science, technology, the human body, the role of finance and personal services could they promote among their fellow workers and business associates without suffering personal identity crises about their current roles or losing their jobs and contracts? It was bad enough during the old Stalinist days of 'proletarian science' when scientists constantly feared having their scientific work censored by the arbitrarily designated label of 'bourgeois science'.

As to an 'environmental consciousness', how is this to be defined and acquired, and who are the 'organic intellectuals' capable of waging a 'war of position' against capitalist *unsustainable* production and consumption? Globally, a post-carbon 'counterculture' is still in a rudimentary and fragmented form. It is possible to piece together various strands of degrowth practices, such as slow food movements, or those creating green sustainable cities, living simplicity lifestyles, and promoting social values based on care and co-operation. Despite annual 'sustainability festivals' and visual and online networks, this post-carbon 'counterculture' is less organisationally integrated and more politically fragile in that it has so far failed to overcome the tensions between green entrepreneurs, supporters of alternative lifestyles and anti-capitalist degrowthers and eco-socialists. Also, in contemporary capitalist societies there are no green political organisations that hold the equivalent political and economic power as that held by earlier socialists and Communists through their unions and parties. Large Green parties such as the German Greens are closely tied to pro-market policies rather than representing a counter-hegemonic position. Green movements consist of cross-class membership but are poorly represented in workplaces, thus limiting their ability to build alternative forms of environmental consciousness amongst wage employees (apart from professions such as teachers) who will be most affected by any transition to a post-carbon society.

A varying percentage of small family businesses, the self-employed and entrepreneurs may be sympathetic to socialism or forms of post-carbon democratic innovation and social justice. The majority of small businesses, however, continue to play very conservative roles in opposing social and environmental reforms. To assume that degrowth 'organic intellectuals' could advance an 'environmental consciousness' of smaller material footprints and establish political relations with millions of small retailers and other businesses is politically unfeasible and bordering on fantasy. This is because the income, use of material resources and survival of retailers and many small businesses depend on the continuation of unsustainable high consumption and high per capita material footprints. Creating a political bond between small businesses, contractors, and wage workers on the future shape of a post-carbon democracy is currently highly unlikely.

In summary, contemporary working classes are remarkably diverse and have little in common culturally, politically, and economically other than that they are dependent on their employers in the private and public sectors as well as on those in not-for-profit organisations. Hence, 'organic intellectuals' cannot be produced by such socially and institutionally diverse layers of society and still articulate a shared and coherent class-consciousness. Workers continue to make the goods, mine the resources and provide services that grow capitalist businesses. Yet, their role up until recent decades has never been to largely provide the organisational, technical, scientific, and ideological foundations of capitalism. Software engineers, marketing personnel or researchers for 'big pharma' corporations could possibly apply their expertise to creating an alternative post-capitalist society. The difference is that according to Gramsci's theory, working class 'organic intellectuals' could develop class consciousness amongst their fellow workers precisely because they did not help manage and sustain capitalist institutions and were an integral part of the working class in which they lived and for which they struggled. No such political consistency is open to contemporary service sector and professional employees who provide the indispensable administrative, technical, and ideological roles used to exploit other fellow workers or prevent the latter from taking control of capitalist institutions. Few have the opportunity to redefine their job specifications so that they cease enhancing capitalist socio-cultural, political economic and technical control.

Not only are employees engaged in crucial roles keeping capitalist production and administrative structures functioning, but as many analysts of the new digital culture have pointed out, the way individuals are accorded recognition and reward is quite distinct from the old public sphere that Gramsci encountered. Most public/private interactions online simultaneously involve being rated or else rating, liking or unliking other people, products, and services.[8] Instead of overt class relations, people are simultaneously rewarded or downgraded through their consumption or networks which all becomes data for digital giants to profit from. Offline social relations are mediated by online interactions that weaken former levels of solidarity as 'platform capitalist' practices reclassify workers as 'contractors' competing with other contractors.

Given the dramatic 'restructuring' of both capitalist production and the workers employed within new private and public service sectors, it is now clear that the concept of 'organic intellectual' has lost all practical political meaning in the struggle for an environmentally sustainable and socially just society. All social change movements need theorists and policy activists. Let us dispense with the illusion that these activists will necessarily arise from some readily identifiable and homogenous working class and be able to advance a singular, comprehensive working-class consciousness. Very importantly, 'consciousness raising' is also a limited and elementary form of political activism. In fact, consciousness raising will only go so far, whether practised by traditional working-class activists or by contemporary advocates of degrowth. The problem remains that just as the majority of industrial workers never supported revolutionary action, so the majority of existing citizens may overwhelmingly support environmental sustainability but do not necessarily equate this goal with post-capitalism. Beyond attempting to unify incredibly diverse populations in developed capitalist societies lacking a common political culture or identity, the so-called 'advanced' or militant individuals and groups will need detailed political economic policies that satisfy quite distinct social constituencies. It is here that the idea of a post-carbon socialism being forged by a single class party with its own 'organic intellectuals' is little more than political nostalgia for a bygone age.

Unsurprisingly, Gramsci, is now invoked as the theorist of 'organising' rather than invoked for his analysis of hegemony. Cultural historian, Michael Denning, argues that the two earlier forms of Gramscian politics are now exhausted: the Gramsci of the 'Modern Prince' which was used to build a revolutionary communist party; and the 'cultural politics' of those engaged in a 'war of position' in education, journalism, popular culture and social movements against capitalist cultural hegemony.[9] While Denning says nothing about 'organic intellectuals', he takes Gramsci's claim that everyone is both an intellectual and a legislator as the basis for his supposed relevance as the new theorist of 'organising'. Clutching at straws, Denning elevates the cacophony of the disorganised voices of the Occupy movement at Zuccotti Park as the equivalent of the workers mass factory occupations in Turin 1919-1920. This romanticisation is little better than the exaggerated illusions of Maoist students who occupied administration buildings or classrooms in different universities during the 1960s and called these 'liberated zones' (after Mao's military campaigns in regional China). Citing Democrat Congress member Alexandria Ocasio-Cortez's self-description of herself as an organiser, Denning declares that "The age of the party is over: this seems true not just in the US, but in the US-ification of other parliamentary election regimes. As a result, young activists think of themselves as organisers (of a variety of stripes) not as partisans (party members)."[10] This may be relevant in the US where 'candidate politics' often overrides weak national party organisations and relies on local organisers to mobilise various social constituencies into effective electoral coalitions. The same tactics and institutional campaigns are less effective in many other countries because candidates are usually selected by party machines rather than through primary election campaigns.

I am not arguing against the need for activist organisers. Rather, it is a long stretch for Denning to imagine that by calling all people 'legislators/intellectuals', that somehow a 'reformation of the national-popular collective will' (in all workplaces, neighbourhoods, households, schools and so forth) is in any way different to Gramsci's old counter-hegemonic politics. Whereas Gramsci saw 'organic intellectuals' as indispensable in developing a radical working-class consciousness and linking ordinary people to the revolutionary party, Denning believes that the age of the vanguard party is over. I absolutely agree. But so too is the notion of a homogeneous work-ing-class consciousness and the notion of organic intellectuals. Denning wants to have it both ways. He wants to revive the obsolete notion of a homogenous 'national-popular popular will' while dreaming that ordinary people as 'legislators' could actually enact legislation without a party or parties winning majority control of legislatures. How the numerous 'organ-isers' combine the quite disparate and fragmented ethnic, racial and other diverse communities and sectional or class interests into a coherent national political force is never spelt out. One thing is certain, Gramsci's theory of organising would be largely ineffective in contemporary capitalist countries based on a range of socio-economic and cultural divisions that he could never have imagined.

The Rise and Fall of Post-Industrial Futurism

The belief in socialist revolution is not the only long-standing theory being kept alive by tiny minorities. Before green growth and ecological moderni-sation became popular with pro-market policy makers, it was the theories of post-industrial society that attempted to counter anti-capitalists in the period from the 1960s to the 1980s. Indeed, post-industrial theories were highly popular amongst a generation of policy makers and academics and evolved into current theories of the 'knowledge economy' and 'networked society'. Despite providing comparative analyses of diverse types of polit-ical economic societies, the earlier post-industrial theories were essentially *nationally* based rather than focussing on what later became known as market globalisation. This was because the world was still divided by the Cold War. It had not yet reduced or swept aside national tariffs on trade, controls over capital flows or instituted the global internet and other value chains or 'networks' of production and consumption.

Some imagine that the post-carbon society will be a post-industrial soci-ety, as the necessary transformation of carbon-intensive industrial society will require production to be largely based on the digital economy of infor-mation and intangible or symbolic data. The question is whether such visions are already being implemented or are only partially true of devel-oped capitalist societies that have shifted many of their dirty industries offshore?

According to the 1960s and 1970s' post-industrial paradigm, human history moved through a variation of essentially three stages: first, the tran-sition from clans and tribes to hierarchical agrarian societies ruled by the

sword; second, the transformation of land-based orders into urban industrial society (whether liberal capitalist, fascist or Soviet Communist) where
power shifted from the aristocracy and religious orders to goods-producing
capitalist industrialists or one-party state bureaucrats and planners; and
third, the rise of knowledge and information-based post-industrial social
orders where most people worked in services rather than in factories.
Hence, post-industrialist theory was an extension or update of nineteenth
century classical sociology that conceived human history as going through
sweeping 'stages' except that the 'end stage' in post-industrial theory was
not 'modernity' in the form of capitalist or socialist industrialisation, but
rather an advanced information and technologically-based society. Today,
there are major divisions over whether future post-carbon societies will be
capitalist or post-capitalist democracies. Will they be the most advanced
technological societies, or will they reject or require either drastic reduction or the stringent regulation of dangerous high-tech industries such as
those associated with military weapons, genetic engineering, and artificial
intelligence?

Not only were post-industrial societies conceived as largely driven by
technological change, but the impression created was that post-industrial
societies were no longer class divided, as capitalists were being replaced by
managers and professionals who now ruled through their ability to control
information and utilise scientific-technical knowledge.[11] Post-industrial
theories were either a mixture of simplistic, class-free scenarios about the
'information economy' or more elaborate sociological scenarios. In 1973,
sociologist Daniel Bell, the 'father' of post-industrial theory published his
book *The Coming of Post-Industrial Society: A Venture in Social Forecasting*, in
which he outlined his vision for the next fifty years.[12] He was far more
conservative than Alvin Toffler who celebrated many of the cultural
changes of the 1960s. Given the passage of five decades, it is now possible
to evaluate his prognoses in relation to the contemporary world and the
current ecological crisis. Bell saw pre-industrial, industrial, and post-industrial societies as based on three axial structures and principals that
governed the action and character of each type of society: one axis was the
'social structure' comprising the economy, technology, and occupations.
Another was the 'polity' concerned with distribution, adjudication, and
enforcement of power. And thirdly, there was the sphere of 'culture' or the
realm of expressive symbolism and meaning whether religious or secular,
high or popular culture.

Bell was proved partially correct to see that industrial societies were characterised by diverse types of political regimes which in the post-1960s began to witness the rise of new occupations in the service sector and the decline of manual workers. But he failed to see that the so-called massive decline in industrial employment was so uneven and did not take place in developed capitalist countries such as Germany, Japan, and the US between 1970 and 1990, let alone across the world. In fact, by 1989, employment in manufacturing in low- and middle-income countries far exceeded the number of jobs lost in developed capitalist countries.[13] The lesson here is that it is necessary to differentiate the types of jobs in 'services', such as those linked to manufacturing, rather than have overgeneralised notions of the 'service sector'. It is also crucial to grasp that any move towards a post-carbon world will be quite different in dozens of countries given the character of their existing industries, their varying levels of dependence on fossil-fuelled or low-carbon intensity trading goods, plus the differing size of their finance sector and need for capital investment. Their ability to become post-carbon societies will also depend on a country's regulatory and tax structures as well as the level of public sector employment and extent of the 'social state' that can absorb unemployment or manage a range of social problems.

In his 1976 book, *The Cultural Contradictions of Capitalism*, Bell argued that three contradictory axial principles governed the economy (efficiency), the polity (equality) and the culture (self-realisation or self-gratification).[14] This was an analysis of Western capitalism with limited applicability to most other nation states outside the Atlantic region or Australia. He was alarmed by the 1960s counterculture and by a generation of American students and dissidents whom he believed threatened social order, capitalist corporations and the traditional values of educational institutions (that is, the culture of 'Western imperialist, white dead males'), even though students benefited materially from market capitalism. It is noteworthy that Bell did not forecast what would happen in the sphere of culture or politics but only in the economy or 'social structure'. He discussed environmental pollution, but like most of his Weberian, liberal, and Marxian contemporaries working within the paradigm of 'capitalism versus democracy', Bell largely ignored ecological factors as decisive in any future social transformation.

Instead, as an ex-Trotskyist, Bell transposed to capitalist societies the old dilemma of the class nature of the Soviet Union that had troubled anti-Stalinists. Could one have classes in a society where private property had been abolished, and were the managers and bureaucrats a 'new class' or a 'new caste'? Bell partly projected this dilemma onto America as the world's most advanced society heading for post-industrialism. Hence, the new managers, scientists, system planners and technicians of post-industrial society that were clustered around universities, bureaucracies and businesses were, he argued, not a 'new class' but a benign caste or elite. He worried that an upsurge of 'populism' from the lower educated population would lead to resentment against the coming power exercised by new 'knowledge elites' and threaten democracy. This scenario has certainly transpired in conjunction with a combination of racist and economic factors that Bell did not anticipate, particularly the rise of nationalism as a reaction to the socio-economic pain caused by market globalisation. Currently, capitalist societies are deeply divided over the desirability of the rapid pace of change, and how any new transition to green growth, let alone post-capitalism will occur. Will it be captains of corporations and governments, the knowledge-based professional and managerial 'class' or mass protest movements that demand solutions to the climate emergency?

As a leading defender of liberal/conservative values, it was Bell, the Harvard professor, who ignored the indispensable role played by universities, researchers, technicians, and other specialists in developing the military-industrial complex as well as conducting numerous wars, not to mention their promotion of market cultural values. Fifty years later, his separation of 'the economy' from politics and culture looks distinctly naïve. Given the increased dominance of capitalist corporations globally since 1973, together with the decline of radical anti-capitalist cultural forces and the political defeats suffered by labour movements, the 'cultural contradictions of capitalism' that Bell feared have significantly diminished and are barely visible except in one crucial area: anti-materialism. Bell was alarmed by the 'hedonism' and 'nihilism' of the 1960s and early 1970s counterculture eroding traditional religious values, the work ethic and also fundamentally weakening the legitimacy of existing political institutions. He attributed these 'negative' developments to the destructive role of 'modernism' but failed to recognise that modernist values were already being eclipsed by the rise of post-modernism which made modernist values look positively conservative.

Importantly, he largely ignored the deep social divisions in America (evident well before 1973) and the anti-rationalism of Right-wing religious and other conspiracy theorists, violent white supremacists and all those who waged culture wars that culminated in the attack on the Capitol building on January 6th, 2021. Similarly, he failed to predict how the anti-materialist and pro-environmental values of the 'back to nature' 'hippie' and other 1960s movements would evolve into large anti-capitalist environmentalist movements in the following five decades.

Bell's emphasis on how a post-industrial knowledge elite would replace capitalist corporations, not surprisingly, completely misread the fusion of capitalism and digital technology that would give rise to Google, Apple, Microsoft, Amazon, Facebook, and other corporate monoliths. The latter have helped shape not only business and occupational spheres, but also the conduct of politics and key aspects of popular culture and social relations. The fusing of digital culture, corporate financial practices (financialisation) and private sector services into deeply integrated forms of capitalist social orders contradicts most of the 'forecasting' by Bell and others. Post-industrial theorists ignored or de-emphasised the threats posed by technocratic government. Yet, for decades we have seen technocrats appointed to run governments in many countries lacking democracy. Today, it is the turn of those nominally parliamentary democracies such as Italy to witness successive unelected technocrats such as Mario Monti and Mario Draghi appointed to run their governments. Technocratic power now constitutes an ever-growing threat to those very limited forms of representative democracy, especially in a climate emergency.[15] Even Bell's analysis of professions and related occupational change, which superficially looks closer to the mark, could be disputed if we count the tens of millions of dirty, polluting manufacturing and mining jobs in offshore low- and middle-income countries that are indispensable in providing the material goods and hardware sustaining information and knowledge workers in 'post-industrial' countries.

Hence, the concept of post-industrial capitalism in OECD countries is both a reality and an illusion. It is both a geographical and technological displacement rather than the disappearance of industrial capitalism. If an industrial society was defined as 'goods-producing', then this ignored the vast numbers of service sector workers which were always indispensable to securing the circulation, protection, and numerous administrative services necessary to sustain and reproduce the capitalist production of goods. Likewise, if the 'post-industrial' society is characterised by 'knowledge and information', then the post-industrial theorists failed to adequately distinguish between the forms of knowledge practice that were dominant. Take for example, technical and scientific knowledge necessary for sophisticated electronics, metallurgy, chemical and synthetic materials, or digital software essential to advanced military sectors, space industries and civilian goods production. These are not equivalent to those theories and forms of knowledge required to teach and learn humanities in schools and universities, or to provide social care and cultural activity. Notably, this distinction is also often ignored by Left technological utopian concepts of post-capitalism.

Networks, Hackers, and Post-capitalism

Post-industrial theorists over-emphasised technocratic changes to 'industrial societies' as they supposedly became post-capitalist nations governed by a 'knowledge elite' and geared to information rather than the production of goods. By the 1990s, a generation of post-Cold War Left analysts focussed on the *global* rather than the national character of the 'network society'. Coming from a neo-Marxist background, Manuel Castells, for example, fused his Marxism with a range of sociological and political economic analyses and became a leading exponent of how labour markets, politics, culture and production were now more integrated into a range of 'networks and supply chains.[16] This transformation of both capitalist and former Communist countries rendered old forms of class politics and social relations increasingly unrecognisable. Accordingly, the 'digital economy' changed everything – from the way many goods were made to the structure of urban life and the connections between developed capitalist countries and developing low- and middle-income societies. While Castells discussed most social movements (including feminist, environmental and social justice movements), the 'network society' also looks dated given the rise of Right-wing racist movements and the crises affecting 'globalisation' since 2007-2008. Nonetheless, the violence, inequality, and social exclusion that Castells documented in African, Asian and Latin American countries are still very much with us after two decades of so-called progress on 'sustainable development goals'.

How the 'network society' will generate moves toward post-carbon social formations is not yet clear. A decade ago, Castells was supportive of the Internet-driven 'networks of outrage and hope' visible in the 'Arab Spring', Occupy movement and Spanish Indignados.[17] These either fizzled out or were crushed and, to date, little has replaced them. Neither is it clear that in a world of growing regional divisions, whether the concept of an interconnected global 'network' will cease being an embracing and inclusive conception of future socio-economic developments. What is clear from the disparate social groups constituting 'networked' protest movements, including more recent ones inspired by Greta Thunberg's actions, is that they are all dependent on parties or governments converting their demands into legislated change.

The Internet has also produced notions of the 'hacker class' of digital workers and the associated rapid development of roboticization and artificial intelligence (AI).[18] There is no doubt that wage and salaried workers are being made redundant, but it is debateable whether AI will produce a new social class separate from workers and employers. More importantly, the growing financialised capitalist digital economies have already produced new social boundaries of inclusion and exclusion. Half the world's population in 2019 were still not connected to any digital devices, whether laptop, tablet, or smart phone. Within leading capitalist countries, we now have a new Lumpenproletariat that sociologist Marion Fourcade calls the 'Lumpenscoretariat'.[19] These are the millions of people under finance capitalism who are 'under-banked' and have no credit score or poor credit scores, thus being denied access to an entire range of everyday forms of consumption, accommodation, and work.[20]

In regard to the question of a new capitalism or post-industrial capitalism, it is revealing that at the end of the 1990s, both the mainstream financial media and investors as well as Left theorists of post-capitalism succumbed to the hype about the 'new economy'. The frenzy on stock markets generated by the belief that information and symbolic capital were rapidly replacing the 'old economy' of tangible goods production cost investors $US4.6 trillion on Nasdaq alone after the dot-com bubble burst in 2000.[21] Left accelerationist theorists such as McKenzie Wark failed to take note. Between 2004 (*A Hacker Manifesto*[22]) and 2019 (*Capital is Dead*[23]) Wark continued to promote the problematic thesis that hackers – that is, everyone who produced information – constituted the new exploited class dominated by the private corporate 'vectoralist class'. This new class owned intellectual property and controlled information through vectors affecting all spheres of the economy and social life. Capitalists in manufacturing, mining, agriculture, finance, commerce, and services were now dominated by a new ruling class that no longer produced goods and services.[24]

Wark simultaneously frames his analysis partly within Marxist categories but overlaid by a culturalist critique that betrays an inadequate understanding of the material structure of contemporary political economic and environmental processes. If Wark and other theorists of information and digital processes are merely pointing to the emergence of new corporate giants such as Alphabet (Google), Amazon, Apple and Facebook having disproportionate impact on socio-economic spheres, there would be no disagreement. However, all these old and new entrants controlling information and intellectual property are still capitalists consti- tuting a sector of the capitalist class rather than a new class. Despite the quest by Wark to identify a new revolutionary subject after the historical demise of the radical proletariat, this new class is not the 'hacker class'. Crucially, the most powerful G20 capitalist countries are still overwhelming engaged in the production of goods and services, including the production of digital hardware without which the 'vectoralist class' and the 'hacker class' could not function. Indeed, the existing 'hacker class' remains an exceedingly small percentage of the total global workforce in goods and services as well as rural agricultural labour.

Similarly overstated analyses of technological and social change are evident in the work of the technological utopians such as Jeremy Rifkin on the liberal centre/Left and Aaron Bastani and Paul Mason on the radical Left. These conceptions of post-capitalism either gives mass movements little or no role as social change agents (see Rifkin) or display minimal awareness of the incompatibility of an automated society with environ- mental sustainability (see Bastani and Mason).[25] The emphasis on high-tech innovation and free peer-to-peer networks is largely promoted without any substantial engagement with the environmental *unsustainability* of the mate- rial resources required for electric vehicles, 3-D printers and multiple forms digital hardware needed for these fanciful notions of post-capitalism. Indeed, it is difficult to actually find contemporary theorists articulating a model of the power wielders in a 'post-carbon society' that would be equiv- alent to the aristocracy in pre-capitalist societies or capitalist industrialists in earlier types of capitalism. Apart from notions of classless, post-work or post-capitalist futures where all seem to have equal power (after the removal of corporations as rentiers preventing democratic free peer-to-peer networks[26]), little analysis is provided today by either anti-capitalists or liberal technocrats about how we get from 'carbon capitalism' to post-capi- talist futures.

Unless there is as yet unforeseen radical change, it is unfortunately clear that capitalist classes will continue to exist and probably remain dominant during the decades-long transition from fossil fuels to a society based on renewables. If, however, there is a growing push by an alliance of social movements, scientists and policy activists demanding the reduction in the use of material resources, it will become increasingly difficult for businesses to maintain their agenda of incessant economic growth or their ability to retain their political and cultural hegemony.

Wark, Mason and others offer important insights into how the management of capitalist enterprises has changed in the current era of control over data and intellectual property. This leaves the question of whether intellectual property laws can be transformed or abolished, and which social forces will lead this important political strategy. In the absence of such fundamental change to information and knowledge, corporations will continue to be run by managers and technocrats committed to profitability and efficiency using all kinds of new techniques. It will remain up to organised workers in the so-called 'platform' or digital economy to fight alongside other workers and their political allies for new labour laws covering conditions and rights.

A 'transitional society' will require new forms of power sharing if sociopolitical institutions are to be re-geared towards environmental sustainability. Bell and earlier post-industrial theorists said little about looming ecological crises driven by incessant growth, even though the Club of Rome's *Limits to Growth* had been published in 1972. Similarly, the global panoramic discussion of 'network' capitalism or 'vectoral' capitalism briefly discusses the Anthropocene but ignores broader and deeper environmental issues involving the extraction, production, and consumption of a range of material resources. Instead, Wark is deeply pessimistic and believes climate change cannot be prevented. Others such as Mason propose exceptionally long time-frameworks for post-capitalism and provide no indication as to whether post-carbon societies will continue to be part of the globalised 'network'. Given growing regional tensions (especially between the US and China), will these result in decentralised pathways in the form of a revived nationalism based on particular socio-economic and cultural power relations, or is the pathway of deeper global industrial, technological, and social integration unstoppable?

How the 'Cultural Contradictions of Capitalism' will Affect Post-Carbon Societies

Like many other social theorists, Daniel Bell was preoccupied with modernism and modernisation and assumed that societies evolved through different homogenous states with coherent or dominant 'axial principles'. According to Bell, the axial principle of culture within capitalist societies was 'self-realisation' or 'self-gratification'. This may be true of large sections of the population in various countries. It is equally true, however, that many contemporary societies are not dominated by a singular axial principle. Rather, the world at present is characterised by a plurality of values, beliefs, and practices co-existing side-by-side, whether in China, the US, Norway, or Turkey. Complex divisions are evident in multicultural societies with democratic or authoritarian political and cultural institutions. These include religiously conservative, socialist, libertarian individualist, communitarian egalitarian, pro-market technocratic, environmental anti-materialist, ethno-nationalist, and other beliefs that cut across a range of issues affecting private and public social relations. Given these divisions, the 'cultural contradictions' of the 'transition period' to post-carbon societies may prompt a clash between various axial principles, for example, individualism versus social co-operation or environmental sustainability versus growth, that will emerge in quite diverse ways in particular countries.

Although I am critical of Bell's conservative propositions, it is still particularly important to consider whether post-carbon capitalism or post-capitalist eco-socialism or some other type of social formation will be threatened or undermined by new cultural contradictions. If this is the case, what will characterise these socio-economic and political axial principles and to what degree will they differ from those currently dominant in developed capitalist societies?

Sociologist Ingolfur Blühdorn argues that in the post-truth age, democratic legitimacy is both hollowed out and based on an ambivalent and contradictory value system. There is now a clash he argues, between the notion of citizens' inalienable right to 'self-realisation' and the incompatibility of this individualist agenda with finite resources and a collapsing biophysical system.[27] In short, individual self-realisation of the affluent 'good life' (promoted by Right-wing and centre/Left parties, as well as by some Left technological utopians) is incompatible with a sustainable biosphere.

Blühdorn's analysis signals some of the new complexities of 'democracy versus sustainability'. He recognises that Right-wing 'populists' also try to legitimise their racist and nationalist ideas by appealing to democracy against the technocratic-bureaucratic elites. Most of the far Right are anti-environmentalist, but there is a long tradition of Right-wing nationalist, anti-immigrant defence of nature against population growth. Others present their ethno-nationalism dressed up in ecological clothing as saving 'European ecological civilisation' from foreign civilisations.[28] Unfortunately, Blühdorn offers no positive solution or pathway out of the current 'post-politics' scene. Instead, he espouses a contemporary pessimistic theory of 'decline' similar to Weber's 'iron cage', the Frankfurt School's 'totally administered society' and other criticisms of 'modernity'.

At the same time that Bell was bemoaning the 'cultural contradictions of capitalism', American historian Christopher Lasch attacked the 'culture of narcissism' whereas sociologist Richard Sennett focused on the 'tyranny of intimacy' and the search for 'authenticity'.[29] Both lamented how the development of capitalism and the corresponding rise of bureaucracy and professional experts led many to retreat to the private self in the quest for meaning; these trends have combined to debase and transform public life. While Lasch defended a conservative notion of the family and longed for a mythical populist bygone era to restore democratic communities in America, Sennett sought refuge in the ideal of the 'craftsman' as an antidote to the specialised division of labour produced by bureaucratic capitalism. Both were either pre-feminist or anti-feminist analyses of essentially white male dominated public life that simultaneously longed for the *gemeinschaft* of small face-to-face associative life while recognising that we lived in the *gesellschaft* of large urban and impersonal relations.[30]

Two decades later, Ulrich Beck, Elisabeth Beck-Gernsheim and Anthony Giddens analysed how 'individualisation' and feminism affected family life, personal relations and the broader public life of democracy, work, and culture.[31] The relationship between sexuality, intimacy and democracy changed the possibility for men and women to develop the right to free and equal self-development. The sexual passion of private life and the sexualisation of public life were distinct and yet related. If intimacy and democracy were to be made compatible, then societies would need substantive rather than mere formal democratic rights in public and private life.[32] In recent decades, the notion of 'individualisation' has extended to same-sex and transgender relations. Zygmunt Bauman's notion of 'liquid modernity'[33] and Beck's concept of cosmopolitanism and the 'risk society'[34] highlighted both the fragility of traditional social relations and institutions and the new threats to all facets of political, economic, environmental, and social life. The positive dimension of greater opportunities and access to global cultures was countered by increasing health and safety risks from toxic products, military, and environmental threats, to name just some of the fear-inducing aspects of daily life. Consumption and production were now inextricably associated with both self-realisation and self-gratification on the one side and the unleashing of global and local dangers, fear of catastrophes, loss of meaning and loss of community traditions.

It is also necessary to note the more pronounced recent cultural changes that Beck and other analysts of 'risk society' could not have predicted when developing their theories of post-modern or post-industrial capitalism. In the era of 'fake news' and conspiracies, large minorities of people accept the 'truth' of all sorts of risks and *non-risks* which are treated as equally dangerous or benign. On social media, there are endless claims about everything from 5G networks as the cause of COVID-19 to gross distortions that governments 'stage' scenes of mass shootings in schools simply to 'take away' the freedom of citizens to own guns. The other side of this cultural syndrome of hyper market individualism is the rejection or denial of scientifically established risks. Take for instance, the defiant protests against COVID-19 quarantines, opposition to wearing masks and other such ideological manifestations of risk-prone behaviour or especially the widespread Right-wing denial of the largest risk facing the world (climate breakdown) that has been overwhelmingly documented by climate scientists. Instead, Right-wing think tanks, parties and social media outlets promoting fossil-fuels and all kinds of critiques of social policies have adopted earlier Left and green critiques of technocratic power minus the latter's democratising agendas. While socialists and greens call for a radical science that safeguards the environment and society against business threats and nuclear war, the Right-wing assault on science masquerades under the cynical and obstructionist banner that democracy via elected politicians should determine policies rather than unelected scientists. At face value, this appears a reasonable demand. However, in many countries, 30% to 40% of the population now refuse to accept any scientific criteria presented to electorates as legitimate guidelines for both politicians and voters to consider.

While the notion of a 'risk society' contains many suggestive and illuminating insights, it is also both dated and politically insufficiently differentiated. One needs a hierarchy of 'risks' identifying those more dangerous than others, rather than a description of endless 'risks'. For instance, if 'democracy and sustainability' are to become compatible, close attention must be paid to the organising principles of any future sustainable democracy. This has proved to be difficult, especially with the lack of democratic scrutiny. Instead, we have witnessed an organisational logic in Communist countries based on corruption whereby managers and local party officials risked causing workers' deaths and environmental destruction due to fear of disobeying or critiquing irrational orders. The failure to use safety measures, such as shutting down production in particular factories to save lives or prevent pollution was linked to fear of not fulfilling commands 'from above' such as the central plan. Similarly, hiding serious local problems (such as COVID-19) is also related to a closed system whereby officials fear losing their privileged positions.

By contrast, 'risks' in so-called 'open' competitive market capitalist systems based on 'shareholder value' and quarterly bonuses for managers tends to prioritise and incentivise highly exploitative and destructive practices affecting countless communities, jobs, habitats and lives. A proportion of the public may increasingly calculate the 'risks' from particular industries, chemical products, environments or diets. This social fear of 'risk' is related, yet quite different from the notion of 'risk' held by managers and entrepreneurs. The latter weigh their potential profits and bonuses against the cost of either preventing or causing toxic spills, producing carcinogenic goods or hundreds of thousands of preventable industrial injuries and deaths. The wilful abuse of hundreds of millions of workers and consumers continues unabated and is part of a destructive organisational logic that long preceded the 'risk society'.

The polarisation of social attitudes over the existence, character or extent of particular 'risks' spells acute political dangers for any social movement trying to simultaneously advance democratic rights and post-carbon sustainability. Paradoxically, it is the notion of democratic rights which legitimises intolerant and anti-democratic Right-wing groups and movements. Still, without these democratic rights, any post-carbon society would be doomed to become an authoritarian state. Therefore, we need to recognise and remove the inbuilt incentives and unintended consequences of existing formal private and public organisational structures which encourage psychotic and other pathological sadistic managerial traits. The onus is on advocates of local, national, or international forms of democratic sustainable institutions to ensure that social forces advancing both 'democracy' and 'sustainability' do not contradict one another or replicate existing highly negative practices.

Looking back on the social theoretical discourse of the 'culture of narcissism', 'liquid modernity', the 'risk society' and 'individualisation/cosmopolitanism' in the decades between the 1970s and the first decade of the new century, one is struck by the mixture of important cultural themes and exaggerated accounts of how much of the old world had been transformed. While Lasch, Bauman and Beck have died, their diagnoses of the 'liquid' world did not lead them to adopt a radical politics. Instead, Sennett along with Giddens endorsed a mainstream social democratic/Third Way politics[35] but opposed radical green movements. Bauman was sympathetic to the post-growth ideas of Tim Jackson, and Lasch simultaneously supported conservative 'lower-middle class' American industrial culture and Rudolf Bahro's warning that extending Western affluence to the rest of the world would result in ecological catastrophe.[36]

For all the problems with their individual positions, what the writings of Lasch, Sennett, Giddens, Bauman, Beck, Beck-Gernsheim and Blühdorn (in their distinct ways) alert us to is the need to be aware of the dangers associated with the quest for 'authenticity', 'self-realisation' and small-scale communities or *gemeinschafts*. We can't all revert to becoming 'craftsmen', and most women across the world are still heavily dominated by patriarchal relations and lack the opportunity to exercise their 'individualisation'. In those countries where women can exercise their 'individualisation', many are simultaneously torn between career market competitiveness and a desire for a relational self in connection with others. Currently, only a minority of feminists are 'maternal feminists' caught between conservatives on the one side and quasi-neoliberal 'careerists' on the other. An alternative society based on care and equality would need to simultaneously reject both conservative notions of gender and neoliberal notions of the mythical 'autonomous individual' that is not dependent on somebody else for care at some point in their life.[37]

If cosmopolitan values continue to be overshadowed by nationalism and racism, the desire for self-sufficient individuals and communities also comes packaged with highly negative narcissistic characteristics. It is common for social change movements to decline and fall apart because of the inability to work with other individuals due to 'personality' clashes despite supposedly sharing common values. Hence, future local communities can easily become a destructive or unhappy *gemeinschaft* just like an open planned tyrannical office based on false intimacy.[38]

The transition to a post-carbon democracy is made more difficult by the erosion of social bonds and personal relationships and the emergence of a new subjectivity in the form of 'non-commitment'. Marx described how in early capitalism 'all that is solid melts into air' and Bauman, Beck, Giddens, Sennett, and company analysed the modernist and postmodernist dissolution of earlier relationships in late twentieth century capitalist societies. Even if we reject Lasch's white-male anti-feminism,[39] his focus on the development of a survivalist 'minimal self' contains an element of truth. The 'survivalist' mentality now crosses gender lines and requires people to manage how to cope in a world of constant economic, social and environmentalist crises. "A stable identity" he observed, "stands among other things as a reminder of the limits of one's adaptability. Limits imply vulnerability, whereas the survivalist seeks to become invulnerable, to protect oneself against pain and loss. Emotional disengagement serves as still another survival mechanism."[40]

Building on these theories, sociologist Eva Illouz goes one step further in the early decades of the twenty-first century. Analysing the impact of forty years of neoliberal practices, whether in financial derivatives, outsourcing of labour, multiple sexual relations on Tinder or 'unfriending' people on Facebook with a click of programmed software, Illouz observes that the "moral injunctions that constitute the imaginary core of the capitalist subjectivity, such as the injunction to be free and autonomous; to change, optimise the self and realise one's hidden potential; to maximise pleasure, health, and productivity"[41] now all combine to elevate 'non-commitment'. Rather than a survivalist 'minimal self', Illouz regards 'optimising the self' as also resulting in non-commitment. Choice, she observes, "which was the early motto of 'solid capitalism', then has morphed into non-choice, the practice of perpetually adjusting one's preferences 'on the go', not to engage in, pursue, or commit to relationships in general, whether economic or romantic. These practices of non-choice are somehow combined with intensive calculative strategies of risk assessment."[42]

If Lasch's and Illouz's analyses are plausible and extend to a substantial proportion of the population, advocates of democratisation and sustainability now face the widespread 'non-commitment' of people to either joining or remaining members of parties and movements. Writing in 1994, psychoanalyst and sociologist, Ian Craib, noted that if the failure to commit to an organisation is narcissistic because it is based on seeing the world in terms of what can be gained for oneself rather than what can be given, this overlooks the crucial point of being able to negotiate commitment. A mindless commitment, he argued, "is as narcissistic as an inability to commit oneself."[43]

Transitioning to a new post-carbon society requires not just political commitment and activism but also building a new social subjectivity that counters the hyper-individualism of 'optimising the self' at the expense of others. It is possible that escalating economic and environmental crises and major events will lead to the development of a new widespread co-operative subjectivity. This new 'self' has so far not emerged apart from tiny alternative 'intentional communities'. Instead, it is a mixture of old individualism and macro-economic social reform and green policies that largely characterises existing political responses and social activity.

It would be unrealistic to believe that in a transitional phase between the existing old society and a new emerging social order that individuals would be able to jettison their old selves and suddenly become 'born again' non-narcissistic altruistic beings. The increasing structural pressures of earning a wage, paying rent or a mortgage, caring for family and relatives in the absence of adequate public social services all militate against or undermine constructing a co-operative sensibility beyond the immediate family circle. In capitalist societies, it is no accident that individuals (especially young social change activists) without children and family responsibilities, are better able to culturally experiment with alternative communal living and work practices.

As decarbonisation will have to take place under quite different parliamentary or non-parliamentary authoritarian regimes, there will certainly be multiple political economic and cultural tensions between religious and secular beliefs, between concepts of private and public life, between traditional notions of education and a work ethic versus co-operative values in a 'post-work' society. Large capitalist countries such as China, India, Indonesia, Brazil, or Nigeria continue to be characterised by increasing social divisions driven by rising individualism and global market influences alongside anti-individualist bonds and commitments based on religious, family, or communal traditions and practices. The notion of a post-carbon democracy is either weak or non-existent, even though technocratic ideas of post-industrialism and digitalised 'networks' circulate within government circles and among affluent and professional segments of the population in urban centres. From post-industrial theorists to advocates of degrowth, much discussion of future post-carbon tendencies and transitions has been geared only to developed capitalist societies with free elections. However, the construction of post-carbon societies will have to be achieved in countries where the majority of the world's population do not resemble the profiles of Western 'modernity', democracy, and affluence.

Some of the 'cultural contradictions' applicable to parts of the population in OECD countries are also relevant to social groupings within authoritarian low- and middle-income societies. Most, however, may be characterised by new tensions and conflicts that will affect their relations with the natural world due to deforestation, water shortages, pollution and other factors exacerbated by the climate emergency. All will need to rethink the purpose and goal of knowledge and economic activity if social and political stability does not descend into violence. Managing domestic political economic and cultural contradictions will not be possible in many low-income countries without changing international market and power relations with developed capitalist countries.

Whether developed or developing countries, we are only at the doorstep of profound changes to all aspects of familiar socio-economic and cultural practices. It is highly likely that automation and machine learning will transform the structure and content of not just vocational and general education but also other institutional practices in ways that today are yet to be recognised. Both pro-market and anti-capitalist policy analysts are struggling to decide whether the threat to jobs and businesses from automation is greatly exaggerated or not. All is guesswork at the moment. Remember that a mere thirty years ago there was much talk about how the 'knowledge economy' based on a new highly educated and highly productive workforce would replace the old industrial 'Fordism' of mass production and create a socially just society. Governments of all kinds, but especially of the 'Third Way', rhapsodised about the dawn of the new era which has now been replaced by the dread of automation wiping out many of these still-born 'knowledge economy' jobs.[44]

Where does it leave those who neither support old concepts of the working class nor the illusions about the 'knowledge economy? It is clear to those desiring an environmentally sustainable society that the old traditional organised class politics and working-class culture (still partly visible) remains too rigid and hostile to degrowth values based on reduced forms of material consumption and production. Conversely, many environmentalists and feminists reject working-class and mainstream middle-class forms of masculinist violence and aggression within the family or in public, whether violence at football, motor sports, horse racing or hunting animals. Over the past thirty years, binge drinking, excessive credit-fuelled consumer debt and public incivility has become widespread amongst both women and men. What may be too easily dismissed as old puritanical or conservative censorship is in fact a crucial issue for the construction of any future caring alternative society. For if the future will be more of the same libertarian commercial 'anything goes' culture, then respect for nature and biodiversity will be much more difficult to achieve without also concurrently developing a culture of care and civility towards fellow human beings.

Two Images of Post-Work Culture

I began this chapter with a brief outline of Toffler's 'future shock' or what Bauman would later call 'liquid modernity' where all forms of formerly 'solid' social relations melted into air. Today, we see two radical variations or responses to five decades of social and technological change. The first response is characterised by Left Accelerationists and technological utopians who embrace all forms of high-tech culture and welcome automation. They desire the end of wage labour and unnecessary 'bullshit' jobs. The utilisation of advanced technology is seen as necessary to help construct a 'post-work' society based on local and global networks of peer-to-peer communities creating new forms of freedom and social co-operation in future societies free of capitalists, especially rentiers such as Google, Apple, Amazon, and Facebook.

The second response is largely seen in degrowth movements that wish to 're-solidify' social relations and institutions by ending the 'throw-away' consumerist culture, ending environmentally destructive growth and reconnecting individuals to new caring communities and socially enriching cultural experiences. They accept some forms of modern technology but are predominantly anti-high-tech and anti-large enterprises which they see as ecological unsustainable. Post-capitalism is thus seen as essentially local based on a sense of place rather than global mobility, trade, and market cultural links. Degrowthers are also divided over accepting cultural liberalism or more conservative traditional cultural practices compared to the Left Accelerationists.

Leaving aside the controversial issues of how to create a post-work society, the goal of more play and less alienated work is highly desirable and attractive. Any attempt to create a vibrant and joyous society also involves being on guard against possible new forms of 'community *joie de vivre*' that might legitimise something entirely different. After all, the Nazi regime's vast leisure organization, *Kraft durch Freude* (Strength through Joy) was also based on the principles of non-materialistic 'community' relations rather than market individualism.[45] Fascism, Communism and anarchism were all critical of individualism and material consumerism. They all valued 'community' above what they saw as decadent bourgeois individualism.[46] While each movement had its own artistic *avant-garde,* they also had a pronounced element of Puritanism manifested in suspicion of those who did not perform manual labour or were 'unproductive'. Like some earlier Protestant religions that regarded dancing and non-religious music as sexually arousing and sinful, a Puritan streak ran through earlier Communist movements in the denunciation of jazz, rock and roll, homosexuality, 'promiscuous' sexuality and other 'bohemian' tendencies.

It is unclear to what extent both the Left technological Prometheans and degrowthers accept or reject the 1960s New Left and the counterculture's critique of old-style Left Puritanism. Prominent advocate of degrowth, Samuel Alexander, is among a minority of degrowthers who have written about the importance of the aesthetic dimension.[47] While influenced by Marcuse and other radical critics, Alexander's call for artistic creativity to help the degrowth movement is important but could possibly be interpreted as still containing residues of the old Communist functionalist conception of art as agitprop. The boundary between a new aesthetics of simplicity and collectively imposed austerity is a difficult cultural set of relations and values to negotiate. These can either liberate people to enjoy a rich set of non-material pleasures or else be used by others to increase domestic and community drudgery based on the ideologically driven rejection of technological labour-saving innovation. A new aesthetics is also closely interrelated with whether the alternative society will be primarily localist or more cosmopolitan in its recognition that the local is enriched by larger non-local resources and institutional relations.

It is also worth recalling that Marcuse critiqued the early twentieth century orthodox Marxist conception of art as tied to a rising class (the proletariat) and a declining class (the bourgeoisie) with its so-called nihilistic, decadent individualism. Today, it is unclear which class is declining and which class is rising, given six decades of falling levels of industrial manual labour in OECD countries. Regardless of the fortunes of different classes, Marcuse believed that a subversive counterculture must contradict the prevailing art industry. He also argued that art must not be judged solely in terms of its 'proletarian' or 'bourgeois' qualities. "The work of art can attain political relevance only as autonomous work. The aesthetic form is essential to its social function. The qualities of the form negate those of the repressive society – the qualities of its life, labour, and love."[48] Alexander agrees with Marcuse, but at the same time also implies that art can be directly or indirectly evaluated in terms of whether it enhances the political possibilities of degrowth.

This is not the place for a detailed analysis of the theorists who advocate a range of visions about the post-work society. Clearly, there is a world of difference between notions of post-work based on simplicity and small artisan co-operatives and the promise of so-called 'fully automated luxury communism'. Both polarised images are unviable. The life of local communities without significant national and international interaction will also constrain education, science, the arts, and cultural expression if the resources necessary to communicate and exchange ideas and creative works (whether high-tech communications systems, film distribution and so forth) are absent due to lack of funding or parochialism. Conversely, notions of 'fully automated luxury communism' are environmentally and fiscally impossible in a world in which nine billion people are to have equal access to 'fully automated luxury'.

Importantly, post-work 'liberation' must try to ensure that significantly reduced working weeks in the future are based on cosmopolitan, pluralist cultural conceptions of joy and pleasure rather than narrow 'politically correct' parochialism. Even if we do not have a repeat of earlier repressive 'reconstructions' of people's personal desires and modes of action (such as the construction of 'Soviet man' or adhering to the prescriptions of particular religious sects), any new alternative social system will need to consider the diverse attitudes of people to the meaning and attraction of 'community' and what they prioritise in their 'leisure' time.

Currently, the prevailing modes of cultural interaction in capitalist societies are heavily weighted against co-operative interaction. Escalating levels of mental illness compounded by growing up in unhappy split families or living stressed lives of job and income insecurity, are just a few of the widespread socio-cultural factors that undermine the time and energy needed for collective action and community participation. Little wonder then, that there is a pervasive belief that 'out of the crooked timber of humanity no straight thing can ever be made' (Kant). While the objective of constructing a new society (or rational 'straight thing') should never be driven by simplistic notions of socialism or degrowth sustainability being a panacea for all ills, the obstacles to social change should also never be minimised. Hence, it would be foolish to believe that all would relinquish their individualism and be happy communitarians actively participating in collective activities. It is also worth remembering that Marcuse warned radicals about the 'psychic Thermidor' (named after the Thermidorian Reaction of 1794 that toppled Robespierre and the radicals of the French Revolution). This was a psycho-cultural condition in which part of the population were still committed to old conservative values and tried to turn back the clock of radical change.[49] Some degrowthers and other radicals tend to have a benign view of their fellow humanity and underestimate the potential violent defence of material and cultural interests when threatened by degrowth or socialist, anti-capitalist policies.

Supporters of degrowth also advance varied notions of 'community'. Most are democratic, caring, and inclusive and should be strongly supported. However, within broad degrowth movements there are also those elements that promote a type of 'zealous naturalism'. These can potentially become tyrannical and restrictive forms of eco-fascism if permitted to be dominated by ideals of organic, 'natural' social relations that metamorphize into nationalist racism or parochial discrimination and exclusivity. The 'commons' like 'the people' is always open to pressure and manipulation. Increased direct democracy in combination with other national and international institutional practices is a desirable goal. Participatory democracy facilitates the discussion of a range of socio-political views but is itself no guarantee that narrow prejudices rather than broader and more tolerant social values prevail. Hence, the need to strongly critique 'organic' claims of being 'at one with nature'. We must foster the care, protection and respect of the biosphere but also recognise that diverse socio-cultural relations and 'strangers' or the 'other' are generally at risk when ideologues begin reducing 'community' and society to natural 'organic' processes.

Cultural creativity should not be judged according to whether it best serves or supposedly undermines the needs of prevailing social and political institutions. A future co-operative society will not thrive if it does not recognise that collectives are hardly ideal arrangements to produce diverse, exciting, or great art, literature, and many other forms of cultural creativity. The interaction between the individual imagination and personal space on the one side and the collective needs of the community on the other will require ongoing sensitivity and negotiation. Above all, it will require mutual recognition that present and past forms of both individualism and collectivism – whether in cultural creativity, work practices or social participation – are contradictory and can be counterproductive to flourishing and tolerant societies.

In capitalist societies, the ideology of individualism has fuelled many wonderful as well as many awful creations. The problem is that thousands of artistic creations are never seen because they are neither marketable nor receive public funding. Communist countries, on the other hand, gave infinitely more support to most branches of the arts than governments in capitalist countries. As we know, they also prevented and suppressed all creativity deemed unacceptable by these regimes. How to avoid repeating these two unacceptable models remains a major challenge. This immediately raises the issue of how to avoid the unequal allocation of resources by markets without encouraging undemocratic planning and cultural censorship.

What kind of socio-cultural practices will enhance or inhibit the creation of post-carbon democracies will remain heatedly contested. The illusion that developing capitalist countries will simply follow the trajectory of socio-economic development visible in OECD countries over the past seventy-five years fails to take into account that this model of development is now incredibly unstable and is itself being transformed. Most think-tank reports and government analyses are seriously flawed or dated even before they are published because they merely project past and present practices into the future. Low- and middle-income countries will not follow the so-called path of high-income capitalist countries. The transformation of capital investment, labour markets, international trade, education and training, levels of public and private services and struggles over everything from carbon emissions to the application of labour-saving technology will make the old 'modernisation' pathway either a dead-end or increasingly impossible to imitate.

Importantly, the accumulation of capital and the development of military power have been the twin interrelated driving motors of many countries in the past 200 years. How are they to be replaced in a post-carbon or post-capitalist society? Short of revolution and demands to end militarisation, defund the police, and abolish capitalism, these goals remain slogans or consigned to the 'too hard basket' of most radical activists and theorists. Much about future post-carbon societies remains unexplored. We do know, however, that unlike benign theories of 'post-industrial' society, any possibility of constructing post-capitalist societies will not be smooth transitions based on new green growth industries or high-tech employment in the 'knowledge economy'. A post-carbon society is not to be confused with the creation of either post-carbon democracies or post-capitalist socialist societies. All will certainly involve major political conflict but constructing post-carbon democracies and/or post-capitalist societies will also entail social convulsion and protracted struggles.

Over the past fifty years, we have witnessed how previous imaginaries or conceptions of the so-called transformation of industrial societies into post-industrial and 'network societies' have failed to realise many promises. Much attention has been paid to the growth of 'world cities' linked to global commodity and value chains. Yet, the previous political forces championing globalisation have now come up against vigorous opposition, mainly from Right-wing nationalists. Culturally, these 'populist' movements cling to reactive national identities that are almost frozen in time. Espousing racist, masculinist, and anti-ecological values combined with stereotypical notions of law and order over democracy, these movements favour coercion over deliberation as methods of conflict resolution. Whether these nationalist movements are effective in reviving national economies and a powerful and divisive regionalism (that is driven by great power rivalry) remains to be seen. The old notions of a progressive universal cultural modernism sweeping the globe is certainly at odds with powerful movements based on strange combinations of religious, racist, market individualist yet also anti-corporate forms of popular nationalist agendas.

Those who want post-carbon democracies to be built on new ecological sensibilities of care to fellow human beings and other species or are supportive and tolerant of a range of cultural identities, will have to struggle against thriving atavistic nationalist elements if post-carbon cultures are not to be shaped by fear and parochialism. Without understanding how social classes are made or make themselves, and why and how they are *unmade* and decline, we will not be prepared for those emerging social forces which will attempt to make future post-carbon societies conform to their own restricted or broader cultural agendas.

3. THE POLITICAL STRUGGLE OVER NATIONAL AND PER CAPITA MATERIAL FOOTPRINTS

IN EARLIER DAYS, social reformers and anti-capitalists never had to worry about greenhouse gas emissions or the size of material footprints and whether adequate living standards for the global population could be achieved within what some call the 'carrying capacity of the earth'. Even today, there are still many amongst the broad Left who either ignore environmental constraints or simplistically assume that all will be possible once workers gain political power. A sizeable proportion of pro-market policy analysts and business groups are even more indifferent to environmental factors, except when they are directly affected. These groups have never worried too much about inequality or the lack of social justice. If we are to support the full range of socio-economic alternatives to prevailing capitalist practices, whether of the reform or radical kind, it is first necessary to ascertain to what extent these policies are compatible with growing levels of extraction and utilisation of material resources. To what extent are pro or anti-market policies achievable without threatening what scientists call the earth's planetary boundaries?

In contrast to most environmentalists who analyse material footprints, I will attempt for the first time to critically address the way per capita and national material footprints and 'ecological footprints' are used by political movements and governments. I argue that these concepts about material resources are seriously flawed and that many reports and analyses of material footprints arrive at conclusions that need to be critically scrutinised or rejected. In the absence of alternative data and ways of organising the voluminous scale of technical information, we are all constrained by problematic concepts, whether 'low-income, lower-middle, upper-middle and high-income countries', 'ecological footprints', and so forth. All these categories and concepts were developed by mainstream economists and environmentalists and deployed by the World Bank, United Nations, International Monetary Fund, and other organisations. While initially formulated as so-called 'neutral' alternatives to earlier extensively criticised distinctions between 'developed' and 'undeveloped' countries, they remain politically loaded.

Like the widely criticised concept of Gross Domestic Product (GDP), the concepts 'material footprints' and 'ecological footprints' are based on theories that fail to consider profound social inequalities as they emphasise calculations based on averaging or aggregate statistics of per capita and national consumption and production. Like many other policy analysts, I have also too readily accepted the concept of 'footprints' and generalised definitions without questioning both how they are determined and their political implications. Hence, while I am effectively forced to rely on flawed empirical data, I will simultaneously endeavour to indicate why these concepts distort our understanding of socio-economic and environmental relations when used uncritically for questionable ends. It is the debate over material footprints – which is still in its infancy – that continues to inform notions of green growth and degrowth. There is a pressing need to critically evaluate the inconsistencies in the 'material footprint' literature. We must keep in mind that crucial world-shaping political implications flow from accepting or rejecting various assessments of material resources and the corresponding solutions proposed.

To illustrate the distortions built into material footprint statistics, take, for example, fossil fuels which are only one small but important part of material resources, yet dominate policy debates. In 1825, the United Kingdom (UK) accounted for about 80 per cent of global CO_2 emissions from fossil fuel combustion due to its advanced level of industrial production and the fact that the rest of the world was largely pre-industrial.[1] By 2018, the UK was responsible for only a tiny 1.2% of global CO_2 emissions compared with China at over 28 per cent, but was still the seventeenth largest emitter of greenhouse gases in the world (depending on different methodologies) and had per capita emissions of approximately 7.5 tonnes per annum. Notably, these emissions were much higher than per capita emissions in low-income countries such as India and Indonesia (approximately 2.2 and 2.5 tons) but much lower than Qatar (49.2 tons), Kuwait (25.2 tons), Australia (22.9 tons) Saudi Arabia (21 tons) or US (20.3 tons) and even

China at 9.23 tons per capita.[2] Actually, most of these national figures are misleading or inaccurate as they often don't count emissions from off-shore production of manufactured or agricultural goods consumed by each individual country. They also do not take into account historical CO_2 emissions which have accumulated in the atmosphere. On this account, the US is the largest emitter responsible for 30.7% of global emissions between 1850 and 1990.[3]

Aside from growing survey data from 13,000 cities, there is scant detailed comparative data that enables us to gain an accurate assessment of one aspect of material footprints, namely, carbon footprints. For example, Daniel Moran and co-researchers argue that: "While many of the cities with the highest footprints are in countries with high carbon footprints, nearly one quarter of the top cities (41 of the top 200) are in countries with relatively low emissions. In these cities, population and affluence combine to drive footprints at a scale similar to those of cities in high-income countries."[4] Thus, measuring per capita emissions functions as a crude averaging process. Despite looking at postcodes or differences between low- or high-income countries, urban and rural populations, this form of measurement largely ignores class divisions within the same postcode of large cities and whether industries and businesses rather than individuals and households are disproportionately accountable for emissions.[5]

Importantly, we should not confuse national and per capita greenhouse gases emission levels with the much more significant resources comprising per capita and national *material* 'footprints'. For instance, countries with small populations but large exporters of fossil fuels and other raw materials, such as Australia, Qatar or Saudi Arabia, usually register as having high per capita emissions even though many individuals and households in these societies have per capita emissions and consumption of resources no greater than that of households in countries that import material resources. The political and social challenge of reducing the use of a range of material resources in order to achieve greater sustainability is partly related to decarbonisation but is also more extensive and complex, not to mention infinitely more difficult politically.

In this chapter, I will discuss why the concepts of national and per capita material footprints and 'ecological footprints' are driven by market individualism and a misconception that 'sovereign national economies' supposedly determine the size of national material footprints. While well intentioned scientists, ecological economists and many environmentalists are the forward thinkers sounding the alarm over environmental unsustainability, there are also many who unwittingly play the role of 'useful idiots' for corporations and governments. This is especially true of material footprint analysts who play highly contradictory roles. While providing insightful ecological assessments of how material resources are used and abused, they also engage in depoliticised or 'neutral' explanations that fail to directly criticise capitalist social systems that drive so-called national and per capita production and consumption.

What's at Stake?

The majority of analyses of material throughput – from the extraction of resources from land or marine environments to production and final consumption – are mainly conducted by scientists, ecological economists, and other social scientists. It is important to distinguish between two factors: definition and deception. There is a growing literature on all facets of material resources and distinctions between ecological, carbon, water and material 'footprints', which often overlap. Some analysts claim that either one type of 'footprint' is more accurate, or conversely, dispute the validity and meaningfulness of both 'ecological footprints' and material footprints. Little clarity or consistency exists when it comes to ascertaining what constitutes either 'overshoot' or abundance of resources. Politically, 'limits' are not Left or Right issues, even though much propaganda and finance is invested in trying to prove that capitalist economic growth is virtually limitless.

How 'ecological footprints' or material footprints are defined is yet to be fully grasped and debated by political movements concerned about environmental sustainability. As to deception, this is a deliberate policy on the part of governments and industry lobbies to prevent major decarbonisation and environmental protection policies from being implemented. Many governments across the world are redefining what net zero emissions means,[6] falsely claiming much higher emissions reductions by using accounting tricks such as using offset credits, exaggerating land and forest 'sinks', ignoring carbon-embodied traded goods and making spurious claims about carbon capture and other technologies.[7]

In the meantime, the dominant view of material resources supported by a wide variety of pro-market or anti-market political groups ranging from capitalist free-market entrepreneurs and social democratic reformers to green growth modernisers and some socialist revolutionaries, is that aside from the climate crisis, there is no major crisis or shortage of material resources. Hence, variations of the dominant perspective either largely ignore the issue (that is, do nothing 'business as usual') or promote the ecological modernisation of industry, consumption, and waste disposal so that resources are more efficiently and effectively used. Remember, that decarbonisation involves some particularly significant changes to material resources production and consumption, especially in energy, transport, construction, and agriculture. Most green growthers view these changes as being achievable without the need for drastic changes to per capita and national consumption levels. Similarly, the socialists who are focussed on preventing climate breakdown, support a fundamental redistribution of power and wealth (so that material resources can be shared more equitably) rather than advocate substantial degrowth in the use of particular material resources.

It is true that a minority of business leaders and policy analysts do recognise the crisis associated with the use of material resources. However, their pro-market solutions, such as increasing the circularity of materials, tend to reject a substantial reduction in the level and character of current production and consumption. It is radical degrowthers and eco-socialists who warn that there are finite limits to certain material resources and, in the case of degrowthers, call for affluent populations to reduce their material footprints by up to 90% of current levels. Hence, between do nothing 'business as usual' and a 90% cut to per capita consumption in mainly affluent OECD countries, there is an enormous political economic policy chasm. The political economic consequences of even halving such a drastic cut to between 25% and 45% of current per capita consumption levels would place most capitalist countries in a state of deep crisis as growth became curtailed for many major corporations, medium and small businesses.

A gigantic gulf exists between various Right and Left advocates of growth and the warnings by degrowthers and eco-socialists about the ecological disasters that will escalate if drastic reductions in the production and consumption of resources do not occur. This chasm means that the very character of contemporary politics is now entering a fundamentally new phase. One reason why most are yet to recognise the role of material resources in the emergence of a new political divide is that the old struggle of 'capitalism versus democracy' still continues to dominate political discourse. Characterised by class struggles over the distribution of wealth and the institutional and power agendas over 'who gets what, when and how', the conflicts between neo-fascists, conservatives, various religious fundamentalists, liberal social democrats, and radical socialists are being increasingly modified and challenged by new overarching, unstable environmental factors. How the advocates of these various political philosophies come to terms with future constraints on material resources use remains an open question.

If and when voters and policy makers begin to recognise the unavoidable need to formulate policies on how to transform the use of material resources, the critical issue will become: should they opt for government-driven reductions that shift away from existing structural economic and social practices, thereby challenging dominant market-defined notions of per capita consumption at individual and household levels? Or should they only modify business practices (ecological modernisation) but still leave largely intact the very market relations that continue to produce deep social inequality and unsustainable extraction, production, and consumption of material resources?

People such as Tim Jackson have done much to popularise the need for us to rethink how we can have 'prosperity without growth' and enrich our social relations on a planet with finite resources.[8] The paradox, he says, is that the mantra of growth has been chanted by supporters of 'business as usual' and green growth modernisers even as actual growth rates have declined during the past fifty years in developed capitalist societies.[9] Capitalist societies are broken, Jackson argues, because the whole institutional structure is geared to growth and is ill-equipped to change socio-economic practices in a new direction of wellbeing. While I agree with much of Jackson's critique of existing dysfunctional societies, his positive alternative vision rests on the seriously flawed assumption that capitalist enterprises in the future will not remain inherently geared to capital accumulation and profit.

In denying what drives the extraction and consumption of resources, Jackson helps create an illusory utopian politics of how people and governments can lead capitalism on a post-growth or post-capitalist path where businesses no longer pursue profit but become organisations committed to social and environmental health and the good life.[10] If so, how are capitalist enterprises and their shareholders to survive if the addiction to growth is abandoned? What happens when companies lose their share of the market and shareholders see their dividends plummet? It is one thing for companies to promote public relations images of the 'socially responsible corporation' and quite another to cease exploiting environments and workers.

Speculation or Science: What is the Carrying Capacity of the Earth?

Currently, political debates between degrowthers and green growthers as well as 'business as usual' conservatives are based on pessimistic or optimistic arguments about whether there are finite limits to material resources. When we delve beneath the polarised political positions concerning future environmental sustainability, much depends on beliefs or assumptions knowingly or unknowingly held by people, governments, businesses, policy analysts and political movements about the 'carrying capacity of the earth'. What is this elusive 'carrying capacity of the earth' and why is there no agreement about what it actually means or how to measure it?

Part of the controversy surrounding this concept is that it has been transposed from measuring the capacity of ships to measuring 'spaceship earth'. A common definition of 'carrying capacity' is the maximum population of a species (human or non-human) that a given land or marine area can support. As to the total earth's 'carrying capacity', if it is to be a meaningful concept does it depend on human population size and particular levels of consumption of natural resources? Does it have more to do with the way production and consumption can be safely managed without damaging the biosphere and geophysical boundaries of the earth system, as well as other factors such as technology available and the degree of social equality and democratisation? What if none of the latter factors are relevant because the very notion of 'carrying capacity of the earth' is either metaphysical or highly speculative and, like the existence of 'God', can neither be proved nor disproved?

To illustrate the empirical difficulty of determining the 'carrying capacity of the earth', a 2012 survey of 65 studies estimating the earth's 'carrying capacity' found that a majority (33) concluded that it was somewhere between either a maximum of 8 billion people or as low as 2 billion. Fourteen assessments nominated 16 billion, while 18 estimated it to be between 32 billion and 64 billion people or multiples well above these figures.[11] It is understandable why it is in the interests of businesses, governments and many social reformers or some technological utopian radicals to err and accept more generous estimates of the 'carrying capacity of the earth' as either being infinite or several times larger than the current total 'throughput' or use of material resources. Conversely, degrowthers would lose their *raison d'etre* if there was no threat to the capacity of the earth to 'carry' a global population of over nine billion people while continuing to grow economies to the fantasy level whereby all were able to consume resources at quantities currently enjoyed only by affluent populations. In other words, why claim that we need the equivalent of one and a half earths or two, three or four earths to satisfy such needs if the 'carrying capacity of the earth' is either unknown or not limited?

The more sophisticated defenders of capitalism such as green growther, Ted Nordhaus of the Breakthrough Institute, reject the notion of the 'carrying capacity of the earth' and regard it as a static, unscientific, and nebulous concept that denies the way the earth has been remade a number of times throughout its long history. He points out that humans are not fruit flies or cattle, endlessly reproducing until they exhaust resources or have to be managed carefully to stay within so-called 'limits'.[12]

The 'eco-modernist' position may be fine as a critique of Malthusian population theory because there is extensive evidence that demographic growth declined in many countries as industrialisation, improvements in the lives of women and affluence increased. However, the 'eco-modernists' conveniently remain silent on other key issues. In fact, Nordhaus and company are alarmingly blind and unscientific to claim that the earth is infinitely resourceful. Instead of focussing on the exhaustion of crucial materials, dangerous levels of biodiversity loss, rampant deforestation, and other forms of degrading land use, they acknowledge the latter problems but at the same time uncritically and optimistically emphasise the market's capacity to provide technological solutions. In other words, rather than implement renewable energy or fundamental socio-economic change in the way that we use and share resources, the Breakthrough Institute supports fossil fuels such as natural gas and heavily promote nuclear power.[13]

While I strongly oppose the energy and political agenda supported by the American Breakthrough Institute, including their attempts to undermine environment movements, some of their criticisms of the serious methodological problems associated with attempts to measure 'ecological footprints' are pertinent. Developed thirty years ago in 1991, the 'footprint network' presents itself as politically and economically neutral. Officially, it pretends to be apolitical and favours neither particular forms of energy use nor particular socio-economic systems and also avoids analysis of all forms of negative land use, depletion of non-renewable resources, unstable environmental conditions, or ecological destruction.[14] Instead, it purports to measure the annual consumption of the global population to estimate whether it exceeds the biocapacity of the earth to regenerate these consumed resources. In 1961 the global 'ecological footprint' was supposedly two thirds of the earth's biocapacity but by 2019 it required over 1.5

earths and each new year continues to reach 'Earth overshoot day' earlier and earlier (except in 2020 when it was August 22, or three weeks later than in 2019 because of reduced activity due to COVID-19).

I do not propose to 'guesstimate' the 'carrying capacity of the earth' as this concept is not necessary to evaluate whether we should oppose or support particular forms and rates of economic growth, the distribution of power and the use of various resources. Regardless of whether there will be two billion or nine billion people in the future, the concept of 'carrying capacity of the earth' does not tell us what the life expectancy and quality of life will or should be, how much material and political inequality will or should exist, whether people will prefer to live in cities or on the land, and numerous other socio-economic and political variables.

Instead, the concept of 'ecological footprints' has put the proverbial cart before the horse. More than ever before, all future socio-economic interactions with raw and manufactured resources – in hostile, damaged or increasingly managed and protected environments – will be the outcome of highly politicised struggles and decisions within capitalist societies. It is not the 'carrying capacity of the earth' that determines future bio-geophysical life into which socio-political life has to 'fit', but rather it is political conflict or the lack of it that determines the character of particular industries, markets, and forms of consumption upon which estimates of 'carrying capacity' are based.

Notions of 'carrying capacity', like notions of 'God', 'equality', 'democracy', 'freedom', 'nation' or 'individual' can be invoked and influence the shape of politics. After all, how we imagine the future helps determine present action (or inaction) and future-orientated policies. Yet, such an overgeneralised and abstract global concept as 'carrying capacity' is not equivalent to the various available local, regional, or international resources and social practices that make particular forms of life possible. Notably, what can be 'carried' in some parts of the world is already unsustainable in other parts of the earth characterised by desertification or other inhospitable conditions. Carbon emissions levels are related to the particular use of material resources, but they are not equivalent to the limits of material resources and whether they will run out or not. Instead of abstract notions of the 'carrying capacity of the earth', it is the conflict between democracy and sustainability or the political interaction with bio-geophysical processes that ultimately determines levels of biodiversity and social conditions even though this interrelationship is far from straightforward or predictable.

Overall, 'ecological footprints' and the associated debates over the 'carrying capacity of the earth' are misleading, confusing, and largely futile in terms of determining what kind of political, socio-economic and cultural systems we need. As a mode of raising environmental consciousness, even pro-footprint analysts themselves acknowledge that when the public were asked about 'ecological footprints', "67% of respondents strongly agreed/agreed that the calculator had left them confused because of the four different results generated by the calculator (i.e., Personal Overshoot Day, Ecological Footprint, Number of Planet Earths and CO_2 emissions)."[15]

The mask of political 'neutrality' means that 'footprint' analyses can be used by people who are either pro-market or anti-market. Indeed, apart from a minority of analysts, a closer examination of the literature shows that most ecological and material 'footprint' analyses shift the emphasis away from explaining how capitalist business practices and government policies account for much of the environmental destruction perpetrated. Once one accepts the logic that *per capita* 'footprints' or the content and form of individual consumption is the cause of why businesses produce what they do (the old business refrain "we are only satisfying consumer demands"), then the onus for change falls largely on the backs of individuals and there is little need to question globally destructive business practices.

Individuals have a certain limited form of agency in terms of how they spend their income and conduct their household practices, namely, whether they wish to 'go green' or not. Overall, there are constraints on their individual political and social choices. The following outlines some structural reasons why material resources use is not simply a matter of individual choice:

- Car ownership is a necessity if public transport is non-existent, infrequent, costly, and unreliable.
- Many forms of clothing and household goods for sale are increasingly imported, cheaper than local products and hence require a large trade in both raw materials and manufactured goods.
- The majority of food consumed in the largest capitalist countries is produced by chemically based agribusiness that is also often dependent on exploited farm workers, delivered by carbon-intensive road freight and sold in supermarket chains whose

selection of items is stringently calculated to maximise profit margins rather than healthy, safe, quality food.

- Organic food is too expensive for a majority of low and middle-income wage workers to buy and is currently incapable of feeding the world's population because the volume of production is too low and too labour-intensive compared to chemically based agriculture.
- Small individual or family farmers, especially in countries from Paraguay to Pakistan have either lost out to large mono crops of soya, maize, etc., or been forced to produce food dictated by large agribusiness and retail chains.
- The property-industrial complex has been the major transformer of land use through capital investment, infrastructure development (especially for road transport) and the expansion of private housing and commercial developments.
- Within developing capitalist countries, the destruction of ecosystems and rural land-based communities has been driven by mining extraction, cash crops and export-led industrialisation.

In short, the structure of most cities and rural areas have been shaped by market forces rather than by individuals deciding where they will live, what work they will do or what kind of material resources they will need or be able to afford.

Not only do 'per capita footprints' have little to do with individual choice, but like 'national footprints' disguise and distort structural constraints in market-driven societies. 'National material footprints' continue to uphold the illusion of 'sovereign nations' determining their own fates and their own use of material resources. Rather, it is the competitive interlocking of resources extraction, manufacturing and international trade through capitalist corporate supply chain networks, the value of national currencies, levels of foreign investment, levels of R & D and educated skilled workforces, intellectual property rights and the application of digital and high-tech innovations that all shape the quantity and quality of material resources used in different countries.

If individuals are highly constrained financially and socially in their ability to change their use of material resources, most nation states also lack the power to go it alone. This is why recycling and other forms of reducing one's 'ecological footprint' can only have minimal impact. Personal 'footprints' may not be irrelevant, but they are equivalent to the minor impact of charities on assisting low-income countries when compared to much larger levels of government foreign aid. Water usage is an important and illuminating example here of the limits of personal 'ecological footprints'. We know that in developed capitalist countries like Australia, agricultural businesses use approximately 70 per cent of annual water consumption, while tens of millions of urban residents account for between only 7 and 10 per cent of water usage and the remaining 20 per cent is consumed by non-agricultural private businesses and public authorities. The quantity and quality of water usage does not largely depend on changes in household consumption, although of course, individuals should cease wasting water. Instead, it is the water-hungry agribusiness practices orientated to exports and domestic consumption that is the key to excessive water usage. The latter would have to be significantly reduced or transformed in order to become ecologically sustainable. Hence, only individuals mobilised in political movements have the power through their struggles to force changes to ecologically unsustainable government and business practices.

While critiques of market individualism may sound like familiar political platitudes, a survey of the literature on 'footprints', 'planetary boundaries' and 'safe operating spaces' quickly reveals that few scientists and ecological economists actually discuss 'what to do' and how major changes in the use of material resources would threaten either particular industries or whole capitalist economies. When analysts do advocate decarbonisation and structural changes to current priorities and practices in transport, agriculture, manufacturing, and other industries, most of their recommendations are either implicitly or explicitly varieties of green growth modernisation. Indeed, major organisations such as United Nations Environment Programme International Resources Panel (UNEP) or the Intergovernmental Panel on Climate Change (IPCC) issue reports that support green growth and underestimate environmental damage.[16] This is because they are either insufficiently critical of capitalist business practices or that they make compromises following objections from various member countries' governments about draft material that should or should not be included in final reports.

Hence, most of the literature on material resources is effectively depoliticised. Outlines of degraded ecosystems are sanitised in an apolitical parade of 'neutral' terms such as industrial civilisation, consumerism, overuse of chemicals and fossil fuels. Few people name and shame major corporate or government polluters, agribusiness and commercial land-use vandals or finance institutions funding property development that has ruined city after city.[17] Instead, fear and timidity related to jobs and promotions are partly responsible for analysts self-censoring themselves.

In fairness to 'material footprint' analysts, they do concede that they do not have sufficient data from across the world to calculate a full range of socio-economic and environmental variables. Instead, they rely heavily on inadequate government statistics, international agencies such as Eurostat, the OECD, WTO, and United Nations plus assorted national or independent studies that are still collecting data heavily orientated to conventional needs of market forces and governments based on the dominant concept of GDP. Statistics covering material extraction, material consumption, trade flows in goods and resources, or non-profit infrastructure, services and social development are overwhelmingly just *aggregate* amounts for each country provided by national and international agencies.[18] We can see the disparities between, for instance, large, industrialised countries such as the US and many low-income societies in Africa. However, global statistics on household consumption are either inadequate or too patchy to enable us to arrive at detailed figures for different social classes within nations let alone between countries.[19]

In a few countries such as Germany, attempts have been made to calculate different household per capita consumption of materials according to income levels, number of members of household, number of children and so forth. The breakup of household material footprints (based on an exceedingly small sample) ranges from 79.15 tonnes per capita for singles in the top income quartile to as low as 11.78 tonnes for two adults and two children in the bottom quartile.[20] Clearly, the averaging of per capita figures is both misleading and inaccurate as 'national footprints' do not reveal major social inequalities within national populations and between countries.

We also have limited information on the disproportionate use of resources by businesses compared to households or those businesses that are export orientated as opposed to those producing mainly for domestic low-income sections of their national population. In other words, we have to calculate the partial or disguised national and international material footprints of industries in low- and middle-income countries such as automobiles and digital hardware that are heavily exported to high-income countries rather than mainly consumed by poorer local populations. National 'carbon' and material footprints are not only insufficiently broken down but fail to show the large use of resources by military complexes. For instance, a recent study of six EU member countries reported that their military sectors had 'carbon footprints' equivalent to the emissions of 14 million cars even though they were disproportionally smaller than the civilian economy.[21]

Politically, social and environmental outcomes depend on how we classify, assess, and formulate policies in regard to the interrelation between ecosystem services and economic goods and services. It has long been abundantly clear that much of what is good for markets is not good for ecosystem biodiversity. Today, however, one can also be an anti-capitalist environmentalist and still not arrive at a consensus about how to measure ecosystem services in terms of healthy soils, air and water quality, sustainable coastal areas, flourishing forests and biodiverse fauna and flora. Methodologically, the disputes over ecosystem services include problems ranging from how not to double count intermediate processes affecting habitats, economic goods, and human wellbeing, right through to issues of underestimating ecological damage. Crucially, major capitalist countries such as the US still fail to adequately measure key aspects of ecosystem services.[22] This incomplete knowledge of key aspects of ecological services is especially important as any political attempt to reduce or equalise national and per capita material footprints must have a set of criteria to assess the relationship between ecosystems and socio-economic systems. My point here is that we need these quality assessments if we are to arrive at policies that do not *falsely* measure attempts at dematerialisation such as green growth claims about technological solutions that purportedly deliver relative and absolute decoupling of economic growth from ecosystems.

Consequently, despite the good environmental intentions of material and ecological 'footprint' analysts, politically, many of these studies offer highly problematic forecasts of future employment, income, and numerous other categories affecting consumption and production. Projections from most commonly cited statistical sources have been proved unreliable and can easily be manipulated to arrive at desirable policies to suit particular movements, governments, or industry groups. Moreover, the categories used by many governments and non-government agencies are seriously deficient or based on environmentally unacceptable market and government priorities. These priorities are only slowly being changed to accommodate classifications and data that would indicate the complexity of measuring all aspects of environmental sustainability. In fact, our knowledge of the use of material resources is far below what is required due to cuts in employment in national bureaus of statistics, research institutes and other assessing agencies.

We urgently need new criteria and far larger staff levels to identify and measure the connection between socio-economic activity and ecological destruction. These are very labour-intensive tasks even with the help of elaborate digital software programs. We need to recognise that government and business priorities tell us much about the undemocratic distribution of political power in contemporary societies and the urgent need for more accurate pictures of material footprints. Current priorities indicate how far we are from understanding let alone delivering environmental sustainability.

Bio-Geophysical Tipping Points or Finite Material Resources?

Two major obstacles confront advocates of environmentally sustainable social change. Firstly, many governments and businesses still ignore or only pay lip service to the need to substantially recycle or reduce materials usage. Secondly, a political and scientific impasse prevails over how to define and measure the use of global material resources, let alone which countries, which industries and what levels of per capita consumption amongst diverse sections of populations need to be reduced, redistributed, or transformed. This latter obstacle is in contrast to an emerging international consensus on the need to cut greenhouse gases, even though there is no agreement on the rate and methods of decarbonisation. Many also recognise that decarbonisation cannot be achieved without reducing or transforming carbon embodied material footprints connected to cement, steel, grain crops for meat production, chemicals and other minerals and metals. These are vital in military and civilian manufacturing, major forms of road, air and marine transport, commercial and residential building construction and key aspects of agribusiness and processed food consumption. For example, oil is a vital ingredient of the massive global petrochemical industry. The annual production of plastics alone grew 200-fold between 1950 and 2015, eclipsing growth rates of other materials such as aluminium, cement and steel, while polyester fibre now accounts for 60% of total global fibre production thus exceeding all other fibres combined, including wool and cotton. Over 90% of petrochemical products such as plastics have been dumped or burned and are exceedingly difficult to recycle.[23] Alternative non-petrochemical based materials such as fungal mycelium (for building materials, clothing, etc) or seaweed offer hope but are still in their early forms of production.[24]

Nonetheless, those who erroneously believe that capitalist systems cannot fully decarbonise their production processes overlook potential innovations. It is quite possible to implement decarbonisation transitions within market societies without either increasing political democratisation or equalising profound social inequalities in the access to and use of material resources. We are currently witnessing massive capital investments in renewable energy, the production of low-carbon machinery, urban plans to make cities carbon neutral, and research and development projects aimed at low or zero-carbon substitutes for cement, steel production, non-meat foods and so forth. Additionally, apart from electric vehicles, it is technically possible to significantly decarbonise transport by banning short air flights within Europe and other continents by requiring greater rail travel (at speeds of no more than 125 mph) for distances of less than one to two thousand kilometres. International capitalist trade can be reduced, and much lower carbon emissions can be achieved by reducing the speed and internal design of shipping, downscaling fossil fuels (which currently constitute over 30 per cent of shipping cargoes) and 'reshoring' manufacturing supply chains in OECD countries and away from China, Indonesia, Bangladesh, Thailand, Kenya, Nigeria and other 'offshore' low- and middle-income countries. Different sectors of business will definitely suffer or go bankrupt, but this has been characteristic of markets for over two hundred years. Similarly, in agriculture, the periodic draining and reflooding of rice paddies plus new species varieties can reduce the release of methane, not to mention numerous other low-carbon land measures through cutting carbon-based fertilisers, reductions in meat production and so forth.[25]

I am not arguing that these and many other changes in a range of industries will make capitalist societies sustainable. Rather, it is necessary to distinguish between feasible and attainable measures within capitalist systems that can prevent climate breakdown and the larger crisis of equality and material sustainability. The climate emergency is an immediate existential crisis. Yet, long-term sustainability will not be achieved if political struggles over switching from fossil fuels to renewables are not differentiated from the larger debate over the quantity and quality of material resources use. It is not an either/or problem. If we don't tackle both simultaneously, there will be no resolution to the climate emergency. Nevertheless, it is possible to have a dramatic reduction in global greenhouses gases during the next five to fifteen years but still have massive threats to diverse component elements of the biosphere with no or slight improvement in current unequal levels of global material production and consumption.

There is a lack of full recognition and acknowledgement that the use of material resources is both a constitutive part of the climate emergency as well as a much larger and more challenging unfolding crisis. For it is the current use and inadequate recycling or disposal of material resources that tells us infinitely more than greenhouse gas emissions about what has to be changed in order to achieve greater social equality, democracy, and environmental sustainability.

This raises the question of whether future possible catastrophic crises will be caused more by cascading tipping points due to inadequate 'sinks' and feedbacks in the biosphere and geophysical boundaries of the earth system rather than by the exhaustion of finite material resources? There is no agreement over which heavily used resources will or will not run out in the coming century, which key biomass (agriculture, forestry, and fisheries), mineral, water, metals, and other resources are in danger of either being degraded and despoiled or not being easily accessible. During the past fifty years, there have been widespread exaggerated and misleading claims that we would have an economic crisis once peak oil, peak copper, peak zinc, and other resources prevented further economic growth. This simplistic notion of 'finite limits' needs to be either jettisoned or refined to account for the complex relationship between economic growth, resources use and biophysical crises.

In 2017, investigative journalist, Nafeez Mosaddeq Ahmed, claimed that "the escalation of social protest and political instability around the world is causally related to the unstoppable thermodynamics of global hydrocarbon energy decline and its interconnected environmental and economic consequences."[26] Instead of economic determinism, Ahmed developed a thesis of 'energy determinism' whereby social conflict, economic growth, food production and geopolitical instability were caused by biophysical triggers (carbon emissions and the destabilisation of the earth system) due to the need for capitalist businesses to accelerate fossil fuel extraction given the declining quality of existing oil fields and so forth. However, this thesis is being rendered untenable by the switch by corporations from fossil fuels to renewables, a process that will escalate in the next decade. A more simplistic thesis was proposed in 2006 by prominent degrowth advocate, Ted Trainer. He was not unusual at the time in hoping that an oil crisis in the coming decade would stop people getting to the shops and thereby transform their attitudes to capitalist consumption.[27]

As this didn't happen, he later adopted Ahmed's thesis on falling energy supplies.[28]

However, the popular environmentalist misconception of 'peak oil' resulting in a supply crisis, will almost certainly never come to fruition. Instead, there is a glut of oil, with production outstripping demand since 2017, leading to a collapse in prices and profits, mass layoffs of hundreds of thousands of oil workers and price wars between the petroleum states compounded by the crisis of COVID-19. 'Peak oil' has now been redefined to mean not oil running out but rather 'peak price' which, despite recent price increases, will probably never again reach former price heights.[29] There would have to be an extraordinary increase in the demand for oil over the next 5 to 15 years before major capitalist countries implement their already legislated mandatory cessation of production of petrol and diesel fuelled vehicles in the years between 2025 (Norway) and 2030 to 2035 in the EU and other major capitalist countries.

The old theory of 'peak oil' fails to adequately consider the political pressures in coming years to reduce dependence on fossil fuels and is also based on a misunderstanding of the fluctuating relationship of the price and availability of oil supplies to levels of capitalist consumption and production. For instance, if easy access to oil supplies should wane by chance or by war or conflict in some countries, major conservative governments will simply increase subsidies to oil and gas corporations to maintain profitability or alternatively, subsidise the rapid switch to electric cars and renewables). Oil is already heavily subsidised by governments in petroleum rich countries to the tune of more than five trillion dollars, as both over-production and caps on production were alternately encouraged or used to help counter falling profits by corporate oil giants. Even within Trainer's and other degrowthers own frameworks, waiting for the 'oil crisis' is hardly the basis for building self-sufficient communities with their own resources, currencies and lifestyles. Crucially, when the shops closed under COVID-19 restrictions, this did not quell the desire of many to consume online or return once the shops reopened. Indeed, the impact of COVID-19 has been very uneven. Many businesses became more profitable during the Pandemic, while others suffered due to mass unemployment and the decline in income and credit.

When it comes to copper, zinc, and lead, it is not that those resources will run out this century, but rather higher demand and accessibility to better quality materials will cause price increases.[30] Paradoxically, the growing switch to renewable energy and low-carbon intensive technology (solar panels, wind turbines, electric cars) requires a much higher use of copper and other metals. Cobalt, lithium and nickel are associated with shocking mining conditions, disastrous environmental impacts on surrounding agriculture, water, and biodiversity. Substitutes such as sodium for lithium and other metals have not yet been found to be as efficient but may possibly improve given their vital role as essential parts of renewable energy needed for capitalist production.[31] In a survey of critical raw materials needed for a scenario of the world based on fully renewable energy, Elsa Dominish, Sven Teske and Nick Florin compare available known global reserves with levels of potential extraction, use and recycling. Demand from renewable energy and storage technologies could exceed the production of cobalt, lithium, and nickel by 2030 and potentially far exceed known reserves of these raw materials by 2050 if recycling is not vastly increased.[32] Currently, 27 critical raw materials used within the EU and other countries are heavily sourced from China.[33] Renewable energy thus depends on peaceful and cooperative relations rather than a world divided by regional geopolitical pathways and conflicts.

Just as we need to differentiate between 'carbon footprints' and the wider character of material footprints (despite their interconnection), so we also need to make the distinction between certain biomass, minerals or metals that could become exhausted, and the crucial threats to bio-geophysical earth system boundaries that come from abundance rather than just scarcity. Like the debates over material footprints, there has been no consensus amongst scientists or social and economic policy analysts over whether planetary boundaries exist, whether there are nine or more boundaries and sub-systems, and importantly, whether any are actually at a tipping point.[34]

When earth system scientists warn us that there are already four out of nine system-boundaries in a threatened state, these are not just caused by finite resources running out as it is with loss of biodiversity or shortages of phosphorous or fresh water. Rather, it is the lack of adequate 'sinks' to absorb high emissions of carbon that threaten a run-away 'hothouse earth' and acidification of the oceans.[35] Similarly, there is an overuse of nitrogen in fertilisers creating pollutants in the form of ammonia and ozone which are destroying soils, plant life, forests and waterways across the world and are also bad for human health.[36] The so-called pristine scenery of New Zealand, for example, is actually suffering from 90% of its rivers being polluted by excess fertilisers used by the dairy industry which is the coun-try's largest export earner. In agribusiness countries such as Australia, the main political parties are still committed to unsustainable agricultural exports which have almost destroyed the main food basket along the Murray-Darling River and helped damage the irreplaceable Great Barrier Reef. A combination of water shortages caused by climate change, and pollution caused by deforestation and excessive use of fertiliser runoffs is not being adequately addressed due to the power of conservative political parties, agribusiness lobbies, and cultural images promoted by the media of farmers being almost sacred parts of the nation. Despite the very fragile state of key ecological areas, for affluent consumers in Asia and the Middle East the illusion persists within and of Australia remaining the sustainable food basket (dairy foods, cereals, cotton, rice, processed meat, plus the horrors of the shipped livestock trade).

With all the disputes over 'planetary boundaries' and 'tipping points', it is hard to decide which terms are most adequate to describe disastrous damage to environments. The concepts of 'planetary boundaries' and 'safe operating spaces' remain useful, in the absence of suitable substitutes. This does not mean that I am uncritical of earth boundary scientists Johan Rockström, Will Steffen and their co-researchers. While they have made invaluable contributions to alerting us about threats to 'safe operating spaces', these scientists have failed to raise serious questions about unsustainable capitalist green growth policies in a world already experiencing massive degradation of biophysical resources and ecosystems.

We have known for a long time that one of the most important natural 'sinks' for the absorption of greenhouse gas emissions is land. As the Öko-Institute in Freiburg put it in 2021:

> The only sector providing options for natural carbon sinks is the sector on Land Use, Land Use Change and Forestry (LULUCF). Carbon sinks are created by biomass growth and the long-term storage of carbon in vegetation, soils and products. However, the sector accounts also for carbon emissions from biomass use, land conversion and vegetation removal. Moreover, the sector suffers from drastic climate and environmental change, potentially leading to reduced rates of carbon uptake and increased emissions. A contribution to the balance of emissions and removals as anticipated by the Paris Agreement *can only be achieved through a long-term overall net negative carbon balance of the land sector* (my emphasis).[37]

Deforestation and construction for housing and industry constitute the greatest threat to natural carbon 'sinks'. The authors propose that the EU implement land management regulations and a raft of other targeted measures to complement much higher cuts to carbon emissions by 2030. Current EU draft laws on agricultural production and anti-deforestation measures have been widely criticised as containing too many exemptions and subsidies for environmentally destructive practices.[38]

What is alarming about the erosion of natural 'sinks' is that while we are becoming more aware of the need to halt deforestation and transform a range of practices in agriculture, forestry and construction, Europe constitutes only a small part of the global land mass. To date, there are still no detailed equivalent land use planning targets in Asia, North and Latin America, Africa and other continents or regions where the bulk of the world's population lives and where extensive destruction of natural 'sinks' are occurring. Apart from assorted studies of deforestation and land use, governments and researchers in most countries have not yet formulated urgently needed land use plans to restrict and rectify the centuries-long disastrous practices of inadequately regulated market forces. In addition to capitalist development, approximately 1.5 billion desperate rural dwellers in low-income countries and regions contribute to deforestation, erosion, and desertification because of their reliance on wood as their main fuel. Much more renewable energy is needed to provide electricity to what the World Bank in 2019 estimated to be 1 billion people without electricity in low-income countries. But this would require a sea change in the priorities of existing governments concerning the use of material resources.

The Conflicting Politics over Material Resources

The political impasse over drastically reducing global social inequalities while simultaneously preventing the transgression of the earth's safe operating systems through the destruction and degradation of natural 'sinks' and biodiversity loss is the paramount crisis of our age. Policy makers in capitalist societies have always treated nature primarily as a 'material resource' to be utilised for the benefit of businesses. Beginning in the nineteenth century, it was reformers and defenders of heritage (usually from aristocratic or bourgeois backgrounds) who fought to preserve 'oases' of nature as 'national parks' or 'reserves' against the ravages of miners, timber loggers, farmers and property developers. While many countries still lack even these islands of so-called 'nature', the political struggle to protect the Arctic, Antarctic, ocean seabeds or the Amazon from mining and development is precariously poised between devastating incursions and the possibility of the political movements and allies of 'nature' winning out over business. Meanwhile, a new stage of political disputation has emerged over the fate of long-conquered terrains of natural wilderness. The debate has shifted away from pristine nature to whether humanity is able to protect the 'nature' that has already been damaged by human exploitation from further unsustainable profiteering and destruction?

Those who reject 'business as usual' remain divided by fundamentally different explanations of the cause of the unfolding crisis and also over solutions to ecological unsustainability. Marxists and degrowthers desire an end to 'alienated nature'. They argue that businesses, governments, and affluent consumers in imperialist capitalist countries (the so-called 'North') remain the main drivers of the overconsumption of material resources and social inequality experienced by populations in low- and middle-income countries (the so-called 'South'). This is also partially acknowledged by other radical critics who nonetheless warn that the old model of capitalist imperialism and affluent consumerism is blind to the contemporary relationship between capitalism and ecology. Importantly, the bulk of global extraction, production and consumption of material resources, plus carbon emissions and the destruction of 'sinks' to absorb all kinds of greenhouse gases and chemical emissions are not just being driven by corporations and consumers in the 'North'. Increasingly, these unsustainable practices are also being propelled heavily by governments, businesses, and populations in the 'South' to satisfy their own industrial, commercial, and social needs.

To produce manufactured goods of which a proportion are then exported to OECD countries (especially to those in Europe and North America), Asian industrialising countries are now heavily supplied with resources from other so-called 'Southern' countries in Africa, Latin America, and the Middle East. This demand for material resources in Asia has changed old trade patterns. By 2017, 58.5 per cent of all materials were extracted in Asia and the Pacific, while most of the balance was divided between Latin America and the Caribbean (8.6 per cent), North America (8.3 per cent), Europe (8 per cent) and Africa (7.3 per cent).[39] Whereas in 1970, advanced capitalist countries received 93 per cent of all imports, by 2017, Asian and Pacific countries accounted for 48% of material imports and high-income countries had dropped by almost half to 52 per cent of total global imports.[40] The critical difference is that high-income societies only have a mere 14 per cent of the world's 7.9 billion population.

Hence, the twin problem for the future use of material resources and its interrelationship with social inequality means that current imbalances cannot continue if environmental sustainability is the goal. Also, romanti-cised spiritual concepts of 'nature' have been replaced by the use of terms such as ecosystems, habitats, and other specific terms rather than 'nature' to describe what are increasingly hybrid areas of human and non-human species interaction. This has raised the philosophical and practical dilemma of what Bill McKibben calls the 'end of nature'[41] or what others label as the Anthropocene: a new geological epoch where nature is being transformed and destroyed by human action.

Even the familiar and long taken-for-granted notion of what it means to be human is being transformed. In the flourishing world of AI and genetic engineering, what does biodiversity mean in a world where nature and culture are being fused, imitated, or intersected by capitalist-driven tech-nologies? If human rights are still conceived as being different to the rights and existence of other biological species, how does democracy become reconciled with future ecological sustainability in a world of constantly shifting notions of social rights, human rights, and species rights? Is it possible to restore a transformed 'nature' or end what philosophers call human alienation from nature if both humans and non-human nature is being reshaped?

Out of these conflicting philosophies and scenarios concerning nature and equality we can identify four quite different political and economic solutions to inequality and sustainability. The first two are variations of the dominant perspective, while the third and fourth proposed solutions are currently championed by reformers and anti-capitalists:

1. Increase market industrialisation, especially export-orientated industries to combat poverty (such as achieved in North-East Asian countries), while implementing green growth decarbonisation.

2. Implement high-tech solutions to make capitalist growth sustainable (such as modernising polluting industries in the 'South') and transform all countries into post-industrial service economies with lower material footprints.

3. Mobilise the working class and rural masses to radically reform or overthrow capitalism and implement post-carbon democracy based on social equality, an equitable sharing of material resources, and care for the planet rather than profit-driven growth.

4. Reduce per capita material footprints in high-income countries

by degrowing capitalist economies so that the global population
has an equal annual 'per capita footprint' of approximately 6 to 8
tonnes of material resources by 2050.

I will not discuss proposals 1 to 3, as they are analysed elsewhere in this
book. Rather, I will examine the widely held notion – extending from
United Nations agencies to degrowth movements – that it is necessary to
cut high per capita material footprints if global ecological sustainability is
to be achieved.

In 2014, the United Nations Environment Programme International
Resources Panel (UNEP) recommended that the world aim for sustainability by reducing the final consumption of material resources from more
than 70 billion tonnes to 50 billion tonnes per annum, or a per capita material consumption rate of 6 to 8 tonnes by 2050.[42] This was an arbitrary
figure based on a mixture of valid and speculative reasons. No adequate
explanation was given for the 50 billion tonnes per annum target, but it
implied that this figure was the 'carrying capacity of the earth'. Importantly,
no differentiation was made between scarce resources and those particular
abundant resources that could be extracted and consumed at much higher
levels. Also, no distinction was made between abundant material resources
that were not harmful and fossil fuels that could not be extracted and
consumed because of dangerous greenhouse gas emissions. The arbitrary
UNEP target (which was itself based on earlier aggregate figures and
dubious analyses of 'ecological' and material footprints) has been so influential because it carries the imprimatur of an important international organisation.

Many degrowthers and others take the UNEP figure as gospel. Also, in
2015, the National Commission on Sustainable Development in Finland
adopted the UNEP 2050 target for per capita material footprints[43] while
other analysts argued for as little as 3 to 6 tonnes by 2050.[44] Whichever
figure is aimed for, it is perplexing why so many concerned environmentalists, especially the degrowth movement and sustainable development advocates, have uncritically latched on to this call for a radical 80 to 90%
reduction of per capita consumption of material resources in high income
countries. The whole exercise of 'ecological footprints' is based on the
crudest and most questionable figures which are widely repeated without
much serious discussion of how they were originally determined.

There is a vast difference between, on the one hand, supporting a
reduction or transformation of biomass that currently damage fragile

ecosystems and, on the other hand, aiming for a 50 billion tonnes annual target which has not been scientifically justified as ensuring future sustainability. Similarly, fossil fuels currently constitute up to 50% of materials traded by sea, road, rail, and waterway transport. They are likely to dramatically decline in the next two decades once renewables take their place. If and when full decarbonisation is achieved, will the target of 50 billion tonnes be adjusted or refined as no longer the global limit?

As already mentioned, 'ecological' or material footprints are misleading because they are based on averaging statistics that take a particular country's material extraction, material production and consumption (including exports and imports), as well as other indicators, and then subdivide these by the size of population to arrive at 'per capita footprints'.[45] This is a very unsatisfactory methodology which defies consensus amongst both scientists and political movements. Importantly, 'ecological footprints' cover up profound social and institutional inequalities in actual rates of per capita material consumption. To give an example of the highly problematic methodologies used by material resources analysts, take for instance, an influential 2012 study and frequently cited analysis conducted by Monika Dittrich, Stefan Giljum, Stephan Lutter and Christine Polzin. Using data from the United Nations, Eurostat, World Bank, and other institutions, in the section entitled 'Consumption: from survival to affluence', the authors display tables of countries showing their domestic material consumption rates of biomass, minerals, fossil fuels, metals and other materials. The top ten countries such as Qatar (114 tonnes per capita), Ireland (51.5), Australia (36), Chile (43.8) Finland (38.6) and Equatorial Guinea (33.5) had very high per capita material footprints compared with high-income countries such as Switzerland (12.9), Germany (14.8) or Netherlands (12 tonnes).[46] More recent published figures revised some of these earlier estimates and claimed that high-income countries had 'per capita footprints' of 18 to 29 tonnes.[47] Nonetheless, both the earlier and later reports glossed over the distortions caused by aggregate national figures and paint an entirely misleading picture of per capita consumption rates and social differences both within and between countries.

Firstly, the authors confuse or deliberately obscure the differences between material resources extracted from particular countries and their claim that they are analysing 'from survival to affluence'. The top ten countries examined have wide disparities in standards of living within countries such as Australia (between the impoverishment of Indigenous people and affluent middle-class citizens) not to mention the poverty of millions in

Equatorial Guinea and Chile compared with the affluent consumption of large majorities in Germany, Switzerland, and other European countries. The latter high-income countries each supposedly have per capita material footprints two to five times lower than the so-called 'high' 'material footprint' countries.

Secondly, while the authors appropriately classify countries according to their extraction and production of minerals (industrial and construction minerals), biomass (agriculture, forestry, fisheries), fossil fuels or metals, all are not equivalent to per capita domestic consumption of these same materials. On the contrary, many of the resource materials in most countries are owned by national or foreign corporations which extract, and export materials abroad, and only employ as low as three per cent of the workforce in countries such as Australia.

Any political strategy that aims for a 'just transition' to a post-carbon democracy must develop policies that take into account quite different income and consumption levels of housing, transport, land use, energy and so forth. This would entail reductions for affluent high-income groups of certain forms of material resources – whether mineral, biomass or metals used in private transport, construction, and food items such as meat consumption – rather than an indiscriminate averaging out process that overlooks significant levels of poverty in affluent societies. Conversely, it would advocate similar cuts in material consumption enjoyed by hundreds of millions of affluent residents in low- and middle-income countries, approximately 10 to 20 per cent of populations in these highly unequal societies.

Thirdly, and this is an important point, we should cease treating the population of an entire country as consuming misleading aggregate per capita figures ranging from 114 tonnes to as little as 1 or 2 tonnes. Even though 'environmental footprints' are also used by anti-capitalists, 'per capita footprints' are politically conservative and, in the absence of detailed data on distinct social classes, need to be abandoned. If governments and political movements continue to use these crude and misleading statistics, they will endorse policies that fail to remedy gross domestic and international inequalities. Instead, they will only aim for a 'one size fits all' global equalisation of per capita consumption (for example, 6 to 10 tonnes per capita) which is itself seriously flawed.

Fourthly, the literature on material resources and 'ecological footprints' makes elementary mistakes because overall it lacks a critical political economic analysis of capitalist societies and why the structure of industries, degrading forms of land use, unequal wages and promotion of financial incentives to encourage diverse forms of consumption are not accidental and not all amenable to reforms. Typically, one can read numerous reports from concerned ecologists that criticise 'economic growth' in general terms and proceed to model scenarios of consumption of resources or emissions based on broad categories of 'business as usual, lower growth or degrowth'.[48] What may appear to be a critical evaluation of material resources is instead either an over-estimation of the capacity of capitalist systems to implement equitable sustainable solutions[49] or an underestimation of the non-negotiable nature of certain 'transitional' policies.

One particular feature of the literature on material resources and 'footprints' is the inadequate attention or unintentional disguise it makes of the disproportionate use of material resources extraction and consumption by corporations, military industrial complexes and large government institutions compared to households from diverse social classes. This blurring of specific differences in the use of material resources means that national aggregate figures often 'level out' and distort social differences in low- and middle-income countries. Without more precise social breakdowns of data, 'material footprint' analyses fail to indicate how the impoverished standard of living suffered by billions of people living in low- and middle-income countries could be improved without simultaneously punishing substantial minorities of poor people in high-income countries. Any clarity of 'footprints' would require quite different statistical and data sources concerning glaring social inequalities and particularly the disproportionate use of minerals, water, biomass, metals, etc., by mining, manufacturing, agricultural and military industries compared to household and individual consumption. In the absence of these more detailed accounts and abandonment of current methodologies, we are currently only offered variations on the politically vague call to equalise global per capita material footprints or implement green growth ecological modernisation.

So far, degrowth movements offer little or no detailed breakdown of how diverse populations in individual countries need to change their use of material resources. Not only do we not have any clear political economic program on which sections of diverse high-income, middle-income, and low-income countries will see their standards of living improve or decline, but there is no consensus about the scale and rate of this change. Consequently, degrowthers are particularly weak on the major issue of whether to degrow or grow the economies in low- and middle-income countries, and what type of growth would be ecologically sustainable so that poverty could be vastly reduced or abolished.

As to the dominant green growth perspective, it is no surprise that most policy advocates favour expanding the circular economy, decarbonisation and decoupling economic growth from negative impacts on ecosystems. For example, the Amsterdam-based group Circle Economy (endorsed by corporations, NGOs, and leading mainstream environmentalists such as Kate Raworth) produces the annual *Circularity Gap Report* which is an assessment of different material resources and the degree to which they are recycled or wasted. These annual reports contain positive policy suggestions to combat climate breakdown despite being primarily geared to making capitalist societies sustainable. The 2021 Report showed that the circular economy went backwards from 9% to 8.6% and that 91% of the more than 100 billion tons of material resources entering global economies was not recycled but consumed or wasted.[50] As Joan Martinez-Alier points out, the massive circularity gap is due to 44% of processed resources that were used for energy and not available for circulation. Secondly, the continued expansion of the built environment accounted for rising material and energy inputs and once built cannot be regularly recycled but in fact require additional resources for maintenance.[51]

Green growthers succumb to the ideology that sustainability can be achieved by the circular economy. Yet not only are the vast majority of material resources consumed, wasted or are impossible to recycle, but little is said about the mode of extraction of resources. Martinez-Alier sums up this deliberate neglect by pointing out that the 'circularity gap' is due to the incessant need of industry for fresh materials and energy which causes ecological distribution conflicts at the frontiers of commodity extraction, transport, and waste disposal (over 3,380 registered conflicts by March 2021). Sometimes compensation is won in national or international courts. Still, the Paris Agreement of 2015 on climate change applies the rule of 'no liability' or compensation to affected countries for damages and injuries.[52]

Using familiar government and international organisational statistics, growth in per capita income and consumption was shown to be the main driver of material use and exceeded population growth as the cause of the unsustainable and unequal growth in the use of material resources.[53] During the previous 25 years, 10% of the world's richest population accounted for over 48% of global greenhouse gas emissions, while the poorest 50% of the world's population were responsible for only 7% of greenhouse gas emissions.[54] However, between 1980 and 2020, 'per capita material' consumption in Europe and North America either declined or remained stagnant.[55] This was an unintended form of partial 'degrowth' driven by stagnant wages growth, unemployment and economic crises. It was also caused by large proportions of populations in OECD countries shifting to the consumption of services and away from 'durable' consumer goods.

Politically, the significant differences in the quantity of material resources used by developed capitalist OECD countries as opposed to emerging capitalist countries, leads to all kinds of confused pronouncements. Take, for example, Kenta Tsuda, staff attorney for the Conservation Law Foundation in Massachusetts, who erroneously projects stagnation in leading Atlantic countries and Japan onto the entire world. Within the context of making a biting critique of degrowth theory, Tsuda claims that:

> the specific character of the environmental crisis and climate change arises not from out-of-control economic dynamism but its opposite: the politics of stagnation. Where degrowthers posit crazed economic expansion, one looks in vain at the data for evidence of that runaway dynamism and cornucopian excess. It may be that degrowth theory is another case of overstatement from misdiagnosis, analogous to the hyperbolic automation discourse that Aaron Benanav has criticised. If this is correct, the struggle to avert ecological catastrophe and irreparable damage to the future of human civilisation arises not from substantive differences over the remedial policy package, but as part of a generalised political crisis that transcends the ecological domain.[56]

What Tsuda overlooks so glaringly is the rapid growth of China and other new industrial powers which now account for the majority of global material resources consumed. Tellingly, between 1970 and 2020, the annual global use of resources more than quadrupled from 26.7 billion tonnes to 100.6 billion tonnes in 2020 and is projected to rise to 180 billion tonnes by 2050.[57] Such is the rate of increase in material resources extracted, produced, and transformed, that Tsuda's Atlantic-centric analysis is completely blind to what is going on in the Asia-Pacific area, currently accounting for almost two-thirds of the global population. It is utter nonsense for Tsuda to say that the environment crisis arises out of stagnation rather than the rapid rate of use of material resources. Think of how incredibly more disastrous ecosystems would be if North America, the EU, and Japan had matched growth rates in China over the past forty years.

Even pro-market green growthers acknowledge that growth of fossil fuel emissions rather than stagnation is causing climate breakdown.

As for Aaron Benanav's analysis of stagnation and job-shedding due to overcapacity rather than automation, this is an historical update of Robert Brenner's narrow productivist thesis[58] that also ignores environmental crises and reduces most state policies to merely economistic policies serving the needs of the capitalist production process.[59] While I share Benanav's criticisms of universal basic income schemes (which is similar to my earlier critique[60]), he says nothing about future employment, investment and profitability, not to mention broader issues of social order and conflict. How will employment be affected by environmental constraints on material resources extraction, consumption, and waste disposal? Another serious omission in Benanav's analysis of stagnation/low growth in manufacturing is that this is not true of urban construction, biomass, and general land use. These latter sectors have witnessed accelerated extraction, destruction and the degradation of vital material resources threatening overall sustainability. Only part of this accelerated destruction can be explained by capitalists seeking new 'sinks' for investing idle capital in urban property development (such as argued by political economist David Harvey[61]). It is the expansion of urban housing and infrastructure needs, especially in China and other middle- and low-income countries, combined with agribusiness and land use crises (deforestation, soil depletion etc.) that are cumulatively affecting ecosystems.

The utilisation and demand for specific forms of material resources (biomass, metals, ores, etc.) are not just driven by capitalist production. Governments are also under pressure to meet conflicting pressures from populations needing housing, essential infrastructure, and services. All of these factors will become crucial as businesses and governments struggle to simultaneously deal with the social crises stemming from *abundant* labour, but *scarcity* of certain raw materials combined with worrying potential planetary boundary tipping points. In short, just as it is necessary to critique naïve degrowthers and simplistic theories of automation, it is also necessary to recognise the dynamics of material resources use in capitalist systems without denying or glossing over the urgency and scale of environmental crises. Unfortunately, far too many anti-capitalists continue to analyse the relations between capital and labour as if they exist in an environmental vacuum.

Reconciling the 'Good Life' with Unequal Global Material Footprints

Currently, the world is characterised by entirely different forms of personal and household consumption which is not to be confused with total national material footprints. In high-income, developed capitalist countries, personal and household consumption accounts for between 50% and 70% of national GDP. This consumption is subdivided into durable goods such as cars and appliances and non-durable goods like food, fuel, clothing, and services. (In reality, many so-called 'durable' goods are deliberately manufactured to be neither durable nor repairable.) Over the past fifty years, durable goods (which accounted for 40% of US GDP in 1968) has declined as part of total national consumption while personal and household consumption of services has risen dramatically and now accounts for up to 60% of personal consumption and approximately 46% of GDP.[62]

If we take the crude aggregate figures (due to lack of data) and distorted concepts used by 'material footprint' and decarbonisation advocates, several noteworthy facts stand out. These include that:

- Seventy percent of carbon emissions are related to material handling and use.
- More materials are used to make possible international trade than is embodied in the goods traded.
- Housing and infrastructure, mobility (transport) and the small sector of consumables (consumer goods) account for 66% of the total 'material footprint', 64% of the 'carbon footprint' and 48% of the 'financial value footprint'.[63]
- Consumer goods (household appliances, clothing, personal care products, etc.) only account for 7 per cent of total material resources used, so the common idea that personal shopping is the main driving force behind depletion of resources needs to be reassessed.
- Instead, nutrition is the largest sector after construction/housing in terms of material use and carbon emissions. All forms of land use in the production of biomass are accountable for not only depletion and degraded material resources, but the production and distribution of biomass is one of the main causes of global social inequality.
- The common image of services as having low negative impacts on ecosystems is misleading. Recurring labour and care activity

have to be differentiated from initial and ongoing resource requirements. Real estate, retailing, finance services, defence, education, health, and hospitality are not low users of material resources. They directly or indirectly require substantial amounts of capital and material resources in the form of shops and shopping malls, offices, military equipment, schools, hospitals, hotels, cafes, connecting transport and energy infrastructure, digital technology and so forth.

According to 'ecological' and 'material footprint' analysts, high-income countries typically exceed their domestic 'carrying capacities' by a factor of three to six or more, thereby imposing a growing burden on low-income countries.[64] This figure is based on the dubious calculation of 1.7 global hectares per capita as each person's equitable or 'fair Earth-share' of global biocapacity.[65] Regardless of the flaws in the 'footprint' calculator, the EU, nevertheless, is the world's largest importer and exporter of food. Not only is 31% of the land required to satisfy EU food demand located outside Europe, but half of EU fish and seafood consumption is caught outside European waters.[66]

The political dilemma about how to equitably distribute global material resources begins when we try to evaluate what is politically feasible in capitalist countries if populations wish to reduce their disproportionate share of resources. It is certainly possible to legislate against food waste (a third of food either lost at site of growth or thrown out by consumers) as some countries have done. We could also reduce meat consumption, rezone land use to protect against deforestation, property development and so forth. The expansion of shared land, 'the commons', by transforming urban streets and roads into parks, food producing areas and recreational spaces is an excellent idea but would entail changes to private property and public land regulations. This could constitute a major threat to key elements of capitalist societies, namely, the property-industrial complex consisting of construction companies, financial institutions, the auto industry and related chemical, metals, and other materials suppliers.

It is also definitely possible for capitalist countries to increase their low rates of recycling. Currently, the circular economy is more advanced in EU countries while very low in most other parts of the world. Modernisation could also drastically clean up the worst forms of industrial production such as chemical leakage and pollution in oceans, lakes, and waterways, minimise destructive mining practices and other despoiling activities causing massive biodiversity loss, shortages of fresh water and millions of lives cut short by fine particle emissions and all kinds of toxic carcinogens in polluted cities. Despite positive outcomes which will be necessary in coming years, the circular economy does not go to the heart of the problem, namely, the character and structure of everyday life promoted by private enterprises. It offers no alteration to the length of the working-week, no change to social priorities or the elimination of massive social inequalities. Essentially, it attempts to 'sanitise' and 'immunise' capitalist production and consumption (for those who can afford most of it now) without transforming the political power relations that drive existing disastrous socio-economic practices threatening environmental unsustainability.

Legislatively, green growthers[67] and degrowthers[68] wish to outlaw non-repairability and the planned obsolescence of manufactured goods to ensure that they last 100 years or more. Repairability can be legislated and is relatively easy to achieve compared to durability. However, if based on maximising profitability, quality, durable goods could make household consumer goods much more expensive and unaffordable for up to 70% of low- and middle-income wage earners in OECD countries, and more than 90% of populations in low- and middle-income countries. Market proposals to switch from buying to renting expensive durables have not yet been costed for most industries. Household debt is already high in many countries and the additional burden of monthly rental payments for appliances could be prohibitive given decades-long stagnant wage rates. Either way, industry groups would bitterly contest the goal of 'durability' for its disastrous consequence on volumes of sales and corporate profitability. If passed, this legislation could see the end of many manufacturing businesses as the accumulation of capital via high turnover of goods would plummet as production volumes decreased and new consumer markets ceased to grow.

Similarly, those advocating the reduction of the large use of resources in housing/construction (to achieve UNEP's goal of 6 to 8 tonnes per capita) usually call for a mixture of substitute materials for carbon-intensive cement and other materials as well as smaller homes or halving housing space. Part of this objective is possible with the development and use of new materials. New construction could also be determined by legislation specifying the size of dwellings and permissible sustainable building materials. Both are achievable despite major political battles with both the property-industrial complex and many voters who will oppose restrictions on their choice. However, profound domestic and international inequality in built environments cannot be rectified by breaking up large houses or transporting infrastructure to deprived communities and poor countries. It would take a political revolution just to force existing occupiers of mansions, let alone millions of middle-income dwellers in existing homes, especially in OECD countries, to share their living space with the homeless or domestic low-income populations.

However, the enormous task of building hundreds of millions of similar small homes and networks of schools, hospitals, public transport, connected electricity, potable water and sewage disposal for the billions of people living in sub-standard or slum dwellings in low- and middle-income countries will require a massive increase in the extraction and use of material resources. Some of these resources can be diverted from high-income countries (to date, we have no global calculations), but it is highly likely that much higher levels of material resources will be needed just to provide sufficient comfortable living rather than affluence. To achieve greater global equality, we need to abandon the arbitrary target of 50 billion tons by 2050 while still aiming for low or carbon-free materials to build housing and social infrastructure for the global poor. If not, one can endorse rigid and dubious concepts of the 'carrying capacity of the earth' but resign oneself to accepting deep social inequality in a so-called post-carbon capitalist world.

Even if all the residents of high-income countries cut their per capita 'footprints' by up to 90 per cent (to 6 to 8 tonnes per annum), the mathematical and political and social realities of distributing material resources to nine billion people within a so-called cap of 50 billion tonnes per annum would be near impossible. As they say, theoretically, you can fit over 100 people into a telephone box once the bullshit has been squeezed out of them. However, in the world that we currently confront, no such tricks are possible. That is why when it comes to 'levelling' up a global population to the same per capita 'material footprint', such objectives are politically unattainable.

Instead, I believe that we can and should implement a wide variety of policies to reduce and transform the extraction, production, and consumption practices of high-income countries without relying on unrealistic and vague aggregate figures about material footprints and 'carrying capacity'. Each one of these necessary cuts to material resources use – decarbonisation, transformation of land and water use, recycling of materials, changes to the character and level of household consumption – are major battles. Even if they are won in coming decades, it is necessary to recognise that the polarised political world we live in will not easily or perhaps never permit a major transfer of global material resources from high-income populations to the poor in low-income countries. That is why advocates of equitable 'footprints' operate with a rose tinted, unconflicted, harmonious model of the world free of geopolitical power struggles, corporate capitalist exploiters or authoritarian regimes that oppress their own people and care little about equality. These advocates of equitable 'footprints' even ignore the fact that voters and governments in developed capitalist countries object to raising tiny amounts of foreign aid to support other countries, let alone implementing the revolutionary move of cutting their own per capita material footprints to just 6 to 8 tonnes per annum.

Should we succeed in overcoming all or some of these major political obstacles, and I hope we do, the population in each low and middle-income country will still have to decide how they will use their local or imported material resources, what population size, ownership and shape of economy or connections to the external world they need to limit or increase. It is time we recognised that global per capita 'footprints' are little more than technocratic criteria formulated by concerned and well-intentioned environmentalists who are often completely divorced from actual political economic processes and the possible formulation of social objectives by a democratic citizenry.

Consequently, the struggle between 'democracy and sustainability' will be partly fought over claims and counter claims as to what constitutes an equitable future per capita level of material consumption. Social justice movements cannot afford to accept misleading 'material footprint' statistics from agencies that prioritise capitalist green growth, whether UNEP, OECD, EUROSTAT, or the World Bank. In a period of rising nationalism, few analysts of material resources examine the interlocking regional structure of material resource use that transcends national boundaries. The notion of 'sovereign' and unilateral government decisions to change what are called 'national footprints' ignores the powerful international political economic constraints on such decision-making.

Given the polarised politics of existing representative democratic processes, it is far from certain that prevailing decision-making institutions will opt for fundamental changes to the use of material resources. Most 'material footprint' analysts gloss over this crucial factor and hope that a 'rational' description of depleted and damaged resources and threats to planetary boundaries will result in appropriate policy remedies. Their remote and distorted aggregate calculations, especially their failure to document social inequalities blurred by per capita 'footprints', will quite possibly be rejected by all those diverse population groups and classes in individual countries. This is because major social change can never be delivered by crude equalising targets of global per capita 'footprints' that neither conform with peoples' diverse urban, rural, class, gender and other social and cultural experiences.

Imagine if governments and businesses in OECD countries shifted the main burden of distributing material resources to low-income countries onto the backs of low- and middle-income people in Europe, North America, Japan, or Australia. Without lengthy discussion and mass education campaigns, any such re-distribution of material resources will be bitterly resisted. Think, for instance, of the 'yellow vest' protests in France which were partly due to people being told to buy unaffordable electric vehicles and carry the fiscal burden while the Macron government provided tax cuts to businesses and the wealthy. Such unequal policy proposals reveal the essence of why 'democracy' as practised in capitalist societies is far from compatible with environmental sustainability.

Unsurprisingly, a widespread cultural transformation in environmental thinking and behaviour would first be needed before diverse populations *democratically* agreed to the standardisation of their access to and consumption of material resources. However, no government currently has any intention of enforcing caps on material consumption at individual or household levels despite good reasons for doing so. Carbon emission trading caps are not equivalent to the rationing of material resources which a per capita target of 6 to 8 tonnes effectively and informally aims to deliver by scaling down much higher rates of consumption. Future governments would need to be politically secure and strongly backed by electorates to reduce extraction and production of materials necessary for various industries. Even in the event that governments agree to international targets and caps on material resources, few national governments are likely to enforce such divisive measures without popular domestic support or the imposition of international penalties and sanctions. Sadly, no international organisation currently has the power to impose such penalties on nation states which fail to sign or adhere to international agreements.

In the meantime, the record of more than two hundred years of private capitalist agriculture across the world has been one enormous irreparable damage and destruction. It is sheer madness to perpetuate massive biodiversity loss through the overuse of chemical fertilisers, deforestation or soil and water loss through inappropriate agribusiness crops, costly crop production for stock-feed meat production and many other commercially driven practices. The solution is not a return to the crude bureaucratised industrial collective farms of the USSR which were disastrous for both human and non-human species. Rather, we need to implement more balanced eco-agricultural practices that require political movements based on public awareness of the unsustainability of current food consumption and production. The transition to agroecology is itself fraught with many obstacles in diverse high-income or low-income capitalist countries. These organisational, cultural, legal and political obstacles usually take the form of resistance from land-owning classes and commercial food processing companies.[69] Any such transformation of public consciousness will not be possible without greater awareness of the inseparable link between food production and the geopolitics of historical 'food regimes'.

Analysts such as Philip McMichael have adopted global panoramic views in explaining the transformation of previous modes of food production and the institutionalisation of new 'food regimes'.[70] While this approach tends to gloss over the many specific historical forms of regional and local food production and consumption that have never conformed to the grand macro perspective of capitalist agriculture, McMichael nonetheless helps us locate and understand the way biomass has been structured and consumed. He argues that the British-centred food regime was the first to link food production and consumption to its expansive world empire built up during the 18th and 19th centuries. This co-existed with and was succeeded by the US-centred food regime during the twentieth century which presided over the intensification of agribusiness (the application of capital-intensive methods, chemicals, and industrial productivity objectives) as well as utilising food as part of strategic aid and 'development policy', especially during the Cold War period. Whether there was a third food regime based on corporate globalisation rather than US state policy is disputed. Currently, McMichael sees a trend towards 'regional food regimes' in Asia, Latin America and elsewhere with China and other new local players. It is corporate neoliberal food practices that have spawned "a contradictory conjuncture: a tension between a trajectory of abstraction in agro-industrialisation (agro-food/fuel from nowhere) and place-based forms of agro-ecological farming (food from somewhere), nurtured by food sovereignty politics – a politics of modernity rooted in a global moral eco-economy."[71]

It remains to be seen whether the link between rural social justice movements and urban ecological awareness of unsustainable food production gives rise to more sustainable forms of food consumption and the end of corporate agribusiness and food retailing. If it is to be successful, the alternative use of material resources such as biomass is a political project that needs to go well beyond both McMichael's old-style anti-imperialist analysis and simplistic 'environmental footprint' analyses that obscure the unequal political economy of the extraction and consumption of material resources. We have already entered a period of environmental challenges that defy the division of the world into the neat geopolitical categories of the 'South' and the 'North'. Unsustainable practices are now driven by both traditional imperial powers and multinational corporations as well as by new local and regional governments, businesses, and consumers.

Although international solutions are preferable and more significant in their impact, it is much more likely that changes to the extraction, production and consumption of resources will come about in a haphazard and uneven manner as the result of local and national populations recognising the immediate threats to degraded ecosystems and biodiversity loss. This will likely prompt calls for limitations on particular forms of economic development and unregulated abuses long before international treaties are agreed to and implemented. Whether liberals, Keynesian social democrats, neoliberal conservatives or Marxist and anarchist radicals, the old distributional struggles between capital and labour will eventually be unable to ignore the interrelated environmental struggles over material resources. On the contrary, it is the coming struggle over unequal per capita and national resources that will help reshape currently narrow political conceptions of the 'economic' and the 'social'.

In 2018, Daniel O'Neill and colleagues carried out a comparative survey of 150 nations to assess whether these countries met a range of social needs, such as education, income, nutrition, health, employment, life satisfaction and democratic equality without transgressing planetary boundaries including carbon emissions, material footprints, nitrogen, phosphorous and other biophysical indicators.[72] The academic survey not only lacked a clear politics and set of priorities but contained a number of problematic concepts including attributing goods consumed to a particular country rather than identifying where they were actually produced.[73] Overall, the findings were not unexpected. No country managed to satisfy social needs without transgressing 'safe planetary boundaries'. Conversely, all countries that stayed within the 'safe boundaries' of biophysical indicators were also the same societies that failed to provide their populations with adequate social services or democratic and egalitarian social relations.

Despite some shortcomings in the comparative research findings, this survey of 'the good life within planetary boundaries' stands as a powerful and sober reminder to all who still adhere to the old paradigm 'capitalism versus democracy', particularly to all those who wish to create an alternative post-capitalist society without adequately considering environmental factors. If markets are not to remain the dominant mechanism whereby goods and services continue to be distributed unequally, any future notion of state planning (whatever the model) needs to specify how both social and environmental indicators can be organised to ensure that success in one area is not at the expense of the other. This vital task is currently given low priority by alternative social change movements, whether radical socialists, social democratic post-Keynesians, technological utopians or advocates of degrowth.

4. DEGROWTH: DIRECT DEMOCRACY IN A POLITICAL ECONOMIC VACUUM

MOST PARTIES from the Right to the Left have yet to confront the implications of the coming political struggle over per capita and national material footprints analysed in the previous chapter. They still reject the need to decelerate economic growth or to curb and reorganise the use of material resources away from the dominant forms of capitalist extraction, production, and consumption. By contrast, the main political groups that place the need to transform the size and quality of material footprints at the centre of their political and social vision of an environmentally sustainable democracy are the degrowth and post-growth movements. I share with degrowthers and post-growthers many of the reasons why we need alternatives to existing capitalist practices that are destroying and degrading the biosphere and social relations. However, I also strongly disagree with various proposed solutions, especially those advanced by degrowth movements. More is the pity that both degrowth and post-growth advocates rest their alternative visions on such problematic political, economic, social, and organisational proposals. When reading the growing degrowth literature one is struck by the paucity of their understanding of democracy. They fail to develop any concepts of what kind of democratic institutions, legal and administrative structures will exist and how they will function aside from the overwhelming faith that most degrowthers place in local communities practising direct democracy. Therefore, the aim of this chapter is to examine why some of their key social and institutional proposals are deeply flawed, counter-productive to their stated objectives of egalitarian and democratic environmental sustainability, and politically ineffective and irrelevant in their current forms.

The Illusions of a Steady State Economy and an Embedded Society

Supporters of degrowth and post-growth promote the 'steady-state' and the embedded society where the economy serves the needs of society rather than society and the environment serving the needs of the capitalist market. The difference is that advocates of post-growth often favour state institutions and 'mixed economies' of private and public sectors whereas most degrowthers reject capitalist social relations and campaign for radical direct democracies based on local communities. Both groups assume that the use of material resources, or size of populations and livestock do not need to incessantly grow. However, degrowthers go further in their support of radical 'energy descent'. The degrowth of material resources is used to justify a more equal form of 'sufficiency' for all, rather than reduced but still significant levels of inequality favoured by some post-growthers.

Allowing for their political and theoretical differences, why do both groups, nonetheless, uncritically share the concept of the 'steady-state' which is so dubious and problem-ridden? When ecological economist, Herman Daly, coined the term 'steady state' in 1973 as a critique of the dominant economic religion of 'growthism', he was building on the collective work of Howard T. Okum, Kenneth Boulding, Ernst Schumacher and Nicholas Georgescu-Roegen. Generations of environmentalists continue to be influenced by Daly but tend to remain silent on his reliance on pro-market, neo-classical economics. Daly believes in a 'steady-state' sustainable society where there is stable flow of population and capital stock adjusted to different countries' needs.[1] Government regulation of material resources throughput – extraction, utilisation, and waste disposal – ensures that natural resources are not depleted or cause too much pollution. While at face value this idea of 'balance' sounds compelling, the problem is that paradoxically, Daly relies on cap and trade and other neo-classical market-orientated economic concepts.[2] His vision is not only based on a mixture of Malthusian population theory, conservative cybernetics ecosystems theory and mainstream economics, it moreover lacks any conception of democracy other than misconceived notions of existing political systems. Daly also relies on the systems ecology put forward by Jay Forrester and others.[3] Their conception of nature and society is governed by a model of interconnecting sub-systems and feed-back loops that with care and the right policies such as 'energy descent', can be restored to a balanced or 'steady state'. These are all well-intentioned goals that rest on what other ecologists regard as highly contentious notions of the internal processes and biodiversity of nature, let alone of human societies.

Despite what neo-classical market economists claim, there has never been *general equilibrium* in industrialised capitalist societies characterised by multiple forms of inequality and conflict. Similarly, it will be revolutionary for nation states just to aim to achieve post-capitalist societies based on very minimal levels of inequality and conflict, even though these potential future societies will *not* be balanced 'steady states'. Daly rejects state planning to control the throughput of material resources and relies on market mechanisms which are currently grossly ineffective in reducing carbon emissions, let alone a range of material resources.

In Daly's case, the 'steady state' is a pseudo solution that does not fully come to terms with capitalist political economy. Writing within an American political culture dominated by various forms of free-market individualism, Daly's 'alternative society' is conceived as having many of the same characteristics of what he ridiculously calls 'socialist democracies' or mixed economies of public and private sectors in capitalist countries such as those in Scandinavia or Switzerland.[4] These countries are neither socialist nor heading towards a 'steady state'. Despite claiming to abandon 'growthism', Daly's model is awfully close to the mythical or utopian 'equilibrium' of markets long promoted by mainstream pro-market economists. Neither the 'invisible hand' of the market nor Keynesian state intervention were ever able to achieve balance and prevent, control, or eliminate major crises in capitalist systems during the past one hundred years.

'Steady state' ecological economists are committed to the illusory idea that post-growth and degrowth can be implemented within capitalist societies by altering the material throughput of resources, waste, and consumption without precipitating a major economic crisis. Earlier crises, such as Japan's protracted low growth/stagnation of recent decades, were misconceived by Daly as though Japan was half-way on the road to a 'steady state'. Ecological economist Daniel O'Neill repeats this nonsense in his 2015 survey of 180 countries.[5] Not only is this a fundamental misunderstanding of Japan's high carbon emissions capitalist economy, but like Sweden and Switzerland, Daly's conception of the 'steady-state' is neither post-capitalist nor an egalitarian society. If these countries are close to the 'steady-state', then this is a goal that will only reproduce more of the same 'mixed economy' capitalism that has caused existing socio-economic and environmental disasters. Instead of drastically reduced income ratios – from the lowest to the highest paid – of no more than two to one, Daly favours inequality that ranges from a ratio of 10 to 1, to as high as 100 to 1, which is still enormous and immoral despite being less than the current obscene levels of inequality between multi-billionaires and the poorest in society.[6] Daly's new society is also conceived as being based on the usual myth of a small business capitalist utopia without existing giant corporations and private monopolies.

While Daly views the 'steady-state' as still largely capitalist, like other Left advocates of 'national social democracy' such as Wolfgang Streeck, Daly is opposed to 'cosmopolitan globalism' and wants to 'renationalise capital' and impose environmental controls and other regulations over capital and immigration flows.[7] This is a largely inward-looking model of future socio-economic relations that aims to minimise external interaction so that national 'steady-state' economies and populations can be regulated. Whether this type of society is introduced in the US or in other countries, in a hypothetical world of diverse economies – whether capitalist, hybrid capitalist/steady state systems or eco-socialist – governments will nonetheless find it difficult to avoid financial, trade, currency, accumulation and investment crises. Daly's 'steady-state' is market-based and does not aim to be self-sufficient, even though it would aim for a balanced throughput of material resources. Hence, it would invariably import external problems because it will still be integrated into international capitalist markets.

It is true that other ecological economists and degrowth proponents put forward more radical anti-capitalist ideas of the 'steady state' that are based on far greater equality and either more international cooperation or more isolation and radical self-sufficiency at local and national levels. Nonetheless, the inherent weakness of Daly's notion of 'equilibrium' still applies to these models. There exists far too much vagueness about exactly how the interaction between national domestic producers and consumers and dozens of international exporters and investors could attain economic balance or equilibrium whether using market mechanisms or state planning. Daly's fictional ideal world presupposes far more symmetry and benign and cooperative relations with like-minded nations committed to post-growth rather than the existing hostile competitiveness and polarised politics over climate policies, trade, material resources, intellectual property rights, immigration, and many other socio-economic issues. As to 'fundamentalist' small, stateless, and largely self-sufficient communities, this version of the 'steady-state' is an impractical solution for a world of nine billion people and would probably eventually implode (even amongst experimental small communities) due to multiple internal stresses of isolation, scarcity, and social conflict.

The problem of the political and economic impossibility of reaching a 'steady state' is that Daly and many other environmentalists share an unrealistic view of how to change capitalist societies. They assume that if only communities and social movements adopted post-growth or degrowth practices and the correct state levers were pulled and a more balanced or 'steady-state' economy was formed, then the world could be made just, stable, and sustainable.[8] Such an ideal image overlooks or minimises the crucial and inseparable relationship between economic growth (especially technological innovation) and military and political power. It is against the background of a profoundly uneven and unequal world, a world characterised by a mere 19 countries out of 195 accounting for approximately 80% of world GDP, a world where almost two-thirds of the global population earn either far less than or little more than US$5 a day. It is also a world where on 2020 figures, the US military budget of $US732 billion was 38.2% of the estimated total global military expenditure of US$1,917 billion and equalled the combined expenditure of the ten next largest spenders by dwarfing China's $US261 billion, India's $US71.1 billion, Russia's $US65.1 billion, Saudi Arabia's $US61.9 billion and France's $US50.1 billion as the next five largest spenders.[9]

Sobering figures revealed that only fifteen countries accounted for 81% of total global military expenditure and yet 32 countries had military conflicts in 2019. It is not just well-known arms exporters such as the US, Russia, France, Germany, China, and the UK that keep elevated levels of violence alive in the world. Spain is now the seventh largest arms exporter and its Socialist/Podemos government continues exporting weapons to notorious countries such as Turkey and Saudi Arabia, the latter using Spanish made arms in its brutal war in Yemen.[10]

In such a divisive and hostile geopolitical world where the top nineteen countries (by GDP) also have about 61% of the global population, including a substantial proportion of the world's poorest people alongside incredible personal wealth for a tiny minority, one has to be blind to not see the enormous obstacles confronting radical degrowthers. Any political analysis that ignores the interconnection between vested government and business interests in developing and maintaining competitive industrial strength in metallurgy, electronics, chemicals, digital technology, and other key industries necessary for military superiority will seriously underestimate the challenges that degrowth and 'steady state' advocates face. Even giants such as China currently only produce about 16% of their semi-conductors and are highly dependent on importing other advanced technologies and materials.[11] Most countries much weaker than China cannot surmount these massive obstacles. Of course, one can reject the modern world and dream of simple technologies in an autarkic 'steady state' society that has minimal connection to the rest of the world. Such visions are a luxury and hardly an option for most people.

Some ecological economists, such as Ann Pettifor, continue to use Daly's concept of a 'steady state' to underpin her case for a Green New Deal based on 'localism'.[12] The notion that one could transform national fiscal policy, social and military expenditure and material resources use to achieve not a national or international Green New Deal, but a 'steady-state' based on a local Green New Deal is daring but highly politically unrealistic. Such rhetoric ignores both existing interlocking capitalist societies and the feasibility of post-capitalist nations trying to survive without multiple socio-economic links beyond local economies. Like Pettifor, ecological economists Tim Jackson, Peter Victor and Ali Naqvi offer many positive features of an alternative society. Yet, crucially, they also ignore the *realpolitik* of military-industrial production in their attempt to go beyond Daly by developing a model of the British economy as a series of stock flows between different sectors.[13] Once again, it is entirely unclear how such a theoretical model of local economies within a national economy can avoid importing major economic problems or prevent domestic economic depression if it disengages from or restricts exchanges with international markets.

Politically, a 'steady state' would require extremely tight controls over economic activity, especially imports and exports. It would require a cultural revolution in attitudes and behaviour that would be exceedingly difficult to achieve within the normally short political electoral cycle. This is one reason why advocates of a 'steady state', especially degrowthers, have little conception of democracy that is not local. As long as there are competitive free elections, it is highly possible that without new cultural values being widely and deeply held, import/export controls and capital controls could be relaxed or abolished by a new incoming government elected on promises that voters would gain more access to foreign goods and services. Currently, it is exceedingly difficult for domestic industry in countries such as the UK to disengage from incessant growth as combined imports and exports constitute over 60% of the latter's GDP. As the largest economy in the EU, Germany has an even greater 'export fetish' than the

UK which lacks comparative industrial strength. Germany's exports alone constituted 43.5% of its economy in 2020, which was much larger than China's 18.4%, Japan's 16.4%, and the US at 12.9% of GDP.[14] America and China have much larger imports in volume and dollar value than Germany. Consequently, all of these large economies would have major problems immunising themselves from imported economic crises. Those who boldly declare that imported goods and resources are not needed, risk forgetting that many domestic industries would plunge into crisis without vitally needed materials, technology, and manufacturing component elements. Covid-19 has shown dramatically how interruptions to supply chains affected many national markets.

Individual countries could possibly transition away from such a heavy reliance on imports and exports over a decade or more, but any significant switch to degrowth could see the stock market continually decline or crash, private investments disappear offshore, and employment and income plummet dramatically as many businesses in most advanced capitalist countries are highly integrated into international value chains and financial markets. This is hardly unexpected given that multinational corporations account for the overwhelming level and scale of international trade in material goods and financial services. The only surprise is that despite widespread and repeated criticisms of the naïve or 'bright-side' accounts of future degrowth societies, far too many degrowthers still persist with Pollyannish accounts of 'steady-state' nirvanas. Largely, they are preoccupied with local or national alternative communities. One is reminded of earlier socialists who believed that 'socialism in one country' could survive in a hostile capitalist world. Similarly, degrowth proponents completely underestimate international pressures and exchanges that make idealised notions of 'steady state' a policy trajectory headed for inevitable failure.

Degrowth policies would therefore not succeed without first identifying and establishing alternative forms of production and political power that were able to counter or control the value and supply chains driven by powerful corporations. Yet, even with government helping stem the fall in income or generating new public employment and services, post-growth scenarios would have trouble surviving in isolated nation states without the staunch support of other leading capitalist countries undergoing similar post-growth transitions. Supranational entities such as the EU would possibly have a greater chance of a successful transition to sustainability – both in terms of resources and political power – providing that cross-national co-operation expanded, and domestic political divisions could be minimised. Brexit has effectively instituted or consolidated UK 'weakness' in international capitalist markets while Left nationalists (who supported Brexit) have made the transition to post-capitalism infinitely harder due to adhering to the myth of national sovereignty.

Conceptions of the 'steady state' are also largely orientated to developed capitalist countries. It is still often overlooked that from the sixteenth century to the twentieth century, 'primitive capitalism' was violent and ferocious in different continents regardless of whether it was backed by monarchies or republics, whether it took the form of domestic upheaval or imperialist 'development' abroad. On the positive side, the formation of post-carbon societies is most unlikely to repeat the slaughter and dispossession of First Peoples and their lands, the forced proletarianisation of millions of people from early nineteenth century rural labourers in England to late twentieth century China. Marx called primitive capitalism 'accumulation by dispossession'. In recent years, Ramachandra Guha, Joan Martinez-Alier and Shulan Zhang have described ecological struggles in India as 'environmentalism of the dispossessed' or 'environmentalism of the poor' in that it is a struggle over inequality and access to natural resources appropriated by landowners and a range of businesses.[15] It is quite different to the political ideas of degrowth sustainability driving environmentalism in affluent OECD countries today.

Despite inflicting shocking suffering and death on uprooted rural populations and urban workers, early capitalist entrepreneurs were able to grow within various empires, kingdoms, nation states and city states without being destroyed by local and international pre-capitalist ruling classes. No such luxury of 'peaceful development' is available to 'steady state', degrowth or other models of post-capitalism in a world of highly integrated capitalist businesses and their political and military allies. This does not mean that advocates of post-capitalist ecologically sustainable societies will be repressed and killed *en masse*. Rather, it does mean that they will encounter strong political opposition while lacking the military, economic, legal, and ideological forms of state power that helped capitalists rise to become the dominant class power. Unlike early Christians who were protected by Emperor Constantine, the fate of radical ecological sustainability will depend on mass mobilisation of people rather than on just the blessings of benign governments. I will return to these questions of strategy in a later chapter.

It is also worth briefly discussing that many but not all advocates of the problematic notion of the 'steady-state' also aspire to the equally unrealistic notion that post-carbon societies should be embedded organic social orders (with or without state institutions). It was Karl Polanyi in *The Great Transformation* (1944[16]) who critiqued the way capitalist markets disembedded pre-capitalist communities by subjugating and subordinating social and community relations to the emerging market economy. Polanyi wished that a socialist society could reverse disembeddedness and restore a new form of embeddedness where politics and social values made the economy serve social needs. This admirable but ultimately utopian objective has been uncritically adopted by all kinds of environmentalists and socialists. In *Capitalism Versus Democracy?* (Book One), I extensively outlined the serious flaws in Polanyi's work. Those who use Polanyi as justification for a future organic embedded society 'at one with nature' are subscribing to a political and socio-economic fiction. It is most unlikely that a future world will be universally socialist. It will, unfortunately, remain characterised by countries with different political regimes based on greater or lesser equality, greater or lesser democracy, and greater or lesser social control over finance, trade, and numerous other crucial activities. Such a world in coming decades will probably have either no or minimal agreement over what it means to 'embed' or control national economies or international markets and whether these objectives are desirable or possible.

Very importantly, the notion of an 'embedded society' tells us little or nothing about the social norms and morality guiding such a society. Consider that during the past seventy-five years, most citizens and national businesses in affluent OECD countries have cared little about the welfare of strangers in former colonies or other exploited countries, except when they impacted their profits and jobs or when they dared to arrive in their home countries uninvited. Hence, it is theoretically possible to imagine a nationally 'embedded society' characterised by full-employment, affluent consumption and overall social contentment that is nonetheless utterly abhorrent. Crucially, such an 'embedded society' could be environmentally unsustainable, based on the blatant exploitation and misery of workers in other countries, and characterised by racism, the absence of democracy and an intolerance of cultural practices that do not conform to the conservative values of the so-called comfortably embedded 'organic community'. We cannot therefore assume that 'embeddedness' is inherently democratic, egalitarian and environmentally sustainable.

Also, the moment that one begins to extend the geographical boundaries of 'embeddedness' beyond the local or to include all those who are *not* citizens, but unemployed or without adequate sustenance or social rights, then the notion of 'embeddedness' becomes something quite different to Polanyi's very limited notion of 'organic' Christian socialism. One can understand why degrowthers and socialist critics of neoliberalism are attracted to Polanyi in their desire to subordinate contemporary capitalist societies to political control. Nonetheless, the problem today is far more complex. Even gaining full socialist or radical green political control over national or international markets is not equivalent to establishing an 'embedded economy'. This is because medium to large cities, let alone nation states, are inherently impersonal and based on distant, abstract relations that are doomed to remain 'disembedded' as daily life experiences.

So much discussion of 'disembeddedness' avoids the key question of what would constitute an 'embedded society' in the twenty-first century. For if we are not talking of small, face-to-face, self-sufficient communities, then all nation-states are to varying degrees, remote and 'disembedded', not to mention supra-national entities such as the European Union or global markets. In addition, there is no clear idea or consensus about what level of social and political control will end 'disembeddedness' and commodification. Some small face-to-face, self-sufficient communes could possibly claim to be fully embedded only if the residents had no major dependence on external goods, services, or income, a near impossibility in the contemporary world. Organising billions of people into small, face-to-face communities is a fanciful notion. It is also possible that future populations might even regard socialist egalitarian societies that engage in global trade rather than just local, self-sufficient, face-to-face interactions, as remote or 'disembedded'. Yet, this would hardly be a sufficient reason to oppose such societies.

It is delusionary to believe that 'embedded' self-sufficient, stateless, small-scale communities are politically feasible or viable as the main form of a global alternative to capitalism. If we are mindful of Polanyi's warning that self-regulating markets are utopian and dangerous, the same warning also applies to socialist or green *stateless* societies based on equally utopian small, self-regulating communities.[17] Despite being characterised by powerful and attractive critiques of bureaucratisation and oppressive hierarchies, there is a high chance that these stateless anarchist and green alternatives to neoliberalism could also degenerate (especially by the second and subsequent generations of communalists) into new authoritarian nightmares or selfish parochial communes that refuse to help other less fortunate communities or 'outsiders'.

On the contrary, we need solutions that will reorganise existing complex national and global institutions to maximise social justice, democratic control, and co-operative cultural values. The goal of 'embeddedness' at either local community or global levels remains then a utopian distraction from the difficult task of combatting inequality, racial and discriminatory social hatred, patriarchy, religious sectarianism or ending and preventing wars and catastrophic ecological breakdown. We need alternative political economic agendas to dominant neoliberal and authoritarian practices, even if these do not conform to a Polanyian unspecified ideal type of organic 'embeddedness'.

Disputing Degrowth

During the 1980s and 1990s, the German Greens were divided into three broad sub-groups: the radicals or *fundis* who were split between those who rejected capitalism and communism and opted for a deindustrialised world of small simple, stateless communities, and *red/greens* who combined environmental policies with Leftist anti-capitalist social policies. The other sub-grouping known as *realos,* or realists later became either green neoliberals or a variation of social democrats supporting ecological modernisation within a capitalist society. It is the *realos* which have achieved electoral success in recent years but at the expense of former radical green policies. Just like the two wings of the original Green party *fundis*, we now see similar divisions play out in degrowth movements. An informal assemblage of various environmentalists, anarchists, eco-socialists, and other critics of unsustainable and destructive capitalist growth has given rise to two types of degrowthers: those *fundis* or fundamentalists who advocate stateless communities and others who recognise the continued necessity and vital role to be played by local, national, and supranational state institutions.[18]

In contrast to Green parties that are organised at national level and participate in electoral politics, most degrowth movements are disengaged from national politics and largely operate within their own networks or in a political vacuum. Moreover, the conceptions of an alternative society promoted by both of the two broad degrowth tendencies are presented as if they are *ready-finished* social orders or functioning realities rather than images and goals that need to be developed and secured against widespread political, economic, and military opposition or repression. Unsurprisingly, like other radical movements, key socio-political objectives of post-capitalist degrowth are often *disconnected* from the extremely difficult political, economic, and environmental obstacles that need to be surmounted. It is this very process of constructing new democratic and sustainable institutions within very hostile political terrains that will inevitably shape and transform the original end goals sought in the first place.

Degrowth continues to be advanced by an assortment of academics via publications and conferences that critique unsustainable capitalist growth. It is also an activist movement based on a number of small experimental communes and networks. Approximately 80 per cent of practitioners of alternative energy, food production and anti-consumerism live in urban settings rather than in rural communes. To date, no distinct degrowth party or coherent movement has emerged (except an earlier failed attempt in France) and there is no clear politics currently manifested in actual national political organisations like socialist parties. Degrowthers are also deeply divided over whether degrowth movements should adopt nation-wide organisational forms or remain local, grassroots groups.[19]

Recently, dedicated supporter of degrowth, Timothée Parrique, provided the most comprehensive study of this diverse political movement that is called degrowth.[20] Surveying the growing literature on the central policies, aims and strategies of degrowthers, Parrique summarised these visions and arguments for what he calls 'degrowthopia', where exploitation of people and nature has ended. This new society rests on three principles: autonomy, sufficiency, and care. The ultimate purpose of a post-work economy is to liberate workers' time for joyous non-economic social and cultural purposes, that is, work less and play more. Life will be organised in small-scale, horizontal communities with their own currencies and goods will be produced in small artisan circles and cooperatives using convivial tools. Voluntary simplicity is to be based on outwardly simple, but inwardly rich lives which emphasise less stuff and more relationships. All are guaranteed free access to essential necessities and services, and political life is to be organised around direct democracy at the town or neighbourhood level and representative democracy at the bioregional and national level.[21]

At first sight, many of these values and practices are desirable. However, as I will discuss, the principles of autonomy, sufficiency and care can be contradictory in potential scenarios and some of the 'degrowthopia' goals are not all compatible with democratic environmental sustainability. Also, while degrowthers do not ignore the plight of billions of poor people in low-income countries[22] and in OECD countries, nonetheless, this is one of their key weaknesses. Apart from general statements, we are yet to read practical political economic degrowth policies and strategies that would remedy mass poverty without resorting to economic growth and/or profound redistribution of wealth.[23]

Two overlapping critiques of degrowth have been made in recent years. Socialist, Leigh Phillips, rejects degrowth and mischaracterises it as 'austerity ecology'. Subscribing to a crude orthodox Marxism, Phillips argues that class struggle leading to the overthrow of capitalism combined with innovative technology will solve inequality and ecological destruction.[24] Like Phillips, social democrat, Branko Milanovic, staunchly defends growth and calls degrowth 'magical thinking'. "Degrowthers live in a world of magic", he argues, "where merely by listing the names of desirable ends they will somehow happen. In that world, one does not need to bother with numbers or facts, trade-offs, first or second bests; one merely needs to conjure up what he/she desires and it will be there."[25] He goes on to claim that degrowthers would not only prevent the vast global armies of the poor from aiming for significant growth to improve their lives, but would also "need to convince 86% of the population living in rich countries that their incomes are too high and need to be reduced. They would have to preside over economic depressions for about a decade, and then let the new real income stay at that level indefinitely."[26]

In reply, degrowth advocates such as Jason Hickel argue that both Phillips and Milanovic base their critique of degrowth on caricatures and straw men, including false claims that degrowthers wish to suddenly cut all sectors of the economy in half. According to Hickel, Milanovic misrepresents degrowth which is not about reducing GDP. "Rather, it is about reducing excess resource and energy throughput, while at the same time improving human well-being and social outcomes; the literature is quite clear on this." [27] It is important to note that my position is different to that of Phillips, Milanovic and Hickel. In contrast to Phillips and Milanovic,[28] I reject techno-fixes and incessant market growth but am critical of the simplistic methods and political institutional arrangements that degrowthers believe will achieve their goals.

Although I agree with Hickel that GDP is a misleading and a poor measuring tool and that international agencies like the World Bank disguise the real levels of inequality, nonetheless, Hickel is evasive when it comes to rates of degrowth. Insofar as GDP prevails as the key national and international indicator, degrowthers still have to convince electorates about how much degrowth per annum they favour in material and energy throughput which are themselves measured in both quantitative terms and as a proportion of GDP. Hickel admits that degrowth may slow growth and cause a recession if the economy is shifted away from a growth imperative. But he is extremely vague about how this 'shift' could take place without causing an economic crisis.[29]

The same is true of those who attempt to reconcile degrowth with cultural critique of Eurocentrism (Buen Vivir). Adrián Beling and co-authors proclaim that degrowth does not promote economic slowdown. Instead, of 'unfettered material consumerism', they advocate "the creation of a different societal structure, transforming current institutions and rules, promoting a different balance of material and nonmaterial forms of prosperity: time prosperity, 'relational goods' (friendship, neighbourliness, etc.), non-capitalistic, community-based forms of production, exchange, and consumption..."[30] The assumption that creating a 'different balance of material and nonmaterial forms of prosperity' will *not* result in an economic slowdown for most capitalist businesses dependent on growth is self-deluding. Either degrowth is conducted over many decades and is so slow and barely perceptible or it is faster and more substantial. The truth is that any contraction of material throughput that threatens profitability, stock market values and capital investment cannot be achieved without seriously harming existing businesses and market values.

As a socio-economic theory, degrowth has to date been unable to convince tens of millions of potential supporters about how an alternative political economy will function or how to implement and measure degrowth. An unplanned recession/depression such as that caused by COVID-19, witnessed GDP decline between 5% and 20% in various countries. Yet, when it comes to 'planned contraction', crucial questions remain unanswered. These include:

- Would the necessary level of 'planned contraction' of material throughput be smaller or greater than the decline in production, consumption and employment caused by unplanned capitalist recessions?
- In conventional terms, would it be equivalent to 2%, 5% or 10% of GDP per annum or over five or ten-year plans (or some other indicator), and would it be confined to the private sector by mainly focussing on private consumption and particular manufacturing or extractive industries? For example, an annual contraction of 5% of military sector expenditure and automobile production or other destructive and wasteful sectors would reduce these by a quarter within 5 years and halve them within a

decade. But would such cuts reduce the per capita or national use of material resources by equal amounts, or would this largely be a reduction of the financial expenditure in these sectors? Would this degrowth be too rapid or insufficient in developed capitalist countries and how much in the way of alternative socially useful goods and services could substitute for the wasteful and damaging material goods scaled back?

- Would planned contraction on such a scale mainly apply to key parts of the private sector and to imported goods and natural resources? If applied to all of the latter, what level of unemployment, change in income and other multiplier effects would flow to the whole society? Without even the slightest indication of which national or local institutions would democratically decide and implement planned contraction, how would 'frugality' differ from the enforced and involuntary poverty caused by recessions, especially in those impacted countries where the majority of people are already extremely poor?

Remember, these questions are relevant to the transition phase from capitalist growth to any post-capitalist society at a time when there is not yet a fully developed degrowth society and we are still in a stage of 'planned contraction' of capitalist societies. Hence, the vague notion of degrowth as 'planned contraction' remains stuck at the level of rhetoric and aspiration. No satisfactory detailed plan has been provided at either particular country or local levels, let alone globally.[31] We are largely in the dark concerning rates of degrowth or the sectors and activities that may be most affected. Identification of items to be targeted, such as weapons, SUVs, bottled water, or advertising will not be sufficient. Nor will it be enough to use other measuring tools such as the Genuine Progress Indicator. Any indicator will still have to measure real declines in the excessive use of material resources! Decisions about which consumer goods and technologies should be either reduced, banned, or exempted will not be made easily. If banned or phased out, which political institutions other than small communities will decide this, as most degrowthers have not yet outlined how democracy beyond the local will actually work.

Degrowth movements are caught in an anti-politics bubble. The fact of being geared to the local community means they function in a political vacuum. Even elementary conceptions are lacking about what kind of electoral processes are favoured at national or local levels or whether there will be political parties. One gets the strong impression that politics will disappear in alternative degrowth societies which are conceived as being run by idealised individuals who will supposedly never be divided or group together in their own parties, movements, or subcultures. Hence, there is no political strategy or agreement on whether degrowth of material resources should first occur in larger private industrial and government enterprises before consumption and waste is significantly reduced in households, especially low- and middle-income households.

Degrowthers reject universities as they currently exist due to their central scientific and technological role in maintaining key economic, military, and administrative practices. However, little is specified about what kind of alternative advanced scientific and medical research centres are needed and the role organised knowledge could play in the transition to a new degrowth sustainable society. Any future society will still need all kinds of scientific laboratories and technological equipment that will require funding and resources not available from small local community sources. The notion that you can maintain a balanced society based on *simplicity* and 'convivial tools' (Ivan Illich[32]) in key areas of daily consumption and production alongside the retention of advanced science and specialised forms of knowledge in other sectors is an illusion. The processes of acquiring advanced knowledge in its different forms is integral to a certain level of scientific, technological, and socio-cultural institutional complexity that is incompatible with 'fundamentalist' degrowth notions of simple, local, communal life. No wonder those sympathetic to degrowth values are quickly turned off by half-baked and ill-conceived notions of an alternative politics and social strategy.

Unsurprisingly, Brazilian environmentalist Roldan Muradian argues that degrowth is destined to be a Eurocentric movement, simply because 'frugality by choice' is not an option favoured by impoverished masses in low- and middle-income countries.[33] The impasse between growth and degrowth is not only due to residents in high-income countries refusing to radically cut their use of material resources. Degrowthers need to rethink their romanticisation of post-colonial ideas and simple or easy to use convivial tools as adequate on their own to solve immense levels of poverty and deprivation. For there can be no improvement of basic services in low-income countries without substantial growth in the use of material resources for socially useful housing, sewage and piped water, electricity, public transport, schools, and hospitals.

The harsh truth is that redistribution of wealth is necessary but not adequate in itself. Simple analyses of capitalism that propose to end poverty by redistributing the monetary wealth and assets of billionaires will only work once, and still not be enough for *sustainable* forms of equality in the years to come. What is needed are systemic solutions that enable people to have employment, essential basic services, and other improvements in the quality of life currently out of their reach. Redistributing political power and financial power is an essential first step. However, one cannot equalise countries by simply uprooting and transposing housing, urban infrastructure, hospitals, and schools from high-income to low-income countries. Most of these facilities and networks have to be constructed within low- and middle-income countries by reorganising both their political economic engines of inequality and the corporations that benefit and drive these market processes. Instead of slogans, we await ideas from degrowthers about how this enormous task will be initiated, developed, and accomplished.

The Limits of Local Power and the 'Commons'

It is often forgotten that the inventory of specific materials, products and technologies used in contemporary societies is enormous. This incredible range of tens of thousands of items and resources produced under quite diverse production conditions across the world, is beyond the current national capacity of most countries. The task of evaluating which 'bad' or undesirable goods and services need to go and which 'good growth' goods and services are to remain or expand, must therefore not be left *only* to local community decision-making. Decisions about the safety, sustainability, and diverse needs of the majority of people living outside particular localities should be a joint process made by national or supranational environmental and social government departments and agencies in combination with the full involvement of local communities and institutions. If left solely to diverse local communities, these vital decisions will almost certainly introduce numerous inconsistencies resulting in domestic and cross-national shortages, disruptions, large informal black markets, and other organisational and material problems that will fuel disharmony, discredit degrowthers and lead to serious political conflict.

There are numerous creative and practical suggestions that span a range of industries and sectors of national economies – everything from agriculture, energy, finance and education to trade, work, and waste disposal – that could constitute the basis of an alternative degrowth society.³⁴ Yet, most of these proposals are unconnected and disorganised. Others, as I have argued are very problematic, like illusory notions of the 'steady state'. Crucially, if those degrowthers who believe in the necessity of state institutions actually succeed in coming to power and implement planned contraction, how would the new government(s) prevent a Great Depression unfolding from falling stock markets, the collapse of private investment, mass unemployment, currency collapse and hyper-inflation? Without any notion of state planning, would degrowth communities and governments 'take up the slack' by somehow dramatically increasing the size of public sector employment, goods production and providing services vacated by or closed down by private businesses? Most degrowthers reject conventional public sectors and assume the 'shared commons' will take care of all essential social needs. The problem with this scenario is that most local communities lack a range of resources. If a planning model is not created, degrowth based on 'planned contraction' would either suffer a still birth or quickly become 'unplanned contraction' with all the negative features of regular capitalist recessions.

Degrowthers support peaceful social change. So, in the absence of co-operation from a majority of businesses, how would conflict be minimised if the lawful or illegal confiscation or appropriation of private land and business resources by local communities need national legislation or the co-operation of police and military and other such national legislative authority? Degrowthers might argue that local non-market solutions will emerge in the form of barter, co-ordinated food production and other co-operative services. It is important to note that in many local and regional settings, these alternative practices would be grossly inadequate to keep a new transitional economy afloat. Unless degrowthers prepared for a combination of national, regional, and local measures — such as strong regulation or nationalisation of corporations (if this is legally possible), controls over capital flows, labour markets and the allocation of resources — then failure is virtually guaranteed. Planning requires preparation and I know of no detailed contingency plans or macro-economic policies conceptualised by radical Greens or ecological economists other than the limited post-growth stock flow models constructed by post-Keynesians such as Tim Jackson and Peter Victor.

Supporters of degrowth seem to assume a benign world as currently their visions say little about how to counter potentially powerful foreign and domestic corporate and political opposition. It is not that they are unaware of the power of military establishments in leading G20 powers. Their social visions do not account for dismantling the vital connection between existing production systems and military and security apparatuses that are closely tied to the incessant logic of capitalist growth. In fairness to degrowthers, this failure to discuss how to deal with military-industrial complexes is common to most social change movements and theorists, including myself.

Those degrowthers who regard national state institutions as necessary, still need to specify how these institutions will interact with local democratic communities and facilitate democratic decision-making at national and regional levels. Without constitutional change, which is itself exceedingly difficult in so many countries, the old political conflict over how much power should be decentralised, centralised, or shared between different tiers of government or local and national communities could continue in new forms. If local power prevails over national government powers or has the power of veto over national decisions – as many degrowthers geared to community grassroots power passionately desire – then it is guaranteed that the larger society will flounder in a series of socio-economic crises caused by inadequate coordination of planned contraction. Conversely, if clear power-sharing and decision-making is not specified, representative democracy at national level will most likely subordinate the political will of local communities or contradict and negate local direct democracy. This old dilemma of the conflict between direct democracy and national state planning faced by earlier generations of socialists has now metamorphized into the new paradigm of 'democracy versus sustainability'.

Very importantly, after forty years, there is still a fundamental lack of clarity about whether there should be a *standard rate of degrowth* for *all* resources, goods and services or a *differentiated* rate of degrowth per annum or per decade based on varied global reserves of vital commodities and the need to achieve specific local, national, or international ecological and social goals. The visions of degrowthers are still divided between those who desire to live in ecologically and socially transformed cities and others who prefer life to be primarily organised in small non-urban local communities.[35] Either way, we need to ask: who would collate and measure the rate of degrowth? Would it be a national bureau of statistics, or supranational, national, or regional planning bodies, or would it be tens of thousands of informal local communities and neighbourhoods collating statistics or 'guesstimating' their annual extraction and consumption of resources? Without adequate information and knowledge of what is happening outside the locality, no informed democratic decision making is possible.

Trusting fellow local communards and strangers in tens of thousands of other 'commons' to not excessively indulge in consumption at the expense of those adhering to shared objectives of frugality is a naïve politics and a recipe for conflict and highly uneven degrowth. A stateless society conceived in this way becomes an absurd dystopian proposal. A bureaucratically-free option is not feasible in complex societies. One can try to minimise the administration of production and distribution but without minimal national statistical and regulatory offices to collate local and regional data on all forms of production, consumption, income and expenditure, loss of biodiversity and numerous other demographic patterns and resource levels, no local population would ever know how to adequately satisfy the needs and shortages within their own city or other cities and local communities. There would be no stored knowledge and data to help prevent dangerous national developments or eradicate inequalities and improve conditions for those suffering neglect, deprivation or overuse of natural resources. Whatever trust in fellow degrowthers might initially exist, would be likely to dissipate once some local communities interpreted 'frugality' in more 'generous' terms or selfish individuals engaged in black markets and criminal activity – an inevitable consequence of either a shortage of goods or a minority of corrupt or selfish people who obstinately refused to share collective values.

Despite being desirable and preferable to alienated labour, relying on volunteerism, self-motivation and co-operation is socially unpredictable. These highly unreliable qualities can alternate from being abundantly available in a crisis, to quickly receding and evaporating just when volunteers and altruistic people are sorely needed to perform mundane daily tasks. No society should solely rely on voluntary behaviour for producing and distributing vital goods and services and maintaining social stability. Active democratic participation has also been shown to be equally fickle. The positive energy and social rewards of co-operative engagement in decision-making are unfortunately not universally appreciated by those members of society who reap the benefits but are reluctant to contribute to sustaining democratic practices.

Alternative visions of the 'good society' have long been dominated by the repeated and uncritical assertion that in contrast to the impersonal, corporate, and bureaucratic character of national and global institutions, the only 'genuine' democracy is local direct democracy. This is because generations of anti-statists, self-management radicals, municipal socialists and now degrowthers claim that only communal participatory democracy enables people to express what kind of community they would like to construct, what social needs should be fulfilled and what kind of relationships with the immediate natural environment and built environment are acceptable and sustainable. These ideals are very important until we begin trying to define 'localist' ideals. Indeed, there is little consensus on what the 'local community' actually means in terms of population size, geographical boundaries, or political institutional structures. Only one thing is clear, namely, that the notion of small communities of no more than a few thousand people is no longer possible in cities with populations of hundreds of thousands and tens of millions of residents. Subdividing these large cities into many local governing units has already produced numerous disputes and inconsistent government over who can have a say over the character, production, and delivery of vital essential services. Think of the megacities across the world characterised by large internal migration from rural areas, and divisions between slum areas and luxury residential areas

In addition to these confusing claims over what constitutes the 'local' is the adoption by many degrowthers living in OECD developed capitalist countries of a set of assumptions about 'folk' and post-colonial knowledge. It is true that we have much to learn from locally based, indigenous practices of how to regenerate and respect the natural world or adopt more appropriate levels and scale of socio-economic activity rather than incessant speed, maximum capitalist productivity and return on investment. However, not all Western knowledge (including the very idea of degrowth itself!) favours high-tech solutions driven by corporations and governments. Conversely, it is important for degrowthers not to succumb to mystical notions that Indigenous peoples, rural women and men practising natural remedies or pre-capitalist communal forms of knowledge somehow have the answers to how to look after the land or create harmonious social relationships.[36] Little is said by uncritical devotees of so-called 'non-Eurocentric' knowledge about extensive forms of superstition, intolerant religious practices and medical 'cures' that are far from benign, harmonious or innovative. Most people (including many supporting degrowth) would not like to go back to a low-tech world without advanced medical and scientific equipment (used for peaceful purposes) and just rely on simple 'convivial tools'.

Any transition from market individualism to communal sharing will require the capacity to democratically enforce the planned contraction of material resources. Without such enforcement of appropriate state rules and regulations beyond the 'local', how would those enterprises providing resources, goods, and services not available at local neighbourhood or community level actually be required to conform to nationally and democratically agreed rates of degrowth? It is utterly naïve to believe that crime, corruption, irresponsible behaviour, incompetence, and preferential treatment will all suddenly disappear or not re-emerge. It is to be hoped that the vast majority of people will be imbued with a new cooperative spirit and ethic of care. But no society can embark on significant social and environmental transformation and assume that all people will share these values and behave accordingly, especially within the context of ongoing scarcity of resources.

Within degrowth movements there are those who fully recognise, yet simultaneously play down the fact that we live in a world of violent regimes with anti-democratic repressive state apparatuses, numerous neo-fascist and other authoritarian and violent movements and deep-seated fundamentalist religious movements intolerant of secular cultural practices. And that is only a brief list of opponents of equality and sustainability! Like some other radical theories, degrowth lacks any practical organisational anchors or institutional possibility of success outside the micro-local. Hence, if post-growth societies do emerge, they will almost certainly develop from within situations of political polarisation and conflict where a clear majority will, for a range of reasons, voluntarily choose to adopt degrowth policies strongly disliked by minorities. A socially sustainable political system cannot avoid the unpleasant topic of how the new society will protect its members and prevent opponents from weakening and destroying its new institutions and social relations. Few advocating degrowth pay sufficient attention to what kind of alternatives to current criminal justice systems are necessary or viable.

The widespread assumption about the superior benefits of direct face-to-face democracy is also only partly valid given this mode of decision making is far from suitable for all aspects of socio-economic life. For example, urban planning could definitely benefit from the enormous input of democratic participation that could help plan neighbourhood needs and overcome the inequality and neglect of existing urban infrastructure policies. However, the delivery of city-wide transport, housing, health, energy, and cultural facilities (especially in cities with populations ranging from twenty thousand to thirty million) needs coordination to ensure accessibility based on equal rights to resources and services. Large population centres need to also minimise waste of environmental and fiscal resources by eliminating duplication, better managing scarce resources and maximising service delivery to those sections and areas of cities currently neglected. Participatory budgeting and other such engagement of local citizens is merely a vitally needed first step rather than a solution. However, this form of increased democratisation and consultation requires vital financial and material resources, as well as experts and citizens with knowledge beyond the 'local' (however narrowly or broadly this is defined). Once this is recognised, we unavoidably enter the world of national politics with large political parties campaigning on the appropriate political economy needed to boost and sustain local communities, cities, and regions. The 'local' now becomes enmeshed in the shape and direction of the national and the international.

Evaluating broader political philosophical issues such as whether we need governments, the possibility of ending all political alienation and why a totally self-transparent organisation of society (at local or national level) is either utopian or potentially dangerous, social theorist, Slavoj Žižek, cuts through a range of illusions and false hopes when he pointedly observes:

> It is no wonder that today's practices of 'direct democracy', from favelas to the 'postindustrial' digital culture ...all have to rely on a state apparatus – i.e., their survival relies on a thick texture of 'alienated' institutional mechanisms: where do electricity and water come from? Who guarantees the rule of law? To whom do we turn for healthcare? Etc., etc. The more a community is self-ruling, the more this network has to function smoothly and invisibly. Maybe we should change the goal of emancipatory struggles from overcoming alienation to enforcing the right kind of alienation: how to achieve a smooth functioning of 'alienated' (invisible) social mechanisms that sustain the space of 'non-alienated' communities?[37]

Just as currently it is mainly women who perform the 'invisible' domestic labour that keeps households functioning, so too, local communities would encounter numerous dysfunctions and collapse of activity if non-local networks of extraction, agriculture, goods production, distribution, revenue collection and delivery of social services were interrupted or ceased. One only has to remember the scenes of empty supermarket shelves when a combination of interrupted supply chains and panic buying of toilet paper and food affected cities during the COVID-19 pandemic. In short, all advocates of either direct democracy or representative democracy cannot afford to base their political strategies on the illusions of a future totally unalienated politics or on the myth of the autonomy or sovereign power of the 'local people' in future post-capitalist societies.

We need neither the undemocratic practices of highly centralised societies with super states nor the illusions that local communities could or should fully control their decentralised, local democracies. The complexity and interdependence of contemporary societies means that even under favourable conditions, local communities could only ever have democratic control over a limited choice of everyday needs and how they are organised, produced, and consumed. There is little prospect that existing countries or nation states would break up or that voters and citizens would permit the implementation of a totally different national constitution that enabled local democracies to disengage from the laws and regulations applicable to the rest of the national or regional society.

As many degrowthers and advocates of direct democracy are aware, politics is not just local community engagement. Politics will inevitably be conflictual, based on competing parties or movements rather than 'good news' harmony and cooperation. Grassroots action goes nowhere without the larger mobilisation of people which in itself requires national and supranational organisations. At this point in time, degrowthers veer between either rejecting national organisations or failing to specify how local democracy is to be linked to larger political, economic, and social institutions. Hence, notions of direct self-management remain attractive at the level of utopian imagery with little or no detail about how they are practically relevant to actual contemporary political struggles. It is one thing to propose radical changes that enhance greater decision-making for all workplaces, and quite another to go to the next step and think that whole cities can be independent local democracies capable of being self-sufficient and at odds with the decisions and needs of the rest of the larger society and world. It is in this sense that autonomy is not always compatible with democracy.

Convivial Tools, Small-Scale Production, and Urban Realities

Advocates of degrowth pay lip service to the need for comprehensive public institutions and services and instead focus heavily on the direct democracy aspect of the local commons. Hence, admirable principles such as 'sufficiency rather than excess' do not in themselves tell us much about the ability of small local co-operatives to satisfy specific large urban infrastructure needs. This is also the case with food production, vitally needed medicines and health care, the availability of non-carcinogenic natural or renewable building materials, household goods, machinery and communications technology or a multitude of other financial and techno-logical resources beyond the 'local'. All too frequently the uncritical assumption that 'small is beautiful' is the default position of many degrowthers. We are reminded of the dangers of this assumption by an example from China. The policy of every rural commune having its own backyard steel furnace during Mao's Great Leap Forward between 1958 and 1962, proved to be a human, ecological and economic disaster as peasants were diverted from agriculture to produce inferior quality steel. Mass hunger ensued, industrial production went backwards, and everyday life was made extremely difficult. While the degrowth movement is certainly not advocating Maoist dictatorial policies, valuable lessons can be learnt about the counterproductive consequences when any political movement pursues either too much decentralisation or too much central-isation.

In a world where a minority of giant enterprises employ tens and hundreds of thousands of workers while millions of businesses are small and medium enterprises, there is no clarity over what 'small local artisan co-operatives' might mean. Does it mean co-operative enterprises of 10 to 100 workers, 500 to 2000 workers, or larger or smaller enterprises? Will there be upper limits on the size of enterprises and what will be the approximate or maximum size of a local community? Will planned contrac-tion only apply to large corporations or to the vast majority of small busi-nesses and worker co-operatives?

Although I support the view that active local communities are much more knowledgeable about their needs as opposed to the imposition of policies by distant and impersonal government agencies, this is not equiva-lent to local communities having the capacity to become economically and socially autonomous. We know that the ability of local communities to raise and coordinate scarce material and human inputs in order to realise locally expressed desires is both extremely uneven and limited without national or supranational revenue raising, adequate research funding and the development of alternative technologies beyond the very small-scale 'convivial tools' idealised by degrowthers. Sustainability should not be auto-matically equated with either small or big enterprises. Rather the complex objective of how to maximise the viability of diverse habitats should be considered on the basis of what most effectively makes possible the values of care, democracy, and the universal satisfaction of essential needs.

Advocates of radical decentralisation in either its stateless or minimal state forms need to come to terms with the reality of urban life in the twenty-first century. Those supporting direct local democracy make a fetish of the decision-making process and often ignore the inability of communities to be largely self-sufficient. Any contemporary city with a population larger than several thousand people, is not capable of having face-to-face direct democracy unless one puts tens of thousands of people into a football stadium to have pseudo-democratic mass gatherings or one conducts decision-making via elaborate digital communication channels. A degrowth society will therefore still need an elevated level of communications technology which at this point of time, like a range of other non-luxury goods, cannot be made in small artisan co-operatives lacking the scale and capacity of substantial R & D, sophisticated metals and electronics, rare minerals, and a very skilled and specialised workforce. Leaving aside fundamentalists, if other advocates of degrowth do not wish to take us back to simple, pre-capitalist technologies and crafts, then far greater specification is needed about which existing technologies and future research activities are compatible with environmentally sustainable urban life.

The widespread advocacy of craft or small industrial rather than mass production also indicates that there is little agreement over the rate and scale of reducing individual and national material footprints in high-income countries. Some degrowthers concede the need for national or regional factories to produce steel, textiles and so forth. But convincing upwards of nine billion people by 2050 (a majority being urban residents) to rely on small local co-operatives for all their needs and supplies without larger regional, national, or city-wide production and distribution enterprises is ridiculously counterproductive and utopian. Instead of likely widespread shortages due to excessive demand and inadequate productive capacities, we need to urgently develop new conceptions of alternative economic models based on combinations of local, regional, and supranational supply chains. It is necessary to restructure the current economies and infrastructure of urban mega cities and small, mid-size towns so that not millions, but rather billions of people have a realistic chance of enjoying and satisfying sufficient essential needs. This is especially true for people living in the numerous geographical areas of deprivation that are blighted by desertification, mass urban slums or impoverished villages with no running water or electricity.

Billions of people in low- and middle-income countries will only benefit from the greater equalisation of material per capita consumption if their often corrupt and dictatorial governments are overthrown and global resources are not diverted into the wealthy pockets of corporate investors, prevailing oligarchs, and the military. In OECD countries, the voluntary commitment of voters to supporting the reduction of per capita consumption over the next thirty years would require significant trade-offs. If individuals and families could not see a gradual increase in universal basic services in exchange for periodic decreases in consumption of private goods and services, any such political commitment would soon evaporate. Until governments began funding and supporting national and local institutions and communities to provide more universal basic services, no substantial transition presided over by democratic communities is possible.

In previous decades, neo-Marxists and feminists had focussed on the household and family as not something that is separate from 'the economy' but vitally integrated into its function and form. Sociologist Wally Seccombe, for example, analysed how capitalist industrialisation changed the reliance of families on multiple breadwinners so that by the time of the First World War the male breadwinner had become the norm and new gender roles were consolidated. Intricately linked to this were the effects on the family of increasingly centralised manufacture, the introduction of compulsory schooling, the separation of workplaces from the home neighbourhood, the introduction of mass transit and changes in domestic labour brought about by urban housing.[38]

The past sixty years have witnessed the restructuring and reshaping of family life in developed capitalist countries due to feminist struggles and large numbers of women in paid employment, new battles over birth control and child-rearing, access to higher levels of mass education and so forth. While families based on single breadwinners have reverted to two or more income earners per family, what has not changed to the same degree is the separation of workplaces from home neighbourhoods (apart from home office work during COVID-19). Households continue to be integrated into debt and credit financed (financialisation) services and consumption. Supporters of degrowth aim to change this by making the household a site of production and not just consumption. For example, Sam Alexander and Brendan Gleeson wish to bring 'degrowth to the suburbs' by developing several new social practices ranging from food production, energy conservation and changing the car-centred form and function of the city. These are all excellent ideas, but they lack at least one

central feature – the connection between work and income.[39] Until alternative forms of employment and income generating production of goods and
services are outlined, the separation of households and local neighbourhoods from 'the economy' will remain the norm. Suburbs can be turned
into green cities and food producing centres, but this is only the tip of the
urban iceberg and does not account for the multiple production and
consumption roles that will be needed in the future.

Fundamentalist degrowthers in Australia, Europe and North America
not only reject capitalism but also high-tech industrial and post-industrial
society. For example, Ted Trainer and associates grouped around the
Australian movement 'The Simpler Way' accept modern science and
modern health. Yet, they also favour a society where the scale of manufacture and building would be enormously reduced and there would be little
need for heavy machinery. Most roads and freeways would be torn up and
converted into gardens, parks and food producing plots. Hence, according
to Trainer, "very few if any big bridges, skyscrapers, tunnels, silos, roads,
freeways, aircraft and airports, big trucks, cars, ships, ports, cranes, mines,
warehouses, forklifts and bulldozers" would need to be produced.[40] There
would be very little international trade and given that most roads would be
torn up, it is entirely unclear how people could even get around on their
bicycles or have goods delivered from so-called small 'regional' factories
within a 5 to 10 kilometre radius (that is only a fraction of the size of many
cities which are hundreds of square kilometres in area) and certainly not
what is commonly defined as a 'regional' geographical zone in most
countries.

Degrowthers such as Ted Trainer also criticise others in the degrowth
movement for failing to recognise that material resources consumption will
have to be cut by 90% in high-income capitalist countries to make for an
equitable world living within sustainable boundaries. This he declares, will
mean that all present industries must be shut down. "How then" Trainer
asks, "could large numbers of workers possibly be taken out of factories,
offices and mines ... to do what? They can't be transferred to other kinds of
jobs in the existing economy since the point is to dramatically eliminate
that economy's volume of jobs and production and GDP. What is to be
done with entire towns and regional economies ... Could such changes be
got through other than by extremely authoritarian governments? But how
would such governments with such policies come to power in the first
place; certainly not through election by publics which at present would
regard the notion of Degrowth as absurd."[41]

Sadly, Trainer's solution is equally untenable and politically absurd in its requirement that the global population needs to live in small, mainly self-sufficient communities. As such alternatives are rejected by the vast majority of people, Trainer envisages future crises leading to a Depression which, he hopes, will lead people to recognise that their only hope lies in building self-sufficient, simplicity communities. In other words, fundamentalist degrowthers have no politics other than catastrophism from which the phoenix of sustainable living will miraculously arise.

Others such as Joshua Lockyer[42] and Timothée Parrique are typical of those who also favour societies geared to simple rural or urban existence, where food and craft production is the dominant form. This concept of degrowth is essentially based on a semi-deindustrialised society where cities are de-modernised from their capitalist property-industrial complex forms, and populations adopt lifestyles that aim for greater household self-sufficiency and various aspects of modern urban contemporary culture. They would work two days a week making money and the rest of the week tending to their food plots, making hardy clothes and crafts with mostly hand tools and recycled materials or get other provisions from small co-operatives. With a universal basic income, community labour would be voluntary and care services would be provided by the community rather than publicly funded child-care, aged care and so forth. Instead of corporate 'culture industries' that are driven by the dollar, local artists, writers, and creators will entertain the populace with many performances, festivals and gatherings.

There are many compelling aspects of this idea of degrowth communities creating and satisfying their own needs. If the worst aspects of mindless consumerism, financially driven property development tied to polluting car-centred cities, plus ecologically unsustainable agribusiness and the destructiveness of military-industrial complexes could be eliminated, it would be a much better world for humans and all other species. However, most of the latter features of contemporary capitalism can be combatted without the need to revert to extremely austere or frugal forms of daily life. Leaving aside the problem of funding a universal basic income without revenue derived from capitalist markets that are supposed to be *degrowing* or cease operating, only a certain proportion of people will be drawn to a life where their current paid work time is reduced to two days, but they will have to perform an additional three to five days of labour devoted to growing food, making essential clothing and homewares. Getting chickens to produce eggs more sustainably[43] or other such innovations mainly preoccupied with food production and crafts are all useful. Yet, the emphasis by degrowthers' on these limited activities will not satisfy those who long for an enriched and diverse society beyond the 'realm of necessity' dominated by either endless paid work or unpaid domestic labour.

Outlawing large publicly owned or co-operatively run enterprises is illogical if most people in big cities or neglected rural regions go without simply because of the extremely limited output capacity of small co-ops. Scarce *essential* non-luxury goods will inevitably foster a roaring black market, corruption, and political disaffection. Remember the historical lesson that hundreds of millions of people in Communist countries were desperate for some consumer choice after decades of drab, minimal offerings inflicted on populations. While we need to cut down the approximately 25 kilograms of clothing that affluent individuals discard each year, consumables (clothing and household goods) are not the main drain on resources and only account for 7 per cent of total global material resources used.[44] There is therefore sufficient sustainable resources to enable greater diversity of clothing and household goods rather than just home-made hardy clothes and crafts.

The future should therefore not be a choice between two extremes: frugal self-sufficiency or rampant and destructive consumerism. It should also not be a choice between either global entertainment corporations or local entertainment that closes the door to international arts and cultural exchanges. One needs limited international transport, or communications technology, international scientific co-operation, and cosmopolitan values if parochial, narrow minded localism and nationalism are not to snuff out tolerance and open-mindedness. Internationalism requires a certain level of material infrastructure in the form of mining, manufacturing, technology, transport, and communication equipment. Even 'convivial tools' need to be made from mined materials or logged timber resources that have to be transported and manufactured. While degrowthers attack racism and oppose all sorts of prejudice, these prejudices do not grow on trees but rather require particular social conditions to flourish. There is more than a strong risk that by advocating much greater local self-sufficiency and dramatically reduced international cultural exchanges and global perspectives (as opposed to global capitalist markets) that parochialism and prejudice will eventually triumph despite the best intentions of degrowthers'.

Crucially, degrowth as a movement is doomed to failure if it can only offer 'voluntary frugality' as an answer to capitalist unsustainability. Instead, degrowth must be based on the specific size, scale and character of diverse populations and political constituencies in particular countries so that the concept of direct participatory democracy enhances social wellbeing for large populations rather than clinging to fanciful notions of small self-sufficient communities. It is true that there are many creative and necessary forms of decentralised production and delivery of services compared to both existing bureaucratic administration and multinational or medium-sized businesses alike. The degrowth movement would be more convincing if it moved beyond holding ideologically pure conceptions of a simple economy based primarily on small artisan co-operatives and self-made necessities.

The Dangers of 'Funny Money'

It is common for critics of finance capitalism to propose alternative concepts of money to end the commodification of labour and essential products and services as well as facilitate democratic social exchange and decision making. Degrowthers are divided over whether a future society could be moneyless or even have alternative currencies as the primary currency. Many advocates of self-sufficient communities and local control have long favoured various forms of alternative 'money' ranging from barter/exchange schemes such as Local Exchange Trading Scheme (LETS) to local currencies based on non-commodified time-sharing and other criteria that treat labour input as equal.[45] However, good intentions can have unintended negative consequences if inadequate consideration is given to the expansion of local 'currencies' to embrace whole societies. Kristofer Dittmer has already shown the failure of local currencies and barter in Venezuela and Argentina to achieve their objectives and also the failure to enhance degrowth policies even with the support of the Chavez government.[46] Several other complications and barriers arise from schemes that attempt to demonetise and 're-localise' money.

Firstly, it becomes extremely difficult to obtain goods and services from non-local sources if the 'currency' is unacceptable nationally and internationally. For a national or local currency to be convertible it must have an intrinsic value beyond its borders or be pegged to existing currencies such as the American dollar or Euro.

Secondly, local currencies are extremely limited in that they can facilitate the exchange of simple services such as body massage, bicycle repair, cleaning, child-minding and so forth. These peripheral services or simple goods fail to substitute for the thousands of other forms of economic activity and income or the payment of goods using national currencies. The needs of people living outside the 'local currency' area will be denied if they are not eligible to participate in the local network.

Thirdly, alternative 'currencies' can actually be a barrier to the transition to a post-capitalist society because they force people to make a choice of either accepting the rules and embodied labour value of the 'local currency' or continue adhering to their legal national currency or supranational currency (Euro). Currently, international trade is facilitated by reserve currencies (the American dollar) and directly or indirectly pegged to this national but globally used currency. Local currencies are incapable of replacing national currencies in a world where many countries may either not be governed by degrowth principles or where the exchange of goods and services is impossible especially if there is no way for a local community to purchase vitally needed resources from a country that refuses to accept 'funny money'.

Fourthly, millions of people are paid national pensions and state benefits and will be extremely reluctant to abandon these for insecure local alternatives. The same is true of the larger population geared to existing forms of central government legal tender or fiat money. If two parallel currencies co-exist (for example, LETS and existing national currencies) then the national currency will always be dominant. Regardless of one's position in regard to a universal basic income, this option would be impossible without a national uniform currency and the monetised taxation revenue necessary to fund this basic income. Degrowth proponents such as Parrique take the straightforward way out by envisioning alternative currencies operating at community level while national state taxation, monetary and financial institutions remain in place in 'phase one' of any transition to degrowth. The question is: how can future transitional stages to degrowth function *after* 'phase one' if the same problems continue to arise without national currencies or national and supranational fiscal institutions? Degrowthers unrealistically assume that in 'phase two', national pensions, state benefit payments and welfare services will be drastically reduced as local communities will either provide these directly to those in need via actual material forms (housing, food, care services) or via vouchers, tokens, or other local currencies.

While local provision can certainly be increased, it would be an illusion to think that all communities will be sufficiently well endowed to not require substantial assistance from national or other institutional sources. Some degrowthers dismiss the notion of 'scarcity' as a myth and argue that in a society (rather than a world) of equals, there will be sufficient for all. Ironically, this contradicts the fundamental reason why degrowth is needed in the first place. Scarcity is either the outcome of involuntary political policies based on institutionalised inequality, or global scarcity is real and hence affluent people in OECD countries will need to reduce their use of material resources by between 25% and 90% – as degrowthers themselves argue. Hence, either scarcity is real and cannot be overcome politically and technocratically (hence the need for degrowth), or we can aim to raise all the world's population to 'fully automated luxury communism' as the technological utopians proclaim.

Fifthly, it was Friedrich Hayek who proposed ending state or fiat money and permitting any institution to issue their own currency. Market competition would determine the value of each currency.[47] This is an extreme form of marketisation (also evident in various bitcoin schemes) and as such, the opposite of social solidarity. Recently, we have seen the rise of utopian blockchain theories that put forward anti-statist notions of 'fully automated blockchain communism' or 'cryptocommunism' and other such fanciful ideas.[48] Implicitly and explicitly the benefit of decentralised currencies that bypass banks and government-issued money is far outweighed by their negative function that monetises all social relations based on contracts. Apart from the environmentally destructive use of energy, bitcoin currencies embody and operate as exchange-value by either being tied to the established value of national government currencies such as the American dollar or calculating all social purchases and contracts according to the particular price or value of labour. This leads to the commodification of every social relation, cultural creation, and human activity – a process that does not concern libertarian or Right-wing anti-statist free-marketeers but should definitely worry all advocates of a decommodified, caring, egalitarian society.

Most supporters of degrowth oppose Hayekian market competition and the commodification of labour. However, they fail to consider the dangers of using multiple currencies that operate as de facto local market currencies (legal tender used by local co-operatives and other production units). What sounds like a persuasive radical alternative on the face of it, actually undermines solidarity and connectiveness at regional, national, and international levels. If the local currency is like a voucher issued by the commons and cannot be traded outside a self-sufficient tight-knit community then without an exchangeable nation-wide government currency people will inevitably confront either bleak or happy futures depending on their scarce or adequate local material resources. On the other hand, if the local currency assumes the de facto role of existing money and can be traded externally, then without non-local government regulation and assistance, most of the problems of inequality will creep back in just like in previous and current market-based currency systems.

Sixthly, many of the proposals for alternative demonetised 'currencies' are utopian schemes for the so-called ready-finished, future decentralised society. Yet, they are entirely inappropriate and counterproductive when trying to implement degrowth transitional strategies within the context of existing capitalist societies. The notion of 'local' currency depends on having a geopolitical conception of the 'boundaries' and size of the 'local'. Will it be a few thousand individuals or one to thirty million residents of a local city? These parameters are crucial to identify as there are many contemporary cities with populations much larger than small countries such as Denmark, Lebanon, or El Salvador. No viable alternative society will emerge if new local currencies are unable to show how a transitional strategy is possible that enables these 'local' demonetised 'currencies' to replace existing national and supranational government-backed currencies. Planned degrowth requires the voluntary and co-operative action of the majority of the population. However, this co-operation may either not be forthcoming or would quickly collapse if the implementation of 'funny money' leads to major shortages, chaos, and disorder due to the poorly thought-through consequences of a monetary system that fails to meet the national needs of millions of people.

As we are not living in the era of city states or medieval barter, it is imperative that any alternative monetary system is able to function in both domestic and international settings. To think that all trade and international exchanges will cease is to regress to a bleak, autarkic and isolated future. A society based on degrowth will still require national and supranational tax structures, fiscal policies, and the allocation of resources beyond the local level. These fiscal and monetary systems will hopefully be designed in quite a different manner to existing capitalist practices of financialisation in order to help minimise environmental damage, overcome glaring inequalities and maximise social justice.

The tension of 'democracy versus sustainability' also manifests itself at the level of symbolic monetary and regulatory processes. Current degrowth proposals lack a more systemic conception of how an alternative degrowth political economy will de-financialise the worst aspects of capitalism and yet also create viable monetary and fiscal processes. Instead, it is almost guaranteed that many of the half-baked, alternative 'mickey mouse' or exploitative currency proposals will end up being social and political disasters that will lead to widespread democratic opposition. As mentioned, far too many radical proposals are situated in a political vacuum. There is no shortage of wish-lists and elaborate flow charts and diagrams without adequate consideration that these idealised models can be undermined in a blink of the eye by the actual political economic struggles that shape transitional strategies.

Monetary systems, like so many other aspects of production and administration are often 'path dependent' in that historical and existing processes significantly shape what can be reformed or substantially changed. Even previous revolutions that overthrew most existing institutional arrangements could not immediately or entirely free themselves from old practices despite trying to start afresh. Degrowthers supporting demonetised local economies fail to recognise the strong likelihood that these micro-economies will become dysfunctional and will need to be rescued by national governments. The possibility of constructing an alternative to money, like other degrowth proposals, requires much more thought and debate if it is not to descend into chaos and fuel widespread popular mistrust of the other vital degrowth values so central to preventing environmental destruction.

The Mixed Goals of Politics from Below

There has always been a recognition by social change activists of the need for grassroots social movements and especially what happens to large parties when they lose their connection to a politics from below. Most recently, for example, Left writer Owen Hatherley commented on the failure of Corbynism and UK Labour. "It was purely electoral. All of the talk we did about being a social movement meant nothing, and was nothing. We did nothing... There was no depth to it."[49] The past two decades have witnessed a revival of anti-statist politics under the banner of the 'commons', federations of quasi-anarchist, post-capitalist and other technological utopian solutions and strategies.[50] Degrowth movements share radical Left notions of the 'commons' but do not critique capitalism from a traditional 'workerist' or class perspective. In fact, degrowth advocates reject forming national parties and believe that social change will only come via local grassroots community politics. Ted Trainer, a leading advocate of alternative 'eco-villages', argues that: "The Simpler Way is death for capitalism, but the way we will defeat it is by ignoring it to death, by turning away from it and building those many bits of the alternative that we could easily build right now."[51] This anti-statist strategy is the mirror image of the neoliberal 'trickle down' effect. Both would take between 120 and 200 years to either deliver benefits to the poor (at current rates of 'trickle down') or undermine capitalism if exceedingly small numbers of people opted out of the system. We do not have the luxury of time given the urgency of the climate emergency.

Without a strategy to link grassroots socio-political change to larger national and international strategies, politics from below can become a dead end. As the main form of social change, anti-statist politics from below is either extremely limited or a guaranteed pathway to permanent marginalisation and irrelevance. The ability of 'eco-villages' or other communal alternatives to expand significantly within the suburbs and cities is virtually impossible given the structural barriers/dynamics of everyday urban life controlled by governments and businesses. It is certainly possible for people to minimise conventional consumerism and adopt a limited range of alternative practices. However, few if any urban or rural eco-villages or 'transition towns' can provide sufficient paid employment or finance their own infrastructure and services should their network population grow. Most are not fully self-sufficient in either food, natural resources or income and the provision of health and other social services. They co-exist with dominant capitalist institutions but are politically irrelevant as a threat to the future of capitalism.

Converting cities and households into food producing centres and new cooperative practices needed for sustainable cities are all necessary and excellent ideas.[52] The problem is that the new urban imaginary can only be achieved on a larger scale by political and legal reforms such as instituting legislative changes to convert private property and publicly owned land into green commons. To make a large city sustainable would involve challenging the sacred notion of the ownership and control of private property which is the foundation of capitalism. Degrowthers recognise the need for changes to state policies and legislation but argue that without grassroots action no larger political and cultural changes are possible. The question is: what kind of political economic changes? Certainly not those that affect the vast majority of wage workers and their families who depend on organised action at workplaces and in the electoral system. Local grassroots changes to household consumption and production are fine if you own your own home, but millions do not. Also, many past and present local actions have not produced the desired affects at state level. Indeed, the historical record shows that is possible to have solar panels on the roofs of most homes, greater production of food in backyards and converted community plots and still have the key political institutions and most forms of production, distribution, digital communication, and control of the military apparatuses of capitalism untouched.

Crucially, to link all the suburban and urban houses based on degrowth principles requires so much more than simply grassroots activity. Degrowth requires political organisations to legislate or demand specific taxation, social welfare, education, trade, employment, and many other key policies rather than stateless community self-sufficiency movements. Without broad based political movements there will be no transition to a society that reduces material footprints. Progressive social change is not an either/or choice between top-down or bottom-up strategies. Both are urgently required.

The strategy of over-emphasising 'politics from below' means that the scale and complexity of 'planned degrowth' is unattainable and obscure if left in the hands of decentralised and fragmented households and communities. Such change needs the democratic support of the majority of people who, as residents, voters, workers, or consumers, may not embrace frugal lifestyles and instead wait for governments to reduce material throughput at larger industry levels. This in turn will not eventuate unless parties push forward these agendas both outside and inside government. The cycle of making changes through the political, economic, and legal systems means that in order to change institutional practices (without revolution) you need access to institutional power. This will be impossible if movements decide to ignore conventional political participation. Apart from defensive actions such as preventing unpopular policies, nothing much gets changed on 'the street' unless grassroots campaigns force mainstream parties to adopt social reforms. Even the mass protests and riots in various countries against austerity measures or higher taxes have failed to deliver positive requisite changes when governments are tossed out of office or merely withdraw their unpopular policies. So long as new policies are not developed and implemented by supporters of alternative movements, then governments from France to Chile merely make cosmetic changes or withdraw the most objectionable parts of their proposed legislation to keep 'business as usual' running unchecked.

Crucially, disengaging from politics never changed any political system. Degrowthers that disengage from opposing conventional institutions and practices via the micro-change processes of building alternative community and household production/consumption are today's 'dropouts'. According to sociologists Ingolfur Blühdorn, Felix Butzlaff, Michael Deflorian and Daniel Hausknost, despite the degrowth movement advocating communal solutions, paradoxically, its rejection of national political movements reinforces a retreat to depoliticised market individualism.

> As the degrowth movement has no well-developed concept of power but seems to champion the deliberate absence of power, it is dependent on individualised, morally motivated action in small groups. It thus has the tendency to happily retreat into private sufficiency and to the field of material practice rather than engaging in political organisation and strategic action. This is consistent with the logic of progressive individualisation and differentiation, and points to the possible absorption and dispersal of the movement as just another private lifestyle choice within the neoliberal universe.[53]

Until degrowthers in each country, region, and locality outline how 'planned degrowth' and the delivery of crucial services and employment will be designed for not dozens, hundreds, or thousands of people, but for millions and billions of people currently dependent on income from capitalist growth orientated enterprises and public sector institutions, no meaningful change will occur. Without these concrete proposals, degrowth movements will fail to attract the mass support that they urgently need.

In conclusion, degrowth movements begin from the entirely valid position that capitalist incessant economic growth is not only environmentally unsustainable but is also destructive of valuable social relations that are essential for more humane and caring societies. Unfortunately, these crucial starting points are undermined by ill-conceived alternative socio-economic proposals that are almost entirely circular and have minimal relevance beyond insular degrowth networks. Degrowthers say little or nothing about how to change present work conditions, social welfare benefits or dozens of other crucial aspects of everyday life. All we have are outlines of the utopian communities of the future but no socio-political transitional pathway for the vast majority of the population other than isolated eco-villages. Consequently, degrowthers fail to provide even elementary indications of how to get 'from here to there'. Most mistakenly assume that living alternative prefigurative practices by creating small experimental communities in urban or rural settings will be enough to eventually persuade millions of people to adopt degrowth principles.

It is ironic that for a social movement which is concerned with democracy, that aside from the face-to-face local model, there has been so little attention paid to how to create and sustain new democracies. Combining the goal of environmental sustainability with new democratic practices at the local, national, and international level is the challenge that will increasingly confront not just degrowthers but all social justice and environment movements. I will now proceed to discuss why parties and movements that are critical of capitalist anti-democratic and environmentally unsustainable practices have so far largely failed to transform dominant institutional practices and political debates.

5. SEARCHING FOR A MODE OF POLITICS TO BREAK THE IMPASSE

IT IS a political truism that collective organised action is the essence of politics. Without it there can be no change of institutional relations and policies. If so, what form of collective action can lead to post-carbon democracies? The dominant conflict in most developed capitalist countries is not one of class struggle between socialist parties and the various conservative and liberal parties representing ruling classes. This earlier historical form of class politics is now confined to Latin American countries and some other societies. Instead, the protracted political impasse in North America, Europe, Japan, and Australia is between various pro-market conservatives and Right-wing authoritarians opposing reform-orientated businesses, centre/Left parties, and social groups. This political impasse is itself a consequence of larger domestic and international events and balance of social forces in the current political conjuncture. What we have lived through in most OECD countries during the first two decades of the twenty-first century is the rejection of bi-partisan neoliberalism by both the 'populist Right' and anti-capitalist social movements.

Although the writing is on the wall for the old political and social worlds based on fossil fuels, far more is at stake than just switching to renewable energy. The political impasse is characterised by disputes over how much restructuring and reform is necessary or desirable in key industries and domestic social institutions, as well as the unequal international power relations between developed capitalist countries and low- and middle-income societies. Businesses and policy makers are divided over how to regenerate capitalist growth without triggering wage growth, inflation, increased carbon emissions and even a renewed militant labour movement. Social democratic and labour parties offer few policy alternatives and appear locked into the dominant agenda of increased trade rivalry and the risk of armed conflict or even nuclear war with China. This cannot be ruled out unless the US and allies change tack and recognise the need for global and regional power sharing, whether with China, or in the Middle East or in other contested regions. With no clear alternative national or international visions to prevailing market scenarios, both centre/Right and centre/Left parties will need to be dragged screaming before they accept the need for emergency climate action.

Some would argue that these disputes are not an impasse, but rather the continued expressions of different strategies pursued by members of the hegemonic political bloc. If so, why is it that so many business leaders, pro-market politicians and policy analysts are divided over future policy paths and constantly warn about the disastrous economic, environmental, and socio-political consequences that will arise if modernising reforms are not implemented? As to opponents of capitalism, the enormous threat of the climate emergency and the COVID-19 pandemic simultaneously either stifle or act as catalysts for political action. Yet, the massive obstacles preventing political breakthroughs all contribute to the disillusionment with the hard grind of both electoral politics and building extra-parliamentary movements. Little wonder that radical activists turn to utopian flights of fancy or contemplate notions of rebellion and sabotage. There is also the understandable tendency of political movements to modify or re-use earlier strategies. Unsurprisingly, these reconfigured approaches are often flawed or inadequate when it comes to breaking the political impasse.

While weakened and quiescent organised labour movements no longer worry ruling classes as much, they do fear and show greater concern about what might trigger social protests, riots, and eruptions. In recent years, these flash events – which are the consequence of decades of built-up anger over business exploitation and state neglect, discrimination, and corruption – have been put down by brutal police and military repression in countries from France and Chile through to Egypt and Colombia. Some of these eruptions have been partly influenced by Leftist organisations but in most instances, they have been triggered by seemingly minor changes like increases to public transport fares, for example.

We thus have two different but interrelated types of political deadlocks in contemporary societies. One is an updated version of the old impasse between reformers and radicals about how to change society via parliamentary or non-parliamentary means. Depending on individual countries, this particular impasse can be seen as either a theoretical sideshow involving small Left movements with no power to change anything, or else an important aspect of the much larger political impasse that covers the conflict between different wings of national political cultures including: conservatives, the neo-fascist 'populist' Right, the liberal and social democratic centre, as well as diverse social movements and Left parties critical of dominant social injustices or environmental practices.

Contrasting the Impasse of the 1920s with the Political Impasse of the 2020s

To better understand the diverse aspects of the current impasse, I will compare it with the political impasse of the 1920s. Both seemingly involve struggles between conservatives, liberals, socialists, and fascists, but their changed goals and the relative strength of these political groupings amongst changed social constituencies tell another story. Whereas degrowth movements are disengaged from mainstream politics, I will discuss the various attempts by contemporary Leftists and social movement activists to break the impasse by re-politicising politically disengaged social classes through strategies such as Ecological Leninism, 'Left populist' parties, and other organisational tactics.

In my earlier book *Capitalism versus Democracy?*, I analysed whether the rise of Right-wing 'populist' or neo-fascist movements was a replay of the rise of fascism in the 1920s. Here I aim to focus on some of the distinctive features of the 1920s political impasse compared with present-day crises. The role, significance and meaning of 'democracy' in young parliamentary systems of the 1920s were quite different when compared to contemporary politics. Similarly, the revival of Left strategies – whether Leninist, Gramscian, anarchist or whatever – are equally irrelevant or inadequate when it comes to explaining and resolving the quite unusual character of the political impasse in the current historical conjuncture.

Sadly, many radicals are still trapped in the old relationship between ideas and action. Indeed, the ideas of nineteenth century revolutionary, Louis Augustin Blanqui (who influenced revolutionaries including Lenin) still linger on even though being replaced by new realities. Despite Blanqui insisting "that education is the sole agent of progress"[1], he was the classical proponent of seizing the moment. "A revolution improvises more ideas in one day", Blanqui argued, "than the previous thirty years were able to wrest from the brains of a thousand thinkers."[2] This is undoubtedly true at the level of simple political action on the street. Nonetheless, Blanqui's celebration of action utterly fails when it comes to devising a set of alternative policies in the midst of major crises we confront today. This was shown by a stunned and ill-prepared Left in the financial crisis of 2007-2008 and more recently during the global crisis caused by COVID-19.

Contra Blanqui, the problem is not necessarily just a shortage of strategic ideas or the will for immediate action. Rather, the crucial problem concerns which set of ideas are likely to gain the upper hand and resolve major socio-economic and environmental problems once the so-called masses have either rebelled or wish for an alternative suite of socio-economic policies to lead them out of the crisis. Even when revolutionaries such as Lenin, Gramsci, Trotsky, Mao, and their generation built political organisations, their endless strategic manoeuvres overshadowed any substantial allocation of political energy to devising alternative policies. The disastrous consequences of an almost 'empty policy cupboard' soon revealed itself after 1917 and 1949. Hence, building a post-carbon democracy cannot be done with simple slogans such as Lenin's 'peace, land, bread'. Herein lies part of the new impasse which differs significantly from the impasse of the 1920s. What can we learn from these old conflicts?

Following the Russian revolution of 1917 and the disasters caused by the First World War, the threat of socialist revolution in the midst of profound economic instability, a weak new parliamentary system and polarised cultural conflict all featured prominently in the Weimar Republic, a defeated but key economic and political power in Europe. Political theorist, Bernard Manin, reminds us that representative government is not to be confused with representative democracy. During the eighteenth and nineteenth centuries, the concept of representative government was originally oligarchic or based on the selection of notables to prevent the common people from having a voice.[3] Now the threat of revolution and disorder after the collapse of empires in 1917-18 gave new meaning to both representative and direct democracy. This period also witnessed many political theorists and social commentators preoccupied with 'the masses', 'the crowd' or 'the mob'. Stefan Jonsson vividly describes how in everything from political theory and psychoanalysis right through to social and cultural analyses, there was much discussion of the rational or irrational aspects of 'the masses' and whether they could be mobilised, controlled or influenced for democratic or fascist ends.[4]

Just as many media commentators discuss whether liberal democracy can survive today, the years between 1918 and 1933, saw prominent German and Austrian figures (who were not just anti-socialist theorists) debating whether the mass politics of liberal capitalism could secure bourgeois power inside a parliamentary system. Take for instance, sociologist Max Weber, who helped draft the Weimar constitution. He was particularly concerned about two different threats to the bourgeoisie: firstly, direct democracy in the form of Bolshevik workers' councils which would exclude the bourgeois middle class; and secondly, the growth of bureaucratic technical rationality that would replace family businesses with large bureaucratic corporate organisations aligned with state administrative power.

As we know, Weber was no democrat and regarded the defence of democracy or the 'sovereignty of the people' as 'ideological trash'. When asked by authoritarian General Ludendorff what he meant by democracy (in their famous conversation concerning the new Weimar republic), Weber answered: "In a democracy the people choose a leader in whom they trust. Then the chosen leader says, 'Now shut up and obey me'. People and party are then no longer free to interfere in his business." Ludendorff warmed to Weber's definition and replied: "I could like such democracy."[5] Weber valued parliament not as the embodiment of democratic power but as a technocratic training ground for political leaders to develop 'statecraft' and curb their more charismatic impulses. It was in the party machines, Weber argued, rather than in parliament where 'chieftains' waged battle with each other in the quest for control of the extra-legal apparatus of power.

When it came to defending the market and property owners from socialists during the 1920s, liberals were seriously divided over whether they should first defend democracy or private property. Right-wing liberals such as Ludwig von Mises were quick to praise authoritarian solutions, as long as the free market was restored after the fascists 'dealt' with the 'revolutionary emergency'. Conversely, cultural liberals feared both fascists and communists as threats to social order and tolerance. Conservative Catholic/Nazi legal theorist, Carl Schmitt, was very hostile to both liberalism and parliamentary democracy. He rejected liberalism and parliamentarism as 'government through talking'. Instead, he later helped draft Hitler's legislation that abolished all parties except the Nazi party. Contemporary political theorist, Ellen Kennedy, observes that like Weber and the elite theorists, Schmitt thought 'the masses' were capable of acclamation, but not fit to make decisions. She argues that "the widespread assumption that a power elite matters more than the people in contemporary democracy, is evidence that these remain problems for liberal democracy nearly a century later."[6]

It was former Austrian Finance Minister, Joseph Schumpeter, who also later developed Weber's concerns about bureaucracy and democracy. He reduced democratic participation to the bare minimum of the electorate only making a choice between which competing party elite should rule.[7] Where Schumpeter differed from other conservatives was in his belief that capitalism would ultimately fail due to individual entrepreneurs being replaced by corporations that were unable to drive capitalism through innovation. He also thought that socialism would triumph because the bourgeois class valued education and ideas, and intellectuals were predisposed to supporting socialism. Alas, Schumpeter was wrong about intellectuals who, despite a minority becoming socialists, overwhelmingly supported versions of liberal capitalism. He was equally wrong about corporations which continued to drive innovation. In addition, his analysis between 1919 and 1927 was even more unrealistic in believing that aggressive imperialism was a consequence of atavistic elements in capitalist societies and that a mature capitalism, such as the US, would be most unlikely to engage in imperialist militarism.[8] The history of violent military interventions by the US and allies since 1945 makes a mockery of this assumption about 'mature capitalism'.

Despite their major political differences, what the liberal and authoritarian theorists and policy makers had in common with the radical Left was that they all focussed on the main action outside parliament, whether in struggles between capitalists and workers or the consolidation of power in state bureaucracies and private corporations. Parliament was regarded as merely the representation of classes through their respective parties. The development of one-party states – whether fascist or Communist – simultaneously broke the illusion that parliament represented 'the people' and yet also kept it alive. Indeed, there was no need for Cold War propaganda against Communism or fascism to convince large sections of Western electorates to avoid these authoritarian parties. Ultimately, if capitalism continued to deliver the goods and to enable a personal space of individual freedom without fear of the secret police, any radical truths voiced about class dominance of state institutions could be ignored in developed capitalist societies. Those minorities who critiqued the capitalist state, such as the large post-1945 Communist parties in France and Italy, were never strong enough to be elected in their own right. Following the collapse of the USSR, some Communist parties were dissolved in the early 1990s or progressively withered away to small parties.

The liberal and conservative theorists of the Weimar years remain influential in shaping the relation between democracy and parliament. The earlier fear of the bourgeoisie losing their wealth and power forced them to prefer fascism over liberalism if this meant stopping socialism or Bolshevism. Such a choice had never presented itself in pre-Second World War Anglo-American countries where the Left were too weak to force capitalist classes to abandon conventional conservative and liberal parliamentary parties. The mass strikes by workers during the New Deal were not ever aimed at bringing in socialism and it was only Right-wing propaganda that presented Roosevelt's policies as 'communist'. Today, there are hardly any serious major public debates between the Left and the Right about whether governments should adopt extensive state planning to solve the climate emergency and other major socio-economic problems. Even proponents of Green New Deals who favour substantial increases in social and environmental public expenditure, tip toe around the vital issue of state planning.

Most of the dominant models of socio-political change that prevailed during the twentieth century are now exhausted. The forty-five-year period between the defeat of fascism in 1945 and the collapse of Communism in Eastern Europe (1989-1991) was noteworthy for its transformation of all types of political parties. By the 1960s, the post-war recovery fuelled by consumer production, marketing, and the promise of social mobility to 'middle-class' suburban lifestyles via rapid urbanisation, were all part of the reason for the steady demise of traditional class politics. It is not that parties suddenly lost their former class characteristics. Rather, traditional working-class parties of the Social Democratic or Labour variety, alongside liberal and conservative parties were transformed in the decades after 1945 into what Carl Schmitt's favourite student, the socialist Otto Kirchheimer, later in 1966, called the 'catch-all' parties that competed for cross-class support in the electoral market.[9]

André Krouwe describes Kirchheimer's anxiety about modern democracy in the West as characterised by "the vanishing of principled opposition within parliament and society, and the reduction of politics to the mere management of the state. This leads to collusion of political parties and the state, severing of the societal links of party organisations, and erosion of the classic separation of powers. Vanishing opposition, cartelisation and professionalisation of politics pits citizens against a powerful state, which increases political cynicism and apathy." [10] In other words, de-democratisation occurred well before the rise of what Leftists Perry Anderson and Wolfgang Streeck called the EU 'Hayekian State' – from the Maastricht Treaty of 1992 to the present day.[11] What Kirchheimer diagnosed in the 1960s, while there were still large labour movements and mass opposition to capitalism by a new generation of Left activists in the streets, became far worse by the end of the 1970s and early 1980s.

The rediscovery of liberal market policies formulated in the 1920s and 1930s, and now called neoliberalism, exacerbated the 'managerial' market character of parties. In their innocent or calculated adoption of neoliberal policies to help stimulate stagnant economies in the 1970s and 1980s, Social Democratic and Labour parties lost large numbers of party members, became disconnected from their grassroots bases and were barely distinguishable in their policies from Right-wing parties. All these changes compounded the disillusionment of electorates with all forms of party politics. These parties still had a minority of members who supported socialism or Keynesian social reforms. However, most of the political leaders of mainstream parties used the constraints of having to function in competitive global markets (free trade and lack of capital controls) to defend the inability of national parties to impose new taxes on business to pay for new electoral promises. It was not just central banks that were made 'independent' of government so that they could better serve the interests of corporate capital. The goal of full employment was now abandoned in favour of fighting inflation and keeping interest rates low. Similarly, in recent decades many parties lowered voter expectations and adopted organisational practices to free the parliamentary representatives of these parties from being controlled by or dependent on sectional interests (especially trade unions) within their respective political bases. It was the cumulative socio-economic problems leading to the Great Financial Crisis of 2008 that produced an internal crisis in centre/Left and centre/Right parties.

The transition from 'catch-all' to 'cartel parties' was also the attempt by large mainstream parties in OECD countries to control the electoral space by limiting or excluding new parties from gaining a strong foothold. This 'cartelisation', like business cartels, used legal and illegal methods of electoral laws (voter registration, electoral boundaries, campaign finance) to consolidate the 'cartel' and make life difficult for small parties and independents. In the US, the suppression of black and Hispanic voters remains a favourite tactic of white racist legislators.

Paradoxically, the dissolution of Left-wing strength in various countries during the last decades of the twentieth century occurred at the very same time that capitalist societies began failing to deliver the goods for an increasingly substantial number of people. Propped up by rising household indebtedness due to stagnant wages and precarious or scarce employment, conservative governments could no longer blame the climate emergency and government austerity measures (following the economic crisis of 2008) on non-existent Bolsheviks or non-existent militant workers. Instead, neoliberalism has been weakened through its own failed policy endeavours, even though it survives in hybrid form in various countries.

Despite the brief momentary growth of the Left within large mainstream parties (notably, Corbynism in UK Labour), the broad Left remains weakened and marginalised. In some Latin American countries such as Bolivia and Peru, there has been a renewed 'pink tide' after the ousting of earlier 'pink tide' governments. However, *none* of the G20 largest capitalist countries – whether Canada, Germany, France, India, Indonesia, Italy, Japan, South Korea, Mexico or the UK and US – have a radical Left or Green party strong enough to get elected on its own. Of the other G20 countries, China, Russia, Saudi Arabia, and Turkey are too authoritarian to permit a free contest, and the Australian Labor Party or Argentina's Peronist Justicialist Party and Brazil's Worker's Party are at present, either too conservative or tainted by corruption to offer real alternative policies, even if they succeed electorally. Most conventional centre/Left parties remain averse to or hesitant about fighting for socio-economic and environmental policies that move societies in the direction of becoming more sustainable and equitable post-carbon democracies. This is particularly true of parties such as the Australian Labor Party that continues to support fossil fuels.

Today, the political impasse differs from the impasse of the 1920s in that it is no longer a conflict in most G20 countries between strong socialist or communist parties, weak liberal/centrist governments and rising fascist movements. Socialist movements have been effectively sidelined but retain a minority presence in the form of either traditional labour movements or newer cultural identity and eco-socialist movements. Current conflicts between parliamentary liberals and conservatives on the one side and Right-wing nationalists and racists on the other are essentially about the future character of capitalist societies rather than about post-capitalism. Some centrist liberal-Left and Green parties defend cosmopolitan cultural policies and ecological modernisation against fluctuating informal political alliances consisting of fossil fuel interests, racist ethno-nationalists, and cultural conservatives. However, they are either quite conservative or cautious when it comes to issues of social and economic equality in workplaces or supporting greater social expenditure.

Since the 1980s, the political battlelines have been increasingly redrawn between various exponents of global marketisation on the one side and a range of nationalists, including Right-wing ethno-nationalists, Left post-Keynesian nationalists and anti-market Green proponents of national 'steady state' societies on the other side. It could be argued that we now have four competing political blocs:

- Neoliberal marketeers of the centre/Right and centre/Left promoting global financialisation, high tech innovation and ecological modernisation.
- Anti-globalisation nationalists of the far Right and assorted cultural and economic conservatives.
- Cultural liberals and Keynesian Left social democrats who defend national social welfare institutions, the public sector and local businesses and their employees against multinational corporations but also oppose the free movement of refugees and immigrants.
- Various Left internationalists, anti-discriminatory cosmopolitans, and those internationalist wings of social justice and environmentalist movements sympathetic to action on issues such as global inequality, anti-militarism, and the climate emergency.

The relative strength of these blocs is partly determined by specific electoral voting systems. In both the UK and US, the main parties are able to win majorities in legislatures without polling a majority of votes. In countries such as France or Italy, there is no dominant political bloc as both traditional Left and Right parties have dissolved or been replaced by new socio-political realignments featuring either technocratic stop-gap government (Italy) or in the case of Macron, hybrid neoliberal/authoritarian practices.[12]

Until now, the main conflict in many countries has been between the heterogeneous blocs of market globalisers and assorted nationalists. Two decades of muddle-through policies have resolved none of the major political, economic, or environmental crises. On the contrary, the more that the climate emergency and stagnant/low-growth economies fail to absorb the unemployed and underemployed while requiring major restructuring of environmentally unsustainable industry sectors, the more likely that existing political blocs will fragment even further.

We are now entering a period of increased uncertainty and danger with the possibility of a break-through in a few countries of a realigned conservative/neo-fascist bloc. Should such Right-wing blocs succeed (or remain in office such as in Brazil, Hungary and Turkey), they are likely to retain formal parliamentary systems but suppress various opposition forces through discriminatory electoral system changes, more use of police and cuts to liberal cultural institutions (education, public broadcasting). The goal will be to simultaneously appease ethno-nationalist cultural warriors and a desperate attempt to prevent a raft of economic and social pressures, as well as hoping major climatic events do not lead to demands for greater government action. Conversely, the prolonged political impasse could be broken by the election of a genuinely socio-environmental reform government consisting of a coalition of parties with a compromised electoral pact. This new coalition or 'social bloc' could also be brought into being by extraordinary climate events or as a response to deteriorating socio-economic conditions combined with fear of potential neo-fascist governments taking power.

Just as the 1930s did not see fascism come to power in most leading capitalist countries, so too, it is currently difficult to see either a neo-fascist or a radical socio-environmental government emerging in most countries. Instead, the 2020s will most likely be characterised by hybrid governments combining neoliberal and post-Keynesian policies in the form of post-COVID stimulus packages of the Biden or EU Green Deal variety. Authoritarian governments will continue to hold power in some countries but will come under severe pressure to implement decarbonisation strategies if they wish to modernise production and avoid trade barriers. The real test for G20 countries will come a few years down the track when these stimulus packages prove to be inadequate and conservative forces attempt to reassert austerity measures. Unless there is a remarkable change in electoral and social movement support, it is unlikely that a Left/Green/liberal social democratic 'social bloc' in most major G20 countries will be strong enough to break the impasse in the coming decade.

Underpinning the loosening of traditional voting patterns in many OECD countries has been the direct and indirect impact of financialisation. Much has been written about elevated levels of indebtedness and the power of the finance sector on national socio-economic policies due to the removal of regulation and controls over international capital flows. At the level of work and family life, financialisation has also led to significant changes over the past four decades. Take for instance, housing, which is so important. In the midst of homelessness, high rents, and the inability of younger people to enter over-inflated housing markets in affluent countries, obtaining a family home is no longer seen by many as the old desire for life-time stability. Economist, Hyman Minsky, analysed the debt-fuelled capi-talism of recent decades based on acquiring and managing liquid assets. Using Minsky, political economists Lisa Adkins, Melinda Cooper and Martijn Konings provide an insightful analysis of the shift from the Keyne-sian concept of housing to the 'Minskyan household' which has affected not only housing but also created new social divisions. Whether upscaling one's home to something larger and better or downsizing in order to use the surplus income from the home sale for retirement purposes or to help chil-dren acquire their own asset, the former permanent family home in the traditional pre-neoliberal era has now become a central feature of the 'asset economy'.[13]

The larger repercussions of the 'asset economy' or financialisation, flow through to new inequalities within wage-earning classes and between employed asset owners and the unemployed, underemployed and those dependent on state social benefits. In a climate of stagnant wage growth, the increased hostility by former working-class voters to Labour or Social Democratic parties is partly connected to a dislike of policies that jeopar-dise the liquid asset value of the home through higher taxes, interest rates and so forth. Former employed workers who become self-employed contractors and consultants are particularly geared to acquiring and increasing the value of property assets due to their insecure futures and lack of employer and state pension contribution schemes.

Despite their valuable analysis, Adkins, Cooper and Konings do not develop the implications of the 'asset economy' on social change strategies such as forming new political blocs or alliances. They also say nothing about the relationship between homes as liquid assets and the crucial issue of the environmental impact of these shifts. In 2017, it was estimated that global real estate was worth $US217 trillion (of which approximately 75 percent was housing) or 60 per cent of the world's assets.[14] As discussed in Chapter Three, the land use and construction sector (LULUBCF) is one of the largest users of material resources. We desperately need national and

international policies to restrict property development, prevent desertification, deforestation and the destruction of natural 'sinks' for carbon emissions. Existing 'asset economy' practices cannot continue in their
quantitative and qualitative fashion once pressures mount to curb the
disastrous consequences of endless new land grabs on outer urban fringes
that are currently forested or used as food producing land.

Proponents of degrowth, Alex Baumann, Samuel Alexander and Peter
Burdon are also caught in a housing dilemma. They recognise that
constructing prefigurative alternative social practices within a market
society is not possible for people who lack their own homes and suburban
land for collective food production and are forced to work in environmentally unsustainable jobs just in order to obtain income to pay off their home
mortgages. Their proposal to break this vicious cycle is for governments to
initially fund public housing on urban land and enable the unemployed and
low-income people to gain access to the material conditions facilitating the
creation of alternative neighbourhoods in exchange for 15 hours labour or
participation income per week.[15] While in principle this idea is very positive, the scale of any such provision of land and public housing would be
very small, as it would quickly come into conflict with both the 'asset economy' (by devaluing the liquid assets of existing homeowners) and the environmental constraints of unsustainable destructive land use. Unless built
mainly on unused public land in cities, it is difficult to imagine how large
scale continued horizontal expansion of urban metropolises would be environmentally sustainable.

Finally, the revival of interest in Karl Polanyi's concept of the 'double
movement' in the 1920s and 1930s is now promoted as a 'counter-movement' against neoliberalism. However, history does not move in cyclical
patterns of first the movement to increase marketisation, followed by the
countermovement of social protection. The socio-political forces of the
period between the 1830s and 1930s that Polanyi analysed are no longer
present in their earlier forms. Even Polanyians such as social theorist,
Nancy Fraser, recognise that Polanyi's 'double movement' is seriously
flawed. "There is no going back", she argues, "to hierarchical, exclusionary,
communitarian understandings of social protection, whose innocence has
been forever shattered, and justly so."[16] The old sexist, racist and exclusionary conservative forms of social relations can never be the basis of a
new 'double movement'.

In response to the question of why there is no unified 'counter-movement' in the twenty-first century, Fraser points out that "the social move-

ments of the post-war era do not fit either pole of the double movement. Championing neither marketization nor social protection, they espoused a third political project, which I shall call emancipation."[17] These are all valid points which leads Fraser to call for a 'triple movement' that includes movements for emancipation. However, she labours under the illusion that a 'triple movement' would encompass the range of contemporary political struggles. Unfortunately, both the 'double' and 'triple movement' do not speak to millions concerned about potential climate chaos. Carbon emissions are not like the conflict between capital and labour or authoritarianism versus social emancipation that oscillate according to who is in power. Once accumulated greenhouse gases in the atmosphere pass dangerous tipping points, there is no way of easily reversing this environmental disaster like countering marketisation and discrimination with social legislation. (See my detailed critique of double movements in Chapter Six of *Capitalism Versus Democracy?*).

Polanyi lacked any clear theory of the politics of social change, especially the interaction of political parties and movements with state institutions and business groupings. Instead, he operated at such a vague, abstract level of 'market, society and state' that the notion of 'social protection' sought by the 'counter-movement' was never specified. Who was actually 'protected' and was this 'protection' forged 'from below', that is, from particular segments or classes in 'society' or was it administratively imposed 'from above' by fascist, New Deal or Soviet state policies? In what way did a 'counter-movement' based on a democratic vote or mass agitation differ from policies implemented from above?

Consequently, the 'double movement' or 'triple movement' is so unclear that it could be interpreted to mean several conflicting things including: the conventional quest for social reform within capitalist societies; the push for a radical neo-fascist regime to curb the unregulated market; the replacement of the entire capitalist system with democratic socialism or some other form of ecologically sustainable post-capitalism. Unsurprisingly, the 'double movement' or 'triple movement' is next to useless in helping us understand the dynamics of how political coalitions are constructed or how labour movements and other social movements under specific historical conditions are both made and unmade. The notion of a 'double movement' is so removed from actual political struggles that it has nothing to say about the common organisational, strategic, and other difficulties facing social change activists. As a general observation, we can acknowledge that many domestic or international policies and practices eventually ignite a 'counter-movement' or some level of resistance. Yet, this generalisation in no way validates the 'double movement' as some quasi-socio-economic law which enables us to predict the character of the reacting social groups or the form such counter-movements may or may not take.

Desperate Politics: from Ecological Leninism to Extinction Rebellion

Existential fears of climate chaos, expressed as 'no future' or 'end times', can become volatile catalysts within a political impasse, or what is now called 'politics as usual'. Despair re-enters the political scene in the form of Extinction Rebellion (XR), Ecological Leninism and the rebirth of sabotage. These are not nihilistic or destructive, but neither are they forms of martyrdom as in the case of Jihadist militants of the Islamic state. The latter have a determined idea of the Caliphate, no matter how simplistic and anti-modernist. The self-sacrificing hardcore of XR know what they wish to prevent, but not the form which the new post-carbon society should take. The same is true of the new anti-capitalist saboteurs aiming to disrupt high-tech and AI innovations. I will therefore briefly discuss why these political analyses and strategies either try to change the world in the political costumes of the past, or else desperately clutch at disconnected straws blowing in a hostile wind.

Historically, the Leninist vanguard party was a classic opponent of absolutist monarchy and early forms of capitalist power. This model of the tightly knit party as a fighting machine was also based on the related concept of 'dual power'. If the state was to be overthrown by the proletariat, then a parallel state of 'workers and soldiers councils' (or soviets) had to be established alongside the capitalist state and effectively undermine the latter's power and authority. A century later, this model is politically obsolete in complex OECD countries and is only vaguely applicable in low-income countries with either 'failed states' or suffering years of civil war that create the possibility of establishing a countervailing system of 'dual power'. Although residents of eco-model communities aim to undermine the growth-orientated state and capitalist economy, they do not pursue this goal by any direct attempt to overthrow the state. In any case, eco-villages and transition towns are too weak and disconnected from the everyday work and life practices of large populations. Hence, they are incapable of establishing 'dual power' as parallel alternative centres of an environmentally sustainable society alongside the dominant capitalist system. Instead, most degrowthers live harmoniously in a political and social bubble largely disengaged from everyday political struggles.

If the notion of 'dual power' lives on in the imagination of some radical activists, it is utterly marginal and ineffective as a method of bringing about the end of carbon capitalism. This has not deterred Swedish Leninist, Andreas Malm, from borrowing past slogans, costumes, and language in his advocacy of 'ecological Leninism' as a strategy to deal with the climate emergency. He makes the pertinent observation that social democracy has no concept of catastrophe because it believes in incremental steps that are completely inappropriate in a 'situation of chronic emergency'. Hence, Malm declares that it is "incredibly difficult to see how anything other than state power could accomplish the transition required, given that it will be necessary to exert coercive authority against those who want to maintain the status quo."[18] While I agree with this prognosis, we part company over the meaning of 'coercive authority'. Passing legislation that coerces businesses to decarbonise is an absolute necessity given that voluntary decarbonisation has moved at little more than at a snail's pace. However, it is quite another thing to imagine that a Leninist party or economic strategy could achieve sweeping political economic transformation by coercive draconian measures that would render society, like 'War Communism' within early Soviet society, denuded of democracy. Even Lenin had to retreat and restore the market in 1921 in order for the Bolsheviks to survive.

Sadly, Malm regresses to political fantasy when he declares: "The whole strategic direction of Lenin after 1914 was to turn World War I into a fatal blow against capitalism. This is precisely the same strategic orientation we must embrace today – and this is what I mean by ecological Leninism. We must find a way of turning the environmental crisis into a crisis for fossil capital itself."[19] Revealingly, Malm conveniently overlooks the fact that Lenin's strategy of a 'fatal blow against capitalism' was an abysmal failure everywhere, even in Russia where the Czarist regime collapsed without Bolshevik involvement in February/March 2017. Moreover, one cannot have 'ecological Leninism' without a vanguard Leninist party strategy and this, as I have argued in Chapter One, is historically obsolete. If Malm is simply promoting the idea of concerted action to transform state policies in the direction of environmental sustainability, then there is no disagreement here. However, he is misguided if he thinks that 'ecological Leninism' will transform the 'crisis of fossil capital' into a socialist revolution.

Like many other Marxist-Leninist radicals, Malm is caught between admiration of the old revolutionary framework and the part realisation that this type of politics is utterly ineffective. What may sound clear, and persuasive, is in fact a longing for a less complex society than the one we currently inhabit. This nostalgia lingers on in other contexts. German Marxist, Ingar Solty is typical of traditional revolutionary Leftists when in an answer to a question about contemporary class struggle, declares that "social revolution in advanced capitalist societies today depends more on 'wars of fixed positions' and less on 'wars of movement', more on transforming the capitalist state into a democratic state rather than storming the Winter Palace."[20] In other words, strip away the 'revolutionary rhetoric' and one finds that most Marxists across the world struggle for a socialist society in very similar fashion to non-Marxists, regardless of the names of the parties or movements they support. This struggle is waged through organised protests, mobilising unions, or other social movements, campaigning electorally for Left or Green parties and so forth. Moreover, radical Left parties, like centre/Left parties and movements, are not currently engaged in revolutionary action but in the necessary defence of political and legal institutional processes of 'bourgeois democracy' against far-Right parties and movements who wish to suspend or tear these down.

In his disillusionment with non-Leninist, peaceful climate movements or what he calls 'strategic pacifism', Malm embraces the need for more extreme action. Surveying the ineffectiveness of former peaceful movements – from anti-slavery, suffragettes, anti-Apartheid, and other campaigns – until they took up violence or militant resistance, Malm argues that thirty years of peaceful climate protests have got nowhere. Sabotage is needed, whether of SUVs by small teams deflating the tyres on thousands of cars during the night or blowing up pipelines or mass confrontations at coal mines and power stations. Malm opposes violence against people even though he celebrates some movements which engaged in such violence. This is a highly controversial strategy that others have described as 'how to blow up a social movement'.[21] During the 1970s, when the Baader-Meinhof Red Army Fraction (whom Malm cites approvingly) and the Italian Red Brigades were active, an anarchist pamphlet appeared with the title 'You can't blow up a social relationship'. History has shown that these small extreme terrorist groups were completely counterproductive and deluded themselves into thinking that assassinating or kidnapping the 'head of state', or business leaders would reveal the class nature of the state and lead to working class revolts. Instead, the 'social relationship' that a majority of workers lived from-day-to-day under capitalism led them to hate terrorist actions and unsurprisingly, resulted in voters backing repressive measures against most of the non-terrorist radical Left.

Social change is not possible until a majority of the population is not only convinced of the need to rapidly decarbonise but is also presented with practical and feasible alternative policies that will secure workers employment, income, and social protection. The largest Left book publisher in the world, *Verso Books*, has unfortunately succumbed to crude marketing practices in producing a clickbait title 'How to blow up a pipeline'. Malm does not offer a bomb construction and demolition manual and instead supports diverse political strategies. Nonetheless, he is a convert to Franz Fanon's notion of 'violence' as a cleansing experience. In child-like fashion, he honestly admits that he was on a high for a few weeks after experiencing a political orgasm by tearing down a fence blocking entry to a power station in Eastern Germany. "I have never felt a greater rush of exhilaration: for one throbbing, mind-expanding moment, we had a slice of the infrastructure wrecking this planet in our hands."[22]

Tellingly, there is no comparison between tearing down a fence and Fanon's defence of national liberation movements fighting against repressive imperialist armies. Instead, Malm and the Zetkin Collective inappropriately use Fanon's *Black Skin, White Masks* which they convert into *White Skin, Black Fuel*.[23] The problem is that fossil fuels are not the exclusive preserve of white capitalists and racist colonialists and are profitably extracted and produced by businesses run by people with multi-coloured skins. As a critique of the links between fossil fuel industries and neo-fascists, Malm is still trapped in paradigms from the 1920s and so exaggerates the power of the far Right in the 2020s. He overlooks the fact that many corporations and their political allies are already beginning to abandon fossil fuels, even though the rate of doing this is far too slow. Politically, in most countries, there are no mass Left movements currently threatening capitalism and no need for fascism to save capitalism from revolution. Rather, the rise of far-Right parties favouring trade protectionism for 'national capital' emerged in opposition to market globalisation, even though ethno-nationalists direct their hate against the Left, non-whites, and non-Christians. Climate denialism has outlived its usefulness even for the far Right who are now shifting to 'patriotic ecology' and 'national climate' strategies against internationalists.[24] Most businesses reject 'fossil fascism' as a counter-productive strategy because it impedes growth through what they see as technological innovation based on ecological modernisation and less confrontational 'greenwash' tactics.

Occupying coal-powered stations as part of a larger mass mobilisation against fossil fuels is a perfectly legitimate tactic. But let us not dress up this tactic in the dated clothing of Leninism. Power stations are extremely limited targets because this is not where most greenhouse gas emissions are produced. However, they do have a symbolic value for protests against the failure to implement rapid decarbonisation. The less visible emitters are dispersed sources in agriculture, transport, manufacturing, mining, trade, and consumption that collectively do not readily lend themselves to serve as neat identifiable focal points for militant occupation. These 'social relations' of production and consumption cannot be 'blown up' so easily and as Malm and others know, it will take much more than tearing down a fence to create a post-carbon world. This is especially true of the hundreds of millions of affluent consumers who sustain the major forms of global greenhouse emissions. It is not new fascist movements that are the main obstacle to preventing climate catastrophe. Rather, it is the pervasive sense of individualistic entitlement fuelled by corporate production and media cultural campaigns that sustains key industries and affluent consumption. These will continue regardless of the fluctuating political strength of far-Right movements.

Very importantly, Malm says much about past and present tactics but little about the society he would like to construct or how the 'ecological Leninist' strategy he promotes can actually undermine rather than achieve its realisation. Remember, Lenin was captivated by capitalist techniques such as Taylorism and had an impoverished vision of how socialism could actually work. Simplistic notions of socialist administration (for example, in *State and Revolution* Lenin claimed it could work like a post office) or his campaign slogans such as 'Communism is Soviet power plus the electrification of the whole country' are barely passable for pre-industrialised countries let alone for contemporary developed capitalist societies. Yet, Malm follows Lenin's technocratic tendency when discussing 'direct air capture' (DAC) or the various multi-trillion geoengineering schemes of removing carbon from the atmosphere. This task, Malm argues, should be socialised, and carried out by governments rather than left to private corporations.

Climate scientists James Dyke, Wolfgang Knorr and Robert Watson warn of the illusions and dangers associated with schemes such as DAC, regardless of whether implemented by corporations or by governments.[25] Leaving aside the highly risky and controversial nature of technocratic solutions, which government(s) would pay the enormous annual cost of $12 trillion in a capitalist world? In short, Malm's inconsistent ecological

Leninism veers between the tactics of mass mobilisation of 'War Communism' and relying on states using the elaborate and elite technical-scientific apparatus of capitalism to solve the climate emergency. This preoccupation with the tactics of decarbonisation is disconnected from the vision and organisation of a post-carbon society.

Other supporters of 'ecological Leninism', such as environmental researcher Max Ajl, combine Leninism with degrowth visions. He attacks Green New Deals as 'green social democracy' that would be imperialist and devastate 'the South', as it is not eco-socialism but based on commodification and managerialism.[26] Others such as Marxist-Leninist, anti-imperialist' Indigenous movement, The Red Nation, call for 'decolonisation or extinction', that is, everything from open American borders, defunding the police to LGBTQ and Indigenous rights.[27] While I agree with Ajl's critique of technological utopians and some of the valuable proposals he makes about alternative agriculture, Ajl's 'people's Green New Deal', like The Red Nation's 'Red Deal', depends on radical land reform and uses old-style anti-imperialist rhetoric about disempowering capitalist classes. This task will supposedly be achieved by all kinds of 'common people'.[28] In short, both 'people's Green New Deal' and 'Red Deal' are a hotch-potch of Leninism, degrowth and 'Left populism'.

A useful warning about the politics of Malm, Ajl and many activists in Extinction Rebellion is found in historian Jeremy Varon's analysis of the despair and delusions of an earlier generation which produced the Weathermen and the Baader-Meinhof group (RAF). Discussing these 1970s groups, Varon pointedly observes that:

> Both groups fell victim to equally flawed, contradictory assumptions, between which they oscillated. In one emphasis, defined by an exaggerated pessimism, they saw imperialism as a monolith. Its power to absorb, delude, and dispirit its subjects was so great that no sustained internal resistance was possible. ... In a second emphasis, driven by an exaggerated optimism, the Weathermen and the RAF saw imperialism as on the brink of collapse. Resistance was everywhere – in the Third World certainly, but also in the institutional fabric of their own societies: in the schools, the military, the factories, the bureaucracies, halfway houses, ghettos, and working- and middle-class homes. Their violence, in this model, needed only to light the spark to ignite mass discontent into revolutionary conflagration. Both views, despite their apparent polarity, had the same effect: to discourage the difficult work of addressing, through redoubled efforts to educate and

organise ambivalent populations, possibilities that lay somewhere in between.[29]

Whereas 'ecological Leninism' attempts to apply the failed strategies of the past to contemporary societies that have long ago rendered the vanguard party and Leninism irrelevant, it is equally necessary to dispel the 'anti-politics' strategy and illusions of movements such as Extinction Rebellion (XR). For example, XR attempts to create the impression that it is apolitical. On September 1, 2020, XR declared: "Just to be clear we are not a socialist movement. We do not trust any single ideology, we trust the people, chosen by sortition (like jury service) to find the best future for us all through a #CitizensAssembly. A banner saying, 'socialism or extinction' does not represent us."[30]

The notion that handfuls of selected people in citizens' assemblies represent the views of the vast majority of 'the people' is no more credible than the claim by self-appointed Leninists that the Party represents the views of the working class. Indeed, the report on the Citizens' Assemblies UK (CAUK) July 2021, showed that 45% of participants thought that 2050 was the right target date for zero greenhouse gas emissions while only 37% thought it was too late.[31] This is hardly good news for XR which puts its faith in citizens' assemblies to bring about urgent action. Although it is certainly possible for valuable ideas to emerge from citizens' assemblies, the path to a post-carbon society is not possible without political organisations mobilising people to change government policies directly or indirectly through either elections or via multiple actions pressuring businesses, governments, and other institutions.

In pursuing a form of 'anti-politics', XR and others are doomed to a series of protests with little or no impact on governments in between elections. The 24-hour media cycle has already made the initial positive impact of XR (especially in raising awareness of the climate crisis) politically dated and ineffective. Various forms of 'anti-politics' are dead ends and only compound despair and disillusionment when rendered no longer shocking but merely a disruptive nuisance to 'business as usual'. These disruptive actions also have an inbuilt logic of failure if repeated often. Each new individual action or period of disruption needs to be larger and more provocative than the last, a difficult tactic to sustain in a long-drawn-out struggle within a very hostile political and media terrain. Like the Baader-Meinhof and other terrorist groups, the preoccupation with evading police capture takes on a life of its own at the expense of developing alternative politics.

So too, it would seem that XR now devotes more energy to developing its tactical relationship with the police rather than to political strategies of how to resolve the climate emergency.

What Politics May Follow the Passing of the 'Left Populist' Moment?

For the past sixty years, a giant chasm has continued to exist between the flowering of anti-hierarchical ideals of alternative movements (espousing environmentalist, feminist, and various anti-discriminatory values) and the practical politics needed for any parliamentary or extra-parliamentary transition to a post-capitalist or post-carbon democracy. The long 1960s has had an irreversible impact on old-style pre-1950s class-based politics which have been consigned to the historical museum and largely replaced by 'non-class' or 'cross-class' social change models. One would have thought that the collapse of Communist regimes (1989-1991) would have been the final straw that broke the back of old Leninist, Trotskyist, Maoist, Gramscian and other political discourses that in the past have been tied to outdated notions of vanguardism and class struggle. Instead, the generation of the 1960s New Left were split into two informal wings: one that never fully relinquished longstanding concepts of the revolutionary overthrow of capitalism, while at the same time engaging with new social movement issues and attempting to form alliances with these movements; and the other wing that moved from a traditional class analysis of society to a more pluralist, intense engagement with environmental, feminist, race and post-colonial or LGBTIQ issues that could not be reduced to class conflict. Occasionally, social movement activists in the second group carried out tentative joint actions with Left parties but neither trusted nor shared the same understanding of contemporary society.

The first informal grouping dominated Left publishing and small media outlets and kept alive the old Communist tradition of vanguard parties and that Leninism and communism were still legitimate and quite separate from Stalinism and brutal dictatorship.[32] French Maoist, Alain Badiou, declared that: "We know that communism is the right hypothesis. All those who abandon this hypothesis immediately resign themselves to the market economy, to parliamentary democracy – the form of state suited to capitalism – and to the inevitable and 'natural' character of the most monstrous inequalities."[33] The dogmatic assertion that communism is the only alternative to neoliberalism and 'monstrous inequalities' is precisely why so many anti-capitalist social movement activists reject Badiou and other Leninists.

Given the widespread unpopularity and understandable dislike of Communism, it was not surprising that attempts were made to salvage and partly repackage Marxism/Leninism as 'Left populist' parties/movements. Depending on the particular countries, 'Left populism' was either a broad *informal* alliance of class and social movements or a *formal* attempt to build an anti-neoliberal political party out of social movement fragments and disillusioned mainstream social democrats and assorted Communists, Trotskyists and other vanguardists. However, it is much harder to develop a non-Leninist 'organisational model' and political platform that maximises the ability of diverse social movements to co-exist within a 'Left populist' party. It is obvious that constructing new political economic institutions and practices that simultaneously promote workers' demands, environmental sustainability and new socio-cultural relations is an exceedingly challenging task.

We have just gone through a second decade (approximately between 2008-2009 and 2019-2020) of a momentous flowering of all kinds of re-energised anti-capitalist movements, from degrowth and accelerationist technological utopians proclaiming post-work scenarios, through to Occupy, the 'Arab Spring', Black Lives Matter, Me-Too, LGBTIQ movements, DIEM 25, Extinction Rebellion and other movements. Although protests against neoliberal policies had been gathering momentum before 2008, it was during this past decade that we witnessed major attempts to reunite social movements formally or informally within new Left parties such as *Syriza, Podemos, La France Insoumise* and the Italian hybrid ('neither Left nor Right') Five Star party or the supra-national movement Democracy in Europe 2025 (DiEM 25). Old nationalist parties such as British Labour were also momentarily swept up in the 'populist moment' with the influx of new members under Jeremy Corbyn. While these 'Left populist' parties continue to exist, it is certainly the case that the 'Left populist' character has either been cleansed from parties such as *Syriza* and British Labour or passed its political moment. It was not just that these parties/movements failed to live up to initial expectations, but more importantly, they were incapable of breaking the political impasse in question, either because they were too weak or because they couldn't surmount internal organisational divisions generated by a range of domestic and international pressures.

The rise and fall of Bernie Sanders' presidential campaigns and the attempt to establish 'socialism' in the US as a politically legitimate value fits into a slightly different category compared to that of the 'Left populism' in other countries. Left or Progressive members of Democratic Party in America also struggle to unite social movements and workers, but their 'socialist' platform is largely social democratic (universal health care, increasing the minimum wage, Green New Deal) compared to the more radical demands of Left parties in Europe. It is unclear whether their peak political moment has also passed, as the ability to grow depends on whether the Biden administration will partly incorporate parts of the Green New Deal and steal their thunder, or whether the Republican far Right expands its power in a disastrous repressive manner.

Like the 1960s, the past decade projected a spirit of optimism amongst a new generation of younger people more receptive to radical ideas and political alternatives to Right-wing neoliberalism and conservative main-stream centre/Left policies. For example, for radical technological utopians, Nick Srnicek and Alex Williams', 'Left populism' combined an embrace of post-work automation with the demand for universal basic income. Every successful movement, they argued, "has been the result, not of a single organisational type, but of a broad ecology of organisations. These have operated, in a more or less coordinated way, to carry out the division of labour necessary for political change."[34] Critiquing what they call 'folk poli-tics', or an obsession visible in social movements and new parties with constructing the most 'democratic' and pluralist alternative to the vanguard party, they went on to pronounce that:

> There is ultimately no privileged organisational form. Not all organisations need to aim for participation, openness and horizontality as their regulative ideals. The divisions between spontaneous uprisings and organisational longevity, short-term desires and long-term strategy, have split what should be a broadly consistent project for building a post-work world. Organisational diversity should be combined with broad populist unity.[35]

In opposition to notions of deliberative democracy, political theorists Ernesto Laclau and Chantal Mouffe influenced activists in *Podemos* and *Syriza* by advocating radical reformism or 'agonistic pluralism' based not on a deliberative rational consensus (Habermas, Rawls, et. al) but rather on the conflictual pluralism of emotional politics.[36] Deliberative democracy is seen as essentially a soft Left/liberal operating principle underpinned by rational discussion rather than confronting a class-divided world. Yet, as with deliberative democracy that prepares information and topics for people to deliberate upon, 'agonistic pluralism' is also pre-shaped by the leadership group within 'Left populist' parties, despite all the rhetoric about popular democracy.

The reality is that advocates of deliberative democracy are not in competition with agonistic 'Left populists'. Instead, deliberative democracy developed from the 1980s onwards as a response to the so-called 'democratic deficit'. Disputes raged about whether people were disengaged from politics because of the sameness of the major parties, or because of a general decline in civic participation, or because of a distaste for conflictual politics or due to multiple other reasons. Advocates of deliberative democracy were a mixture of liberal social democrats and anti-capitalists who wished to regenerate democracies by experimenting with randomly chosen citizen assemblies to deliberate on all kinds of socio-political issues.[37] By contrast, 'Left populism' was an attempt to reinvent a post-workerist or post-vanguard party/movement that was still immersed in an anti-capitalist counter-hegemonic strategy by trying to link the social fragments.

It is clear that both deliberative democracy and 'Left populism' have severe limitations and remain unable to overcome the political impasse. Practical examples of deliberative democracy may work very well in small group settings where people can discuss the merits and disadvantages of particular proposals in depth. This option is either limited or unwieldly in national political forums involving potentially thousands of people.[38] Crucially, contemporary political struggle is not conducted in rational terms where orderly, detailed policy explanations are presented to the participants for their deliberation. Instead, distortions, fake news, exclusion of radical proposals by conservative media outlets, unequal financial resources to fund campaigns and other obstacles have become the norm. Secondly, deliberative democracy remains powerless to tackle class power in the form of unequal corporate control of the economy unless combined with radical mass mobilisation that challenges private wealth and power. As with all proposals of direct democracy or deliberation in complex capitalist systems, the failure to replace day-to-day bureaucratic and corporate power leaves deliberation nominally in the hands of 'the people' while the administration and implementation of policies (or real power) stay in the hands of corporate management and political or bureaucratic and technocratic minorities.

While I agree that politics in capitalist societies cannot be conducted like a university seminar, the notion of 'agonistic pluralism' is fraught with different problems. Only those academics with minimal experience of the day-to-day realities of organisations could come up with a politics based on abstract linguistic political theories. It was fine for Laclau and Mouffe to argue that there was no unified subject, namely, the proletariat with its own party, that could overthrow capitalism. It was also valid to reject a politics of 'emancipation' or 'liberation', as if politics ceased 'after' the revolution. Instead, a 'populist reason' was founded on the existence of plural subjects representing diverse political, cultural, and socio-economic subjectivities and constituencies.[39] Rather than class struggle based on an economic determinism, Laclau and Mouffe argued that all was temporary and nego-tiable rather than predetermined by the inevitable triumph of the working class.

Consequently 'Left populism' went to the opposite extreme and advo-cates of 'agonistic populism' or radical democracy became stuck at the level of organisational relations. Unity through diversity is supposedly acquired by baldly stating one's policies rather than searching for a false consensus. All this is fine at the level of political rhetoric. It falls apart once intractable divisions emerge over crucial socio-economic questions of what environmentally sustainable economic program (such as tax, industry, social expenditure, and fiscal policies) should replace existing policies. Organisa-tional issues became secondary once the leaders of *Syriza* succumbed to the EU financial ultimatum to Greece in 2015 and the anti-neoliberal platform collapsed.

One of the slogans used by the Spanish *Indignados* or 'Real Democracy Now' movement (which erupted across Spain in 2011) was 'our dreams don't fit into your ballot box'. Reacting to mass unemployment and austerity following the crisis of 2008, they protested against the narrow solutions offered by the Spanish mainstream parties through the electoral system. Like many other movements across the world, the *Indignados* sought a mixture of practical immediate policies and utopian solutions to poverty, inequality, and ecological destruction.[40] These popular demonstrations gave rise to the new coalition or 'Left populist' party, *Podemos*, which captured over 20% of the vote and much media attention. Although it initially trans-formed the political landscape by helping to mobilise country-wide disaf-fected citizens in numerous campaigns over housing, jobs and care, its emphasis on electoral politics came at the expense of local community activists.[41] Like so many parties in the past, local community members eventually played little role in the formation of policies. Ten years after the *Indignados* and following internal splits over policies and 'agonistic' internal conflicts, *Podemos* has rapidly declined. It now faces the same fate as other radical movements/parties, namely, how to sustain grassroots extra-parliamentary activity while simultaneously trying to increase electoral representation and participation in government.

Both *La France Insoumise* and the British Labour Party were restricted or foundered on the issues of nationalism and EU membership, levels of immigration and refugees. *La France Insoumise* never really broke its confinement to the French Left political ghetto despite competing with Le Pen's National Front/National Rally for votes. Leader Jean-Luc Melenchon voiced anti-German/anti-EU mixtures of Left nationalist and xenophobic policies, claiming that migrants "are stealing the bread of French workers."[42] Working-class nationalism and racism were even more visible amongst sections of the white English working class because of the polarised Brexit debate. Like a ball and chain, it hung around the neck of British Labour and divided the multicultural working class. Labour was reduced to near irrelevancy in Scotland due to the rise of Scottish nationalism and remains a minority in the rest of the UK, given the electoral system and the Labour leadership rejecting a progressive united platform with other parties.

No level of agonistic emotional politics or continual negotiation of differences and particularisms can secure a common language and programme in 'Left populist' parties if the members are either divided over degrees of national or cosmopolitan tolerance while at the same time endorsing social and environmental policies that are unsustainable. Most commentators refer to Right or Left 'populism' which is defined in narrow or broad terms. Others such as Paula Biglieri and Luciana Cadahia, using political experiences in Latin America, reject this particular division of 'populism'. If Right and Left 'populism' consist of the same features, then, they argue, 'Left populism' is misconceived as being associated with authoritarianism, ethno-nationalism, and other Right-wing characteristics. Instead, they see Right 'populism' as a form of fascism that has little to do with democracy and equality, while 'Left populism' is a strategy to democratise 'the popular' by advancing anti-capitalist policies.[43]

Despite it being necessary to make these distinctions between Left and Right, Biglieri and Cadahia still remain trapped within the same abstract forms of agonistic politics that have failed to prevent 'Left populist' parties from having an initial burst of enthusiastic support followed by familiar splits over policies, strategies, and organisational forms. Between 2008-2009 and 2019-2020, 'Left populism' as a vague, constantly shifting model confirmed that it was going nowhere, fast. As a response to the exhaustion of twentieth century Left organisational models, involving a mix of old and new radicals, it remains to be seen whether 'Left populism' itself withers away or is revived in new guises.

The 'Left populist' moment is also linked to recent debates about a 'social' or 'historical bloc'. Whether it is better to create a new party, or a new 'bloc' of different social and political constituencies remains a divisive issue amongst political activists. Could the call to establish a Gramscian or non-Leninist 'Modern Prince' actually work? Such a non-Communist, broad-based party of different social movement tendencies (without all the old Left hierarchical baggage of a vanguard party) would supposedly be able to manoeuvre and advance a post-carbon transition to post-capitalism. Leftists, Martin Bak Jørgensen and Óscar García Agustín, may defend 'Left populist' parties as the 'Post-Modern Prince'[44] but new labels are of little help when it comes to 'populist' parties overcoming the problems discussed above. The question stands as to what parts of the Gramscian 'Modern Prince' would be retained or jettisoned. As I argued in Chapter Two, an updated Gramscian strategy is not possible if based on the leading role played by 'organic intellectuals'. These 'organic' constituent elements of the working class are politically obsolete in contemporary capitalist societies, given the profound social and cultural differences amongst the working classes and all other strata classified as non-capitalists. If members of this potential 'Modern Prince' or 'Post-Modern Prince' wished to mobilise diverse social constituencies, they would need to be able to communicate a coherent alternative to existing hegemonic power that appeals to quite diverse social groups. Such an important agenda to reconcile democratic anti-capitalism with environmental sustainability has so far eluded 'Left populist' parties.

Why emphasise environmental sustainability above other issues? The simple reason is that none of the other socio-economic policies directed against inequality and injustice are viable or durable if the complex measures to maximise environmental sustainability fail to be implemented. It is therefore necessary to rethink previous radical assumptions that were based on first developing elementary forms of solidarity in the form of trade union consciousness before the acquisition of a deeper and broader political or revolutionary consciousness. Today, acquiring a revolutionary consciousness is inadequate because any critique of capitalist systems is not equivalent to equipping workers to fight for specific environmentally sustainable economic policies in any so-called transition to socialism or to a pluralist post-carbon democracy. For example, let us imagine that workers are successful in either nationalising privately-owned industries or gaining political control over these corporations. Will they then pursue export-led or consumption-led growth or neither of these macro-economic strategies as degrowth policies may be required. Unions and Left parties have often needed to deliver short-term benefits to workers in return for their support. But this could become counter-productive if a broad national strategy requires transforming existing environmentally unsustainable employment, consumption, investment, and production in order to prevent ecological crises. Conversely, advocates of degrowth or green growth are also likely to antagonise those in a 'social bloc' to the degree that they focus more on long-term environmental policies at the expense of the immediate need for jobs, improved workplace conditions and irradicating poverty.

Currently, there is little agreement between the socio-environmental goals pursued by degrowth movements, defenders of immigrants, refugees, and multicultural social and cultural identity movements as opposed to the agendas pursued by nationalist labour movements. The latter tend to champion growth and a greater but more exclusive share of the ecologically unsustainable national economic pie. Internal party divisions over conflicting priorities are bound to create problems between members and leaders. Gramsci's 'Modern Prince' was not democratic (being a Leninist party) and was based on 'democratic centralism' which required all members to adhere to the party line. By contrast, contemporary activists want democratic organisations which permit their voices to be heard and their participation in decision-making recognised. Such non-Leninist democratic parties could lack the capacity for quick strategic manoeuvrability in a crisis situation requiring a rapid response. Hence, socio-political diversity and the need for internal democracy makes a non-Leninist 'Modern Prince' or 'Post-Modern Prince' theoretically attractive. However, this attractiveness has to be juggled against potentially cumbersome organisational structures regarding quick decision-making processes. Nonetheless, it is preferable to have the complexity of internal party democratic decision-making rather than party leaders who sacrifice democratic participation for quick, policy decisions by the inner circle. Any shift to 'efficiency' and 'control' over decision-making is usually a sign that the deradicalised political rot has set in.

Most countries no longer have Left parties that are either large enough to win elections on their own or lead mass movements based on a unified counter-hegemonic 'working class' platform or agenda. Furthermore, the old radical strategy of 'entryism' of Leftists with the goal of eventually converting large centre/Left parties into radical parties has been an abysmal historical failure and waste of energy. The Corbyn experiment within British Labour based on mass new party members seemed to momentarily invalidate previous experiences only to prove that Left control was brief and insecure. Importantly, no party or set of 'organic intellectuals' can speak for diverse segments and classes in capitalist societies because 'catch all' mainstream parties consist of cross-class elements that have regularly produced splits once particular factions tried to shift party policies to the Right or to the Left.

The quest for a new politics to break the political impasse is largely connected to the demise of the old belief in a single, undifferentiated social class (the industrial proletariat) having the will and capacity to transform contemporary developed capitalist societies. If such a view of class is no longer able to either represent diverse social identities and interests or inspire millions into class action, are the political prospects for a 'social bloc' or cross-class coalition advancing a post-carbon democracy any better? After all, the political economic strategies associated with both green growth and degrowth are not derived from a single class position similar to working class support for trade unions. Anti-capitalist reform or radical consciousness raising in limited or more extensive forms is now only possible by building cross-class alliances or coalitions. Yet, alliance building is difficult and not very stable given the fluctuating need to sustain the mutual support of diverse groups, each espousing different political interests under a delicately negotiated broad banner.

A contemporary 'social bloc' or historical 'political bloc' must be understood as something quite different to Gramsci's attempt to construct a bloc between the Northern Italian working class and Southern peasantry in the 1920s. By contrast, during the past decade, mainstream centre-Right parties in the UK, Australia, the US, Austria, Sweden, Denmark, and other countries have either courted far Right movements and voters or embraced authoritarian policies on refugees, law and order and other social issues. Centre/Left mainstream parties and policy makers have made rhetorical gestures signalling their concern about inequality and climate change but, with the exception of minor tinkering, have continued to adhere to many neoliberal policies. They have rejected radical change and refused to form electoral coalitions or 'social blocs' with Left parties, apart from exceptions such as the five-party coalition government in Finland, the Socialists (PSOE) and *Unidas Podemos* government in Spain and the 2021 Norwegian Labour coalition with centre and Left parties.

Given that in the foreseeable future, no single Left party is likely to be electorally strong enough or inclusive enough in most of the G20 countries, a 'social bloc' needs to be based on a political alliance of parties and movements that share a mutual understanding of what they need to *prioritise* and which parts of their own political agendas they need to temporarily suspend or compromise. Being separate parties rather than diverse parts of a single 'Left populist' party, agreement needs to be reached on a minimal programme such as a Green New Deal, that outlines clear legislative objectives should they win office. The 'political bloc' can either be based on equal weighting of the participating member parties and movements or built around a recognition that the largest member party or movement will have more influence over policy direction. However, if the largest member of the coalition uses its political weight to harm the interests of other smaller players, then the 'bloc' is certain to collapse.

Secondly, a 'social bloc' will fail if it is merely a repackaged collection of existing wish lists. Instead, it must identify and prioritise a few key policy areas that unify various movements around a minimum program. Rather than appearing to be all things to all social movements in a repeat of populism, it must emphasise the sustainable use of material resources and social justice that is underpinned by an urgent replacement of fossil-fuel based industries and the implementation of universal basic services legislation and a job guarantee. Thirdly, such a 'bloc' can either be predominantly electoral or a mixture of parliament and 'the street' in its campaigning and social mobilisation. This is where 'social blocs' have often been found wanting due to lack of internal democracy, accusations of sexism and racism, too much decision-making concentrated in the centralised negotiations between representatives of the constituent parties and factions. Conversely, the desire of a certain proportion of the 'bloc' to pursue more radical activist campaigns can be at odds with the conventional parliamentary politics of others.

No Ecologically Sustainable Socio-economic Agenda, no Viable 'Social Bloc'

In 1935, Stalin ordered that Communist parties cease attacking socialists and the non-Communist Left as 'social fascists' and form a Popular Front against fascism with these same former 'class traitors' as well as with liberals and conservative anti-fascists. The notion of a 'social bloc' has often been used to advocate temporary political alliances to defeat or stop a common enemy. Today, radicals such as Paul Mason call for a temporary alliance between centrist and Left parties to stop rising neo-fascism.[45] This is a valid political strategy in Europe but has limited applicability elsewhere. Any successful 'social bloc' against climate catastrophe or neo-fascism must be more than a temporary political alliance, as the targets of authoritarian neo-fascism are quite different in Europe compared to those scapegoated people in India, Brazil, Nigeria, Turkey, and other countries. The survival of any new electoral 'bloc' must also be based on a clear environmentally sustainable political economy to underpin its political strategy. The problem is that an ecologically sustainable political economic program needs to be simultaneously incompatible with racism, anti-Islamic, anti-cosmopolitan and socially unjust policies. This is far from easy in countries with deep-seated and divisive institutional and cultural prejudices.

To date, 'Left populist' parties have emphasised creating organisational and political cultural formations but sadly, de-emphasised or ignored ecologically sustainable political economic strategies. This is a neglected issue that has profound consequences. Neo-Keynesians and neo-Marxists are still largely trapped in a pre-environmentalist framework when they argue that the 'social bloc' must have a clear notion of the primary driver(s) of economic growth and how this benefits the movements and parties constituting the 'social bloc'.[46] For example, when export-led growth policies are adopted by governments, this often means restrictions on wages and domestic consumption with the purpose of making local industry lean and internationally competitive. Consumption-led growth is used by Right and centre/Left governments to boost domestic consumption in an economic downturn and is heavily reliant on private households borrowing in order to fund their consumption.[47] This 'disguised pain' is often politically effective in the short-run. Eventually, trade deficits from higher levels of imported goods and accumulated private household and individual debt leads to constraints on retail spending, forced currency devaluation, cuts to imports, stagnant wages and/or higher prices for households. These characteristics have all been evident in recent decades.

Most mainstream parties are reluctant to upset consumers and voters by restricting consumption-led growth. On the contrary, governments are currently preoccupied with COVID-19 stimulus packages to generate and sustain consumption and jobs. However, the failure to impose curbs on affluent consumption will prevent dealing with the environmental crisis. By contrast, low- and middle-income countries still lack adequate domestic sources of capital formation necessary for investment in essential services and infrastructure. They are either unattractive to foreign business investment or heavily dependent on foreign capital for any economic growth. These countries are also severely constrained in international markets because of the need to import elaborately manufactured goods and large capital goods due to the absence of industries such as heavy engineering and sophisticated electronics, as well as being short of adequately skilled workforces. Little wonder that over six decades of the unequal market exchanges between 157 low- and middle-income countries and developed, high-income countries since 1960, only a handful of the former have become high-income countries.[48]

If the various 'drivers of growth' have failed to raise the living standards of most low- and middle-income countries, this conventional conception of development has also plagued stagnant/low-growth, high-income countries in recent decades. No adequate and durable growth dynamic has been successful in recent decades despite decades of talk about innovation, high-tech, 'knowledge economies' and other so-called panaceas. Even more fundamental is that the political logic underpinning 'drivers of growth' policy making is no longer appropriate or acceptable in an era where degrowth and environmental sustainability is a key goal for an increasing number of social movements.

Hence, when it comes to developing a political coalition or 'social bloc' committed to environmental sustainability, economic strategy options such as export-led or consumption-led growth will prove unacceptable to opponents of incessant growth. This is because export and consumption-led growth contradict the need for lower carbon emissions or the need to curb the negative social and ecological consequences of agribusiness, toxic manufacturing processes and the extraction and consumption of material resources. The question therefore becomes: how is a future 'social bloc' to be formed or kept together if the 'drivers' of economic growth are replaced or modified by including some degrowth objectives in the policy program? This may upset other member parties of the 'bloc' which champion conventional job-creating export-led and/or consumption-led policies to please their constituencies. Which parts of the policy platform will be compromised if electoral success is to be achieved and a coalition government formed?

In a non-revolutionary era, social change activists must confront the timeworn and familiar choice of theoretical purity but political impotence or agree to a political strategy that delivers only part of their agenda. All parties and movements continue to have maximalist and minimalist programs or goals. Alternative 'social blocs' are unlikely to accommodate too many 'fundamentalists' who wish to promote their 'maximalist' socialist or environmentalist agendas via electoral coalitions. Sadly, the character of contemporary fractured political life favours minimalist programs precisely at a time when fundamental change is desperately needed. This does not preclude extra-parliamentary movements agitating for sweeping reforms and putting pressure on a 'social bloc' or coalition government to adopt much more than a minimalist political program. Nonetheless, building and sustaining a viable political coalition that delivers more than a minimalist pact is the dilemma facing any transitional strategy to a post-carbon society. Avoiding splits and destabilisation will ultimately depend on how well the 'social bloc' parties first prepare voters and activists with mass cultural and educative campaigns to explain why new forms of production and consumption are necessary for both community wellbeing and environmental sustainability. It is difficult enough to form an alliance to combat neoliberal austerity in OECD countries or massive poverty and inequality in low-income countries without the added goal of creating a whole new society. Herein lies some of the difficult choices facing both reformers and radical social change activists.

Crucially, the connection between the possible political success of a 'social bloc' and its endorsement or rejection of particular economic 'drivers of growth' confirms why both oppositional Keynesian and Marxist policies need to be either overhauled or modified. Most policy makers have failed to register, let alone integrate into their political models, the ways in which environment crises will affect the viability of all future growth strategies. Eventually, environmental damage caused by implementing updated versions of Keynesian increased consumption or aggregate demand to combat austerity will begin to register with policy makers, businesses, unions, and households. The high probability that ecological modernisation goals in the form of techno-fixes decoupling economic growth from nature will fail, has not yet been factored in by most mainstream policy analysts. It is therefore the task of future 'social bloc' activists and negotiators to reject conventional export-led, consumption-led, or conservative state-led (China) 'drivers of growth' and develop alternative agendas to existing ecologically unsustainable growth models. If the 'social bloc' is merely a defence of variations of old forms of employment, social welfare, and conventional political representation, then few new alternative policies will emerge to break the old capitalist order's destruction of the biosphere and built-in social inequalities.

In this chapter, I have tried to show that strategies based on vanguard parties, politics from below, and 'Left populism' are unable to succeed because they are essentially reworked and amalgamated concepts that originated in both the pre-1945 era and in the 1960s. The era of a single radical party and even of a mainstream centre/Left party winning on its own has finished in many countries. Rare are the left-of-centre parties in the twenty-first century that manage to regularly win majorities in both lower and upper legislatures. The rise of social movements from the 1960s merely delayed the political recognition that the Schumpeterian notion of democracy as two sets of competing elites, was an era that had already passed in most OECD countries, except in a few countries such as the US with undemocratic electoral systems propping up Republicans and Democrats. Even in the US, the 'shell' of the formal party structures continues to barely paper over a range of regional and ideological internal party divisions. The rise and decline of 'Left populist' parties in Europe, Latin America and elsewhere were attempts to bring under the one party umbrella the disunited fragments of old vanguardists, social movements, post-colonial anti-imperialists and newer socio-cultural and environmental anti-neoliberal groups. This era has ended even if the news has not reached the disparate advocates of 'agonistic populism' still caught up in old debates and defunct political paradigms.

Following Engels and Lenin, Marxist/Leninists continue to argue that a "democratic republic is the best possible political shell for capitalism..."[49] as the universal vote disguises the reality that workers remain wage slaves. Two factors have rendered this analysis of voting redundant. Firstly, rather than being duped by the 'universal vote', the same sections of the less-educated working class who have lost out to marketisation and austerity are disengaged and disillusioned with 'politics'.[50] The electoral system is regarded as delivering few social and work benefits, thus enabling authoritarian parties rather than socialist revolutionaries to successfully appeal to their collective discontents and nationalist and racist sentiments. Secondly, the shift from Left parties to Right-wing parties by significant sections of the working class is indicative of the conservative beliefs held by many workers with lower levels of formal education in regard to environmental, law-and-order, immigration and cultural issues concerning gender and sexuality. There is a disconnect between income and voting patterns. Class is not dead but has been 'buried alive'[51] by electoral contests between centre/Right and centre/Left parties that mainly deliver benefits for the capitalist class and higher educated segments such as professionals.

A recent detailed study by Amory Gethin, Clara Martínez-Toledano, and Thomas Piketty of elections in 21 countries between 1948 and 2020 shows how traditional alignments of workers and the educated middle classes have changed since the 1980s.[52] Despite the use of crude aggregate data based on low-, middle-, high-income, or less-educated compared with tertiary-educated people, the trend across the 21 countries is clear. Such is the cross-cutting effects of class realignments – especially the embrace of Right-wing parties by significant sections of low-income working-class voters and the corresponding loss by conservative parties of those segments of the professions with higher formal education qualifications – that those earlier political blocs have been weakened.

The question for centre/Left parties and social movements is what do they need to do to win back the 10% to 30% of low-income working-class voters that have deserted them or don't bother to vote? Would these new social and economic policies be environmentally sustainable? If concerted efforts were made to end precarious jobs by providing secure and better paid conditions, improving social welfare for families and so forth, would these policies undermine the hospitality, tourism, digital and gig economy sectors, agriculture, and retailing that rely on low-paid jobs especially for young and immigrant workers? Would such targeted policies increase food, entertainment, travel, and other prices thus alienating middle-income voters? If professional, higher-educated voters are increasingly anti-Right-wing, it is logical to focus on an ecologically sustainable political economic program that also delivers significant benefits for low-income working-class voters. Otherwise, the latter will continue to abstain from voting or remain captured by Right-wing and neo-fascist parties. This will ensure that social democratic parties fail to win majorities on their own or in coalition with other reform orientated parties in a 'social bloc'.

Radical political activists must therefore face the hard truth that current socio-political conditions make winning on one's own most unlikely. The quest for the 'winning organisational model' is a mistaken and unrealisable goal. Alliance building between parties and movements is one of the few options left to advocates of social change. Central to this new political reality is that many parties still fail to take seriously the problematic relationship between mainstream and alternative concepts of democracy and environmental issues seriously as something far more extensive and more complicated than the climate crisis. It is not only 'Left populist' parties that still lack a policy strategy that comes to terms with how any alternative program on employment, production, taxation, social services, and other issues must reckon with environmental constraints within capitalist systems. Post-carbon capitalism is an emerging and volatile reality that will need to be secured by internally divided business and political leaders. These pro-market forces face external demands from diverse political constituencies that ecologically modernised capitalism be converted into more socially just post-carbon democracies.

However, the character of future political struggles will depend on the degree of awareness amongst reformers and anti-capitalists as to the future limits that must be imposed on ecologically unsustainable capitalist growth. Meanwhile, the advocacy of a borderless world and versions of post-growth, post-work or a degrowth society will continue to remain utopian goals. As fringe ideas supported by marginalised social movements and handfuls of radical academic theorists and students disconnected from political engagement, they are most unlikely to be adopted as major features of conventional electoral politics any time soon. However, they need to persist as important goals by which to measure the inadequacies of mainstream socio-economic policies and as catalysts for more extensive social change.

Despite two major crises having shaken the globe since 2007-08, the political situation in most countries is still very much in a state of interregnum where the old prevails and new major reforms are yet to take hold. The institutional structure and culture of centre/Left mainstream parties is highly contradictory. On the one hand, their structure means that they cannot be radicalised, as generations of hopeful radicals have learnt through bitter experiences. On the other hand, these parties are based on diverse constituencies, shifting positions and internal conflicts which can still result in formal or informal roles in any potential reform-orientated 'social bloc' of various parties and movements.

The immediate task confronting all reform and radical parties and movements is to prevent climate chaos. To prevent such a dangerous outcome, there is a pressing need for those favouring social change not to opt for 'anti-politics' in the form of a retreat to micro-changes at household level, or sabotage, or violence or 'street politics' that rejects electoral politics. Even the most successful extra-parliamentary social movements have still needed parties to pass sympathetic legislation in state institutions. By abstaining from what is called the sphere of the state, all social change politics, or philosophical and socio-cultural critiques of capitalism become romantic in the belief that people can change the world without organised politics beyond the local. Semi-organised politics is also rendered aimless if most energy mobilised in protest marches soon dissipates unless it is channelled into parties/movements with democratically defined agendas. Until these time-tested truths are recognised by new generations of activists, it is unlikely that social change advocates will be able to break the damaging political impasse preventing the transition to greater social equality and environmental sustainability.

6. ALTERNATIVES TO WELFARE STATES: BEYOND 'DEPENDENT BEGGARS AND WAGE SLAVES'

ANY TRANSITION to a post-carbon society that goes beyond the minimum objective of replacing fossil fuels with renewable energy, raises the question of how the restructuring of key industries, labour markets and trade will affect the provision of sufficient income, decent secure work, and adequate social care for growing numbers of people who currently lack these basic social conditions. Today, there is a growing recognition that the obstacles to greater equality and democratic choice do not just come from powerful propertied social classes resisting change. Achieving social equality must also overcome what many environmentalists see as the limited capacity of the biophysical world to sustain the growth in the use of material resources necessary for comprehensive, radical egalitarian programmes. In affluent OECD countries with social welfare institutions, these welfare regimes vitally depend on tax revenues raised from what are currently environmentally unsustainable forms of capitalist production and consumption. Shifting to ecologically sustainable economic processes will not be possible without significant political struggles between businesses, wage workers and constituencies dependent on state welfare benefits. While the 'just transition' may be an oft-quoted political demand, little is said about what kind of policies and socio-economic institutional forms would make possible a 'just transition' to an environmentally sustainable post-carbon democracy.

Hence, the shape and future character of what is called social welfare, or the 'social state' is not a peripheral policy issue that only affects low-income, marginalised sections of the population. Rather, the 'social state' will become central to all major policy debates and strategies in coming years. Without an understanding of how bio-physical capacities will affect not only sustainable production and consumption but also government revenue and expenditure needed for essential services and income, all public policy is likely to be established on shaky foundations. Consequently, in this chapter, I will discuss why we need to move beyond much of the conventional discourse about welfare regimes (mainly confined to affluent countries), and why previous notions of decommodification are inadequate to an understanding of what is needed to change existing capitalist welfare regimes. I will then focus on why anti-statist conceptions of enterprise-based welfare, the 'commons' and other self-sufficient, anti-bureaucratised solutions such as universal basic income schemes will fall far short of meeting critical essential needs. Finally, I will conclude with a brief outline of more hopeful strategies that are worth pursuing.

Disputing the Geo-Political Dimensions of Democratic Social Care

Until recently, the clash between market globalisation (permitting the free movement of labour, capital investment and cultural and technological exchanges) and various anti-globalisation local and nationalist demands to protect jobs, welfare entitlements and ecological habitats was perhaps the dominant political feature of our times. Now the emergence of regional blocs built around trade, military and other geopolitical tensions between the US and China, with Europe and other regions forced to either fend for themselves or join in closer socio-economic alliances with one or another of the superpowers, threatens to shape future regional 'social states'. In the EU, for example, the ability of member governments to deliver social welfare will increasingly depend on the economic health of key industries caught in potential high-tech and trade wars. Political support for an egalitarian EU-wide democratised 'social state' has been too weak. Even after decades of the limited attempts to breakdown national inequalities, it is clear that income and social care disparities within the EU are as wide as ever. Only the owners of capital enjoy a borderless EU between member countries. Either the EU becomes even more marketised and the last vestiges of social democratic and corporatist welfare disappear, or the EU is democratised, and social and labour processes are made much more equal across the EU.

Neoliberal policies are at a crossroad. Growing political pressures to decarbonise EU industries and implement the 2017 'European Pillar of

Social Rights in 20 Principles' (equal opportunities, fair working conditions and social protection and inclusion) may have more chance of success in a prolonged economic crisis. At the moment, a progressive template awaits substantive action and expenditure if it is not to remain 'feel good' rhetoric. If the EU as a 'social state' becomes the dominant operative model for other regions, then national criteria of welfare eligibility would need to be broken down as EU citizens and residents become entitled to social benefits and supra-national services regardless of where they reside. This would mean a fundamental reorganisation of national, local, and supra-national welfare budgetary allocations with profound consequences on labour processes in terms of wages, social insurance contributions and the relation between state institutions and business sectors.

Such a 'social state' could not be introduced without a significant loss of private corporate and small and medium business power. It could also not be introduced without the EU increasing its own borrowing and revenue raising methods such as new EU-wide taxes and issuing bonds or mutualised debt. Currently, businesses in member states can compete for 'social state' contracts across the EU. Any push for substantial decommodification of essential services (see below) would need to end profitable market competitiveness and restore the delivery of these social services to non-profit public agencies or local community co-operatives.

Yet, Europe is only a small part of the globe. Most of the world's population living in bordered, antagonistic countries do not desire or are unable to imitate a so-called borderless European Union. Across the Mediterranean, there is no African country that has comparable welfare services to those in Northern Europe. Most have been unable to surmount the legacy of artificial nation state boundaries bequeathed by colonial conquest. Some countries such as Ghana have the formal legislative commitment to providing health, education, and other social welfare, but not the resources. Similarly, in 2004, Lesotho introduced the old age pension for people 70 and over. However, with an average life expectancy of 44 (and still only 54 years in 2021) this reform is largely meaningless for most of its citizens. It should not be forgotten that up to 39% of the GDP in low-income countries like Lesotho is made up of migrant workers in other countries supporting their families by sending remittances back home (privatised informal welfare support!). From Botswana to Uganda, Mozambique to Nigeria or Angola to Libya, African countries *exclude* far more of the total 1.2 billion people on the continent from social benefits than the minority who are able to access their woefully under-resourced social programmes. Add numerous civil wars, climate induced drought and a catalogue of debilitating diseases from HIV to malaria and tuberculosis, and there is no possibility of these low-income countries constructing European-style social welfare programs without massive foreign aid, cleansing corrupt governments and a cessation of civil conflicts.

African countries are not alone in suffering from mass unemployment and inadequate or virtually non-existent public welfare provision. There is no shortage of countries in Asia or Latin America with large informal sectors based on poorly paid precarious labour and squalid social conditions. Governments now face a brewing storm of continued stagnant/low economic growth, climate induced natural disasters and major threats to food security in key food producing regions. Add the need to rapidly decarbonise and restructure industries, and it remains to be seen how many governments will survive. Amid these simultaneously occurring crises, if the familiar resort to violent repression is avoided, it will be the strength of national 'safety nets', namely the scale and comprehensiveness of particular social programs, that will heavily determine political outcomes. Let us not forget that approximately 160 out of 197 countries do not have universal welfare systems, let alone adequate government income schemes and essential services support programs. This means that most of the world's population are already in a precarious and grossly disadvantageous position concerning their capacity to cope with impending crises generated by climatic events and socio-economic crises.

Degrowthers such as Joan Martinez-Alier[1] and eco-socialists have long combined social justice, biodiversity, and sustainability in their strategy of 'environmentalism of the poor'. Local villagers, Indigenous communities and poor urban dwellers in many countries have to battle against rapacious developers, violent landlords, businesses generating toxic industrial waste and fumes from mines and factories, to mention just a few of the struggles waged for environmental justice. Without mass campaigns for state-provided universal basic services or basic income, low-income people are left defenceless and isolated to fight fragmented local battles against those who wish to deprive them of land or render them homeless or slum dwellers working in the exploitative informal sectors of large cities.

In developed capitalist countries, radicals have generally regarded 'welfare states' as mere band-aids for capitalism that perpetuate poverty and inequality while trapping recipients of benefits in labyrinths of state bureaucratisation. Unsurprisingly, we have witnessed a proliferation of ideas about fully automated post-work societies based on universal basic incomes or self-sufficient, small communities providing care and wellbeing. Yet, in many countries in Asia, Africa and Latin America with large rural populations and urban slums, there has long been a tension between those social change activists who wished to develop the benefits of social welfare systems like those in northern Europe, and others who advocated various forms of ecological agrarian communitarianism. The South Korean example is a relevant case in point. During the 1980s, Korean activist Gyu-seok Cheon, argued that state welfare made self-sufficiency impossible and converted people into dependent beggars and slaves while 'community communitarianism and associationism' in the form of agrarian self-suffi-cient communes or associations would simultaneously reject capitalism, industrialism, and welfare statism.[2]

It is extremely difficult for villagers in a range of countries to become self-sufficient in areas of increasing desertification, infertile land and depleted or polluted marine or freshwater habitats. Rural labourers working in agribusiness cash crops suffer from low wages or prices even when compared to poor standards of living experienced by urban workers. Glob-ally, movements that campaign for sweeping land reform to win the right of millions of rural people to run their own villages without landlordism and expropriation are still weak. It remains to be seen whether these move-ments can form political alliances with urban movements seeking to replace export-led manufacturing with a 'social industrial' strategy of building essential housing, electricity, sewage, water and other infrastructure, and social services.

When we look at the possibilities of sustainable welfare systems in China and India that account for almost 40% of the world's population, it is not just that these countries lack adequate universal welfare systems. This is true of the US as well. However, the standard of living in India is far lower. (I will discuss China shortly.) Caught between relying on meagre family and communal support in thousands of poor villages, barely surviving on the streets or in the urban slums while working in the large informal sector, or fortunate enough to get a job in the formal private and public sector, India is a *social disorder* of daily degradation, deep layers of shocking poverty, discrimination, violence, and prejudice.

Since the birth of modern India in 1947 and China in 1949, analysts have continued to compare their development, socio-political systems, and quality of life. Both have poisoned their soil, water, and air but with quite different impacts. Social analyst, Richard Smith, is scathing about both countries when it comes to environmental sustainability. He notes that in comparison to China:

> India's dysfunctional ruling class can't even provide toilets for its citizens, or pick up the trash, let alone provide electricity, modern container ports, high-speed trains, or a skilled industrial work force. In the twenty-first century, hundreds of millions of Indians remain unconnected to an electrical grid. Unmanaged refuse accumulates into 'mountains' that collapse killing people and cause tuberculosis, dengue fever, and poisoned ground water. India's air pollution is now as bad as if not worse than China's despite having far less industry. Minister Narendra Modi wants to compete with China?"[3]

Add the absolutely tragic, catastrophic mismanagement of COVID-19 in India compared to China, and we have the worst of worlds in the fusion of Indian capitalism with religious communalism, authoritarianism, and corruption. Also, the prospects for reform are bleak as the nexus between class position, level of education and voting is weak in India where ethno-religious and caste cleavages dominate.[4]

In recent years, governments in Mexico, Brazil, Iran, Egypt, Tunisia, and other countries have paid cash transfers or subsidies for fuel and energy rather than a universal basic income (UBI) to families, some in return for ensuring school attendance, immunisation against diseases and other requirements. Riots and mass protests have ensued in Ecuador, Chile, Colombia, and other countries when these subsidies or pensions were removed or threatened. We know that shocking poverty compounded by lack of elementary health and other care facilities continue to ravage many countries. South America has only 5.53% of the world's population but by May 2021 had suffered 32% of COVID deaths globally. India is following close behind. A few years ago, the Modi government's 2016-17 Economic Survey proposed a targeted basic income, to minimise existing misallocation of funds and corruption (about twenty per cent of eligible people fail to receive their tiny government support). However, this targeted basic income would have been a replacement for most food, fuel and other subsidies going to the poor rather than an additional and more generous payment.[5]

Instead of more extensive social care provision, in 2020 the Modi government proceeded in the opposite direction and legislated an extensive program of market commodification for its poorest people. The Indian

Farm bills will marketise and deregulate the *mandi* or public market price system of essential commodities, expose farms to private contractors and large international agribusinesses[6] while threatening the already very meagre livelihood of 46% of India's workforce on small farms of 1 to 2 hectares. Such is the level of unequal land ownership that the top 10% control 50% of farming land while the bottom 50% own less than 1% of agricultural land.[7] Little wonder there have been mass protests by poor farmers during 2020/21 as this proposed transformation of farming will lead to death, despair, and increased landlessness. Rampant market restructuring of rural India will compound existing inequality. This underscores the reason why universal basic services and basic income schemes are an essential part of any alternative socio-economic strategy and must be fully integrated with an environmentally sustainable political strategy. So far, these two crucial components of decommodification and sustainability have been marginalised in a country whose government and ruling class shows appalling contempt for the most needy and vulnerable. As so many others have concluded, India desperately needs a revolution.

Beyond Narrow Views of Decommodification

To understand how debates over statist and anti-statist alternatives to existing welfare regimes have changed, I will briefly discuss earlier conceptions of decommodification in contrast to more recent notions of post-growth wellbeing. During the 1970s, the concept of capitalist welfare systems simultaneously crisis-managing the flaws of market capitalism and yet also helping to decommodify social relations by partially freeing people from being dependent on commodified labour in the marketplace, was developed by sociologist Claus Offe.[8] He called the sector of 'residual labour power' the extreme pole of decommodification. The unemployed, pensioners, university students, prisoners, and all others outside the labour market receive social benefits or payments that are politically determined and do not correspond to a relationship between the work performed and remuneration paid.[9]

Building on Offe's analysis of decommodification, sociologist Gøsta Esping-Andersen famously divided welfare regimes into three types: Anglo-American liberal capitalist countries (including the US, UK, Australia, Canada and New Zealand); the social democratic Scandinavian bloc; and the conservative corporatist countries such as Germany, Austria, France.[10] Each of the liberal, social democratic and corporatist types of regimes had welfare delivery based on means-tested or universal benefits or promoted religiously influenced welfare that upheld conservative concepts of women and the family. The level of decommodification differed in these 'three worlds of welfare'. According to Esping Andersen, "decommodification should not be confused with the complete eradication of labour as a commodity; it is not an issue of all or nothing. Rather, the concept refers to the degree to which individuals, or families, can uphold a socially acceptable standard of living independently of market participation."[11]

Offe also argued that the extension of universal voting, parliamentary government, and recognition of trade union interests in the early twentieth century resulted in legal welfare entitlements becoming relatively 'rigid' or even irreversible.[12] This view from the 1970s turned out to be premature and certainly wrong in the light of neoliberal assaults on welfare during the past forty years. He also underestimated how business groups and their political allies ensured that *decommodification* was strictly controlled or reduced.

Decommodification is partly related to the size of the 'social state'. In *Capitalism Versus Democracy?* I argued that there is no uniform size of the 'social state' or level of social expenditure and environmentally sustainable policies as a percentage of GDP beyond which capitalist political economic orders are threatened and begin to disintegrate. What is tolerable for businesses in countries such as France or Norway may be regarded as beyond the pale by capitalists and governments in the US, Japan, or Australia. For example, in capitalist Finland, one third of the economy is in the public sector which employs a third of the workforce and almost 90% of private and public sector workers are covered by a union contract. For America to match Finland in similar percentage terms, Matt Bruenig of the *People's Policy Project* argues that the US government would have to "not only build a social-democratic welfare state, but also socialise $35 trillion of assets, unionise 120 million workers, and move 25 million workers into the public sector."[13]

Why is this lack of a clear tipping point between size of public and private sectors so important? Two reasons. Firstly, given the short- to medium-term impossibility of revolution or radical degrowth, any transition to an environmentally sustainable post-capitalist society would initially have to begin within existing capitalist societies. Secondly, all schemes for universal basic services, basic income schemes or job guarantees under programs called 'Green New Deal' or other names would almost certainly involve a process of some level of decommodification or freeing up certain social relations from the dictates of the market.

Notably, before the 1980s, growing state social expenditure that loosened the dependence of most people on private markets for daily care, sustenance, and income was seen as a threat to capitalist commodified relations. Yet today, these developments have been scaled back or halted altogether in various OECD countries. Thomas Piketty argues that well before the crisis of 2008, if there had been no curbing of the growth of the 'social state', the rate of tax as a percentage of GDP before 1980 would have seen social expenditure and tax collection increase to between 70 to 80 per cent of national income by 2050-2060 in European countries.[14] Therefore, between 1980 and 2010, neoliberal EU governments stabilised the tax collected to between 40 and 50 per cent of GDP (still well above tax collected in the US, Japan, Australia). Nonetheless, short of 90 to 100 per cent of GDP, nobody knows what the limits of tax, as a percentage of national income would have to be in capitalist countries before major political conflict erupts. Four decades of neoliberal mythmaking based on privatisation, austerity policies, small government, 'balanced budgets' as signs of good heath have been blown out of the water since 2008 with massive increases in government quantitative easing programmes, and trillion-dollar rescue packages during the COVID-19 pandemic.[15]

It would be a big mistake, however, to think that a nominal increase in government expenditure on health, housing, income support, social insurance protection for the unemployed, pensions, child-care, and aged care, automatically leads to decommodification. Certainly, it is preferable to have a society spend a larger proportion of GDP on social expenditure. Nevertheless, the standard and prevalent comparison of nation states by their level of fiscal spending on welfare services is a very crude device that only tells us what these countries allocate rather than the *quality* of particular services. Indeed, most social welfare budgets do not tell us whether services are publicly provided or contracted out to private businesses, and especially whether public sector agencies imitate and uphold market practices or undermine capitalist commodity relations by providing services based on need rather than profit.

It is true that Offe recognised the changing character of capitalism. There were by the mid-1990s, more aged pensioners than blue collar workers in Europe and more unemployed persons than farmers. One could no longer identify people's political views by their location in the mode of production or by their forms of consumption.[16] Like other analysts from the 1970s onwards, Offe focused on how endless demands on state resources coupled with stagnant or diminished revenue forced governments to offload responsibilities to numerous 'para-corporatised' or 'para-constitutional bodies', whether churches, trade associations and professional bodies, trade unions or 'social entrepreneurial' groups. This 're-feudalisation' of the state witnessed many governments abandoning their roles as direct providers of goods and services and delegating these functions to intermediary organisations.

However, despite these important insights, both Offe and Esping-Andersen advanced a narrow view of decommodification because they failed to adequately consider or anticipate the degree of marketisation of essential public services. Hence, their dated analyses mainly viewed decommodification through the prism of the labour market, namely, whether people had to sell their labour power to survive or were outside the labour market and on welfare benefits. Importantly, these theorists said little or nothing about the other key aspect of decommodification, that is, the difference between whether health, social care, education, pensions, and other services were delivered as non-market, decommodified social relations by public institutions, community co-operatives and agencies or whether they were transformed into profit-making commodified services.

Today, many former non-market public welfare services such as health, housing, transport, aged-care, child-care, and other services have either been commodified through privatisation or the *de facto* privatisation of the latter via outsourcing the delivery and provision of these services to private contracting businesses. Take, for instance, aged care. Investigative journalist, Juliet Ferguson, recently reported that OECD figures indicated that states transferred around €218 billion to care home operators each year, with a further €65 billion paid by the residents or their relatives.[17] The disastrous death rates from COVID-19 continue to reveal lack of adequate public health system capacity in the US and especially the large outsourcing to private providers of services across the old 'three worlds of welfare' whether in Australia, the UK, France, the US, or Sweden, all countries employing low-paid precarious labour in health systems and aged-care.[18] An incredible 41% of all deaths from COVID-19 in Europe by February 2021 were care-home residents.[19]

Families and individuals have thus incurred higher costs and also continue to be subjected to harsher profit-making market criteria. In the US where civilian welfare had always been grossly inadequate, the switch from military conscription to a volunteer force in the 1970s was accompanied by a significant boost to 'army welfare' (designed to attract recruits with families) that was far more comprehensive than the civilian 'welfare state'. By the 1990s, this welfare provision was scaled back and privatised so that in the 21st century, US military and civilian social welfare services were both de-facto privatised to private contractors.[20]

Across the world, financial institutions, and private providers of everything from job retraining to medical care are also able to siphon off scarce public fiscal resources in the form of contract fees per 'case load' and tax subsidies, all in the name of 'market efficiency'. The outcomes are usually inferior and less secure services, such as reducing the number and quality of care providers (often through lower paid casual employees or contract case workers, cleaners, private prison guards and so forth) while increasing the number of patients, the aged and others in need of care.

Retirement income or pensions are now divided between those with remaining large public contributory schemes but growing private pension systems (such as Germany, France, Norway, Italy), and a range of private pension systems (in Anglo-American countries, Switzerland, the Netherlands and elsewhere) which account for up to 42% of pension assets alongside public systems. For example, the 1981 privatised Chilean system is highly unpopular, fosters increased poverty due to years of poor market earnings plus ineligibility criteria, all compounded by the COVID-19 economic slump. It is clear that globally, with over USD$45 trillion in private pension assets in 2019, pension funds have played an increasingly powerful role in equity markets over recent decades.[21] Workers are thus becoming more dependent on fluctuating equity market performances as well as their pension fund's property, bond, and infrastructure investments. Most new workers are no longer entitled to partially decommodified fixed pensions or 'defined benefits' based on number of years of contributions, age and income earned. Instead, pension fund benefits are now often determined by members selecting different asset classes that constantly fluctuate as markets make gains or losses.

In short, decommodification entails far more than whether a person is independent of the private capitalist labour market or only partially reliant on the wage labour process. Today, decommodification will only occur if the social relations between the providers of care and social income are not constrained by market mechanisms or disciplinary measures. We are now in the era of pseudo-care and time limits on social benefits that do not undermine market relations. Notable examples include the quick 'turnover' of patients and larger numbers of children to each carer in private child-care, or contract providers of dead-end job retraining schemes for the unemployed who are treated as little more than new commodities. Most contemporary private or public welfare services do *not primarily* aim to improve the welfare and wellbeing of the recipients, despite the good intentions and demanding work of many underpaid and overworked staff.

Consequently, there will be future struggles in many countries over the extent to which vitally needed social welfare services, free of private market criteria, can be won by political movements. Creating a 'social space' for decommodification, despite opposition from businesses and conservative political forces is also highly relevant to the future character of either green growth or ecological sustainability. If we are to develop a political strategy that is more than a mere shopping list of desirable objectives, any such strategy must consider the wider picture of 'democracy versus sustainability' and how this could play out within capitalist societies and between capitalist global and national powers. Our political responses need to be structured in ways that go beyond both the old inadequate liberal social democratic policies of yesteryear and the prevailing mixture of neoliberal and paternalist authoritarian forms of enterprise-based welfare and market driven green growth. Importantly, any conception of the 'social state' in post-growth societies must also consider crucial issues of financing and delivering services.

There is growing discussion of the connection between environmental policies and social welfare in OECD countries. In fact, there is a standard formula on display in welfare policy literature. Nearly all the authors state from the outset that they are not going to discuss welfare services in the rest of the world. They then proceed, ironically, to make pronouncements on *global* sustainability, carbon and material footprints that precisely depend on the actions and needs of 86% of the world's population outside North America, Europe, Japan, and Australia that they deliberately exclude or refuse to discuss. Recently, ecological economists Christine Corlet Walker, Angela Druckman and Tim Jackson made the valid observation that, "the problem of state welfare provision in a post-growth economy is, in many ways, a microcosm of the general post-growth challenge: how to ensure the sustainable prosperity of a population in a non-growing economy, in a way that does not compromise the ecological integrity of the planet, or the ability of others around the world (and in the future) to meet their own needs."[22] Like many other analysts of OECD welfare states, they unfortunately undermine their own case by refusing to discuss social welfare dynamics outside what they call the 'Global North'. Nonetheless, many of their questions are particularly important. Surveying the literature on welfare and sustainability, they identify five core dilemmas:

> One, how to maintain funding for the welfare system in a non-growing or shrinking economy.
> Two, how to manage the increasing relative costs of welfare, compared to other goods, without relying on economic growth.
> Three, how to overcome structural and behavioural growth dependencies *within* the welfare system.
> Four, how to manage increasing needs, and therefore demand, on a finite planet.
> Five, how to overcome political barriers to the transformation of the welfare state.[23]

In similar fashion to most other ecological economists, all these important questions about social change assume a certain degree of political stability in European and other OECD countries with free electoral systems. While Corlet Walker, Druckman and Jackson canvas a range of mainstream welfare policies as well as degrowth and neo-Marxist approaches, they also assume largely benign capitalist class forces that will not turn to authoritarian and violent solutions when facing crises of profitability. Moreover, they are sympathetic to greater regulation of private suppliers to the health system and other aspects of the 'social state', in order to keep costs down and make services more sustainable. The idea of the 'entrepreneurial state' (Mariana Mazzucato) is also uncritically supported concerning state innovation in the production of services.[24] One notable omission is the failure to discuss state planning as opposed to greater regulation of markets.

Given that local communities lack the political and economic resources or power to combat corporate giants, the potential chaos of climate breakdown and dysfunctional markets can only be dealt with by state intervention and some form of state planning of how to meet social needs. Yet, there is still much suspicion and caution about planning and controlling. Social theorist, Hartmut Rosa, argues that instead of improving our lives, the desire to control all aspects of our world has led to unforeseen environmental crises and new social problems. He contrasts 'controllability' – the modern desire to control nature, political and economic institutions, cultural practices, and personal physical and mental health – with the rise of 'uncontrollability' in the form of volatile markets, unpredictable and dangerous processes stemming from digital technologies and so forth.[25] As a general reflection on the 'modern condition', Rosa's insights are both suggestive and perceptive. As an explanation of what could be done to remedy 'uncontrollability', however, his theory lacks a politics and any sense of the way forward.

In opposition to Rosa's warnings about 'controllability', I would argue that we need to be more specific about what needs to be brought under greater political control, including financial practices, deforestation, exploitative labour markets, polluting chemical factories, destructive mining ventures or congested, car-dominated cities. Conversely, we also need far greater public discussion about the socio-economic, political, and ecological processes we need to 'liberate' from current bureaucratic, abusive, or discriminatory state and private practices, especially relating to people's eligibility and the delivery of social services.

It is not an either/or situation of planning in post-capitalist society on the one hand but no planning within capitalist countries on the other. Let us not forget that planning is currently indispensable in key logistical areas of contemporary capitalist societies (transport, communication, military weapons, energy grids and so forth). Planning could be extended to a wider range of essential social services, habitats, and products. Currently, the public have little or no say about priorities and expenditure allocations other than occasionally at elections. Instead of just thinking about how whole countries could be planned, social change activists could also identify which areas of existing political economic activity – from health systems and housing, right through to revenue collection or natural resources use – are amenable to alternative, more equitable and sustainable policy planning models, and practices. This would involve movements, communities and policy analysts rethinking the production and delivery of particular goods and services, so that they are planned in accordance with input from relevant constituencies rather than by governments, thinktanks and businesses offering familiar but narrow market solutions.

One such attempt at local and regional planning is called the 'foundational economy'. This group of theorists based in Manchester, Barcelona, London, and other cities start with the following premises about the 'foundational economy':

- Central or national governments should not abdicate responsibility and leave cities and regions suffering from decades of under-development to deal with inequality and lack of resources. However, because most central or national governments lack the imagination and knowledge to deal with local and regional problems, it is necessary to reinvent, empower and develop the micro-level capacities of local and regional governments who are most familiar with their own needs in regard to employment, services, industries, and ecology.[26]

- Instead of beginning with abstract concepts of 'the market' or an 'undifferentiated capitalism', it is crucial to recognise that the basic materials of everyday life "are exceptionally diverse in their production cycles, their economic geographies, the complexity of their inputs, their spatial relations and reliance on land..."[27]

- Rather than focus on the tradeable and competitive parts of the production system as if they were the whole economy, the 'foundational economy' approach divides each local, regional, and national economy into zones of which the tradeable and competitive market businesses are only one zone. The other zones consist of essential services in health, education, transport, housing, energy and so forth, the family or household core zone, and the occasionally used zone of activities, such as holidays or haircuts.

While the Foundational Economy group are not all geared to radical post-capitalist change, they do emphasise the need to develop essential services and those zones of regional and local economies. These would help shift social and economic activity away from commercial tradeable commodities to decommodified services, or employment and infrastructure that would reduce poverty and inequality in a manner that is compatible with environmental sustainability.

In recent years, some socialists have argued that all large corporations such as Amazon, Apple, Walmart, and thousands of other businesses engage in extensive forward planning across different subsidiaries and supply chains in their production, marketing, and other departments.[28] Hence, these planning models could supposedly be adopted and modified for use in post-capitalist societies. While sounding persuasive, these market socialist models are also far from problem-free. The notion of utilising planning models borrowed from private multinational corporations overlooks the vastly different profit-making logic built into corporate plans. Once democratic governments either reject or try to avoid imitating narrow corporate objectives based on exploitative labour conditions, environmental destruction, tax avoidance and numerous other strategies designed to enhance 'shareholder value', the tricky problems begin. Corporate planning largely excludes workers. If workers demand self-management rights or planners not only prohibit exploitative wages and environmentally polluting products and practices, but also enforce other such socially responsible objectives, it is doubtful whether corporate planning could be easily transposed to eco-socialist and other types of democratic public planning.

Market socialists must also consider how a post-growth society can reconcile leaving key parts of the economy in the hands of small and medium private enterprises or co-operatives while the 'commanding heights' of large enterprises were state planned. If market growth were allowed to determine demand in both publicly and privately controlled sectors, it is likely that non-market values such as degrowth of resources, social need and equality would either encounter major obstacles or cease being the primary operative principles guiding key industries. Without a national plan specifying limits on the volume of material resources going to small and medium businesses, market practices would undermine ecological sustainability. Similarly, without a national incomes policy and also prices policy for key commodities, in other words, politically legislated 'ceilings' limiting private wealth and income as well as 'floors' preventing poverty, it is almost certain that major forms of inequality would remain. Importantly, if such policies were implemented only by local communities in a post-carbon democracy, it is highly likely that regional and national inconsistencies and inequalities would also arise.

Some market socialists such as David Schweickart propose models of 'economic democracy' for the US which retain key aspects of capitalist markets except that the labour market is controlled to eliminate unemployment in the interest of workers, and capital investment markets are also controlled in the interest of public goods and services to negate the worst aspects of neoliberal financialisation.[29] This would still be essentially a capitalist society with better labour conditions and state control over aspects of market activity. The question remains as to whether political control over financial markets would eventually lead to greater development of post-carbon democratic social institutions or not?

Workers' Control: Sustainability and the Dangers of Enterprise-Based Welfare

Prominent alternatives to neoliberal social policies take the form of radical workers' control at enterprise level or social democratic state reforms. Take, for example, liberal social democrats such as Dani Rodrik, Branko Milanovic, and many other policy analysts either writing for journals such as *Social Europe* or working with centre/Left parties and labour movements. They favour green growth strategies and advocate a range of reform policies which aim to reduce inequality *without* a major restructuring of key parts of the environmentally destructive character of capitalist systems.[30] Some of their proposals include the extension of up to 50% of worker representation on corporate management boards and variations of the discontinued Swedish Rehn-Meidner model of 'wage workers funds' where shares are allocated to all workers in businesses over a certain size.

These policies are combined with state policies such as the provision of fixed sums of money or 'lifetime accounts' for education to each child or adult as 'seed money' for better 'life chances'; wealth taxes and various revenue schemes to counter offshore tax evasion, and other such proposals designed to redistribute proportions of capital to non-capitalists and also to help regulate and outlaw bad corporate behaviour.[31] Most of these proposals either aim to remedy past and present excesses of neoliberal capitalism or institute defensive labour and social laws to protect workers and consumers. They also assume that changes to the law defining 'the firm' as well as shareholder and management rights will help democratise capitalism and give workers a personal stake in the businesses that employ them.

Thomas Piketty advocates similar policies. He is representative of those Left social democrats/socialists who stand between radical Marxists and neo-Keynesian reformers. In Piketty's view, capitalism and private property can be superseded and replaced by 'participatory socialism', an ambitious quasi-market socialism based on competing enterprises (rather than state planning) and characterised by the redistribution of wealth, education and other social resources via steep wealth taxes and other measures.[32] Being a mixture of market socialism and social democratic reform, Piketty, like many liberals and Left social democrats, proposes reforms that are top-down proposals largely disconnected from struggles by social movements.

The argument that either a substantial or majority shareholding owned by workers will change society is highly questionable if considered *only at the enterprise level* while leaving the macro-political economic decisions beyond the individual enterprise largely unchanged. These enterprise management arguments only appear credible if a change in worker owner-ship is linked to larger political and social movements that explicitly advo-cate environmentally sustainable social justice policies and institutional practices. Nonetheless, any increase in worker representation, controls over capital investment and wealth taxes would be a welcome change from decades of growing inequality. A very modest wealth tax and cap on extreme wealth, for instance, would raise almost 1.3 trillion Euros annually to finance greater social and environmental expenditure.[33]

As to environmental sustainability, even radical versions of pension and other worker funds largely ignore the environmental limits to incessant market growth. Earlier critics of existing pension funds, such as Robin Blackburn, provided ample evidence of the inequality and appalling conse-quences resulting from finance capital's management of pension funds.[34] However, such alternative proposals unfortunately were framed within an *environmental vacuum* as to the long-term sustainability of investments needed to provide adequate pensions. The old paradigm of 'capitalism versus democracy' was based on a struggle between capitalists and workers over redistribution of wealth and control of decision-making. However, greater worker representation on boards or the ownership of shares by workers will be ineffective and meaningless if the latter changes to deci-sion-making and ownership result in workers largely endorsing ecologically unsustainable growth trajectories adopted by market-orientated managements.

In short, state-owned, or worker-controlled enterprises and pension funds operating under market conditions are highly constrained as alterna-tives to capitalist markets. They mimic the limited capacity and contradic-tion of trade unions within capitalist societies. In order to protect workers, most union leaders, leaving aside their conservative views, cannot afford to go all the way and support revolutionary action for fear of the devastating impact of social convulsion on their members' jobs and living conditions. We are still in the early stages of developing policy ideas and strategies that link workers' struggles to the development of state planning of environ-mentally sustainable 'social state' policies and new community institutional processes. Few anti-capitalists have paid sufficient attention to how to reconcile the need for democratic state planning with the desire to maximise local community and workers' control over their workplaces and social institutions.

Not only is it clear that the discussion about planning is extremely limited at the moment, but most of the contributors to these debates operate with outworn assumptions that belong to social conditions prevalent in the first half of the twentieth century. We no longer live in the era when manufacturing was a very large employer of labour and notions of socialism revolved around the leading role of the industrial proletariat. Today, few conceptions of planning consider that more than 80% of workers in leading capitalist countries do not produce goods in factories and do not produce surplus value in offices, shops, hospitals, schools, public transport vehicles, police and military apparatuses, and numerous other private and public workplaces. While manufacturing remains a vital part of most developed capitalist countries, it would be highly undemocratic for the small and declining proportion of workers employed in this sector, as well as the small numbers employed in mining, construction, and agriculture in OECD countries, to make decisions about the allocation of material resources on behalf of the vast majority of workers and their families dependent on employment in service sectors or relying on state benefits. In low and middle-income countries with large rural workforces employed in agriculture or in the urban informal economy, the imbalance between different sectors of employment and income sustenance would make workers' control of industrial enterprises even more undemocratic. It would also lead to a repeat of 'enterprise welfare', which, as I will go on to discuss, is an unequal model best avoided.

Revolutionary conceptions of socialist self-management or workers' control assumed that as workers produced the surplus that was appropriated by owners as profit, a post-capitalist society would end this undemocratic process. Workers would now make the decisions about how the surplus was produced, distributed, and invested in the form of social welfare, community facilities, retirement income and general wellbeing for all. Although it is easy to envisage all workers in service sector employment democratically organising their offices, universities, hospitals and so forth, this model of workers' control is necessary but does not translate into the democratic allocation of goods and resources without the co-existence and heavy involvement of social planning by local, regional, national, and international state institutional structures and processes. It is here that earlier models of planning provide an inadequate understanding of how both a post-neoliberal economy and any transition to a post-carbon democracy could function. This is because models of full worker self-management of enterprises are essentially anti-statist and incompatible with either democratic state planning or with viable well-run societies that fulfil complex and essential social needs.

Like self-managed degrowth communities, self-managed enterprises that don't just organise and run workplaces but decide on who is to receive allocated resources are anti-democratic and counter-productive to social equality. For the contemporary world, where most people do not produce surplus value and do not work in factories or mines, self-management must be adjusted and redefined as a necessary but limited objective (that is, self-administration co-shared with community and state planning bodies) to avoid being ineffective, conflictual, and chaotic. In the absence of as yet an uninvented solution to the notion of self-managed planning, people in the future may have the following choices. Firstly, they can strive to take full democratic control over their own employing enterprises *without* being constrained by national planning or concern for all other communities, including all those who do not produce a surplus in their own cities or communities. While this choice may appear democratic, it is short-sighted because it could well guarantee the growth of deeper social inequality without state distributive and allocative functions overriding selfish, ill-informed, or narrowly focused workplace decisions. Mass discontent would lead to the eventual modification or curtailment of worker's self-management and its replacement by either nation-wide socialist planning or in the worst-case scenario, a restoration of old capitalist market practices. Secondly, employed workers can democratically decide on how to co-share powers with democratically elected local and national state institutions over how national and imported material and social resources can be planned and distributed in the most equitable manner. This would also mean strict limitations on the range and types of decisions made exclusively by workers in self-managed enterprises.

Similarly, it is also crucial to recognise the dangers of enterprise-based welfare. This is a failed template for future social equality. Any future reorganisation and development of social welfare within capitalist societies needs to learn the lessons from how past and present Communist regimes funded and still organise social welfare. One of the key differences in the quantity and quality of social welfare between different capitalist and former Communist countries concerns the sources of revenue and whether their services and social insurance income are provided by central or sub-national governments or by state-owned or private enterprises. Within capitalist countries, there are significant differences between the proportion of total annual revenue collected coming from *direct* taxes on wages and company profits as opposed to *indirect* taxes, such as consumption taxes. High consumption and other indirect taxes are highly regressive as they fall most heavily on low and middle-income people.

By contrast, the old Communist system in the USSR had a welfare system that was heavily based on state-owned industrial enterprises and collective farms. The non-independent Soviet trade unions helped administer welfare provision alongside management in enterprises. Workers and their families were provided with health services, pensions, holidays at communal resorts and other such social provisions. Standards of living were low due to low wages. But direct taxes were low, as were public transport fares, rent, utilities and other basic service charges. For those not connected to an enterprise, there was a minimal government pension which was not enough for survival and gave rise to extensive poverty, and many became beggars. The Soviet 'social wage' cost enterprises about 25% of their labour costs. In the decades before the collapse of the Soviet Union, the 'social wage' increased faster than the money wage. Following the collapse of the USSR in 1991, the 'social wage' increased to 50% of labour costs as the transition to market capitalism put tremendous pressure on both former Soviet enterprises and millions of workers to survive. Growing food on small residential plots also constituted up to 50 per cent of the post-Soviet 'social wage'. Food from these plots was essential when wages fell, a devalued currency impoverished people, life expectancy declined, and social convulsion swept former Communist countries in the ten to twenty years during and after the 1990s. Millions of people in the former USSR and Eastern European Communist countries were made destitute when their enterprises collapsed and cost them not only their jobs but also their social welfare, accommodation and increased prices for essential utilities, rent and other services.

The lesson here is that any non-universal social welfare system based on a person's employment (or former employment) at any enterprise can turn into a disaster once the enterprise faces prolonged difficulties, shuts down, or is privatised. Moreover, specific employer-tied social benefits, such as in key aspects of the US health system, become vehicles of inequality. Under this patchwork of benefits and entitlements, many workers may get health insurance from their employers (so long as they are employed), but millions of others are left with no protection or inadequate health coverage. What developed in the US from the 1930s onwards was union bargained enterprise welfare in the form of health plans, retirement benefits and so forth rather than a comprehensive social welfare program for all Americans. In post-fascist Europe after 1945, unofficial political compacts witnessed more extensive social welfare programs implemented by both conservative and social democratic governments. Similarly, the 'social wage' deal struck between 1983 and 1996 by the Australian Hawke and Keating Labor government Accords with the union movement meant national health, child-care, retirement income and other social benefits for both workers and non-workers.

However, the notion of a 'social wage' that was championed globally by labour movements during the twentieth century, either in its restricted American enterprise bargaining form or in its broader European and Australian state-delivered policies, still retained strong residues of commodification in that they were a form of 'wage' in return for increases in productivity, 'rationalisation' of industries (meaning job cuts) or compensation for modest wage increases. Consequently, any alternative social welfare system that is both democratic and universal is preferable, as long as it breaks the wage/welfare nexus and leads to society-wide decommodification of values and services. The crucial problem is how to finance such a system and ensure that the revenue it needs does not come from environmentally unsustainable economic growth. More will be said on this shortly.

Very importantly, any proposed scheme for future self-managed worker's or community control that is not based on national or supra-national universal taxation revenue and universal eligibility criteria should be rejected as an inbuilt engine of inequality resting on insecure foundations. There is a common illusion long held by anti-bureaucratic anarchists and socialists, or more recently by degrowthers and technological utopians, that communities and workplaces will look after their fellow members by providing a full range of care from the cradle to the grave. In an ideal world, this model could possibly satisfy small community needs if these self-managed entities were simultaneously blessed with adequate material resources, enough demographic diversity so that people could look after the aged, young children, the disabled and the ill. It would also require sufficient specialists in health care and other essential practices to ensure high quality, attentive and loving care. In reality, employment more than likely will be scattered across enterprises of varying size and resources. Diverse levels of long-term viability and provision of social income will depend on having to operate in regions of abundant resources or profound scarcity.

Even if new post-capitalist co-operatives and community services consciously set out to avoid the worst aspects of the old Soviet enterprise provided welfare, if most resources, staffing, and community support has to largely come from within the limited capacities of local enterprises and community facilities, little will be able to be done to prevent the generation of new inequalities. Democracy and self-management are only as good as the ability to distribute and manage *available* resources. The danger is that the negative side of democratic self-management of enterprises can result in unsustainable practices if workers put their social income needs ahead of safeguarding the wider environment. Also, when needs cannot be met from within the community – due to scarcity of resources or because existing community-owned enterprises run into unforeseen operational difficulties (a frequent problem) and become burdens rather than supporting social needs – conflicts arise, and demands are made to satisfy local deficiencies beyond the enterprise and beyond the local community. This is precisely the reason why the local delivery of social care and community facilities should be funded out of national or supra-national revenue and resources rather than just by local revenue. This could be in combination with far greater and more direct involvement of local populations who best know what they are lacking and how to meet these needs. So long as the political illusion prevails that local communities will all be able to look after their fellow residents without some form of community institutionalised care, and that existing enterprises will somehow last forever (or even half the average life span of healthy people) regardless of market conditions or local resources, social inequalities will not be resolved. Indeed, they could become worse as we have seen from past and present experiences in both capitalist and Communist countries.

The Global Impact of China's Future 'Social State'

It is imperative that we understand Chinese planning and the power of the Communist Party, as the fate of the world is bound up with the largest user of material resources and the largest emitter of greenhouse gases (currently 28% of total global emissions). Any progress towards sustainable democracies in OECD countries will be based on false premises if we do not consider China's vital role in making the earth either environmentally sustainable or not.[35] India may be hailed as the 'world's largest democracy' in name rather than in practice, but as Chinese society analyst, Daniel Vukovich has argued, China is *not* a society in transition towards a liberal market democracy as was mistakenly thought by earlier Western liberal analysts.[36]

China has global economic interests, but it has no desire or ability to replicate the history of Western imperialist military and colonial conquest. In this massive society where national planning prevails, the consequences of a 'hybrid bureaucratic collectivist-capitalist economy' are already ecologically disastrous. It is not just that China's industrial development has come at a shocking price of domestic environmental catastrophe, but that it is also 'cooking the planet' with its hyper development agenda driving dangerous emissions. Richard Smith calls this system the 'engine of environmental collapse'.[37] However, this is only one side of the picture. There are also obvious signs that China's government is moving away from just relying on earlier forms of dirty, hazardous production. China is also the world leader in the production of renewable technology. The rapid growth of a 'cleaner' digital economy in financial, health, education and other services has driven urban employment[38] alongside shockingly polluted rare earths mining (needed for digital and renewable energy equipment) and massive non-recycled e-waste. High numbers of younger 'independent professionals' have now joined a workforce with inadequate social protection.

Despite major socio-economic changes during the past forty years, both India and China still have hundreds of millions of extremely poor people, especially in rural areas. In 2019, the Hong Kong based *China Labour Bulletin* observed:

> The problems in China's social security system can be traced back to two key events: The break-up of the state-run economy, which had provided urban workers with an "iron rice bowl" (employment, housing, healthcare and pension), and the introduction of the one-child policy in the 1980s, which meant that parents could no longer rely on a large extended family to look after them in their old age. In other words, as the economy developed and liberalised in the 1990s and 2000s, both the state and social structures that had supported workers in their old age, ill-health and during times of economic hardship gradually vanished, leaving a huge vacuum to fill.[39]

By 2021, it was clear that China had conspicuously failed to either fill the vacuum left by the demise of the 'iron rice bowl' or replace it with a socially just care system, even though the 'iron rice bowl' was based on an extremely poor society with inadequate services. In forging the greatest industrial development in human history, it failed to create a universal social welfare system for its people. China currently offers a 'social state' that is highly unattractive as a model for other low- or middle-income countries. Instead, China has a range of state-provided and enterprise-provided social insurance, health and other services that are governed by employment, residency, age, and other criteria. These diverse entitlement schemes have institutionalised widespread inequality as hundreds of millions of people continue to be caught between entitlements according to their status as permanent urban residents, transient migrant contract workers or residents in rural communities with allocated land plots. Like the internal passport system in the former USSR that restricted rural and regional population movements to large cities, China retains a version of this divisive system. Several key factors determine the deeply unequal conditions of either insecurity or well-being of the Chinese people.

Firstly, their residential registration status or *hukou* is all important as this determines whether urban residents receive social benefits and welfare from their employer. Rural migrant workers are excluded from these urban benefits even though they may be long-term residents and regularly employed. Instead, they have user rights over collectively owned land in their rural towns and villages. Hundreds of millions of migrant workers fear losing their entitlements to rural land without obtaining *hukou* status in cities. In response, the Communist Party decided in 2014 to increase urban residents from 54% to 60% of China's approximately 1,430 million people by 2020. Of these, 100 million more urban residents with urban *hukou* were raised from 35% of the total working population to 45% thus shifting these people permanently to urban areas.[40]

Secondly, China has a number of social welfare funds that cover housing, pensions, health care and so forth. These are based on contributions made by workers, employers and central or provincial governments that entitle workers to services and income according to the years of contributions made and other eligibility criteria. What nominally looks good on paper in providing degrees of welfare is far from the grim reality experienced by tens of millions of people. This is due to many private employers fraudulently avoiding contributing their legal requirements, provincial governments deliberately or neglectfully failing to enforce legislation for years on end, hospitals woefully underfunded or corruptly selling services and medicines to those who can afford to pay, and numerous other such widespread erosions of a patchwork system that is inherently flawed.[41]

Thirdly, and closely tied to the first two points is the incompatible dynamics driving the public and private sectors that has produced conflict in urban and rural areas. Labour law analyst, Mary Gallagher, points out that:

> The two leading causes of social unrest in China are labour disputes and rural land disputes. ...The declining access to land security among rural residents drives the increasing demands and expectations of rural migrant workers. As access to land security decreases, demands for social security climb. Farmers pushed out of villages by land expropriation must seek out jobs and employment security in cities to replace what they have lost in their hometowns.[42]

Here we have the social security system of the most populous country in the world that directly pits the growth of its state planned capitalist economy against the security of its population and the environmental sustainability of the whole society and planet.

The more that workers lose their land and sustenance due to provincial governments failing to provide adequate social welfare and employment while permitting property developers (in conjunction with local officials) to seize land and transform ecological habitats into concrete towers, the more tens of millions seek employment in cities but are denied access to social benefits. Once in the cities, many of those with *hukou* status are robbed of their entitlements by private businesses which are increasingly geared to exploitative practices and the cutting of labour and social welfare costs. This is a dynamic that has explosive consequences for the entire world. Unless both the Chinese central government and provincial governments can institute and enforce a non-corrupt nation-wide universal social welfare system that provides workers and their families with adequate entitlements, the greater the danger of major socially and politically explosive disturbances.

The Chinese government needs to break the cycle of decades of increased inequality due to private business growth fuelling a substantial proportion of the population left without adequate social protection and facing looming environmental catastrophe. It must establish a universal social welfare system that replaces the corrupt existing system whereby enterprises provide most of the social welfare. The regime's planning model is increasingly geared to green growth. Yet, this option is not sustainable once deeper emissions cuts and reductions in the use of material resources by its substantial but minority middle-class of several hundred million people necessitates limiting unsustainable consumerism. With or without democratisation, the government will be forced to expand state social welfare and increasingly subordinate private sector practices to greater regulation.

China now faces serious socio-economic imbalances that could exacerbate already enormous existing social problems. If a shortage of workers arises because China's over 65 ageing population will more than double between 2020 and 2050 (from 13.5% to 26% of total population) then either productivity will have to increase to make up for the shortfall in labour or internal and foreign migration will have to grow. Opening borders to foreign labour would entail more socio-political problems for the regime. Either way, millions more will be impoverished in their old age unless the government changes the existing structure of the economy from one of industrial growth to a new expanded 'social state'. With an additional 150 to 200 million over 65s needing adequate health care, pensions and a range of services, the government will come under enormous pressure to institute a more universal decommodified care structure that does not depend on the failed system currently run by private businesses and state industrial enterprises.

If, on the other hand, the private sector grows at the expense of environmental sustainability and adequate funding of social welfare, the regime will be increasingly called upon to use force as social disturbances increase. There are already obvious signs that economic growth is relying more on increased credit to fund investment and household consumption. As debt levels increase rather than productivity, China is in danger of sliding down the road of low growth that has long characterised OECD countries.[43] The recent collapse of property development corporations could signal a repeat of the Japanese era of deflation and low growth (that followed the bursting of the property bubble in the early 1990s) unless the Chinese government implements more non-market economic policies. If by some unexpected development, the Communist Party loses its power and democratic institutional processes emerge, it is most unlikely that these would be socialist-inclined if the pattern of post-1989 marketisation in Eastern Europe is repeated in China. We could thus see even greater levels of inequality and social problems common in other countries but magnified many times over in the absence of strong social democratic, green, or eco-socialist parties.

As China tries to avoid major political, economic, and environmental crises, its current 14th Plan (2021 to 2025) aims to reduce its heavy reliance on international trade (due to ongoing tensions with the US) and develop greater regional power and domestic production and consumption of goods and services. Despite environmental sustainability featuring prominently in official rhetoric, the Plan's emphasis on the incessant growth in consumption could well exacerbate the deterioration of many fragile habitats and a dangerous increase in carbon emissions.

Unlike Soviet command planning, China's hybrid form of state planning and capitalist business practices can be loosely characterised as 'command capitalism' subject to domestic and international pressures and conflicting agendas. In 2021, foreign relations analyst, Mark Leonard, described China's new strategy as based on 'dual circulation'. "Instead of operating as a single economy that is linked to the world through trade and investment, China is fashioning itself into a bifurcated economy. One realm ('external circulation') will remain in contact with the rest of the world, but it will gradually be overshadowed by another one ('internal circulation') that will cultivate domestic demand, capital, and ideas."[44] Essentially, China aims to compete globally in high-tech digital and elaborate manufacturing sectors while becoming less reliant on imports.

If enhancing its legitimacy while promoting 'nation building' and 'regional power building' are the primary motives of the ninety-five million-strong Communist Party, then for purely pragmatic reasons it could implement a multi-pronged strategy of anti-corruption, universal social welfare and improving ecological sustainability. These policies would improve the well-being of its people even if full democratic reforms were not implemented. The thorough removal of corruption and abuse by officials goes hand-in-hand with enforcing a comprehensive state-run universal welfare system by taking over all the highly unpopular private and state-enterprise-based schemes that abuse and cheat workers of their entitlements. Significantly improving social conditions in rural areas by providing adequate income and social support for the large but very poor rural population must include curbing forcible land appropriation for property development. These policies should be enhanced by cleaning up the worst forms of rampant pollution and environmental destruction. President Xi's recent 'common prosperity' program is aimed at curbing the power of billionaires, reigning in high levels of debt and extensive corruption generated by the private finance, digital marketing and property sectors that threaten economic stability and the power of the government. However, anti-corruption strategies are only as effective as the degree of freedoms given to citizens to first be able to expose corruption and abuse. Conversely, democratisation will not achieve greater equality if people interpret democracy and greater freedom to mean the right of individuals and businesses to increase their own wealth at the expense of community wellbeing and ecological sustainability.

Overall, we should not underestimate the enormous multiple tasks facing any Chinese central government. On the energy front, for instance, China will have to close nearly 600 coal-fired plants and convert them to renewable energy by 2030 just to reach its declared net zero carbon strategy by 2060.[45] The powerful heavy industry blocs aligned with provincial governments will need to be convinced that rapid decarbonisation is in their political and socio-economic interests. Internal Party politics will be fuelled by the need to provide alternative employment and revenue generating sectors other than debt-fuelled property and other current carbon-intensive industries. Private market forces will have minimal interest in providing a comprehensive 'social state' at the very time China needs to reorientate its whole carbon capitalist model.

While China's national GDP ($US14,722 trillion) in 2020 put it second to the US ($20,936 trillion, the Chinese government admitted that 600 million people (75% of whom live in rural areas) have a monthly income of barely $US155 per month ($1,860 per annum).[46] China is still ranked as a poor country with a per capita GDP in 2020 averaging between $US8,242 and $US10,516 or between 63rd and 86th in the world depending on the data collection used. This means it is closer to countries such as Brazil or Botswana, and well below average per capita income of $65,298 in the US.

Solving China's immense social welfare and environment problems is a challenge that faces both the Chinese government and people, and it has vital implications and consequences for the entire world. Without Chinese decarbonisation there is no chance of the world preventing catastrophic climate breakdown. Countries in Asia account for 60% of the global population or over 4.6 billion people. The 1.9 billion people living in countries outside China and India, from Indonesia to Pakistan or Bangladesh to Vietnam are all strategically part of the Asia-Pacific (renamed Indo-Pacific) expansionary capitalist world. This 'region' now embraces every continent except Europe and has shifted east and south from the Atlantic, Baltic, and Mediterranean. Across the Indian and Pacific oceans, several major African, Latin American countries and Australia have made their economies increasingly insecure by becoming dependent on unsustainable extraction industries and the export of resources and agriculture to Asian countries.

Apart from Brazil, most other countries in Latin America such as Chile, Bolivia, Argentina, Columbia, or Venezuela do not have large manufacturing export industries compared to Asian countries. They are heavily reliant on the export of fossil fuels, minerals and agriculture and will be hit hard in coming years once drastic cuts to carbon emissions become mandatory. Radical theorist, Thea Riofrancos, has already shown how Left movements with histories of collective political struggles are now bitterly divided over extractivism. Leftist governments and one part of a divided Left movement in Bolivia, Ecuador, Venezuela, and other countries continue to espouse a state-centric resource nationalism. This is opposed by indigenous and popular environmental movements (*ecológismo popular*) which struggle against the ever-expanding extractive frontier and advocate a post-extractive future.[47] How to reconcile the global need for non-fossil fuel raw materials such as copper with the needs of indigenous populations will continue to remain an extremely complex problem.

With desperately needed land reform and land rights for Indigenous populations required in several countries, reactionary oligarchies and backward state governments presiding over corruption, clientelism and deep-seated inequality, pervasive violence is never far from the surface. The prospects for establishing comprehensive social welfare systems in these Latin American countries are hardly bright. A forced change in Chinese domestic social policy could possibly trigger domestic reforms in Latin America once an environmentally sustainable agenda in China forces a reduction in the demand for imports of material resources from current extraction-based economies. Also, the dominant model of 'modernisation' based on industrial development geared to the export of manufacturing goods is environmentally and socially unsustainable. Nearly all governments on the political spectrum in Asia, Latin America and Australia subscribe to the mantra of incessant industrial growth and material resources extraction while sleepwalking towards disaster.

Differentiating Utopian from Practical Proposals

The dominant neoliberal ideology of competitive market individualism is based on the myth that dependency is shameful and that as autonomous, self-sufficient persons we should live unencumbered lives rather than be 'burdened' with the care of others.[48] This is why an alternative society based on care and communal co-operation must combine the latter values with the provision of essential social services and related infrastructure such as hospitals, schools, community care facilities, housing, energy, water and communications systems. Social welfare policy is still largely conceived as piecemeal national incrementalism (within constrained international

settings) characterised by minor changes to health, education or state benefits for pensioners, the unemployed and other categories. The global
COVID pandemic momentarily boosted ideas about a universal basic
income, changes to work patterns and more local production as lockdowns
disrupted employment, consumption, and trade. Although many countries
returned to familiar capitalist practices, a future ecologically sustainable
'social state' will increasingly become *the* political issue that governments
will not be able to easily avoid. Little wonder then that decommodified
essential basic services and income are now at the centre of both reform
and radical strategies.

Currently, there is no country in the world that has a system of social
welfare and essential services that is intentionally or unintentionally seriously eroding market social relations. No country provides a 'decommodified space' for people to become independent of the market for the
duration of their lifecycle from birth to death. At best, various social
welfare systems provide partial 'safety nets' in the form of pensions, child-
care, healthcare, and other support at distinct stages of a person's life, but
these do not free people from the constraints of market relations, especially given the way private contractors deliver inferior services and police
welfare recipients. We therefore need to ask what an alternative system
based on significantly decommodified capitalist social relations would look
like? How could it be funded and developed, and would it be compatible
with both democracy and environmental sustainability?

Many analysts either hostile to or supportive of degrowth and eco-
socialist social relations have already drawn attention to the inherent
contradictions of relying on capitalist growth to fund the transition to
degrowth and decommodified relations.[49] If degrowth is successful in
reducing production and consumption, this will result in lower taxation to
fund alternative schemes unless taxation rates or levels of borrowing are
increased. For example, degrowth at 1% to 5% percent reduction of GDP
per annum could possibly result in economies being 10% to 50% smaller
within ten years, thus generating less revenue from a much smaller
economic revenue base. There also appears to be confusion over whether
non-material digital, symbolic and care services will grow or decline. If they
grow, taxes on these services as well as taxes on financial transaction could
replace other forms of material production and consumption and possibly
become an alternative source of revenue.

I have already made clear in earlier chapters, that we need to abandon
universal notions of social life based on small communities and production

confined mainly to craft-based co-operatives. These are fine for a limited number of people but would be inappropriate and impossible solutions for a world of at least nine billion people in coming years. Of course, local provision should be encouraged wherever possible. However, any model that assumes that a local community can provide all of a person's or a household's needs is dangerously foolish. In order to deliver greater equality, most communities will require complex levels of organisation, supply chains and tax revenue well beyond 'the local'.

As I discussed in detail in *Fictions of Sustainability* (Chapter Six), the belief that existing welfare states can be replaced by an adequate universal basic income scheme (UBI) is the prevailing illusion widely held across the world. It is a seductive illusion because it directly taps into the ideology of individualism and desire for individual self-control. While it is within the financial capacity of many governments to provide a very austere UBI,[50] this would hardly decommodify market social relations given that the UBI would be far too little to live on and require people to find additional paid work or welfare services to supplement their income. Such low UBI schemes could undermine wages by allowing employers to offer precarious low-paid work as a supplement for an inadequate UBI.[51] Hence, at present, most existing UBI proposals are undesirable or utopian for the following reasons:

- A UBI requires additional tax revenue that would fall most heavily on workers and consumers (consumption taxes) rather than on businesses unless there was a revolution. This would create major political divisions within different segments of the working class between those receiving a UBI and all other wage and salary workers having to pay higher taxes and/or possibly suffer cuts to their own welfare services.
- There is no agreement amongst advocates as to whether a UBI would only apply to citizens or to all people over a certain age, whether people would continue to receive state benefits (pensions, unemployment benefit or student allowance) as well as a UBI, and whether all those living within supranational entities such as the EU would get the same UBI.
- Although a UBI sounds attractive in terms of ending bureaucratic policing of people on welfare, encouraging individuals to engage in voluntary community care activities, artistic and self-realisation pursuits, this decommodification of

social life would only be partially possible if large numbers of workers continued performing alienated wage labour in order to deliver the tax revenue needed to fund a minority of the population receiving UBI.

- Instead, a UBI is likely to boost market individualism as it would be paid to individuals already living within existing hyper-individualistic cultures. Performing co-operative social labour and other care work would be voluntary and large numbers of recipients would have little incentive to change their behaviour. The scheme would progressively require exceptionally large increases in taxes or collapse as more people crossed the viability threshold and received an adequate UBI rather than engaged in wage labour.

- Finally, a UBI can also be used by Right-wing governments to abolish a range of social welfare services without fearing that people will adopt co-operative socialist values and practices. This is the reason why it is endorsed by so many free marketeers and other defenders of social inequality.

Currently, most radical proposals for a UBI are linked to the call for Green New Deals or degrowth alternatives that are based on unrealistic notions of how to fund an adequate UBI without revenue from environmentally unsustainable economic growth. As to those fully automated, techno-utopian post-capitalist scenarios where the vast majority are assumed to live on a UBI, these are based on the fantasy that sufficient tax revenue will somehow magically flow to state coffers or to self-managed local communities. It is certainly possible to see a significant reduction in the paid working week and the increasing automation of production and administration to reduce unpleasant, hard, dirty, unsafe, or boring labour. Whatever kind of taxes will be collected in the future, these will be affected by environmental pressures that require reductions in the use of material resources. This could well result in less consumption and fewer businesses which in turn will reduce consumption tax revenue needed to fund UBI schemes.

Most UBI proposals are trapped in a fiscal dead end that either disregards environmental sustainability or ignores the highly fluctuating dynamics of capitalist investment and accumulation. Funding UBI schemes are presented as static and fail to account for significant changes in either the number of new recipients of basic income or the changing capacity of governments to raise revenue. Typically, advocates add up all the existing forms of revenue and subsidies that could be cut or diverted to fund a UBI. This assumes that in capitalist societies such high levels of tax restructuring will not have negative consequences on future business activity and levels of consumption that could well result in major shortfalls needed to fund an adequate UBI. The end result is either a very austere and inadequate UBI or a fiscal paper castle doomed to collapse.

How Universal Basic Services Policies Could Decommodify Social Relations

What kind of alternatives to existing capitalist welfare regimes could simultaneously undermine competitive individualism, reduce widespread inequality and poverty, and lay the foundations of genuine decommodification? I believe that a *universal basic services scheme* (UBS) would help do precisely what a UBI is unable to do, but it would not in itself achieve decommodification on its own. While still in a developmental stage, early advocates of UBS (including this author) believe that all should be eligible for any of the essential services necessary to achieve comparable standards of living to that enjoyed by their fellow citizens or residents.[52] A UBS in its less radical form is supported by post-Keynesian social democrats seeking an alternative to neoliberal austerity and is conceived as an extension of the 'social wage'. I support a UBS scheme as part of a broader anti-capitalist strategy. Some elements of UBS have been advocated for many years. These include the demands for universal healthcare, education, childcare, and other essential services. Feminists have long campaigned for the provision of public community services to alleviate the profound global care crisis and the care burden carried by women performing unpaid domestic labour.

It is easy to gloss over the simple fact of how revolutionary it would still be to ensure that impoverished people across the world have an adequate diet, access to health care, decent housing, education, public transport, connection to water, electricity, and other essential utilities necessary for communication, whether telephone or internet. I will therefore outline what I perceive to be the key reasons why the development of a broad UBS strategy simultaneously offers the most viable 'just transition' to a decommodified and environmentally sustainable alternative to existing grossly inadequate capitalist welfare regimes.

In contrast to most universal income schemes that are indiscriminately aimed at all individuals regardless of income and wealth, a UBS would initially prioritise lifting the quality of life for the bottom 30% to 50% of low- and middle-income people in OECD countries and 70% to 85% of people in low-income countries. While all people would be eligible for services, preference would first be given to those who could not afford privately-run services and had no access to essential public services because none exist, or they are in short supply or grossly underfunded and under-staffed.

A UBS would also cost less compared to the prohibitively expensive cost of a UBI and be much more effective than a UBI in combatting poverty and inequality. For example, instead of spending $3 trillion per annum on a sub-poverty level UBI of $10,000 in the US, the equivalent amount on basic services would lead to dramatic improvements in the qual-ity-of-care services, housing, and healthcare over a five to ten-year period. Thirty trillion dollars of additional expenditure over a decade would deliver a vastly improved 'social state' for tens of millions of low and middle-income Americans. Similar levels of public expenditure as a proportion of GDP in dozens of countries would also vastly improve the quality of life for countless millions of people living without adequate basic services.

In contrast to universal income schemes, a UBS is more likely to promote social co-operation, deeper connections between members of households and communities and solidarity compared to the individualist values of a UBI. The improvement and creation of essential services would simultaneously provide jobs in many care sectors, enhance the quality of life for the recipients, and undercut the market provision of these services that millions of people currently can't afford. Although a UBS will not be cheap, it will not create similar major political divisions amongst wage workers compared to the divisiveness of a UBI because it will benefit most workers directly and indirectly. Improved essential services would also facil-itate political coalitions between the recipients of basic services and those who pay the taxes for these services because many will be simultaneously both taxpayers and beneficiaries of a UBS.

Improving the lives of women and men currently performing domestic labour and care work would feature prominently in UBS schemes. The claim by some feminists that a UBI will improve the lives of most women is only partially true at best. COVID-19 has already shown that government income supplements for workers in lockdown at home witnessed an increase in domestic violence and abuse, increased mental illness and so forth. The lesson here is that proposals such as a UBI would do little to change the masculinist and depressed socio-cultural relations that continue with or without a UBI. The illusion that such minimal basic income payments would give women independence and transform their lives without an extensive support network of basic services (such as childcare, housing, healthcare, and other social support services) ignores the current evidence of what it is like to survive on inadequate welfare services or no welfare. By contrast, UBS schemes providing essential services and infrastructure would help counter the isolation of overburdened carers otherwise left to cope alone at home with only a poverty level or sub-poverty level UBI.

Importantly, a UBS would help eliminate unemployment and underemployment. It would, however, eliminate unemployment and have much greater impact if it were linked to government job guarantee programs offering a living wage by governments to all who voluntarily desired to work. In contrast to those advocates who propose paying workers on job guarantee only minimum wage rates, I believe that all prospective workers should be given the choice of either full-time or part-time work with prevailing minimum wage rates being only the base level. Instead, workers should be paid rates earned by workers with different skills, training, or professional qualifications.

A UBS scheme would complement a full employment society by providing a rising level and range of social services. If social goods and services remain heavily privatised or outsourced to private contractors, full employment would not necessarily decommodify social relations. The higher percentage of the work age population employed in job guarantee programs, the higher the level of decommodification of labour from the market determined wage relation. If ten to twenty-five per cent of a country's labour force is initially freed from competitive labour market conditions, this could give all those employed in private sector businesses greater political bargaining strength. Eliminating unemployment, under-employment and precarity through a job guarantee would thus restore the capacity of workers to face employers on a more equal footing. It is the newly employed workers under the job guarantee who will simultaneously help deliver and also benefit from the expanded UBS programmes at national, regional, and local levels. Whereas the cost of a UBI requires raising revenues from unsustainable business practices, a UBS scheme in conjunction with a job guarantee, will help deliver essential basic services that would be partially funded by taxes on workers employed in all kinds of care work, constructing community housing, ecological restoration, and other sectors. This ethical and cultural dimension of UBS schemes would link the provision of jobs and essential services, goods, and infrastructure, and help break the prevailing cycles of ecological unsustainability.

Any 'just transition' to an environmentally sustainable political economy would be facilitated by a UBS scheme. The crucial advantage of a properly implemented and wide-ranging UBS program is that it will not repeat the negative consequences of earlier labour market booms. One of the negative features of high employment is that it has usually fuelled ecologically unsustainable consumption. By contrast, a UBS will assist in the necessary reduction in the use of material resources in those countries where per capita consumption is already unsustainable. It will do this by shifting the present emphasis on mainly money wages and individual consumption to a higher percentage of *social consumption* in the form of comprehensive healthcare, housing, public transport, and a range of socially provided needs. In conjunction with campaigns to reduce the length of the paid working week to first 30 hours and later 25 and 20-hour full-time working weeks over a transitional period, the relationship between existing consumption driven economies and unsustainability would be repaired and rectified.

Welfare analysts are aware that the cost of providing services is rising faster than the cost of producing other goods and services. This is partly due to the heavy presence of private providers and contractors in areas such as health (big pharma, expensive pathology and screening technologies and inadequate regulation of doctors' fees). Aged-care, housing construction and other social services are equally subjected to profit driven excessive costs. Restoring these services to non-profit co-operatives or recommencing public production of medicines and other essential goods and services would eliminate many of the unnecessary higher costs built into expensive public/private enterprise ventures. The latter generate high returns on private capital investment rather than prioritising the satisfaction of non-commercial social needs.

Transforming households and local neighbourhoods from purely sites of consumption to new sites of alternative consumption and production (such as growing food and providing shared services) would be made much easier if people initially worked a reduced four-day and then a three-day week. Currently, in OECD countries with more developed welfare provisions, approximately 20% to 30% of household income comes from state provided benefits. Lifting this to at least 50% of household income over a transitional period would fundamentally alter the balance between commodified wage labour and decommodified social services. Also, apart from the capital infrastructure and maintenance of schools, hospitals and so forth, most of these essential services would not require the same level of material resources as existing major capitalist industries such as private automobile production.

The old dilemma of how to fund social welfare systems that depend on the revenue derived from the continued growth of unsustainable commodity production is partially solved by developing a UBS. This does not mean that a UBS scheme would begin its existence independent of capitalist production. But it does mean that the growth of employment in the various 'social' sectors or the 'care economy' would simultaneously generate taxation from employees, help change existing patterns of consumption and reliance on state revenue principally derived from private enterprise activity. Additionally, the sudden 'discovery' of 20 trillion to 30 trillion dollars across the world to fund stimulus packages to combat the COVID global recession has stripped away the decades-old ideological claims made by conservatives that 'we can't afford' social expenditure. Although Modern Monetary Theory (MMT) may be optimistic in asserting that there is no deficit or debt problem so long as inflation is controlled, MMT has been partially vindicated by conservative governments in their instantaneous abandonment of concern about debt fuelled inflation once the economy had been locked down. On the other hand, most low-income countries lack the fiscal resources to fund a UBS scheme. Additional funding could be partly found just by cancelling their growing debt levels that in some countries now require almost 20% of their national budgets in debt servicing payments to foreign banks and governments. Nonetheless, substantial foreign aid will still be desperately needed.

Diverse political economic conditions ranging from outright repression to fluctuating levels of democratic participation make it ludicrous to specify any general political strategy for how to implement a UBS in over 160 non-OECD countries. Hence, there is no such thing as a general uniform political strategy possible for non-homogeneous countries in what anti-capitalists call 'the South'. Unless there is extensive targeted foreign aid to support such reforms plus a variety of policies, including political campaigns within developed capitalist countries to ensure that their governments act against abusive practices by corporations in numerous low-income countries, we will not see much social change. Only one thing is certain, political movements in many low-income societies will not achieve greater equality without the radical mobilisation of rural and urban populations. Some Latin American countries offer better prospects, but most countries in Africa, Asia and the Middle East are years away from developing powerful social change movements capable of implementing UBS programs.

A UBS requires interventionist states with enhanced capacities to help plan, co-ordinate, fund and implement the many facets of a basic services strategy. I am not talking here about the old centralised and monolithic state apparatuses of yesteryear or today. Instead, there are many ideas being developed about how to introduce new conceptions of the relationship between UBS programmes and local and regional planning schemes. We are also seeing proposals for hybrid versions of universal basic services which combine it with *targeted* basic income for low-income people rather than an indiscriminate *universal* income scheme. These strategies of decommodification are also proposed to assist excluded groups such as Indigenous people with different social needs and suffering greater discrimination than others. Each city, region or country has varying levels of dilapidated, scarce, or unavailable infrastructure and public resources – from parks and social housing to running water – and hence needs specifically formulated transitional strategies. These could be provided initially as free goods and services or for very low fees by public sector and non-profit social providers such as cooperatives conforming to strict social guidelines.

The benefit of a broad UBS strategy is that it could provide targeted goals at local and national levels for workers and families in conjunction with reducing per capita and national material footprints. Typical forms of mainstream welfare incrementalism offered by centre/Left parties during election campaigns usually aim to maximise electoral support instead of coherent planning that best resolves major social and environmental problems. By contrast, a UBS strategy could facilitate public participation in local, regional, and national government annual, five and ten-year planning targets to maximise essential services and shift employment towards core and foundational ecologically sustainable economic zones. New specific and broader conceptions of community and regional planning could be initiated in conjunction with delivering a UBS.

No environmentally sustainable economy is possible without a major cultural shift in both the attitude of citizens and the various socio-political movements that are often set in their ways. A broad UBS strategy has the potential to strengthen union movements through the job guarantee and full employment. Nonetheless, such an achievement could easily be undermined by the continuation of conservative trade union policies narrowly and solely aimed at wage increases rather than the deliberate development of social services. Whether it be unions or other civil society movements and organisations, it is exceedingly difficult to make the transition from the excluded position on 'the street' (protests and oppositional action) to the decision-making institutions and forums of power at local and national levels. Fear of being either incorporated or excluded necessitates a change of political consciousness and action. Few movements have made this transition in consciousness and practice and yet the very democratisation of society depends on it.

In this chapter, I have discussed the limits of old conceptions of decommodification that were largely tied to decreasing reliance on wage labour. Decades of neoliberal policies have transformed welfare service delivery by privatising and re-commodifying the actual relationship between private service providers and populations dependent on a range of services. Rather than drastically cut social welfare budget allocations – although this has also certainly happened in various countries – governments have tended to combine the privatisation of welfare delivery with strategies designed to either deter people or suppress the use of social services with new techniques of 'self-reliance' such as providing loans or financial credit rather than comprehensive support services and secure jobs. These individualist strategies perpetuate poverty, personal shaming, and other forms of stigma. They also create new methods of self-humiliation when these techniques of 'assisting' people to break free of the poverty cycle inevitably fail. By contrast, a UBS program is a strategy to break the ideology of 'self-reliance' and pseudo autonomy.

Whether and to what extent a UBS strategy will be adopted depends on the form new political movements will take, an unknown direction to be determined by people in each country and locality. However, what we do know is that without a notion of how to plan the shift from commodified to decommodified social relations, all political practice will remain merely 'oppositional' and trapped within the parameters of existing capitalist political economies. The key question is how could a UBS scheme be implemented without the proverbial can opener? Canadian sociologist, David Calnitsky, recounts the joke about the physicist, chemist and economist stranded on an island with a can of beans. It is the economist who 'assumes' the existence of a can opener that will solve the problem.[53] No such imaginary solutions can overcome major obstacles for political movements today. Indeed, there should be no illusions about the likely reception given to a broad UBS strategy. Various business groups, governments and sections of the electorate will bitterly resist a broad UBS program. A significant minority of the electorate in countries with free elections or those workers in authoritarian countries will most likely oppose an increase in what they see as the 'social wage' at the expense of higher money wages. Imbued with individualism and notions of the 'sovereign consumer', they will resist the need to reduce their use of material resources and shift consumption from glittering objects to essential needs for all.

The climate emergency will almost certainly force changes to existing levels of production and consumption. Phased-in reductions of material production and consumption in OECD countries will only be supported by electorates if governments can simultaneously promise job and income security alongside basic universal services. Similarly, shifting low-income countries away from current export-led industrialisation to production geared to satisfying and servicing neglected domestic needs is a radical strategy. Despite intense opposition from a minority, developing a broad UBS program lends itself to unifying disparate social movements under a combined coalition umbrella in each country or region. It simultaneously promises work, social care, renovating dilapidated urban environments or neglected rural areas that lack basic infrastructure and services. Importantly, it aims to ensure that the focus is on providing UBS programs within sustainable biophysical boundaries. Without a notion of what we are aiming for, politics is reduced to the daily scenario and ritual of ad hoc policies and reactive, counter responses. At least the goal of universal basic services alongside a job guarantee gives people an objective to aim for and an agenda that strives to meet specific social and environmental needs. This set of goals and framework is crucial to any politics attempting to construct alternative institutions and social relations to those currently dominant in existing capitalist societies.

CONCLUSION

IT IS OFTEN CLAIMED that political dreaming and utopian thinking are what help us aim for more socially just and sustainable futures. However, complex societies with multiple problems require much more than attractive but unworkable imaginative visions. There are no simple ways to resolve the tension between democracy and sustainability. We cannot afford to uncritically accept alternative proposals with glaring defects, just because we long to replace existing destructive and unequal capitalist societies. This book has attempted to outline some of the complex factors that are often camouflaged or ignored in proposed alternatives to existing forms of carbon capitalism. The alternatives I have analysed here range from degrowth solutions to Left technological utopian and green growth social democratic forms of ecological modernisation. Each of these movements and political economic strategies offer something of value. Yet as I have argued, they fail to provide an adequate or detailed way forward to urgently address and resolve deep-seated national and international problems. They either propose solutions to democratise and make society more equal while ignoring the need for environmentally sustainable socio-economic policies, or conversely, they focus on environmental sustainability at the expense of a viable democratic political economy.

Given the exhaustion of old party forms, I also examined the quest for new political organisations and strategies. The principle of 'form follows function' has long been debated in discourses about architecture, design, and engineering. Whether the *function* or purpose of a building, a machine, a piece of clothing, a web page or a community space limits the *form* it can take or whether a new aesthetic form can both create new functions and meaning as well as serve its original purpose is an ongoing part of the creative process. So too, with 'democracy versus sustainability'. The difference is that both are functional processes with inbuilt conscious or unconscious end goals informed by quite different values which take many different forms.

Organisationally, if we strip away all the rhetoric and daily activities, the political function of the historical socialist party was conceived as a vehicle to capture state power and bring about the emancipation of the working class through the peaceful or revolutionary overthrow of capitalism. As we have seen, the *organisational form* of particular Communist, Socialist, Labour, or other Left parties followed the *purpose* spelt out by various theoreticians of social change and the circumstances they encountered. Mainstream centre/Left parties have long abandoned the objective of a post-capitalist society. Today, most labour or social democratic parties are comfortable with varying degrees of pro-market policy agendas and attempt to mirror the functions of capitalist states to the best of their abilities and resources. In other words, opposition parties, like the party or parties that occupy government office, have a division of labour that is determined by the structure and function of contemporary state apparatuses at local, regional, national, and even supranational levels. Shadow ministers for education, finance, defence, transport, environment, and other departments interact with both party members and outside lobbies in their attempt to design the 'form' which their government will take should they win the next election or participate in either local government decisions or supranational bodies such as the EU, the IMF, or the UN.

By contrast, the crisis of social movements, radical parties and degrowth movements is partly related to the confusion over function and form. Is their 'form' exhausted or limited given that they are divided over whether they are anti-statist or simultaneously desiring to shape state administrative policies? Some social movements have no desire to mirror, shape or replace existing state institutional practices. Others naively hope that their actions will ultimately lead to the disintegration of existing institutions without any need for direct confrontation with governments or capitalist corporations.

In the case of the degrowth movement, I have attempted to critically discuss the way degrowthers can be too reliant on the so-called power of face-to-face community relations. This not only involves an undeveloped notion of politics beyond the 'local' but also displays a benign or unrealistic concept of the 'local'. Advocates of degrowth want the 'local community' to be simultaneously the primary 'function' and 'form' of a sustainable society. Diverging from mainstream parties, most degrowth proponents begin at the opposite end of the state-society spectrum. Instead of top-down solutions, they advocate bottom-up or grassroots forms that contradict the existing function and structure of power and social organisation in contemporary societies. Moreover, in contrast to political parties, they tend to have little or no engagement with, or interest in managing state institutions and policies other than to oppose them or ignore them. Hence, to date the degrowth movement has avoided developing any systematic analysis or alternative conception of the role of contemporary state institutions, even though paradoxically many degrowthers simultaneously recognise that planned degrowth will be impossible to achieve without state institutions.

As to 'Left populist' parties, their 'form and function' is one of confusion affecting both theoreticians/policy makers and ordinary members. For theorists and party leaders, their 'function' is to replace the historically obsolete old vanguard or class-based party with a broader or more 'publicly acceptable' organisation consisting of plural constituencies. The 'function' of 'the popular' – despite the veneer of pluralist rhetoric – is to primarily advance socialism, or more accurately a new 'form' of Left Keynesian social democracy in opposition to neoliberal centre/Left or centre/Right parties. However, given the diversity of members and voters for 'Left populist' parties, there is no unity around this objective. The endless disputes and crises within 'Left populist' parties arises from the fact that members pursue multiple agendas. An earlier similar crisis affected various Green parties in the 1980s based on a rainbow of social and environmental interests before the radical Reds and anti-statist 'fundis' were cleaned out or departed. It is not surprising that many people are initially attracted to 'Left populist' parties in the belief that they are the expression of multi-voiced labour, feminist, ecological, post-colonial, LGBTQI and other interests rather than a traditional workers' party dressed up in new clothes. Consequently, the record of 'Left populist' parties is one of disaffection of early supporters, as the leadership either rejects socialism, or grassroots activism in the quest for electoral success. As these parties gradually abandon a pluralist identity or quasi-vanguardism, 'Left populists' begin to decline as they take the 'function' and the 'form' of either more traditional Left or mainstream centre/Left parties.

Democratisation and the Challenges of Sustainability

Two contrasting approaches to national and global change – reform orientated or utopian – dominate contemporary debates even before we consider
their compatibility with environmental sustainability, democracy, and non-
market institutional processes. Italian philosopher Donatella Di Cesare
bursts the bubble of national complacency despite offering a largely utopian
perspective on democracy and equality. Discussing what she calls 'immunodemocracy' in a time of pandemic fear, Di Cesare observes that:

> Debates on democracy examine how it can be defended, reformed, and
> improved. But what they do not put into doubt are its borders, what it
> means to belong to a democracy, or – still less – the bind that holds it
> together: namely, the fear of contagion, the fear of the other, the terror at
> what lies outside of it. This means overlooking the reality that
> discrimination is always-already there, latent and concealed. Even those
> citizens who do fight against racism (a very powerful virus!) – for instance,
> by demanding the opening of their country's borders – take for granted
> their 'ownership' over their 'own' country, which is to say, their national
> belonging.
>
> There is thus a presupposition at work, that of a closed natural
> community prepared to safeguard its own sovereign integrity. This potent
> fiction, which has been dominant for centuries, has driven the belief that
> birth – in the guise of a 'signature' – is a sufficient basis for national
> belonging. Even if globalisation has loosened such connections, the political
> perspective does not seem to have changed any great deal. The discussion
> focuses on matters of internal administration: reforming laws, improving
> efficiency, modernising the tools of deliberation, providing guarantees for
> minorities – that is, democratising democracy.[1]

Despite Di Cesare's insightful observations, the notion of a borderless
global democracy free of all forms of discrimination where all people work
or receive a minimum income and essential services, unfortunately remains
utopian. Unless we have the nightmare of a singular, distant world government, all future political entities will require some form of communal or
state administration which automatically align with defined rights and
borders. How exclusive or open these borders and political rights become is
not yet predetermined. On present indications, global socio-economic
inequalities between and within countries are doomed to remain enormous

so long as capitalist social values and economic practices continue. This 'elephant in the room' has not deterred advocates of social justice. Historically, proposals to overcome inequality and provide social care and wellbeing have assumed several geographical or spatial dimensions based on local, regional, national, and international frameworks. Today, broadly speaking, we see variations of these ideals in the following anti-statist and statist conceptions of social care and wellbeing:

- Anti-statists such as degrowthers and anarchists favour direct care and social co-operation in small-scale, anti-bureaucratic, self-sufficient *local* communities or multiple local communities in a bioregional area.
- Left nationalist social democrats, some liberals and conservatives, as well as neo-fascist ethno-nationalists favour *national* social welfare states with strict criteria of eligibility founded on 'national sovereign economies', whether predominantly market-based or with large public sectors.
- Neoliberal market globalists, assorted technocrats, radical eco-socialist cosmopolitans and communists support supra-national or *international* frameworks based on either open markets or socialist planning. These may take conventional market forms like the EU, or a future socialist world based on integrated federal, local, and regional entities which supplant the primary roles taken by nation states.

During the past two decades we have witnessed the growth of anti-globalisation movements, including calls to 're-nationalise' capitalism so that production, employment, control over capital flows, taxation revenue and provision of adequate national social welfare serves people in need rather than footloose corporations. Some of these calls for 'national civilised capitalism' are a reaction to centre/Left parties having long ago lost their vision of the 'good society' as something distinct from centre/Right neoliberal market values. New political controls over financial practices, labour markets and harmful social practices can certainly be implemented at national level if the political will exists. However, it is neither possible nor desirable to restore many aspects of pre-neoliberal social democracy or the vanguard workerist party. The social and cultural basis for such parties and political economies no longer exists.

What is ignored by those who call for a return to some form of nationally regulated or 'civilised capitalism' is that this requires much more than the reimposition of state regulations on capital movements, labour markets and so forth. Most of these 'national social democratic' visions are bereft of a corresponding environmentally sustainable national economy. Many countries cannot restart their defunct steel mills, car industries, mines, textile, and appliance industries of the pre-1970s, as not only would this be environmentally disastrous but also would be unprofitable (due to integrated supply lines in low-cost countries) and they would be unable to re-employ the same level of workers given decades of labour-replacing technology.

We cannot go backwards to pre-1970s levels of sexism, racism, low levels of formal education and conservative cultural and gender practices. Crucially, many 'national capitalist' countries would not be able to manufacture most contemporary digital hardware and software due to lack of skills, intellectual copyright, and the dominance of this sector by a handful of giant corporations that would require international regulation to disband or control. Add the extensive global supply chains and contemporary processes of disbursed production/assembly, and apart from some countries, it is unlikely that a majority of nations could successfully pursue a new 'national road' to full employment, post-carbon capitalism. For instance, eighty per cent of global automobile production now depends on component parts made in China.[2] Equally telling is the extreme difficulty of de-financialising national economies that are heavily integrated into international corporate financial structures driving credit, debt, and mass employment in many sectors. This de-financialisation can be achieved through national and international regulatory measures, but even a giant such as China is struggling to de-leverage dangerous debt levels driven by the private property sector and digital financial services.

Given the difficulty of restoring or sustaining successful 'national capitalist' economies, it is not possible to fund more extensive social welfare schemes. This means that political movements will need to campaign on platforms that significantly increase the size of non-profit driven national public sectors and facilitate this process by implementing supranational technological, production, trade, and other arrangements with like-minded countries. Instead of 'sovereign national capitalist economies' that cannot be restored to a pre-neoliberal imaginary 'independence', far greater standardisation of international tax rates, regulatory conditions over industries and trade will be required to make societies more sustainable and more equal.

It is the clash between democracy and environmental sustainability that is still not adequately recognised by either reform or radical parties and movements promoting unrealistic models of local self-sufficiency or autonomous national economic democracy. Designing and implementing planned democratic social change that is also ecologically sustainable requires open and vigorous public discussion. It is something that cannot be formulated solely by individual authors or decreed by governments or know-all party leaders. Most opponents of market globalisation need to consider political economic solutions that advance equality and sustainability beyond outdated and sterile notions of national sovereignty. No country can control and maintain incessant 'national market growth' without threatening ecological sustainability. While there is increasing public awareness that major environmental problems cannot be solved within national borders, the widespread myth of national markets solving socio-economic problems is yet to be demystified. Political parties are still unprepared to launch detailed discussions about how to establish new international non-capitalist institutional mechanisms to facilitate more open and democratic multilateral problem solving, whether based on broad planning objectives or specifically targeted interventions. Images of post-carbon economies are still trapped in either national or global market notions of the 'good life'.

Extensive democratisation is necessary if people are to run their own institutions and workplaces. Nonetheless, I have attempted to show that 'democracy' itself needs to be defended and one way of doing this is to expose simplistic versions of 'democracy'. It is common for people on the Left or in social movements to believe that democracy is incompatible with capitalism. This is only true of more radical forms of democracy rather than what passes as 'democracy' in the present-day world.

I began this book by noting the differences between what David Spratt and Philip Sutton called 'normal political-paralysis mode' (or politics-as-usual) and the necessary action required to deal with the climate emergency. Representative democracies are semi-paralysed and too geared to institutional inertia to easily break the pattern of 'politics-as-usual'. There is still a pervasive and dangerously reckless belief amongst governments, business groups and many civic organisations that there is no emergency. This false and complacent attitude seriously underestimates the potential for highly volatile and irreversible shocks to conditions needed for a safe climate. Rather than voluntary and/or ineffective market mechanisms, new society-wide planning and regulatory processes need to be introduced that involve the suspension of normal market practices for an indeterminate period (as has happened in COVID-19 lockdowns). The specific content of these measures needs to be widely debated and could include:

- Government regulation of business use of material resources, especially the cessation of new fossil fuel extraction sites and processing plants, the enforced reduction of fossil fuels used by *each* enterprise in *each* industry, plus the phased-in limits on fossil-fuel exports and carbon-embodied goods that could be traded between countries.
- Carbon rationing on particular types of carbon-intensive individual and household consumption (such as private road vehicles, air transport, level of meat consumption) provided this 'rationing' is not counterproductive and can be implemented in a socially just manner that takes account of people's unequal wealth, income and needs.
- Strict government guidelines on the reorganisation and retooling of particular industries so that enterprises could not return to former destructive and wasteful practices after the emergency.
- Measures to prevent dangerous geo-engineering solutions should corporations opt for quick-fix panaceas that could be disastrous and irreversible.

In those countries with free electoral systems, the climate emergency will still require free elections as in wartime America or Australia during the 1940s. It will be up to electorates to determine whether the implementation of emergency climate planning requires continued strong regulation of capitalist systems or evolves into a post-carbon capitalism once the dangers of severe climate breakdown have been averted.

My own position is that democratic processes are much more preferable, provided that they can quickly prevent looming disaster. The authoritarian temptation to disregard public deliberation of necessary emergency measures sets up a pathway that is difficult to reverse. We are therefore caught in the dilemma that democracy as practiced today is either paralysed or complacent, while authoritarianism defeats the purpose of creating any new democratic society. Therefore, emergency measures must not only be adopted by elected legislatures but also should be rigorously evaluated in terms of preventing or enshrining the spread of authoritarianism to socio-cultural beliefs and activities that are separate to climate policy.

Ultimately, without any conception of desired forms of state planning and which areas of society are either best planned or left to diverse types of decentralised decision-making and allocation of resources, no political movement will be able to specify how to achieve positive alternative outcomes to prevailing destructive market practices. Currently there is little public discussion amongst social change advocates about what proportion of small or medium enterprises should be left unplanned and which key industries and sectors should be planned in any post-carbon society. Hybrid post-carbon social formations based on mixtures of state planning, non-profit sectors, and rural and urban small businesses have been proposed by radicals. Yet, without more discussion and analysis of different models, we will not know whether the Goldilocks' 'just right' balance is a goal worth pursuing or will result in one or another sector dominating the others.

Crucially, the historical conflict of 'capitalism versus democracy' assumes an inbuilt political finality: either capitalism wins and ends democracy by instituting some form of fascism, or else democracy wins and ends capitalism. By contrast, the conflict of 'democracy versus sustainability' has no such end point. Even in the event of a sudden miraculous transformation that ends major capitalist societies, a constant tension in the future is likely to remain. This tension will be between the democratic desire of many people to maintain rates of consumption that may exceed the need to keep the use of material resources below the threshold of unsustainability.

Meanwhile, the conflict of 'capitalism versus democracy' will continue to shape both present and future relations between 'democracy and sustainability'. The reality of violent, massively unequal societies intrudes into every aspect of national and global political economic life and guarantees that existing forms of political, business, and military power will not be surrendered easily, if at all, across the world. Take, for example, the persistent conflict zone of labour/capital relations which remains largely unfree. Sharon Burrow, head of the International Trade Union Congress, observed in June 2020 and July 2021 that a staggering 87 per cent of countries have violated the right to strike while the right to organise has been impeded in 89 countries in 2020 and 109 countries in 2021. Strikes and demonstrations have been banned in Belarus, Guinea, Senegal, and Togo and met extreme brutality in Bolivia, Chile, and Ecuador. In Iran and Iraq, mass arrests were made at protests.[3] The worst violators of workers' rights in 2020 and 2021 were Bangladesh, Belarus, Brazil, Colombia, Egypt, Honduras, India, Kazakhstan, Myanmar, the Philippines, Turkey, and Zimbabwe.[4] Without the freedom to organise and strike, citizens will be restricted in their ability to freely campaign on most other social and environmental issues.

Hence, the obscene levels of inequality and exclusion of billions of people from decision-making will neither end simultaneously nor within a short period of time. If, and when it ever does end, politics will not cease because any genuine new democracy will embody debate, disagreement, and the articulation of either minority or majority interests. Just to repeat, this book has *not* been an argument against democracy but rather an opposition to simplistic conceptions of democracy. There is a reasonable likelihood that in any uneven transition to various forms of post-capitalism, some local or national populations and governments will democratically or undemocratically decide to produce and consume more than other communities. They may possibly decide to continue to exclude strangers, prioritise their own needs and not reduce their use of material resources in line with what they may claim are unacceptable global guidelines for sustainability. In other words, even if capitalism is replaced in some or even in many countries, 'democracy versus sustainability' assumes never-ending negotiation and dispute over what 'sustainability' means and how local and national social and natural resources are to be democratically shared.

We therefore have to ask ourselves, how best to begin the task of minimising social inequality while altering the current environmentally unsustainable use of material resources? This is a question that most Marxists and liberals historically did not consider asking, let alone answering. Given the political fragmentation of social and political movements and the highly unlikely emergence of a single party able to mobilise majority support, I personally support the creation of a multi-party/social movement 'political bloc' to campaign for alternative policies including the introduction of universal basic services schemes and job guarantees plus emergency decarbonisation policies. The possibility of a new 'socio-political bloc' emerging will depend on the future health of existing large mainstream parties and how the latter deal with multiple economic, environmental, and geopolitical, regional military and trade tensions. Some of these mainstream parties will become more democratic or more authoritarian, less committed, or more committed to social justice, more interventionist against threats to ecological sustainability or more committed to green rhetoric rather than green action.

The malaise of the political impasse is simultaneously due to the weakness of the Left and the reluctance or inability of dominant parties and business groups to disregard formal judicial and electoral constraints. Even when various authorities ban or crush oppositional forces, these repressive measures notably fail to alleviate pressures to reduce carbon emissions, restore biodiversity and guarantee food, water, and material resources security. Recent displays of political violence and intolerance driven by angry Right-wing forces is unlikely to disappear. This is especially the case if the necessary transition from carbon capitalism to post-carbon societies is not accompanied by extensive ameliorative and pro-active new state-funded policies to support low and middle-income people.

Seasoned observers claim that there is little new in the endless warnings about impending crises. William Butler Yeats' famous poetic declaration that when things fall apart, 'the centre cannot hold' has become both a political cliché and a portend of events to come. Let us not forget that societies and political systems *do* fail and *do* fall apart. Restructuring carbon intensive industries and cities, providing sufficient social welfare and employment, adjusting tax revenue, currencies, and fiscal allocations in the light of forthcoming declines in fossil fuel-driven industries, exports, and imports, are all just a small part of the unavoidable massive problems that will fall on the shoulders of mainstream parties and governments. And these crises are likely to form a perfect storm of concurrent national and international instability and disruption unless appropriate economic and emergency climate measures are taken. Will non-mainstream parties and movements have the answers?

Unfortunately, an examination of the current policies of centre/Left parties and radical movements shows that they have glaringly failed to both identify and prepare policies to cope with existing and forthcoming crises. Instead, marginalised degrowth movements and revolutionaries offer few practical solutions to immediate crises. As for liberal social democrats, there is a myopic optimism that green growth ecological modernisation will unleash a new era of economic growth to rival the years between 1945 and 1975. This optimistic policy agenda conveniently overlooks the ecological unsustainability of such a repeated growth spurt. It also overlooks the substantial segments of social classes within OECD countries, not to mention low-income countries, that missed out on the benefits of the so-called 'boom' years after 1945. Hence, it will take profound changes in existing market-driven macro-economic policies for any benefits from green growth to be shared across social classes and between unequal nations. We saw how social democratic governments naively adopted neoliberal policies in the hope that market growth would deliver jobs for their working-class supporters during the stagnant 1970s and 1980s. These governments did not bargain on all the negative features of increased inequality brought about by deregulation of financial and labour markets. Now the highly dubious promises of green growth are seducing these same social democratic centrist parties and even some anti-capitalist parties.

As I have argued elsewhere, green growth is based on the myth of never-ending environmentally sustainable capitalist economic growth. It is also dependent on denying the coming global and national struggles over material resources that threaten biodiversity. These domestic and geopolitical struggles will redefine new conceptions of democracy and possible levels of equality. There is still widespread lack of awareness by citizens in capitalist countries concerning the seemingly separate and disconnected processes of extraction and consumption. Governments, corporations, and media promote campaigns aimed at city voters that attempt to sanitise and disguise the shocking practices in extractive industries and agribusiness production which are largely unseen or unfamiliar to most urban residents. Complementing this disconnect about material resources is an uncritical and pervasive optimism about so-called 'clean' ecologically sustainable, high-tech digitalised solutions.

As marginalised viewers on the sidelines, Marxists such as John Bellamy Foster and Intan Suwandi argue that COVID-19 has seen the emergence of 'catastrophe capitalism' via interlinked ecological, epidemiological, and economic crises.[5] Nancy Fraser calls it 'cannibal capitalism'.[6] Such doomsday labels are understandable and typical of those who live in the US and confront a daily dose of irrationality in the form of Right-wing political monstrosities, conspiracy cults fused with celebrity culture and the stench of socio-economic decay alongside obscene levels of private wealth. Nonetheless, these evocative labels are unhelpful unless accompanied by explicit policies about how to deal with one or all of the simultaneously occurring crises. One central policy issue for all governments is how to implement decarbonisation strategies and sustainable material resources extraction and production policies that don't leave low- and middle-income people unfairly carrying the burden of much higher consumer costs. Leaving such crucial policies to market forces is a recipe for conflict and failure. Globally, it is clear that until we see both mainstream parties and alternative movements develop political, economic, and social practices that minimise or overcome the conflict between 'consumer democracy' and environmental sustainability, little will change in the transition from carbon capitalism to post-carbon societies. We should not expect Right-wing parties to change their values and agendas. How long will it take other parties and movements across the political spectrum to recognise both the enormous price of environmental inaction and the narrow definition of sustainability which helps frame their policies?

Despite 'environmental sustainability' having become a hackneyed phrase constantly invoked by public relations apparatuses working for businesses and mainstream politicians, it continues to remain the absolutely major political challenge that most parties and businesses are very unprepared to defend or secure. Ultimately, all economic and social policies will depend on coming to terms with how to live with or resolve environmental constraints. Whether authoritarian or democratic, it is in the narrow self-interest of all governments to safeguard their immediate biophysical resources even if they are reluctant to cooperate globally. Also, we certainly cannot assume that an increasing number of dangerous climatic events will lead to a realignment of mainstream politics in the direction of greater democratisation and social equality. Any such political change will require mass political mobilisation with clear socio-economic and environmental agendas. Hopefully, these political campaigns will prompt populations to rethink the existing capitalist institutional connections between what is currently called 'democracy' and the future character and level of ecological sustainability. Whatever the outcome, the ongoing political tension of 'democracy versus sustainability' will become increasingly difficult to ignore.

Boris Frankel
30th September 2021

NOTES

Introduction

1. For example, on the 12th of June 2021, the Swiss people narrowly rejected an inadequate and flawed law on climate change (that exempted the biggest polluters in the finance sector) despite gaining the support of parties across the spectrum, except for the Right-wing Swiss People's Party. Many voters rejected the proposed complex law because it was seen as increasing the cost of living – see Florian Skelton, 'Switzerland's dead-lock on climate change mitigation', *Brave New Europe*, September 23, 2021.

2. David Spratt and Philip Sutton, *Climate Code Red: the case for emergency action*, Scribe, Melbourne, 2008.

3. Johannes Friedrich, Mengpin Ge and Andrew Pickens, 'This Interactive Chart Shows Changes in the World's Top 10 Emitters' World Resources Institute, December 10, 2020.

4. Branko Marcetic, 'Joe Biden Is Almost as Pro-Drilling as Trump', *Jacobin*, June 3, 2021.

5. Adam Tooze, 'America's race to net zero', *New Statesman*, April 23-29, 2021.

6. Dean Baker, 'Financial Transactions Taxes: The Perfect Way to Pay for Infrastructure Programmes', *Brave New Europe*, May 3, 2021.

7. Sandra Laville, 'G7 nations committing billions more to fossil fuel than green energy', *The Guardian*, June 2, 2021.

8. Climate Action Tracker, 'Global Update: Climate targets slow as science demands action', September 15, 2021, climateactiontracker.org.

9. Laurence Delina and Mark Diesendorf, 'Is wartime mobilisation a suitable policy model for rapid national climate mitigation?', *Energy Policy* 58, 2013, pp. 371–380.

10. Without discussing Spratt and Sutton, eight years later, Laurence Delina, *Strategies for Rapid Climate Mitigation: Wartime mobilisation as a model for action?* Routledge, London, 2016, compares the administrative, fiscal, and socio-economic emergency measures of wartime with possible rapid decarbonisation strategies but is inconclusive in his final recommendations about how to achieve this objective.

11. Giorgio Agamben, 'Bare Life - Interview with Ivar Ekman for Swedish Public Radio, 19 April 2020' published in Giorgio Agamben. *Where Are We Now? The Epidemic as Politics*, translated by Valeria Dani, Eris, London, 2021. There have been many criticisms of Agamben's position. For a discussion of how philosophers have interpreted the pandemic, see Gerard Delanty, 'Six political philosophies in search of a virus: Critical perspectives on the coronavirus pandemic', *LSE 'Europe in Question' Discussion Paper Series*, May 2020. Also see Benjamin Bratton, 'Agamben, Having Been Lost' ch.16 in *The Revenge of the Real: Politics for a Post-Pandemic World*, Verso, London, 2021, who declares that: "It is possible that Giorgio Agamben destroyed whatever was left of his reputation as a public intellectual with his many agitated, delusional, and frankly embarrassing published responses to the COVID-19 pandemic."

12. Bruno Latour, 'Is this a Dress Rehearsal?', *Critical Inquiry*, March 26, 2020.

13. Stephen Rammler, 'I'd rather die in a democracy than live in a sustainable dictatorship', interview with Claudia Detsch, *International Politics and Society*, 30 May 2019.

14. Naomi Klein, *This Changes Everything: Capitalism vs. The Climate*, Simon & Schuster, New York, 2015.

15. For a global overview, see Adam Tooze, *Shutdown: How COVID Shook the World's Economy*, Viking, New York, 2021.

16. For a critique of green growth see Jason Hickel & Giorgos Kallis, 'Is Green Growth Possible?', *New Political Economy*, vol.25, no.4, 2020, pp. 469-486.

17. Philippe Aghion, Céline Antonin, and Simon Bunel, *The Power of Creative Destruction: Economic Upheaval and the Wealth of Nations*, translated by Jodie Cohen-Tanugi, Harvard University Press, Cambridge, 2021.

18. Michael Jacobs and Mariana Mazzucato (eds.) *Rethinking Capitalism: Economics and Policy for Sustainable and Inclusive Growth*, Blackwell-Wiley and The Political Quarterly, Oxford, 2016 and Mariana Mazzucato on Corbyn's 2019 Labour Platform, 'Labour knew austerity was wrong. Now, at last, it also has a vision for growth', *The Guardian*, November 15, 2019.

19. See, for example, *Social Europe* writers in Maria João Rodrigues and François Balate (eds.) *Our European Future Charting a Progressive Course in the World*, Foundation for European Progressive Studies, London 2021.

20. Rebecca Henderson, *Reimagining Capitalism in a World on Fire: How Business Can save the World*, Penguin, London, 2020.

21. Jeremy Rifkin, *The Green New Deal: Why the Fossil Fuel Civilization Will Collapse by 2028, and the Bold Economic Plan to Save Life on Earth*, St. Martin's Press, New York, 2019.

22. See for example, Kate Aronoff, Alyssa Battistoni, Daniel Aldana Cohen and Thea Riafrancos, *A planet to win: why we need a green new deal*, Verso, London, 2019.

23. Riccardo Mastini, Giorgos Kallis and Jason Hickel, 'A Green New Deal without growth?', *Ecological Economics*, 179, 2021, article 106832.

24. Alfons Pérez, *Green deals in a time of pandemics: The Future will be Contested Now*, Libros en Acción, Madrid, 2021.

25. Max Ajl, *A People's Green New Deal*, Pluto Press, London, 2021.

26. The Red Nation, *The Red Deal: Indigenous Action to Save Our Earth*, Common Notions, Brooklyn, 2021.

27. Andrew McAfee, *More From Less: The Surprising Story of How We Learned to Prosper Using Fewer Resources – and What Happens Next*, Simon & Schuster, New York, 2019.

28. See Nafeez Ahmed, 'Green Economic Growth is an Article of 'Faith' Devoid of Scientific Evidence', *Resilience*, July 15, 2020, and Jason Hickel, 'A Response to McAfee: No, the 'Environmental Kuznets Curve' Won't Save Us', jasonhickel.org, October 10, 2020.

29. Johan Rockström, et al. 'Planetary Boundaries: Exploring the Safe Operating Space for Humanity', *Ecology and Society*. Vol.14, no.2, article 32, 2009.

30. On the 'four cheaps' (labour power, food, energy, and raw materials), see Jason W. Moore, 'World accumulation and planetary life, or, why capitalism will not survive until the 'last tree is cut", *IPPR Progressive Review*, vol 24, no.3, 2017, pp.176-202.

31. See Stuart Rosewarne, 'The Structural Transformation of Australian Agriculture: Globalisation, Corporatisation and the Devalorisation of Labour' *Journal of Australian Political Economy* No. 84, 2019, pp. 175-218.

32. For the most detailed examination of 179 reports that claimed decoupling, see T. Vadén, V. Lähde, A. Majava, P. Järvensivu, T. Toivanen, E. Hakala and J. T. Eronen, 'Decoupling for ecological sustainability: A categorisation and review of research literature', *Environmental Science and Policy*, 112, 2020, pp. 236-244.

33. See the latest detailed statistics on inequality analysed by a range of contributors such as Robert Wade, Jayati Ghosh, et al in 'The Inequality Crisis', *real-world economics review*, issue no.92, June 2020.

34. See for example, Jason Hickel, 'Is it possible to achieve a good life for all within planetary boundaries?', *Third World Quarterly*, vol. 40, no.1, 2019, pp.18-35.

35. Iago Otero, et al., 'Biodiversity policy beyond economic growth', *The Conservation Letters*, Wiley Online, April 13, 2020.

36. For a global overview of all political economic, technological, and social aspects of waste, see Kate O'Neill, *Waste*, Polity Press, Cambridge, 2019.
37. See Richard Smith, 'Elon Musk's electric planet-suicide vehicle: Automobiles, emissions and degrowth', *The Ecological Citizen*, vol.3, Suppl B, 2020, pp.47-53. Electric vehicles will be more material hungry than petrol-cars, have shorter lives like other battery-driven products such as mobile phones and create enormous waste-disposal problems.
38. Max Ajl, *A People's Green New Deal*, p.98.
39. Even non-radical organisations such as the UN and OECD recognise the complex aspects of global food production systems and the difficulty of overcoming major problems facing agriculture. See for example, *A Multi-Billion-Dollar Opportunity: Repurposing agricultural support to transform food systems*, The Food and Agriculture Organization of the United Nations Development Programme and United Nations Environment Programme, Rome, 2021.
40. Guillaume Pitron, 'Dirty Rare Metals: Digging Deeper into the Energy Transition', *Isles of the Left*, March 22, 2019.
41. For major technological obstacles in the near future to replacing fossil fuel for airlines, see National Academies of Sciences, Engineering, and Medicine, *Commercial Aircraft Propulsion and Energy Systems Research: Reducing Global Carbon Emissions*, The National Academies Press, Washington, DC, 2016. For carbon emissions from aviation, see Mark Carter, *The Elephant in the Sky: The Hazards of Aviation Emissions and How We Can Avoid Them*, Melbourne, October 2018.
42. Aaron Bastani, *Fully Automated Luxury Communism A Manifesto*. Verso, London, 2019.
43. Joshua Clover, 'The Roundabout Riots', *Versobooks Blog*, 9th December 2018.
44. Paul Ehrlich, *The Population Bomb*, Ballantine Books, New York, 1968.
45. Lyla Mehta, Amber Huffa, Jeremy Allouchea, 'The new politics and geographies of scarcity', *Geoforum*, vol.101, 2019, pp. 222-230; and Ian Scoones, Rebecca Smalley, Ruth Hallc, Dzodzi Tsikatad, 'Narratives of scarcity: Framing the global land rush', *Geoforum*, vol.101, 2019, pp.231-41.
46. Jason Hickel, 'Degrowth: a theory of radical abundance', *real-world economics review*, issue no. 87, March 19, 2019, p. 66.
47. Michael Bloomberg, Saleemul Huq and Agnes Kalibata 'The Race to Sustainable Abundance', *Project Syndicate*, July 9, 2021.
48. Murray Bookchin, *Post-Scarcity Anarchism* (1971) 2nd edition, Black Rose Books, Montreal, 1986, with a New Introduction in which Bookchin recognized much of the environmental damage caused by both corporate capitalism and Communist regimes. In fairness to Bookchin, he did not envisage affluent market consumerism for all when he talked about 'post-scarcity'.
49. Leigh Phillips, *Austerity Ecology & the Collapse-Porn Addicts: A Defence of Growth, Progress, Industry and Stuff*, Zero Books, Alresford, 2015.
50. See for example, T. Parrique, J. Barth, F. Briens, C. Kerschner, A. Kraus-Polk, A. Kuokkanen and J. H. Spangenberg, *Decoupling Debunked: Evidence and Arguments against green growth as a sole strategy for sustainability*, European Environment Bureau, July 2019.
51. David Spratt, Paper presented to 'Unsustainable Past – Sustainable Futures?' conference, Humanities Centre for Advanced Studies, University of Hamburg, 12 February 2021.

1. From Carbon Capitalism to Post-Carbon Democracies

1. For an overview, see Eva Horn and Hannes Bergthaller, *The Anthropocene Key Issues for the Humanities*, Routledge, London, 2020. The authors' survey of politics and the Anthropocene Ch.6, says extraordinarily little about public policies, democratic political strategies or how to deal the negative aspects of the Anthropocene.
2. Nick J. Fox and Pam Alldred, *Sociology and the New Materialism: Theory, Research, Action*,

Sage, London, 2017 use Bruno Latour, Gilles Deleuze, Donna Haraway, Rosi Braidotti and others to develop a 'new materialist' sociology. However, when they give examples of actual social disputes, they fall back on conventional language that could easily be explained by concepts in the so-called 'old materialism'. Action theory, 'assemblages', 'cyborgs' etc., are all superfluous abstractions when it comes to identifying problems, formulating policies to combat climate breakdown or social inequality, and mobilising social movements to act on these policies.

3. Dipesh Chakrabarty, *The Climate of History in a Planetary Age,* The University of Chicago Press, Chicago, 2021, ch.7. p.179.

4. Christophe Bonneuil and Jean-Baptiste Fressoz, *The Shock of the Anthropocene: The Earth, History and Us*, translated by David Fernbach, Verso, London, 2013, p.75.

5. *Ibid*, p.83.

6. See Jason Moore (ed.), *Anthropocene or Capitalocene?: Nature, History, and the Crisis of Capitalism,* PM Books, Oakland 2016, p.5 where Moore mentions how Andreas Malm, Donna Haraway, David Rucio and others independently developed the concept of the Capitalocene from 2009 onwards.

7. Jason W. Moore, *Capitalism in the Web of Life: Ecology and the Accumulation of Capital*, Verso, London, 2015.

8. Jason W. Moore, 'World accumulation and planetary life, or, why capitalism will not survive until the 'last tree is cut", *IPPR Progressive Review*, vol 24, no.3, 2017, pp.176-202.

9. John Bellamy Foster and Brett Clark. 'The Capitalinian The First Geological Age of the Anthropocene', *Monthly Review*, September 1, 2021, have reduced complex, diverse political economic processes and ecological processes to simplistic scientist and economic determinist jargon. Accordingly, 'the Capitalinian', which is the so-called monopoly capitalist phase of the Anthropocene will either lead to civilisation collapse or be succeeded by 'the Communian' phase or socialist civilisation. These quasi-metaphysical concepts are so generalised and devoid of actual specific political movements (apart from the mention of very weak peasant and Indigenous movements) that their 'global universality' is of very limited value to the politics of the major G20 capitalist countries.

10. See the contributions by Neil Davidson, Heide Gerstenberger and Charles Post in the symposium on Davidson's book *How Revolutionary Were the Bourgeois Revolutions?* (2012) in *Historical Materialism,* Vol, 27, no.3, 2019. Also see Heide Gerstenberger, *Impersonal Power: History and Theory of the Bourgeois State* trans by David Fernbach, Brill, Leiden, 2007.

11. Concerning the disputes over capitalist agriculture and feudalism see Keith Tribe, *Genealogies of Capitalism*, Humanities Press, Atlantic Highlands, 1981.

12. For a survey and analysis of the competing accounts of the origins of capitalism see Ellen Meiksins Wood, *The Origin of Capitalism A Longer View*, Verso, London, 2002.

13. Jason A. Josephson-Storm, *The Myth of Disenchantment Magic, Modernity, and the Birth of the Human Sciences*, University of Chicago Press, Chicago, 2017, p.301.

14. E. P. Thompson, *The Making of the English Working Class*, Victor Gollancz, London, 1963.

15. *Ibid*, p.213.

16. See Tom Nairn, 'The English Working Class', *New Left Review*, no. 24, March-April 1964, pp. 43-57 and Perry Anderson, *Arguments Within English Marxism*, New Left Books, London, 1980, ch.2.

17. Priya Satia, 'History from Below', *Aeon*, December 18, 2020.

18. Priya Satia, *Time's Monster: History, Conscience and Britain's Empire*, Penguin Random House, London 2020, p.11.

19. *Ibid*, p.18.

20. See figures in Aaron Benanav, 'Demography and Dispossession: Explaining the Growth of the Global Informal Workforce, 1950-2000', *Social Science History*, 2019.

21. Gilles Deleuze, *Negotiations 1972-1990*, translated by Martin Joughin, Columbia University Press, New York, 1995, p.20.

22. Aaron Benanav, *Automation and the Future of Work*, Verso, London, 2020.

23. Clyde W. Barrow, *The Dangerous Class: The Concept of the Lumpenproletariat,* University of Michigan Press, Ann Arbor, 2020. Barrow provides some good discussion of Marxist and post-Marxist notions of the lumpenproletariat but says nothing about Bakunin's theory of their historical role or how the contemporary lumpenproletariat will affect any transition to a post-carbon democracy.

24. *Ibid*, p.17.

25. See Sabine Hake, *The Proletarian Dream: Socialism, Culture, and Emotion in Germany,1863–1933*, de Gruyter, Berlin, 2017, for a fine study of the gap between the power of symbolic and emotional hope vested in the 'proletarian dream' and the reality of the political weakness of revolutionaries.

26. Rupert Read and Samuel Alexander, *This Civilisation is Finished Conversations on the end of Empire—and what lies beyond*, Simplicity Institute, Melbourne, 2019.

27. See Sebastian Strunz, Melissa Marselle, Matthias Schröter, 'Leaving the "sustainability or collapse" narrative behind', *Sustainability Science*, vol.14, 2019, pp.1717-1728.

28. See Wolfgang Streeck, 'The Post-capitalist interregnum: The old system is dying, but a new social order cannot be born' *Juncture*, vol.23, no.2, 2016, pp. 68-77.

29. See Chris Wickham, *The Inheritance of Rome A History of Europe from 400 to 1000,* Allen Lane, London, 2009.

30. On Barak, *Powering Empire: How Coal Made the Middle East and Sparked Global Carbonization*, University of California Press, Oakland, 2020.

31. *Ibid*, pp.24-25.

32. *Ibid* p.52.

33. See Marc Levinson, *The Box: How the Shipping Container Made the World Smaller and the World Economy Bigger*, Princeton University Press, Princeton, 2006. The transformation of rail freight and shipping by containers began in the US in the 1960s before it moved to other countries. Although the teamsters became a powerful road-based union, they were not supportive of radical social reforms as earlier Left-wing rail and dock-worker unions across the world.

34. Laleh Khalili, *Sinews of War and Trade Shipping and Capitalism in the Arabian Peninsula*, Verso, London, 2020.

35. See Karl Marx, *Capital A Critique of Political Economy, Volume One*, translated by Ben Fowkes, Penguin and New Left Review, Harmondsworth, 1976, p.574.

36. World Employment and Social Outlook – Trends 2019, *International Labour Organization*, Geneva, 2019.

37. ILO Monitor: COVID-19 and the world of work. Seventh edition Updated estimates and analysis, *International Labour Organization*, Geneva, January 25, 2021.

38. Alberto Posso (ed.), *Child Labor in the Developing World: Theory, Practice and Policy*, Palgrave Macmillan, Singapore, 2020.

39. See Antony Bryant, 'Liquid uncertainty, chaos and complexity: The gig economy and the open source movement', *Thesis Eleven*, vol.156, no.1, 2020, pp. 45-66.

40. In the EU the definition of 'worker' has been hotly contested. See Martin Risak and Thomas Dullinger, *The concept of 'worker' in EU law: Status quo and potential for change*, European Trade Union Institute, Report 140, Brussels, 2018.

41. Andre Gorz, 'Redefining Socialism' in *Capitalism, Socialism, Ecology*, trans. by Chris Turner, Verso, London, 1994, pp. 60-61.

42. Michal Kalecki, 'Political Aspects of Full Employment, *Political Quarterly*, no. 4, October 1943, pp. 322-330.

43. Simon Kuper, 'The Myth of Green Growth', *Financial Times*, October 24, 2019.

44. Fiona Harvey, 'US returns to global climate arena with call to act on 'emergency', *The Guardian*, January 25, 2021.

45. Andreas Malm, *Fossil Capital: The Rise of Steam-Power and the Roots of Global Warming*, Verso, London, 2015.

46. Andreas Malm, 'Long Waves of Fossil Development: Periodizing Energy and Capital', in

Brent Ryan Bellamy and Jeff Diamanti (eds.) *Materialism and the Critique of Energy*, MCM Publishing, Chicago, 2018, pp. 161-95.

47. Mariana Mazzucato and Carlota Perez, *Innovation as Growth Policy: the challenge for Europe*, Science Policy Research Unit, Working Papers Series, University of Sussex, July 2014. See my critique of neo-Schumpeterian analyses in *Fictions of Sustainability*, Ch.1.

48. See my arguments in *Fictions of Sustainability*, pp.24-26.

49. Andreas Malm, 'Long Waves of Fossil Development: Periodizing Energy and Capital', p.176.

50. Hartmut Rosa made these points in a lecture at the London School of Economics, January 12, 2017. Also see his book *Social Acceleration: A New Theory of Modernity*, trans.by Jonathon Trejo-Mathys, Columbia University Press, New York, 2013.

2. Intellectuals, Networks, Culture: Shaping Future Post-Carbon Societies

1. Alvin Toffler, *Future Shock*, Random House, New York, 1970.

2. Giacomo D'Alisa and Giorgos Kallis, 'Degrowth and the State', *Ecological Economics*, no. 169, 2020, article 106486.

3. Jürgen Habermas, *Structural Transformation of the Public Sphere An Inquiry into a Category of Bourgeois Society* (1962) translated by Thomas Burger with Frederick Lawrence, Polity Press, Cambridge, 1989.

4. In response to Habermas, see Alexander Kluge and Oskar Negt, *Public Sphere and Experience: Toward an Analysis of the Bourgeois and Proletarian Public Sphere* (1972) translated by Peter Labanyi, Jamie Owen Daniel, and Assenka Oksiloff in 1993 and reprinted with Foreword by Miriam Hansen, Verso, London, 2016. Also see critiques of Habermas's concept of the public sphere in Mike Hill and Warren Montag (eds.) *Masses, Classes, and the Public Sphere*, Verso, London, 2000.

5. György Lukács, *History and Class Consciousness: Studies in Marxist Dialectics*, Merlin, London, 1971, p. 330.

6. Antonio Gramsci, *Selections From the Prison Notebooks* edited and translated by Quintin Hoare and Geoffrey Nowell Smith, Lawrence & Wishart, London, 1971, pp.123-205.

7. Stefan Jonsson, *Crowds and Democracy: The Idea and Image of the Masses From Revolution to Fascism*, Columbia University Press, New York, 2013, p.11.

8. William Davies, 'The Politics of Recognition in the Age of Social Media', *New Left Review*, no.128, March/April 2021, pp.83-99.

9. Michael Denning, 'Everyone a Legislator', *New Left Review*, no.129, May/June, 2021, pp.29-30.

10. *Ibid*, p.44.

11. For an analysis of post-industrial theories see my critique in *The Post-Industrial Utopians*, Polity Press, Cambridge, 1987.

12. Daniel Bell, *The Coming of Post-Industrial Society: A Venture in Social Forecasting*, Basic Books, New York, 1973.

13. For figures on the transformation of work and employment between 1920 and 1990, see Manual Castells, *The Information Age Economy, Society, and Culture, Volume I The Rise of the Network Society*, second edition, Wiley-Blackwell, Oxford, 2010, ch.4.

14. Daniel Bell, *The Cultural Contradictions of Capitalism* (1976), second edition, Basic Books, New York 1978.

15. See Eri Bertsou and Daniele Caramani (eds.) *The Technocratic Challenge to Democracy*, Routledge, London, 2020 .

16. See the three volumes by Manual Castells, *The Information Age Economy, Society, and Culture, Volume I The Rise of the Network Society* (1996), *Volume II: The Power of Identity* (1997) and

Volume III: End of Millennium (1998), Second edition, Wiley-Blackwell, Oxford, 2010 with new preface.

17. Manuel Castells, *Networks of Outrage and Hope: Social Movements in the Internet Age*, Polity, Cambridge, 2012.

18. See McKenzie Wark, *A Hacker Manifesto*, Harvard University Press, Cambridge, 2004; Yann Moulier Boutang, *Cognitive Capitalism* Translated by Ed Emery, Polity, Cambridge, 2011; Vincent Mosco, *Becoming Digital Toward a Post-Internet Society*, Emerald Publishing, Bingley, 2017; Nick Couldry and Ulises A. Mejias, *The Costs of Connection: How Data is Colonizing Human Life and Appropriating it for Capitalism*, Stanford University Press, Stanford, 2019; Catherine Besteman and Hugh Gusterson (eds.), *Life by Algorithms: How Roboprocesses Are Remaking Our World*, The University of Chicago Press, Chicago, 2019; Luca Follis and Adam Fish, *Hacker States*, MIT Press, Cambridge, 2020.

19. Marion Fourcade, 'Ordinal citizenship', *British Journal of Sociology*, 72, 2021, p.161.

20. Marion Fourcade and Kieran Healy, 'Classification situations: Life chances in the neoliberal economy', *Accounting, Organizations and Society*, vol. *38*, 2013, pp.559–572.

21. Figure cited by Adam Tooze, *Shutdown: How COVID Shook the World's Economy*, Viking, New York, 2021, ch.3

22. McKenzie Wark, *A Hacker Manifesto*, Harvard University Press, Cambridge, 2004.

23. McKenzie Wark, *Capital is Dead*, Verso, London, 2019.

24. McKenzie Wark, 'A Rave Just for Friends, Interview with Anders Dunker', *Kunstkritikk Nordic Art Review*, May 21, 2021.

25. Jeremy Rifkin, *The Third Industrial Revolution: How Lateral Power is Transforming Energy, the Economy, and the World*, Palgrave Macmillan, Basingstoke, 2013; Aaron Bastani, *Fully Automated Luxury Communism A Manifesto*. Verso, London, 2019 and Paul Mason, *PostCapitalism: A Guide to Our Future*, Allen Lane, London, 2015.

26. See Paul Mason, *op.cit.*

27. Ingolfur Blühdorn, 'The legitimation crisis of democracy: emancipatory politics, the environmental state and the glass ceiling to socio-ecological transformation', *Environmental Politics,* vol.29, no.1, 2020, pp. 38-57.

28. See Lise Benoist, *Green is the new brown: Ecology in the metapolitics of the French far right today*, Master of Science thesis in Human Ecology, Lund University, 2020 and her work with the Zetkin Collective. Also see Andreas Malm and the Zetkin Collective, *White Skin, Black Fuel On the Danger of Fossil Fascism*, Verso, London, 2021.

29. Christopher Lasch, *The Culture of Narcissism: American Life in An Age of Diminishing Expectations*, Warner Books, New York, 1979 and Richard Sennett, *The Fall of Public Man*, Cambridge University Press, Cambridge, 1977.

30. See Julie Walsh, *Narcissism and Its Discontents*, Palgrave Macmillan, Basingstoke, 2015 for an insightful critique of Lasch and Sennett.

31. Ulrich Beck and Elisabeth Beck-Gernsheim, *The Normal Chaos of Love* (1990), translated by Mark Ritter and Jane Wiebel, Polity Press, Cambridge, 1994; and Ulrich Beck and Elisabeth Beck-Gernsheim, *Individualization: Institutionalized Individualism and its Social and Political Consequences* (2001), translated by Patrick Camiller, Sage Publications, London, 2002.

32. Anthony Giddens, *The Transformation of Intimacy: Sexuality, Love and Eroticism in Modern Societies*, Polity Press, Cambridge, 1992, ch.10.

33. Zygmunt Bauman, *Liquid Modernity*, Polity, Cambridge, 2000 and 2012 edition.

34. Ulrich Beck, *Risk Society: Towards a New Modernity* (1986) translated by Mark Ritter, Sage, London, 1992.

35. See the position of Giddens and Beck in Jane Franklin (ed.), *The Politics of Risk Society*, Polity, Cambridge, 1998.

36. Christopher Lasch, *The True and Only Heaven Progress and its Critics*, W. W. Norton, New York 1991.

37. See Julie Stephens, *Confronting Postmaternal Thinking: Feminism, Memory and Care*, Columbia University Press, New York, 2012.

38. Richard Sennett developed these ideas in *The Fall of Public Man*, Cambridge University Press, Cambridge, 1977.

39. See for example, Elizabeth Lunbeck. *The Americanization of Narcissism,* Harvard University Press, Cambridge, 2014 and Vivian Gornick's review, 'In defence of narcissism' in *Boston Review*, May 5, 2014, plus George Scialabba, The Weak Self: Christopher Lasch on Narcissism A response to Vivian Gornick', *Boston Review*, May 6, 2014. Gornick's review was reprinted in V. Gornick, *Taking a Long Look: Essays on Culture, Literature, and Feminism in Our Time*, Verso, London, 2021 without the title 'In defence of narcisssism'.

40. Christopher Lasch, *The Minimal Self: Psychic Survival in Troubled Times*, W. W. Norton, New York 1984, p.98.

41. Eva Illouz, *The End of Love: A Sociology of Negative Relations*, Oxford University Press, New York, 2019, p.22.

42. *Ibid.*

43. Ian Craib, *The Importance of Disappointment*, Routledge, London, 1994, p.161.

44. Nick O'Donovan, 'From Knowledge Economy to Automation Anxiety: A Growth Regime in Crisis?', *New Political Economy*, vol.25, no.2, 2020, pp. 248-26.

45. See Julia Timpe, *Nazi-Organized Recreation and Entertainment in the Third Reich*, Palgrave Macmillan, London, 2017.

46. See Sabrina P. Ramet, *Alternatives to Democracy in Twentieth Century Europe: Collectivist Visions of Modernity*, Central European University Press, Budapest, 2019.

47. Samuel Alexander, *Art Against Empire: Towards an Aesthetics of Degrowth*, Simplicity Institute, Melbourne, 2017.

48. Herbert Marcuse, *The Aesthetic Dimension Toward a Critique of Marxist Aesthetics*, Beacon Press, Boston, 1978, p.53.

49. Herbert Marcuse, *Five Lectures: Psychoanalysis, Politcs, and Utopia*, translated by Jeremy J. Shapiro and Shierry M. Weber, Allen Lane, London, 1970, p.38.

3. The Political Struggle Over National and Per Capita Material Footprints

1. See Andreas Malm, *Fossil Capital: The Rise of Steam Power and the Roots of Global Warming,* Verso Books, London, 2016.

2. See varying figures in Australia Institute report using Potsdam Institute for Climate Impact Research figures cited by Peter Hannam, 'Emissions surging to high after fires', *The Age*, January 25, 2020, and Union of Concerned Scientists, 'Each Country's Share of CO_2 Emissions', August 12, 2020.

3. Michael Davies-Venn, 'Biden's America is no climate leader', *International Politics and Society*, May 13, 2021.

4. See Daniel Moran, Keiichiro Kanemoto, et. al, 'Carbon Footprints of 13000 Cities', *Environmental Research Letters*, Volume 13, no.6, June 2018 for a discussion of the complexities associated with gathering data.

5. For an analysis of the difficulty of measuring carbon footprints, see Mike Berners-Lee, *How Bad Are Bananas? The Carbon Footprint of Everything,* Greystone Books, Vancouver, 2011.

6. Wolfgang Knorr, 'Trickery in Climate Neutrality – How Net Zero is Secretly Being Redefined', *Brave New Europe*, May 26, 2021.

7. For a sample of liberal and radical views see Daron Acemoglu, 'Climate Change vs. Techno-Utopia', *Project Syndicate*, April 28, 2021; Oliver Howes, 'Tracing the carbon loophole and other trade secrets that lead to unaccounted emissions', *Pearls and Irritations*,

May 27, 2021; George Monbiot, 'Britain has promised net zero – but it's on track to achieve absolutely nothing', *The Guardian*, May 26, 2021.

8. See Tim Jackson, *Post Growth, Life After Capitalism*, Polity, Cambridge, 2021.

9. Craig D. Rye & Tim Jackson, 'Using critical slowing down indicators to understand economic growth rate variability and secular stagnation', *Scientific Reports Nature Research*, June 26, 2020.

10. Tim Jackson, Prosperity without Growth, Podcast, YouTube, April 14, 2021.

11. UNEP, *One Planet, How Many People? A Review of Earth's Carrying Capacity*, UNEP Global Environmental Alert Service, unep.org. June 2012, p.3.

12. Ted Nordhaus, 'The Earth's carrying capacity for human life is not fixed', *Aeon*, July 5, 2018.

13. Linus Blomqvist, Barry W. Brook, Erle C. Ellis, Peter M. Kareiva, Ted Nordhaus, Michael Shellenberger, 'Does the Shoe Fit? Real versus Imagined Ecological Footprints', *Plos Biology*, Vol.11, Issue 11, November 2013.

14. See the Global Footprint Network's own outline of issues covered and not covered, *Ecological Footprint Accounting: Limitations and Criticism*, Global Footprint Network research team, footprintnetwork.org, August 2020

15. See Andrea Collins, Alessandro Galli, Tara Hipwood and Adeline Murthy, 'Living within a One Planet reality: the contribution of personal Footprint calculators', *Environmental Research Letters*, Volume 15, Number 2, 2020.

16. See David Spratt and Ian Dunlop, *What Lies Beneath?*, Breakthrough - National Centre for Climate Restoration, Melbourne, 2018, p.34.

17. A minority of analysts discuss capitalism and degrowth but still abstain from voicing strong political views. See for example, Thomas Wiedmann, Manfred Lenzen, Lorenz T. Keyßer & Julia K. Steinberger, 'Scientists' warning on affluence', *Nature Communications*, June 19, 2020, online.

18. See methodologies discussed in Stefan Giljum, Monika Dittrich, Mirko Lieber and Stephan Lutter, 'Global Patterns of Material Flows and their Socio-Economic and Environmental Implications: A MFA Study on All Countries World-Wide from 1980 to 2009', *Resources*, no. 3, 2014, pp.319-339.

19. Recently, Yannick Oswald, Anne Owen & Julia K. Steinberger, 'Large inequality in international and intranational energy footprints between income groups and across consumption categories', *Nature Energy* 5, 2020, pp.231–239, analysed energy use in 86 countries. This report was heavily skewed towards fossil fuel footprints and did not go much further than concluding with the obvious, namely, that 5% of high-income people consume far more energy than the bottom 20% of low-income people.

20. Frank Pothen and Miguel Angel Tovar Reaños, 'The Distribution of Material Footprints in Germany', *Ecological Economics*, 153, 2018, pp.237–251.

21. Stuart Parkinson and Linsey Cottrell, *Under the Radar: The Carbon Footprint of Europe's Military Sectors*, Prepared by Conflict and Environment Observatory and Scientists for Global Responsibility for The Left group in the European Parliament - GUE/NGL, February 2021.

22. See the report on disputes over ecosystem classification in Tammy Newcomer-Johnson, Andrews, F., Corona, J., DeWitt, T.H., Harwell, M.C., Rhodes, C., Ringold, P., Russell, M.J., Sinha, P., and G. Van Houtven, *National Ecosystem Services Classification System (NESCS) Plus*, U.S. Environmental Protection Agency. 2020, EPA/600/R-20/267.

23. See Adam Hanieh, 'Petrochemical Empire: The Geo-Politics of Fossil-Fuelled Production', *New Left Review*, no.130, July-August 2021, pp.25-51.

24. See Eben Bayer, 'The Mycelium Revolution Is Upon Us', *Scientific American*, July 1, 2019 and Eduardo Souza, 'Mushroom Buildings? The Possibilities of Using Mycelium in Architecture', *ArchDaily*, October 12, 2020.

25. For various solutions within and beyond capitalism, see Jonathan Neale, *Fight the Fire:*

Green New Deals and Global Climate Jobs, Resistance Books, London and The Ecologist, Devon, 2021.

26. Nafeez Mosaddeq Ahmed, *Failing States, Collapsing Systems: BioPhysical Triggers of Political Violence*, Springer, Cham, 2017, p. 2.

27. Ted Trainer, 'On eco-villages and the transition', *The International Journal of Inclusive Democracy*, vol.2, no.3 June 2006.

28. Ted Trainer, 'Simpler way transition theory', *real-world economics review*, issue no. 93, 2020, pp.96-112.

29. On why the old thesis of 'peak oil' lacks credibility, see Antonia Juhasz, 'The End of Oil is Near', *Sierra Magazine*, September/October 2020. In *Fictions of Sustainability* (2018), I deliberatively avoided subscribing to the 'peak oil' thesis as it had long been clear that this thesis was based on a flawed methodology. The current oil glut might well decline in the next few years due to cuts in production, but this will not indicate that we are running out of oil.

30. Harald Ulrik Sverdrup, Anna Hulda Olafsdottir, Kristin Vala Ragnarsdottir, 'On the long-term sustainability of copper, zinc and lead supply, using a system dynamics model', *Resources, Conservation & Recycling: X*, Vol.4 December 2019.

31. See Frances Coppola, 'From Carbon To Metals: the Renewable Energy Transition', *Brave New Europe*, March 17, 2021.

32. Elsa Dominish, Nick Florin, and Swen Teske, *Responsible Minerals Sourcing for Renewable Energy*. Report prepared for Earthworks by the Institute for Sustainable Futures, University of Technology Sydney 2019. Also see *The Role of Critical Minerals in Clean Energy Transitions*, International Energy Agency, May 2021, for a disturbing analysis of the extremely high future demand for minerals driven by renewable energy and especially electric vehicles.

33. European Commission, *Report on Critical Raw Materials in the Circular Economy*, Luxembourg, 2018.

34. See Frank Biermann and Rakhyun E. Kim, 'The Boundaries of the Planetary Boundary Framework: A Critical Appraisal of Approaches to Define a "Safe Operating Space" for Humanity', *Annual Review of Environment and Resources*, vol. 45, 2020, pp.497-52. Also see José M. Montoya, Ian Donohue and Stuart L. Pimm, 'Why a Planetary Boundary, If It Is Not Planetary, and the Boundary Is Undefined? A Reply to Rockström et al.', *Trends & Ecology and Evolution*, Vol. 33, No. 4, April 2018, p.234. and Johan Rockström, Katherine Richardson, Will Steffen, and Georgina Mace, 'Planetary Boundaries: Separating Fact from Fiction. A Response to Montoya et al.' *Trends & Ecology and Evolution*, Vol. 33, No. 4, April 2018, pp.232-33.

35. Johan Rockström, et al. 'Planetary Boundaries: Exploring the Safe Operating Space for Humanity', *Ecology and Society*, Vol.14, no.2, 2009, pp.1-33 and Will Steffen et al, 'Trajectories of the Earth System in the Anthropocene', PNAS, pnas.org, July 6, 2018.

36. Moddassir Ahmed, Muhammad Rauf, Zahid Mukhtar, Nasir Ahmad Saeed, 'Excessive use of nitrogenous fertilizers: an unawareness causing serious threats to environment and human health', *Environmental Science and Pollution research Journal*, December, 2017.

37. Hannes Böttcher, Judith Reise, Klaus Hennenberg, *Exploratory Analysis of an EU Sink and Restoration Target*, Öeko-Institut e.V., Freiburg, March 18, 2021, p.5.

38. Jennifer Rankin, 'Leaked EU anti-deforestation law omits fragile grasslands and wetlands', *The Guardian*, September 15, 2021.

39. Stephan Bringezu et al., *Assessing global resource use: A systems approach to resource efficiency and pollution reduction*, A Report of the International Resource Panel. United Nations Environment Programme. Nairobi, 2017, p.29.

40. *Ibid*, p.34.

41. Bill McKibben, *The End of Nature*, Anchor, New York, 1989. This is also the common theme of an extensive literature on the Anthropocene.

42. UNEP, *Managing and conserving the natural resource base for sustained economic and social devel-*

opment. A reflection from the international resource panel on the establishment of sustainable development goals aimed at decoupling economic growth from escalating resource use and environmental degradation, United Nations Environment Programme, Nairobi 2014.

43. Sanna Ahvenharju, 'Potential for a radical policy-shift? The acceptability of strong sustainable consumption governance among elites', *Environmental Politics*, vol. 29, no.1, 2020, p. 137.

44. Jason Hickel, 'The contradiction of the sustainable development goals: Growth versus ecology on a finite planet', *Sustainable Development*, vol. 27, no.5, 2019, pp.873-884.

45. Jan Matuštík and Vladimír Kočí, 'What is a footprint? A conceptual analysis of environmental footprint indicators', *Journal of Cleaner Production*, October 27, 2020.

46. Monika Dittrich, Stefan Giljum, Stephan Lutter, Christine Polzin, *Green economies around the world Implications of resource use for development and the environment*, Seri, Vienna, 2012, p.20 and pp.78-80.

47. For example, UK 'per capita footprint' was estimated to be 18.5 tonnes - see 'Material Footprint in the UK: 2017', *Office of National Statistics*, 2 April 2020.

48. Iago Otero et al., 'Biodiversity policy beyond economic growth', *Conservation Letters A Journal of the Society for Conservation Biology*, February 2020, online edition.

49. It is not just the Breakthrough Institute in California that promotes an uncritical ecomodernism. Institutes such as the Wuppertal Institute for Climate, Environment and Energy are also geared to green growth and making businesses and societies in the EU more efficient and rational in their use of resources. See for example, Raimund Bleischwitz, 'International Economics of Resource Productivity - Relevance, Measurement, Empirical Trends, Innovation, Resource Policies', *International Economics and Economic Policy*, vol. 7, nos. 2-3, 2010, pp. 227-244 and Raimund Bleischwitz, Paul J. J. Welfens, Zhong Xiang Zhang (eds.) *International Economics of Resource Efficiency: Eco-Innovation Policies for a Green Economy*, Physica-Verlag, Berlin, 2011.

50. See Laxmi Haigh, Marc de Wit, Caspar von Daniels, Alex Colloricchio, Jelmer Hoogzaad, et al., *The Circularity Gap Report 2021*, Circle Economy, Amsterdam, January 2021.1

51. Joan Martinez-Alier, 'The circularity gap and the growth of world movements for environmental Justice', *Academia Letters*, March 2021, p.3.

52. *Ibid*, p.4

53. Figures cited by Heinz Schandl, 'Contribution of the 3Rs to achieving the Sustainable Development Goals – Science and Policy for the 2030 Sustainable Development Agenda', Presentation at the Seventh Regional 3R Forum for Asia and the Pacific, Adelaide 2-4 November 2016.

54. *Circularity Gap Report 2021*, p.23.

55. See Monika Dittrich, Stefan Giljum, Stephan Lutter and Christine Polzin, *Green economies around the world: Implications of resource use for development and the environment*, Sustainable Europe Research Institute, Vienna, 2012.

56. Kenta Tsuda, 'Naïve Questions on Degrowth', *New Left Review*, no.128, March/April, 2021, p.130.

57. *The Circularity Gap Report 2021*, p.37.

58. Robert Brenner, *The Economics of Global Turbulence*, Verso, London, 2006. Brenner was Benanav's Ph.D supervisor and influenced him greatly.

59. Aaron Benanav, *Automation and the Future of Work*, Verso, London, 2020.

60. See my analysis in Ch.6 of *Fictions of Sustainability*, 2018.

61. David Harvey, *Marx, Capital and the Madness of Economic Reason*, Oxford University Press, New York, 2018, pp.187-193.

62. See 2018 figures provided by World Bank in 'Household consumption, percent of GDP by country, around the world', *The Global Economy.com*.

63. *Circularity Gap Report 2019*, Circle Economy, Amsterdam, January 2019, p.26.

64. See e.g., Jennie Moore and William E. Rees, 'Getting to One-Planet Living' in *State of the World 2013 Is Sustainability Still Possible?*, The WorldWatch Institute, 2013, Ch.4. p.42.

65. *Ibid*, p.40. For a critique of 'footprint' methodology, see Robert Richardson, 'Resource depletion is a serious problem, but 'footprint' estimates don't tell us much about it', *The Conversation*, July 24, 2019.

66. Commission Staff Working Document, 'Leading the way to a global circular economy: state of play and outlook', *European Commission*, Brussels, March 11, 2020, p.8.

67. Green growthers such as Carlota Perez propose renting durable consumer goods. See her article, 'Using the history of technological revolutions to understand the present and shape the future', in *The Progressive Post*, Winter 2021, pp.44-49.

68. Jason Hickel, 'Degrowth: a theory of radical abundance', *real-world economics review*, issue no. 87, 2019, p.62.

69. See for example, Lou Plateau, Laurence Roudart, Marek Hudon, Kevin Maréchal, 'Opening the organisational black box to grasp the difficulties of agroecological transition. An empirical analysis of tensions in agroecological production', *Ecological Economics* 185, 2021, online edition.

70. Philip McMichael, *Food Regimes and Agrarian Questions*, Fernwood Publishing, Black Point Nova Scotia, 2013.

71. *Ibid*, p.168.

72. Daniel W. O'Neill, Andrew L. Fanning, William F. Lamb and Julia K. Steinberger, 'A good life for all within planetary boundaries', *Nature Sustainability*, Vol 1, February 2018, pp.88-95.

73. See evaluation from a degrowth perspective by Jason Hickel, 'Is it possible to achieve a good life for all within planetary boundaries?', *Third World Quarterly*, vol. 40, no.1, 2019, pp.18-35.

4. Degrowth: Direct Democracy in a Political Economic Vacuum

1. Herman Daly, 'A Steady-state Economy. Opinion Piece for Redefining Prosperity', Sustainable Development Commission, UK. 2008.

2. Troy Vettese, 'Against steady-state economics', *The Ecological Citizen*, vol.3, Suppl B, 2020, pp.35-46.

3. Jay W. Forrester, *World Dynamics*, WrightAllen Press, Cambridge, 1971, developed the systems dynamic models used by the Club of Rome report *Limits to Growth* published in 1972. There are finite material natural limits to infinite growth but not strictly as conceived by Forrester who presented insightful but problematic analyses of capitalism and the interaction between political economy and ecosystems.

4. Herman Daly and Brian Czech, 'In My Opinion: The steady state economy – what it is, entails, and connotes', *Wildlife Society Bulletin*, no.2, 2004, pp.598-605.

5. Daniel W. O'Neill, 'The proximity of nations to a socially sustainable steady-state economy', *Journal of Cleaner Production*, Vol.108, 2015, pp.1213-1231. O'Neill has a more nuanced notion of steady-state and degrowth than Daly. Nonetheless, he provides a comparative analysis of existing capitalist societies that assumes that with the right balance of policies they will be able to reach the steady state. Such a perspective misunderstands the inbuilt dynamics of capital accumulation and inequality which no single country can abandon on its own, given the interconnection of trade in material resources, goods, and services.

6. Herman Daly, 'From a Failed Growth Economy to a Steady-State Economy' *The Solutions Journal*, vol.1, no.2, 2010, pp.37-43. For an analysis of Daly's and degrowth proposals on income caps, see Hubert Buch-Hansen and Max Koch, 'Degrowth through income and wealth caps?', *Ecological Economics*, no.160, 2019, pp. 264-271.

7. Herman Daly, *Beyond Growth: The Economics of Sustainable Development*, Beacon Press, Boston, 1997, Ch.10.

8. Ekaterina Chertkovskaya and Alexander Paulsson, 'Countering corporate violence: Degrowth, ecosocialism and organising beyond the destructive forces of capitalism', *Organization*, December 2020, pp.1-21.
9. See Nan Tian et al, 'Trends in World Military Expenditure, 2019', *Stockholm International Peace Research Institute (SIPRI)*, Solna, April 2020.
10. Núria Bassa and Toni Strubell, 'Spain's "progressive" bombs for Saudis', *Brave New Europe*, April 23, 2021.
11. George Magnus, 'China's Go-It-Alone Five-Year Plan', *Project Syndicate*, March 25, 2021.
12. Ann Pettifor, *The Case for the Green New Deal*, Verso, London, 2019, ch.5.
13. Tim Jackson, Peter Victor and Ali Naqvi, *Towards a Stock-Flow Consistent Ecological Macroeconomics*, WWW for Europe, Working Paper no.114, March 2016. Also see Tim Jackson et al, 'Modelling Transition Risk Towards an Agent-Based, Stock-Flow Consistent Framework', *Rebuilding Macroeconomics Working Paper Series*, no.40, London, February 2021 which also says nothing about international factors and how they impact the national model.
14. Figures cited in Andreas Nölke, 'Germany's dangerous export fetish', *International Politics and Society Journal*, April 2, 2021.
15. Shulan Zhang, 'Conceptualising the Environmentalism in India: Between Social Justice and Deep Ecology', in Qingzhi Huan (ed.) *Eco-socialism as Politics: Rebuilding the Basis of Our Modern Civilisation,* ch.12.
16. Karl Polanyi, *The Great Transformation: The political and economic origins of our time*, (1944) Beacon Press, Boston, 2001.
17. I have discussed the many socio-political problems associated with small, self-sufficient communities in *The Post Industrial Utopians*, Polity, Cambridge, 1987.
18. As an example of degrowthers who recognise the importance of state institutions, see Giacomo D'Alisa and Giorgos Kallis, 'Degrowth and the State', *Ecological Economics*, no.169, March 2020, online edition, and James Scott Vandeventer, Claudio Cattaneo and Christos Zografos, 'A Degrowth Transition: Pathways for the Degrowth Niche to Replace the Capitalist-Growth Regime', *Ecological Economics*, no. 156, 2019, pp. 272–286 who map the various degrowth tendencies.
19. For a discussion of different definitions of degrowth and divisions over degrowth see Timothée Parrique, *The political economy of degrowth.* Economics and Finance. Université Clermont Auvergne; Stockholms universitet, 2019. English. NNT: 2019CLFAD003, Hal Id: tel-02499463.
20. *Ibid.*
21. *Ibid*, pp.315-18 and p.464.
22. See for example, Jason Hickel, *Less is More How Degrowth Will Save the World*, William Heinemann, London, 2020.
23. See for example, Jason Hickel, The Imperative of Redistribution in an Age of Ecological Overshoot: Human Rights and Global Inequality', *Humanity: An International Journal of Human Rights, Humanitarianism, and Development*, Vol.10, No.3, Winter 2019, pp. 416-428.
24. Leigh Phillips, *Austerity Ecology & the Collapse Porn Addicts: A Defence of Growth, Progress, Industry and Stuff,* Zero Books, Winchester, 2015; 'The case for growth', *Spiked*, June 30, 2017; 'The degrowth delusion'. *Open Democracy,* August 30, 2019 and 'How much stuff is just enough', *Le Monde Diplomatique*, February 21 2021. For a critique of Phillips see Andrea Grainger, 'In defence of degrowth', *Open Democracy*, September 5, 2019; and Kevin Carson, *We are all Degrowthers. We are all Ecomodernists Analysis of a Debate*, Center for a Stateless Society, Tulsa, November 18, 2019, for a discussion of the debate between Phillips and degrowthers and how Phillips mischaracterises degrowthers.
25. Branko Milanovic, 'Degrowth: Solving the Impasse by Magical Thinking', *Brave New Europe*, February 20, 2021.
26. *Ibid.*
27. Jason Hickel, 'Degrowth: A response to Branko Milanovic', jasonhickel.org October 27, 2020.

28. Branko Milanovic, 'Towards global progressiveness', *Brave New Europe*, July 5, 2021.
29. See Hickel's vague discussion of how capitalist growth can be 'shifted' in the section 'Degrowth' in *Less is More*.
30. Adrián E. Beling, Julien Vanhulstb, Federico Demaria, Violeta Rabi, Ana E. Carballo, Jérôme Pelenc, 'Discursive Synergies for a 'Great Transformation' Towards Sustainability: Pragmatic Contributions to a Necessary Dialogue Between Human Development, Degrowth, and Buen Vivir', *Ecological Economics*, vol. 144, February 2018, p. 308.
31. See Giorgos Kallis, 'In defence of degrowth', *Ecological Economics*, vol. 70, issue 5, 2011, pp. 873-880.
32. Ivan Illich, *Tools for Conviviality*, Harper & Row, New York, 1973.
33. Roldan Muradian, 'Frugality as a choice vs. frugality as a social condition. Is de-growth doomed to be a Eurocentric project?', *Ecological Economics*, 161, 2019, pp. 257-260.
34. See Parrique, *op.cit.* Appendixes 1 to 6, pp.820-860 that cover invaluable suggestions for transforming existing societies.
35. See Samuel Alexander and Brendan Gleeson, *Degrowth in the Suburbs: A Radical Urban Imaginary*, Palgrave Macmillan, Singapore, 2019.
36. See various contributions in Ashish Kothari, Ariel Salleh, Arturo Escobar, Federico Demaria and Alberto Acosta (eds), *Pluriverse: A Post-Development Dictionary*, Columbia University Press, New York, 2019.
37. Slavoj Žižek. *A Left that Dares to Speak Its Name: Untimely Interventions*, Polity Press, Cambridge, 2020, p. 21.
38. Wally Seccombe, *Weathering the Storm: Working-Class Families From the Industrial Revolution to the Fertility Decline*, Verso, London, 1993.
39. Samuel Alexander and Brendan Gleeson, *Degrowth in the Suburbs A Radical Urban Imaginary*.
40. Ted Trainer, '*Remaking settlements* for sustainability: the Simpler Way', *Journal of Political Ecology*, Vol. 26, 2019, pp. 202-23.
41. Ted Trainer, 'Degrowth: How Much is Needed?', *Biophysical Economics and Sustainability*, vol. 6, article no. 5, 2021.
42. Joshua Lockyer, 'Community, commons, and degrowth at Dancing Rabbit Ecovillage', *Journal of Political Ecology*, Vol. 24, no.1, 2017, pp.519-542.
43. T. Trainer, A. Malik and M. Lenzen, 'A Comparison Between the Monetary, Resource and Energy Costs of the Conventional Industrial Supply Path and the "Simpler Way" Path for the Supply of Eggs', *Biophysical Economics and Sustainability, no.3*, June 2019.
44. *Circularity Gap Report 2019*, Circle Economy, Amsterdam, January 2019.
45. See the survey of various alternative schemes in Parrique, *op.cit.*, Ch.11.
46. Kristofer Dittmer, *Alternatives to Money-As-Usual in Ecological Economics: A Study of Local Currencies and 100 Percent Reserve Banking*, Ph.D thesis, Universitat Autònoma de Barcelona, September 2014.
47. F.A. Hayek, *Denationalisation of Money – The Argument Refined: An Analysis of the Theory and Practice of Concurrent Currencies* (1976), Institute of Economic Affairs, Third Edition, London, 1990.
48. See Mark Alizart, *Cryptocommunism*, trans. by Robin Mackay, Polity Press, Cambridge, 2020.
49. Lola Seaton, 'Owen Hatherley: "I really hoped that with Grenfell the 'metropolitan elite' debate would just die", *New Statesman*, March 12, 2021.
50. See for example, Pierre Dardot and Christian Laval, *Common: On Revolution in the 21st century*, Translated by Matthew MacLellan, Bloomsbury Academic, London, 2019.
51. Ted Trainer, 'On eco-villages and the transition', *The International Journal of Inclusive Democracy*, vol. 2, no.3, June 2006.
52. Samuel Alexander and Brendan Gleeson, *Degrowth in the Suburbs A Radical Urban Imaginary*.
53. Ingolfur Blühdorn, Felix Butzlaff, Michael Deflorian, Daniel Hausknost, Transformation

Research and Academic Responsibility. The social theory gap in narratives of radical change', IGN-Interventions, March 2018, Institute for Social Change and Sustainability (IGN), Vienna University.

5. Searching for a Mode of Politics to Break the Impasse

1. Quoted by Philippe Le Goff, *Auguste Blanqui and the Politics of Popular Empowerment*, Bloomsbury, London, 2020, p.5.
2. Quoted by Peter Hallward in Preface to Philippe Le Goff and Peter Hallward (eds.) *The Blanqui Reader Political Writings, 1830–1880 Louis Auguste Blanqui,* translated by Philippe Le Goff, Peter Hallward and Mitchell Abidor, Verso, London, 2018.
3. Bernard Manin, *The principles of representative government*, Cambridge University Press, Cambridge, 1997.
4. See Stefan Jonsson, *Crowds and Democracy: The Idea and Image of the Masses From Revolution to Fascism*, Columbia University Press, New York, 2013.
5. Quoted by H. H. Gerth and C, Wright Mills, *From Max Weber: Essays in Sociology*, Oxford University Press, New York, 1958, p.42.
6. Ellen Kennedy, *Constitutional Failure Carl Schmitt in Weimar*, Duke University Press, Durham, 2004, p. 186.
7. Joseph Schumpeter, *Capitalism, Socialism and Democracy,* Harper & Row, New York, 1942, Taylor & Francis e-Library with an introduction by Richard Swedberg, 2003.
8. Joseph Schumpeter, *Imperialism and Social Classes two essays*, Translated by Heinz Norden, The World Publishing Company, Cleveland, 1955, ch.5.
9. Otto Kirchheimer, 'The Transformation of the Western European Party System' in Joseph LaPalombara and Myron Weiner (eds) *Political Parties and Political Development*, Princeton University Press, Princeton,1966. Kirchheimer broke with Schmitt after the latter became a Nazi. Along with other emigres Franz Neumann and Herbert Marcuse, he devoted much energy during the war years inside the OSS (Office of Strategic Services) to defeating Hitler and trying to restore democracy in Germany. Their radical advice on necessary de-Nazification of Germany was rejected by the US government in the period 1945-1946. All three continued to analyse the new authoritarian trends during the Cold War period and why the conflicts in the Weimar years would not be repeated in developed capitalist countries. Instead, de-democratisation was occurring in the late 1940s onwards, even as the West proclaimed itself the 'Free World'.
10. André Krouwe, 'Otto Kirchheimer and the catch-all party', *West European Politics*, vol.26, no.2, 2003, pp. 23-40.
11. See Perry Anderson, 'The Europe to Come', *London Review of Books*, 25 January 1996; and Wolfgang Streeck, *Buying Time: The Delayed Crisis of Democratic Capitalism*, German edition 2013, translated by Patrick Camiller, Verso, London, 2014.
12. See Bruno Amable and Stefano Palombarini, *The Last Neoliberal: Macron and the Origins of France's Political Crisis*, Translated by David Broder, Verso, London, 2021.
13. Lisa Adkins, Melinda Cooper and Martijn Konings, *The Asset Economy: Property Ownership and the New Logic of Inequality*, Polity, Cambridge, 2020, pp.62-79.
14. United Nations figures cited by Samuel Stein, *Capital City: Gentrification and the Real Estate State*, Verso, London, 2019, p.9.
15. Alex Baumann, Samuel Alexander and Peter Burdon, Land Commodification as a Barrier to Political and Economic Agency: A Degrowth perspective', *Journal of Australian Political Economy,* No. 86, 2020, pp. 379-405.
16. Nancy Fraser, 'A Triple Movement? Parsing the Politics of Crisis after Polanyi', *New Left Review*, no. 81, May/June, 2013, p.131.
17. *Ibid*, p.128.

18. Dominic Mealy, 'Interview with Andreas Malm: "To Halt Climate Change, We Need an Ecological Leninism", *Jacobin*, June 19, 2020.

19. *Ibid*. Malm develops his notion of applying Lenin's 'war communism' in *Corona, Climate, Chronic Emergency: War Communism in the Twenty-First Century*, Verso, London, 2020.

20. Ingar Solty interviewed by Darko Vujica, 'German Deunification', *Monthly Review*, June 2020.

21. For critical reviews from activists see Simon Butler, 'Can sabotage stop climate change?', *Climate & Capitalism*, April 28, 2021, and Lars Henriksson, 'Should we blow up pipelines? Once again on sabotage and climate change' *Climate & Capitalism*, May 22, 2021.

22. Andreas Malm, *How to Blow Up a Pipeline: Learning to Fight in a World on Fire*, Verso, London, 2021, Ch.3 Fighting Despair.

23. Andreas Malm and the Zetkin Collective, *White Skin, Black Fuel: On the Danger of Fossil Fascism*, Verso, London, 2021.

24. See for example Lluis De Nadal, 'Spain's VOX party and the threat of 'international environmental populism", *Open Democracy*, August 9, 2021.

25. James Dyke, Wolfgang Knorr and Robert Watson, 'Climate scientists: concept of net zero is a dangerous trap', *The Conversation*, April 22, 2021.

26. Max Ajl, *A People's Green New Deal*, Pluto Press, London, 2021, p.94. Ajl's book has too many inconsistencies and bloopers.

27. The Red Nation, *The Red Deal: Indigenous Action to Save Our Earth*, Common Notions, Brooklyn, 2021.

28. *Ibid* pp.168-69.

29. Jeremy Varon, *Bringing the War Home: The Weather Underground, the Red Army Faction, and Revolutionary Violence in the Sixties and Seventies,* University of California Press, Berkeley, 2004, p.10.

30. Extinction Rebellion UK @XRebellionUK, September 1, 2020, quoted by Mark Montegriffo, 'Yes, "Socialism or Extinction" Is Exactly the Choice We Face', *Jacobin*, September 4, 2020.

31. See C.E. Cherry, S. Capstick, C. Demski, C. Mellier, L. Stone, C, Verfuerth, *Citizens' Climate Assemblies: Understanding public deliberation for climate policy*, The Centre for Climate Change and Social Transformations, Cardiff, July 2021.

32. This position is promoted in journals such as *Historical Materialism*, *New Left Review*, and other publications. See also Sebastian Budgen, Stathis Kouvelakis, and Slavoj Žižek, (eds.) *Lenin Reloaded: Towards A Politics of Truth,* Duke University Press, Durham, 2007; Marta Harnecker, *Rebuilding the Left*, Zed Books, London, 2007; and Paul Le Blanc, *Unfinished Leninism: The Rise and Return of a Revolutionary Doctrine,* Haymarket Books, Chicago, 2014.

33. Alain Badiou, *The Communist Hypothesis*, Translated by David Macey and Steve Corcoran, Verso, London, 2010.

34. Nick Srnicek and Alex Williams, *Inventing the Future: Postcapitalism and a World Without Work, Revised and Updated Edition,* Verso, London, 2016, p.163.

35. *Ibid.*

36. See Ernesto Laclau, *On Populist Reason*, Verso, London, 2005; Chantal Mouffe, *Agonistics Thinking the World Politically*, Verso, London 2013 and 'Interview with Chantal Mouffe on Left Populism', *Verso Blog*, 4 August 2017.

37. See for example, the discussion of issues in Mark E. Warren and Hilary Pearse (eds.) *Designing Deliberative Democracy: The British Columbia Citizens' Assembly*, Cambridge University Press, Cambridge, 2008.

38. See special issue on deliberative democracy in *Dædalus, the Journal of the American Academy of Arts & Sciences*, no.3, Summer 2017.

39. Ernesto Laclau and Chantal Mouffe, *Hegemony and Socialist Strategy: Towards a Radical Democratic Politics,* Verso, London, 1985 and Ernesto Laclau, *On Populist Reason,* Verso, London, 2005.

40. For an analysis of the connection between conceptions of democracy, autonomy and

degrowth, see Viviana Asara, *Democracy without growth: The political ecology of the Indignados movement*, PhD Thesis, Universitat Autònoma de Barcelona, Ph.D. Programme in Environmental Science and Technology, May 2015.

41. Paolo Gerbaudo, 'To Recapture the Spirit of the Indignados, Podemos Has to Speak to Working People', *Jacobin*, May 15, 2021.

42. Quoted by Yanis Varoufakis in Foreword, to David Adler and Rosemary Belcher (eds.) *A Vision for Europe*, Eris Press, London 2019.

43. Paula Biglieri and Luciana Cadahia, *Seven Essays on Populism For a Renewed Theoretical Perspective*, translated by George Ciccariello-Maher, Polity, Cambridge, 2021.

44. Martin Bak Jørgensen & Óscar García Agustín, 'The Postmodern Prince: The Political Articulation of Social Dissent' in Martin Bak Jørgensen & Óscar García Agustín (eds.) *Politics of Dissent*, Peter Lang, Frankfurt, 2015, pp.29-50.

45. Paul Mason, *How to Stop Fascism: History, Ideology, Resistance*, Penguin Books, London, 2021, ch.8.

46. Lucio Baccaro and Jonas Pontusson, 'Rethinking Comparative Political Economy: The Growth Model Perspective', in special edition of *Politics & Society*, vol.44, no 2, 2016, pp. 175-207.

47. In *Fictions of Sustainability*, Chapter Five, I discussed the 'varieties of capitalism' theorists, such as Lucio Baccaro and Jonas Pontusson, who analyse the 'drivers of growth' and 'social blocs' but completely ignore environmental issues.

48. Reda Cherif and Faud Hasanov, *The Leap of the Tiger: How Malaysia Can Escape the Middle-income Trap*, Working Paper 15/131, IMF, Washington DC, 2015. Also see Jason Hickel, Dylan Sullivan, and Huzaifa Zoomkawala, 'Plunder in the Post-Colonial Era: Quantifying Drain from the Global South Through Unequal Exchange, 1960–2018', *New Political Economy*, March 2021, online.

49. Vladimir Lenin, *The State and Revolution*, translation published by Foreign Languages Publishing House, Moscow, 1952, p.22.

50. See Claus Offe, 'Participatory Inequality in the Austerity State: A Supply-Side Approach' in Armin Schäfer and Wolfgang Streeck (eds.) *Politics in the Age of Austerity*, Polity, Cambridge, 2013, as well as other contributions in this book.

51. Jeroen Van Der Waal, Peter Achterberg and Dick Houtman, 'Class Is Not Dead—It Has Been Buried Alive: Class Voting and Cultural Voting in Postwar Western Societies (1956–1990)', *Politics & Society*, Vol. 35 No. 3, September 2007, pp. 403-426.

52. Amory Gethin, Clara Martínez-Toledano, Thomas Piketty, *Brahmin Left versus Merchant Right: Changing Political Cleavages in 21 Western Democracies, 1948-2020*, World Inequality Lab Working Paper, July 2021.

6. Alternatives to Welfare States: Beyond 'Dependent Beggars and Wage Slaves'

1. Joan Martínez-Alier, *The Environmentalism of the Poor A Study of Ecological Conflicts and Valuation*, Edward Elgar, Cheltenham, 2020.

2. See Do-Wan Ku and Hyoung-Beom Yeo, 'Alternative Development: Beyond Ecological Communities and Associations' in Qingzhi Huan (ed.) *Eco-socialism as Politics: Rebuilding the Basis of Our Modern Civilisation*, Springer, London, 2010, Ch.11.

3. Richard Smith, *China's Engine of Environmental Collapse*, Pluto Press, London, 2020, p.2.

4. Abhijit Banerjee, Amory Gethin, Thomas Piketty, *Growing Cleavages in India? Evidence from the Changing Structure of Electorates, 1962-2014*, World Inequality Lab, Paris, March, 2019.

5. See Economic Survey, 2016-17, Government of India Ministry of Finance Department of Economic Affairs, Economic Division, January 2017, pp.173-195.

6. Bikrum Gill, 'India's data harvest', *Red Pepper*, August 25, 2021.

7. Vijay Jawandhiya and Ajay Dandekar, 'Three Farm Bills and India's Rural Economy', *The Wire*, October 1, 2020.

8. Claus Offe, *Modernity and the State: East, West*, MIT Press, Cambridge, 1996, p.x and Claus Offe, *Contradictions of the Welfare State,* edited and translated by John Keane, Hutchinson, London,1984.

9. Claus Offe, 'Crisis of Crisis Management: Elements of a Political Crisis Theory', *International Journal of Politics*, Vol. 6, No. 3, Fall 1976, p.43.

10. Gøsta Esping-Andersen, *The Three Worlds of Welfare Capitalism*, Princeton University Press, Princeton, 1990. See Interview with Esping Andersen by Maya Adereth, 'The Postindustrial Welfare State', *Phenomenal World*, May 14th, 2020, in which Esping-Andersen discusses Polanyi's influence on his work.

11. Esping-Andersen, *The Three Worlds of Welfare Capitalism,* p.37.

12. Claus Offe, *Contradictions of the Welfare State*, p.264.

13. Matt Bruenig, 'No, Finland Is Not a 'Capitalist Paradise'', *Jacobin*, December 9, 2019.

14. Thomas Piketty, *Capital in the Twenty-First Century,* translated by Arthur Goldhammer, Harvard University Press, Cambridge, 2014, ch.13.

15. See for example, Ludovic Suttor-Sorel, *Fiscal Mythology Unmasked: Debunking eight tales about European public debt and fiscal rules*, Finance-Watch.org, Brussels, July 2021.

16. Claus Offe, *Modernity and the State: East, West, pp.viii-ix.*

17. Juliet Ferguson, 'Europe's elderly care problem', *Open Democracy*, July 22, 2021.

18. Lisa Pelling, 'Sweden, the Pandemic and precarious working conditions', *Social Europe*, June 10, 2020, and Evan Jones, 'COVID-19 Hits the French Health System', *Journal of Australian Political Economy* No. 85, 2020, pp. 94-100.

19. See Juliet Ferguson, 'Europe's elderly care problem', *Open Democracy*, July 22, 2021.

20. See Jennifer Mittelstadt, *The Rise of the Military Welfare State*, Harvard University Press, Cambridge, 2015, for a comprehensive analysis of the political economic factors that produced 'army welfare' followed by the neoliberal deconstruction of these services.

21. For country-by-country figures, see *Pension Markets in Focus 2019*, OECD, Paris, 2019.

22. Christine Corlet Walker, Angela Druckman, Tim Jackson, 'Welfare systems without economic growth: A review of the challenges and next steps for the field', *Ecological Economics*, no. 186, 2021, p.3.

23. *Ibid.*

24. *Ibid*, p.6.

25. Hartmut Rosa, *The Uncontrollability of the World*, Translated by James C. Wagner, Polity, Cambridge, 2020.

26. Justin Bentham, Andrew Bowman, Marta de la Cuesta, Ewald Engelen, Ismail Ertürk, Peter Folkman, Julie Froud, Suhkdev Johal, John Law, Adam Leaver, Michael Moran, Karl Williams, *Manifesto For the Foundational Economy*. Centre for Research on Socio-Cultural Change, Manchester, CRESC Working Paper No. 131, 2013.

27. Stephen Hall and Alex Schafran, 'From foundational economics and the grounded city to foundational urban systems', *Foundational Economy*, Working Paper No.3, 2017, p. 8.

28. Leigh Phillips and Michal Rozworski, *The People's Republic of Walmart: How the World's Biggest Corporations Are Laying the Foundation for Socialism*, Verso, London, 2019.

29. David Schweickart, *Economic Democracy*, Next System Project, 2015, the nextsystem.org.

30. See for example, Christian Gollier, Mar Reguant, Dani Rodrik, Stefanie Stantcheva, Axel Börsch-Supan, Claudia Diehl, Carol Propper, *Major Future Economic Challenges*, Olivier Blanchard and Jean Tirole Rapporteurs, *International Commission*, June 2021.

31. See for example, Branko Milanovic, *Capitalism, Alone The Future of the System That Rules the World*, Harvard University Press, Cambridge, 2019; Dani Rodrik, 'New firms for a new era', *Social Europe*, February 19, 2020, and Paul Collier, *The Future of Capitalism: Facing the New Anxieties,* Allen Lane, London, 2018.

32. See Thomas Piketty, *Capital and Ideology,* trans. by Arthur Goldhammer, Harvard Univer-

sity Press, Cambridge, 2020, Chapter 17 and Conclusion on proposals for 'participatory socialism'.

33. See figures in Jakob Kapeller, Stuart Leitch and Rafael Wildauer, 'A European wealth tax', *Social Europe*, April 9, 2021.

34. See for example, Robin Blackburn, *Banking on Death or, Investing in Life: The History and Future of Pensions*, Verso, London, 2002.

35. See Richard Smith, *China's Engine of Environmental Collapse*, Pluto Press, London, 2020

36. Daniel F. Vukovich, *Illiberal China: The Ideological Challenge of the People's Republic of China*, Palgrave Macmillan, Singapore, 2019, pp. 8-11.

37. Richard Smith, *China's Engine of Environmental Collapse*, Pluto Press, London, 2020.

38. Zhang Jun, 'China's Rapid Shift to a Digital Economy', *Project Syndicate*, September 7, 2020.

39. 'China's social security system', *China Labour Bulletin*, October 15, 2019.

40. See Mary Gallagher, *Authoritarian Legality in China: Law, Workers, and the State*, Cambridge University Press, Cambridge, 2017.

41. See details of how workers are denied their entitlements and rights in 'China's social security system', *China Labour Bulletin*, October 15, 2019.

42. Mary Gallagher, *op.cit.*, p.9.

43. Michael Roberts, 'China: demographic crisis?', *Brave New Europe*, May 23, 2021.

44. Mark Leonard, 'The New China Shock', *Project Syndicate*, March 31, 2021.

45. Fiona Harvey, 'China 'must shut 600 coal-fired plants' to hit climate target', *The Guardian*, April 15, 2021.

46. Nancy Qian, 'The Two Sides of Chinese GDP', *Project Syndicate*, April 30, 2021.

47. Thea Riofrancos, *Resource Radicals From Petro-Nationalism to Post-Extractivism in Ecuador*, Duke University Press Durham, 2020, p.5.

48. See Julie Stephens, *Confronting Postmaternal Thinking: Feminism, Memory, and Care*. Columbia University Press, 2011 for a discussion of how neoliberalism has suppressed maternal values and practices.

49. See T. Parrique, *The Political Economy of Degrowth*, pp.430-32 for a survey of various criticisms of those who rely on growth to make possible the transition to degrowth.

50. See for example, Ross Garnaut's proposal for a AUD$15,000 UBI combined with tax claw back on incomes above certain low thresholds, in *Reset: Restoring Australia after the Pandemic Recession*, La Trobe University Press and Black Inc, Carlton, 2021, and David Calnitsky, 'Does *Basic Income Assume a Can Opener?*', *Catalyst*, vol.2, no.3, 2018, pp.137-156 for similar UBI schemes which reduce by 50% or 33% once people earn between US$5,000 and $40,000.

51. See Anna Coote and Edanur Yazici, *Universal Basic Income - A Report for Unions*, New Economics Foundation, Friedrich Ebert Stiftung and Public Services International, April 2019.

52. Institute for Global Prosperity (IGP), Social Prosperity for the Future: A Proposal for Universal Basic Services, UCL, London, 2017; Anna Coote, 'Building a new social commons', *New Economics Foundation*, 2017; Boris Frankel, *Fictions of Sustainability*, 2018, ch.6; Anna Coote, Pritika Kasliwal and Andrew Percy, *Universal Basic Services, Theory and Practice: A Literature Review*, London, UCL Institute for Global Prosperity, 2019; Ian Gough, 'Universal Basic Services: A Theoretical and Moral Framework', *The Political Quarterly*, vol.90, July-September, 2019, pp.534-42; Katharina Bohnenberger, 'Money, Vouchers, Public Infrastructures? A Framework for Sustainable Welfare Benefits', *Sustainability*, vol.12, no.2, 2020, pp.596-624.

53. David Calnitsky, 'Does *Basic Income Assume a Can Opener?*', *Catalyst*, vol.2, no.3, 2018, pp.137-156.

Conclusion

1. Donatello Di Cesare, *Immunodemocracy Capitalist Asphyxia*, translated by David Broder, Semiotext(e)/ MIT Press, South Pasadena, 2021, pp.23-24.
2. C. Shepherd, 'Coronavirus: Chinese carmakers struggle with disruption', *Financial Times*, 24 February 2020 and for extent of global interdependence of manufacturing, see *The Asia-Pacific Trade and Investment Trends 2020/2021 Report,* United Nations ESCAP Economic and Social Commission for Asia and the Pacific, 2021.
3. Sharon Burrow, 'A New Social Contract', *Social Europe*, June 24, 2020.
4. International Trade Union Confederation, *2021 ITUC Global Rights Index*, Brussels, June 2021.
5. John Bellamy Foster and Intan Suwandi, 'COVID-19 and Catastrophe Capitalism Commodity Chains and Ecological-Epidemiological-Economic Crises', *Monthly Review*, June 2020.
6. 'Nancy Fraser: "Cannibal Capitalism" Is on Our Horizon', Interview in *Jacobin*, September 10, 2021.

INDEX

www.ingramcontent.com/pod-product-compliance
Lightning Source LLC
Chambersburg PA
CBHW021853020426
42334CB00013B/307